Exploring Shapes Creatively

Dedicated in Gratitude
to
Fritz C.A. Koelln
and
David Mitchell

Two irrepressible human volcanoes
of enthusiasm

Exploring Shapes Creatively Through Pure Form Modeling
by Arthur Auer
Illustrations by Elizabeth Auer
Photos by the author

Published by:

Waldorf Publications

Research Institute for Waldorf Education

351 Fairview Avenue, Unit 625

Hudson, NY 12534

ISBN: 978-1-943582-23-5

Selections from the Introduction to *Art as Spiritual Activity: Rudolf Steiner's Contribution to the Visual Arts* (1988), with kind permission from Michael Howard and Steinerbooks.

Picture credits: Embryo Chart Illustrations Rows 3-4: *By Permission from Wooden Books, 8A Market Place, Glastonbury BA6 8LT, UK.*

Please contact patrice@waldorf-research.org with feedback on this publication as well as requests for future work.

Exploring Shapes Creatively

THROUGH PURE FORM MODELING

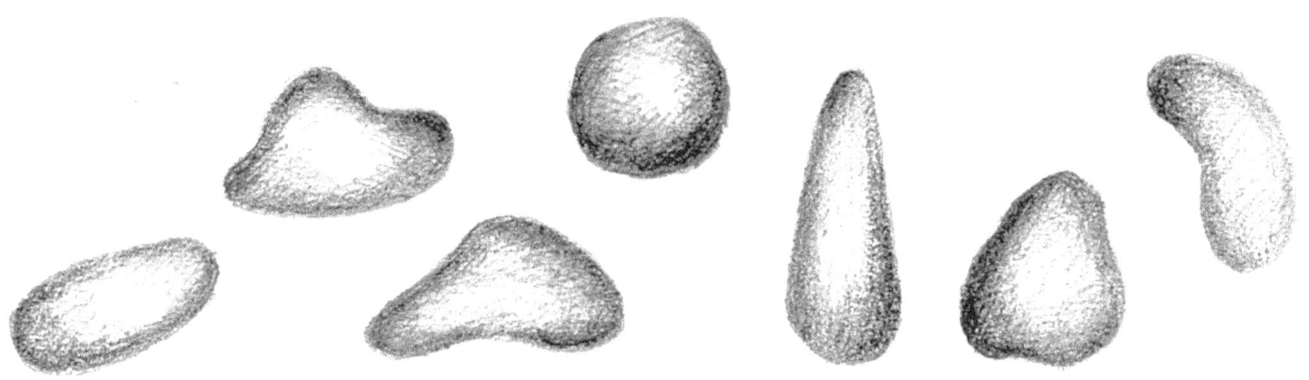

by

Arthur Auer

Illustrations by Elizabeth Auer

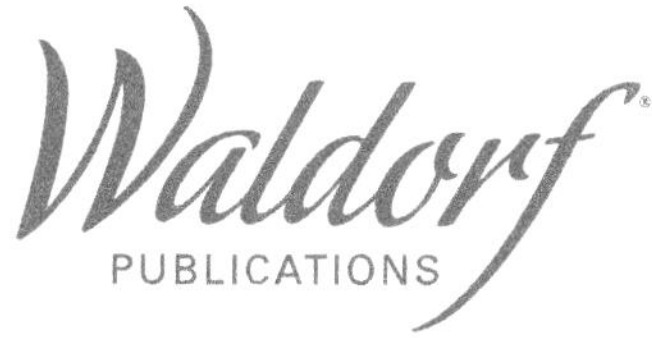

Waldorf
PUBLICATIONS

Table of Contents

Expanding Whole Intelligence

THIS BOOK is a companion volume to *Learning about the World through Modeling: Sculptural Ideas for School and Home* (AWSNA Publications, Fair Oaks, CA, 2001) The first book focused on modeling familiar objects from nature and human culture. This second manual extends the first into the exciting new area of sculpturally modeling pure "non-representational" forms with children and includes over 200 exercises with photos, as well as advice on method and other supplementary materials related to sculptural modeling. The contents of this book may be used in teaching and learning at many different levels and in many different settings, large and small: home and school, public or independent, elementary, secondary, Waldorf, Montessori, and homeschools—or for your own adult artistic self-education and pleasure.

Here are some features of pure form modeling's potency for education and increasing intelligence:

- It teaches children and adults to actively perceive, observe and learn the universal language of forms Nature herself uses in her ongoing, dynamic creation of the world.
- It involves us all in an absorbing and energizing process of exploring and discovering ever new configurations of shapes and above all the remarkable transforming capabilities of our human spirit-permeated hand.
- It is an excellent motivational enlivener of the senses, mind, heart, and limbs
- And it promotes closer relationships to all kinds of subjects: science, math, history, geography, the arts and Life!

Everywhere we look we see natural and man-made forms consisting of flat and curved, convex and concave surfaces. Form is as primary as color; flat and curved surfaces are as fundamental as straight and curved lines. Given this fact, we might ponder why we do not introduce our children to the world of flat and curved surfaces parallel to our introducing the world of straight and curved lines. Form Modeling should be as integral a part of the lower [grade] curriculum as is Form Drawing. For this to come about class teachers must awaken to the vital importance of engaging the children in the tactile world of wavy surfaces as much as wavy lines. With a clear and deep commitment, we discover a whole new discipline opening before us. All that Rudolf Steiner gave us in regards to Form Drawing can serve as a foundation upon which we can build the elements of a Form Modeling curriculum through the grades.

—Michael Howard, *Educating the Will*

A Call to Action: Bring out the Clay!

Ways to Use This Sourcebook

Starter Seed Ideas are to be rendered not copied!

Central to this manual is a call to activity and to:

- **Bring out the clay** or any other modeling material you have (beeswax, plasticine, play-dough, etc.)
- **Start moving your hands** and your children's hands freely into the world of form.

To spark and focus your efforts, I have designed and collected inspiring "seed" or starter exercises in twelve sets called Series. Each individual exercise has the potential for spawning countless other ideas, variations and modifications.

- Each exercise is intended as a beginning point for your own explorations and form-making creativity.
- Start to design your own forms as soon as possible.
- The photos and descriptions are there to give you a motif and to point you in possible directions.
- Freely render the motifs provided in your particular versions and variations.

Rendering leaves you and your children free "to breathe" in the creative process whereas trying to copy something exactly can be constricting and unnecessarily frustrating.

The Order and Selection of Exercises

I created the exercises in a Series 1-12 format with the grades and developmental stages in mind.

- Teachers may find it useful to follow the sequence of the Series in order as the children progress from age group to age group (Series One for first grade, etc.)
- Since all of the forms are in reality *universal* and each may be adapted to any age and to a variety of educational purposes, you may want to hunt around in the entire selection, pick and choose, and create your own approach and order.
- High school teachers can take the primal forms of the Series 1-8 and translate them into more sophisticated exercises for teenagers.

Demonstrating

- For teachers, I recommend that you experiment and practice modeling exercises as part of your preparation *before* the lesson.
- Then demonstrate the creation of a particular form in front of the class.
- You may show the students the whole exercise or just a part to get them started. (Once your students are modeling regularly you can decide how much of an exercise should be demonstrated before they start.)
- On occasion, give only verbal descriptions or instructions and let them work out much for themselves.
- There are a variety of ways of inspiring and guiding projects from imitative rendering to individual choice and a whole range of variations in between.
- Parents may want to work alongside their children and figure out forms as they go along. Children love adults to model with them and share in the excitement of discovering and experiencing emerging forms.
- Display and admire results! Children should always be encouraged to feel that what they make with their hands is good and beautiful. There is nothing "wrong" with their charming creations.

Guiding

Once you set children in motion, it is often crucial to circulate among them to give individual advice. This is particularly so with pure non-representational forms that are more difficult to show and describe in comparison with, for example, the form of an elephant.

In cases where a child has real forming difficulties, you can even take up the piece and help it partially along and/or show your modeling example up close so they can render and copy it if necessary. In general, however, you can leave most students to their own resources in exploring the form assignment.

Basic forms can be practiced more than once before moving on. In this way the forms "sink into our hands and hearts" and we learn them "by heart." Our hands know how to feel, "speak" and "think" particular shapes out of form memory. Our hands are organs of intuition; they perceive and capture spirit forms.

In the Beginning Was the Sphere: From Wholeness Into Parts

Children in kindergarten and early childhood are often builders who love to build up figures piece by piece (people, houses, trees, etc). When they enter the grades, it is educationally and developmentally meaningful and practical to complement this so-called "synthetic" modeling approach with an "analytic" one (the whole differentiated into parts). This may mean that a child starts by forming her lump of clay first into a sphere, as one possibility. Then, without adding more material, she gradually and organically differentiates its parts and features by pushing and pulling. This leads to many possible shapes and surfaces: convex or concave, rounded or angular, smooth or rough. While this is not the only way, it is practical in several respects. Children like swinging into action right away and are better able to listen to further instructions while preparing their spheres. Keeping the piece of clay whole avoids having added parts dropping off easily. The sphere form meaningfully embodies the archetype of wholeness in the world (earth, sun, water drops, turtle eggs, etc.)

And a sphere fits so nicely in the round space naturally created between the facing cupped hands. Many pieces described in Series One through Four can begin as spheres in the hands cradled up by the heart and close to the eyes. Starting with spheres absorbs the children into immediate action with an "old friend" and has a "centering," focusing effect. (There is no dogma about always beginning with a sphere.) As their hands enlarge after age 10 and children want and are able to model larger heavier figures, pieces can *come down to earth* and be started off on a base on a table.

Making Up Form Stories for Younger Children

Younger children love their teachers and parents to make up and tell stories. Such tales can be about the dynamics of pure colors in painting: "One day sad Blue was quietly sulking in the corner. Along came gentle Yellow and cheered her up." Similarly, you also can tell tales about the character of forms in modeling: "Bumpy met Deep Hollow sitting and thinking about something." Hand awareness exercises may precede and introduce form stories (see examples in First and Second Series).

Keeping to Pure Form Language

In Series One through Four, exercises keep for the most part to a language of pure form and avoid giving the shapes a realistic, representational "thing" name. For example "sphere" is used instead of "ball" or "ovoid" instead of egg. If a form reminds a student of some "thing," he can verbalize a name as concept, "It's an egg!" Pure forms, after all, are meant to stimulate the imagination and connect us with the world! While practicing form modeling the instructor, however, stays within the realm of language of pure forms and de-emphasizes talking about actual "things" that can be taken up in other subjects. Class teacher Hella Loewe recommends that a teacher *"become aware of one's own way of speaking. The movement process while sculpting with clay can most vividly be described by using verbs such as 'form, turn, rotate, press, stretch, push, even out, explore,' and many others. The adjectives make the verbs subtler and differentiate them: 'push gently, stretch carefully, turn slowly,' and so forth. The teacher should, if possible, avoid too many nouns, using them only when there is no better choice, for example 'direction, bump, hollow hand, thumb.' In order to educate ourselves in this way of speaking, we have to practice."* (Loewe 2006, 76)

As thinking and self-awareness develop in ages 11–12 and up (Grades 5-8 and high school) you can more reflectively and intellectually explain that in form modeling we are not copying nature's actual forms, but we are joining nature in developing and exploring certain movements and motifs that lend themselves creatively to all kinds of shapes. In Series Five through Eight and beyond, exercises will involve terminology that refers to forms nature herself may be working with: leaf-like, crystal-like, organ-like, bone-like, etc. Older children should be able to go back and forth between the "World of Pure Forms" and "World of Nature Objects." Of course, the practice of modeling pure forms does not exclude, in other contexts, rendering nature forms "realistically." For example, modeling a femur or ear in clay as part of anatomy. The pure form work should enhance the anatomy exercises.

Although form modeling has a different emphasis, in the end, it sharpens our ability to penetrate deeply with our consciousness into the creative movement and form-making dynamics of nature; it develops the capacity to discern how the world is made.

Part II: More Perspectives

In addition to the core exercises of Part I, this handbook provides a number of chapters and articles at the end to help you ponder what you are doing as you proceed. For example, there is a chapter on the use of clay with very young children.

I suggest, however, that you avoid getting bogged down in studying all the chapters in Part II. *Instead, bring out the modeling material and start moving your hands as soon as possible!* Thoughts and questions will emerge as you proceed. Experience will make further parallel reading and study more and more meaningful as you **teach yourself and learn through doing!**

For still more advice on modeling techniques and choice of materials, see *Learning about the World through Modeling: Sculptural Ideas for School and Home*. The two manuals complement each other and I recommend that serious modelers own both.

Clarification of Terminology

- I use the terms "form" and "shape" synonymously in both their noun and verb forms.
- "Sculpture" encompasses both modeling and carving (although the word sculpture confusingly comes from the Latin "*scalpere*" meaning to "carve away. "Carving" per se is a subtractive process only taking away substance).
- In modeling you can differentiate a "whole into the parts" by pushing and pulling a fixed amount of material (analytic method) or build up a whole by adding material (synthetic method).
- The "whole to parts" approach and starting with a sphere is emphasized in this book because it simulates an organic process of one entity going through a series of changing stages of form.

History: Further Complications of Terms

- "Modeling" unfortunately often has the connotation of copying and working from a "model."
- The original Greek name for sculpture was "plastic art," derived from *"plastikos"* and *"plassein"* meaning "to mold" and "to form." In art histories the term "plastic arts" is still used. Today, you also hear of brain "plasticity," meaning the capacity to be altered or molded.

- The most comprehensive word for modeling/sculpting would be "**plasticizing**." (The Germans use the word "*plastizieren*" for modeling and "*Plastik*" for sculpture.

- Unfortunately, in the English world the plastics industry has taken over "plastic" and "plasticizing."

- If I could change the language usage, I think I would choose a new word for modeling adopted from the English nature poet Kathleen Raine: *Shape-shifting by Shape-shifters!*

> *…Those abiding essences the rocks and hills and mountains*
> *Are to themselves and not to human sense.*
> *Persons they appeared, but not personified…*
> *Shape-shifters they are, appear and disappear,*
> *Protean assume their guises and transformations*
> *Each in as many forms as eyes behold.*
>   —Kathleen Raine, "The Elementals," in *Selected Poems*, 1989

Handhelds and Finger Reliefs

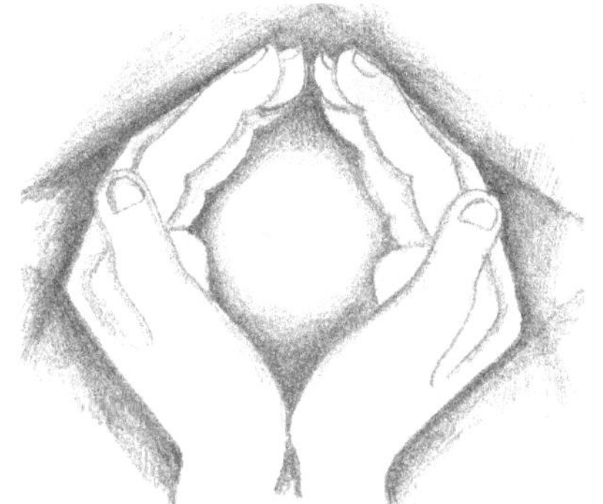

Modeling in Your Hand-Heart Space

The space between our two cupped and moving hands is a creation space, a womb-space in which forms are birthed.

Holding up and modeling a form between the two hands in front of the chest allows us to turn it every which way and experience it intimately as a sculpture "completely in the round." The first human sculptures of 30,000 years ago were small and could be held in the hand—the first handhelds!

At any given moment you are having three main sense experiences. You are touching, moving and seeing the piece. There is always one side, however, that is invisible to the eyes and only sensed through touching and moving. This has a balancing effect because our very conscious eyes often predominate and are a driving force in the shaping process.

Feeling but not seeing a form calls on and educates our "haptic" perception, a capacity combining exploratory touching with moving the hands and fingers over surfaces. Just holding a stationary object in the hand can also give us a haptic sense of its shape, but moving around it adds a fuller sculptural dimensionality. With this sense of form, people can readily identify objects without using their eyes. It is our quintessential "modeling sense." Periodically, it is vitalizing to close our eyes and experience forms just with our very perceptive hands. (See the chapter in Part II: En-*live*-ning Our Senses.)

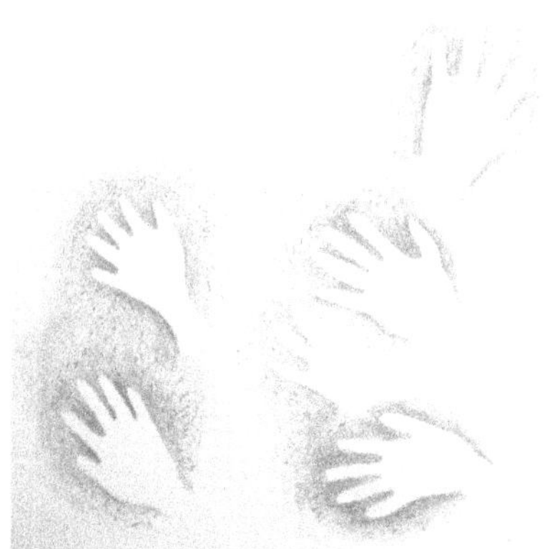

Hand stencils on cave walls 40,000 years old

Modeling on a Table

Modeling a piece standing upright on a modeling board on a table means that the base is hidden, but you are working on most of its surface. The piece is more distanced and separate from you, "out there" standing on its own on the earth. You do not feel its mass and ponderousness unless you lift it. You can, of course, shape out a piece completely in the hands first, then set it on a table and work on it further.

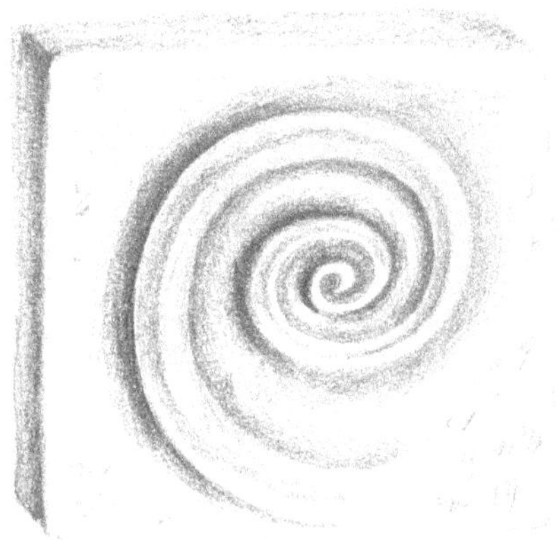

Spiral tool-shaped

Modeling in Relief with Bare Fingers and Tools

Modeling in Relief means that the back half of a piece of material is flat, hidden and not modeled. Relief sculpture is much less three-dimensional and tends to be more picture-like, abstract, and less of "whole-mass-object experience." It is surface sculpture and goes in the direction of form drawing and graphic art. Relief modeling is not whole-handheld but rather emphasizes the fingers as shapers. Fingers are the more nerve-sense, intellectual parts of our hands and even have little skullcaps over one side.

Children in the first five grades can use their bare fingers to push and press geometrical motifs in the clay. As students reach a more intellectual stage in the upper grades, the number of reliefs can be increased. They are eager for new modes of modeling and some tool use can be introduced, although it lessens direct hand-sense contact. (This is similar to the transition from freehand geometry to the use of compasses as instruments in geometry around age 12.)

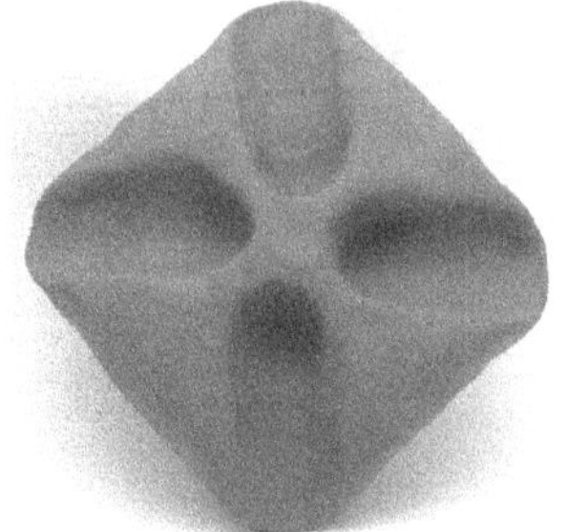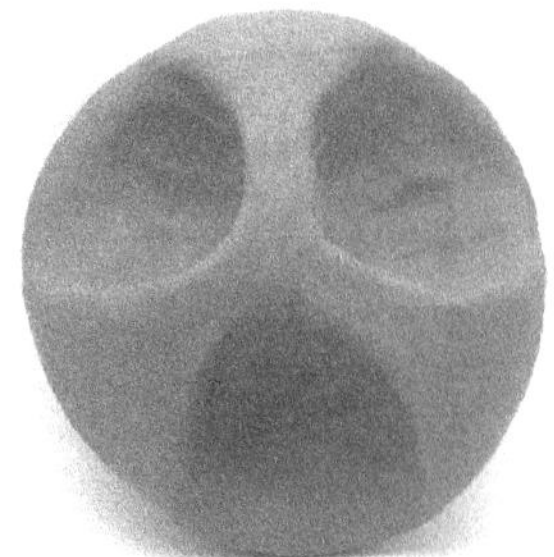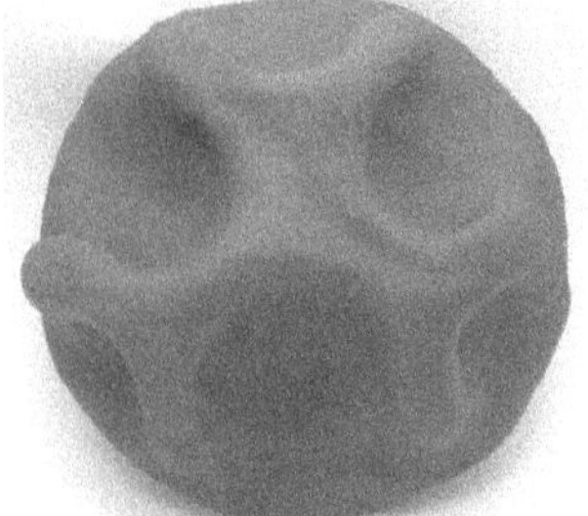

Reliefs for Series Three through Five

Awareness of Our Wonderful Hands

It is very educationally valuable for teachers in modeling lessons to regularly make their children aware in various ways of *how special their hands are*—their marvelous shape, their incredible flexibility of movement, and what they are capable of. We have the whole world and its forms in our hands!

Below I offer a list of brief hand awareness descriptions and actions that can occasionally precede modeling exercises, especially in the younger grades. Teachers are encouraged to spontaneously improvise and make up their own as they work with the children.

- Hold up one hand. Look at its shape. The palm side likes to curve and make a hollow so it can hold things (concave). Its palm and fingers have pads to cushion what it holds. Now take up your piece of clay and feel how it is held and cushioned in the hollow of your hand.

- The other side of the hand tends to curve in an opposite way (convex) and appears bumpier and bonier with knobby knuckles. It is not cushioned and can't really hold anything.

- Of course you can stretch your hand out as straight as you can to make a flat hand. And you can spread your fingers out wide to make a star or tightly curl them up again in a spiral to make solid fist. The hand is capable of all kinds shapes—curves, flat and straight, and even a spiral—all of which we combine in movement to model. So let's see how our hands are going to move today and what form will be born

- Now look, children how we have two hands who love to do all sorts of things.

- Raise them high and greet them this morning—Right and Left. They love to work together. Take up your piece of clay in front of your heart like this and watch how Right and Left move together to shape a sphere. See how they spiral round and round making it smoother and smoother.

- But oh there are still cracks and little holes. Call on strong Thumb to the rescue! He has separated from his more delicate sisters the four Fingers and become very muscular so he can do heavier work. Have him wander over the sphere and press rough spots smooth with his wide pad and even them out. And then the Fingers can help too. They can a follow and touch up places with their gentle pads. And now roll the sphere around between your two hands again until all is smooth and round and ready to become a ___________!

- Our hands are so good at smoothing that we don't need to roll the sphere around on a flat table…

In Part II, there are additional hand awareness exercises and a list of curriculum themes.

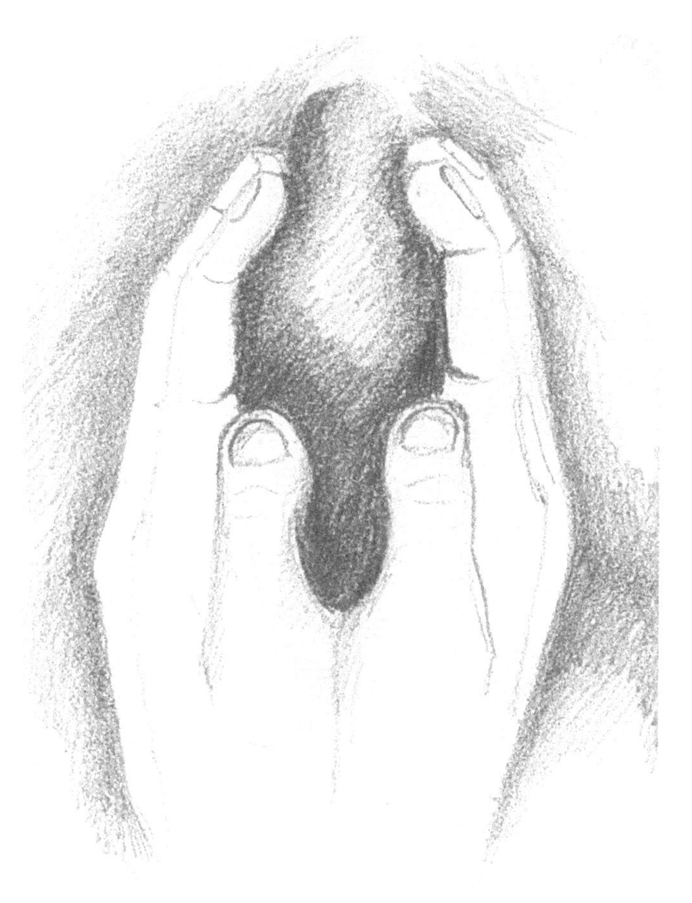

Part I
Exploring

What use is nature shining before your eyes,
What use are all those art works around you,
If creative power does not lovingly fill your soul
And flow into your fingertips to shape new works of beauty.
–Goethe

The Proteus Exercise
Spontaneous Discovery of Pure Forms by Your Exploring Hands

PROTEUS, born in the surging sea as son of Poseidon, possessed the power to change shape at will and to take on the guise of many forms. He was able to foretell the future.

This general exercise may be practiced at intervals as a fundamental experience of our intuitive hands, engaging in free, creative exploration. It may be done on its own as a main exercise or used as a brief warm-up or "creative loosener" prior to modeling a main subject. Modify it according to what works best for you.

Large Format

- Take up a piece of clay* that fits comfortably between both hands and round it into a sphere. After using your whole hands, end by using the pads of your thumbs and other fingers to smooth rough spots.
- Hold your sphere between both cupped hands. Close your eyes and feel its roundness.
- Count to three and spontaneously squeeze the sphere gently so that a new shape arises. (Experiment with different types of random squeezes and applications of pressure on subsequent occasions).
- Look at the form as a new beginning and very gradually articulate and transform it into an interesting, non-representational sculpture. It may often look quite organic!

Small Format

- Take up a piece of clay that fits comfortably in one hand (walnut or plum size) and round it into a sphere with one hand.
- After using your whole hand, end by using both hands and the pads of your thumbs and other fingers to smooth rough spots.
- Enclose your sphere in one hand and feel its roundness. Give it a random squeeze.
- With two hands, develop the resulting form further.
- This small format can serve as a warm-up and/or "loosener."

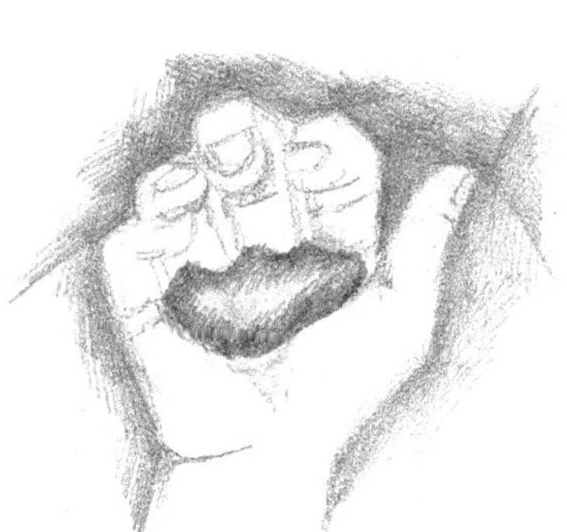

The aim of the Proteus Exercise is for you to develop the capacity to discover free forms

---

* Materials: Clay and playdough work with both formats; beeswax and plasticine with the small format.

without a lot of preconception. The artistic process is full of wonderful surprises. Allow your hands to playfully invent new shapes! Trust in these spirit-permeated organs of will. They are risk-taking explorers of forms streaming to us out of the future—and never seen before!

Series One: Form Stories

There once lived in the Land of Forms
All kinds of shapes
All kinds of forms.
For forms are shapes
And shapes are forms
We see them in everything!
In stars and worms!
Curved or flat, hollow or round,
Everywhere 'round us
They can be found.
Just take in your hands a lump of clay.
Turn it and mold it in a special way
And see! A new form will be born today!

Sphere
Ovoid
Bumpy
Little Hollow
Hand Hollow
Twins
Stretcher
Long Stretcher
Little Curl
Spiral Curl
Pointer
Curved Pointer
Magic Mirror
Roll Up and Oval Mirror
Center and Edge
Raying from Center
Widening and Pointing
Flat and Curved
Curled Up Beside Each Other
One Two Three
Crescent
Wavy and Zigzag
Sphere on Two Disks
Magic Rescuing Ring
Straight and Curved

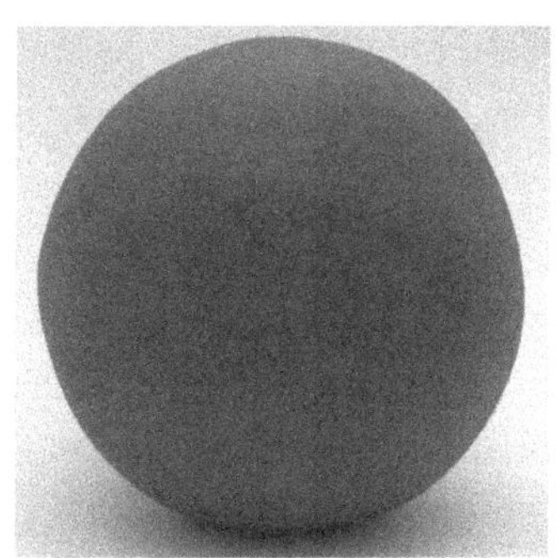

Sphere

Hand Awareness: Hold the cups of your two hands in front of you. Put them side by side and make a bowl. Face your two curved hands opposite each other to form a round space inside.

Once upon a time there was a Lump of clay. She wanted to become as round as the shining sun. Let us help her turn and turn into smooth curves all over until she is a round shape with a new name—Sphere!

Give your creations geometric "form names" like "Sphere" and "Ovoid" rather than "Ball" or "Egg" which then intellectually fix the forms to "things" too quickly. Teachers may elaborate upon the form story sketches in this book according to the ages and needs of their students. Make most of these stories longer.

The sphere can serve as the archetypal progenitor of and starting point for the development of all kinds of forms. Teach your children to take up their lumps of clay automatically and begin working on a sphere before evolving it into a further form.

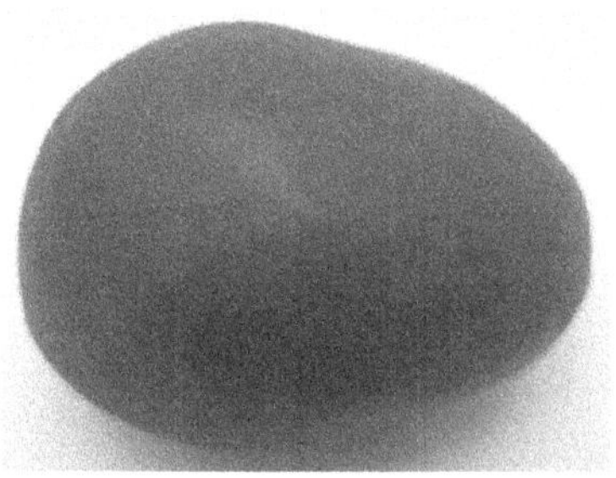

Ovoid

Hand Awareness: Make an ovoid-shaped space between your two facing hands.

One day our friend Sphere wanted to stretch out into the world. Let us help her twist at one end and grow a little longer like this. But oh, how she has become so different! She must change her name to Ovoid. She is learning how to play with others, to share and not just to keep to herself.

The Sphere is the form representing universal wholeness; the Ovoid is the first archetypal step of extending into life. The "egg" shape is a mythical form associated with the creation and genesis of the world from unity into multiplicity.

From Chronos (Time) came Chaos the Infinite and Ether the Finite. By the creative action of Ether, cosmic matter was slowly organized and finally was shaped as a Universal Egg. In the center of this gigantic Egg was born the first being, Phanes—the Light! who united with Night and created Heaven and Earth and Zeus.

—Greek creation myth

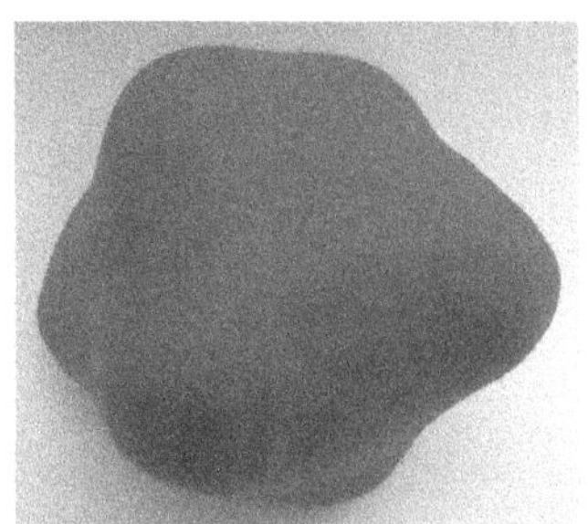

Bumpy

One day Sphere felt herself bursting on all her sides with so much joy that she turned into Bumpy! She never lost her smoothness, however, and did not want to be teased as Lumpy Bumpy.

From Convex Bulging to Concave Hollowing

The preceding basic forms involve the fundamental gesture of extending and bulging out toward the world imagined as a growth process from inside pushing outward. The next exercise works with concavity and the hollowing out of an inner space from outside inward.

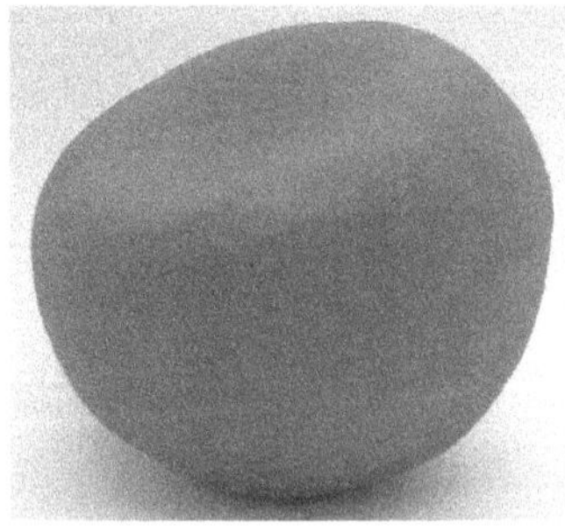

Little Hollow

Sphere felt Thumb pressing gently and changed into Little Hollow.

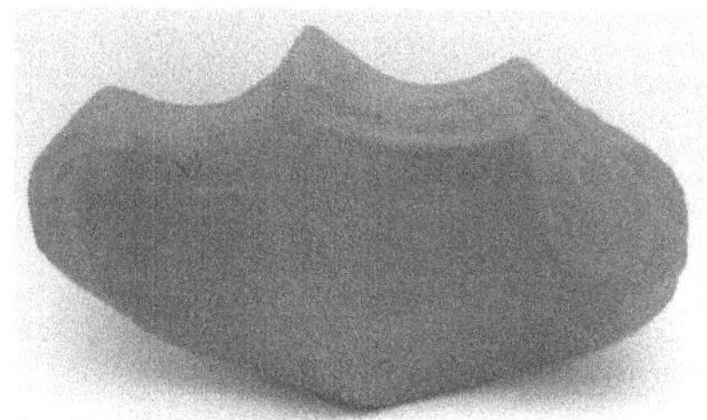

Hand Hollow

Hand Awareness: Children, close one of your hands but leave a slight crack open between your fingertips and the heel of your hand. Peek into the little space in your hand. How does it look? Soft, warm and dark—a cozy place in which to fall asleep?

Sphere went to sleep inside of Hand who held her very, very tightly. When Sphere awoke and Hand opened, she felt longer with curves going this way and that. She knew that she had become Hand Hollow.

(This form may remind children of a "shell" and cause them to verbalize such "concept." Such "it-looks-like" associations, made *after* doing an exercise, need not distract from the pure form experience which naturally stimulates associations and imagination!)

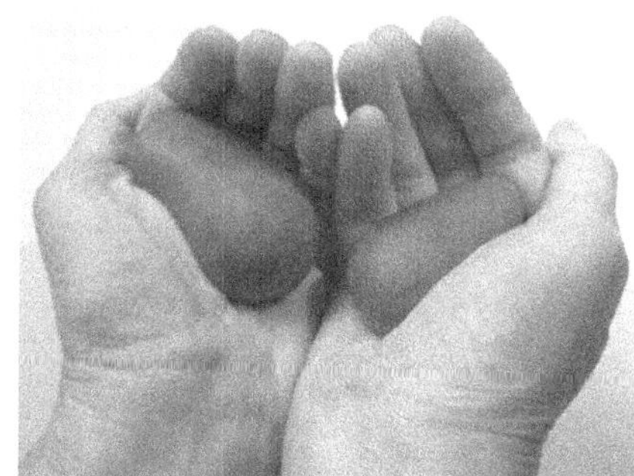

Twins Cradled in Hands

One Twin loved to nestle in the right hand and the other in the left hand.

Cradle elongated twin forms in two cupped hands side by side to feel convexity in concavity and symmetry.

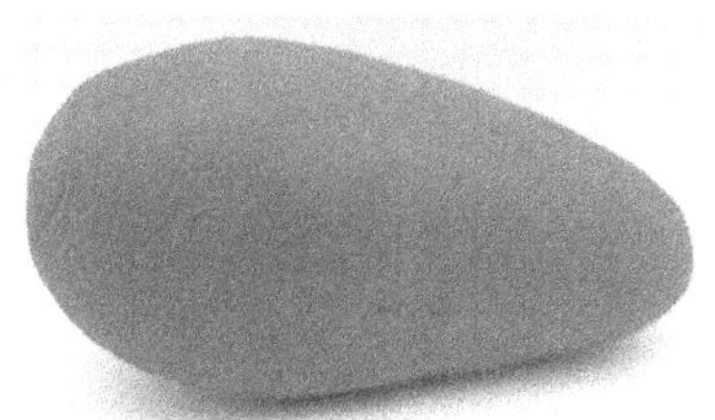

Stretcher (Convexity)

Hand Awareness: Make a sphere shape with your two cupped hands. Stretch it slightly into an ovoid. Let's see what happens when it is stretched further!

Once there was a form that wanted to go out into the world farther and farther—farther than any of his friends, Sphere and Ovoid. She stretched and stretched and stretched and soon found herself poking into all kinds of corners. Her name was Stretcher.

Long Stretcher

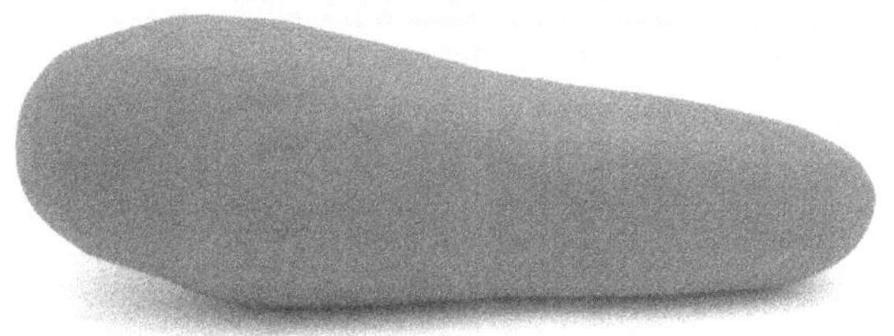

Stretcher was even more curious and one day stretched herself even further into Long Stretcher.

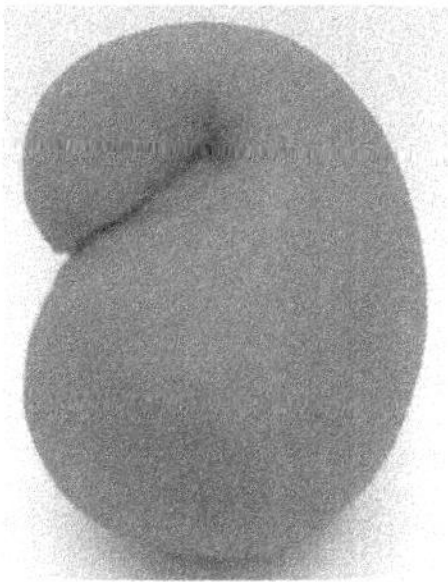

Little Curl and Spiral Curl

Stretcher curved into Little Curl.

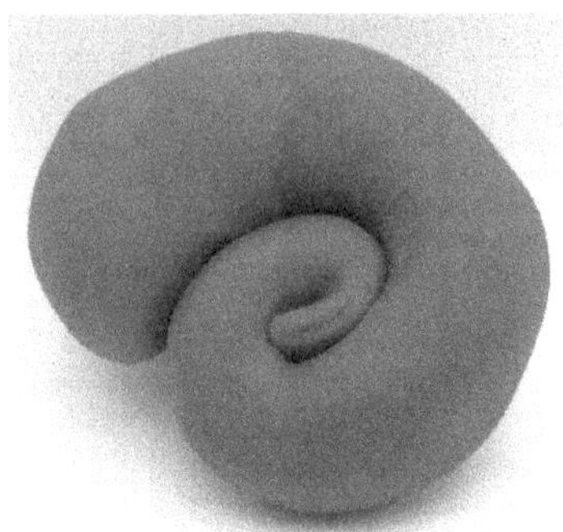

Long Stretcher curled into a Spiral Curl for a nap.

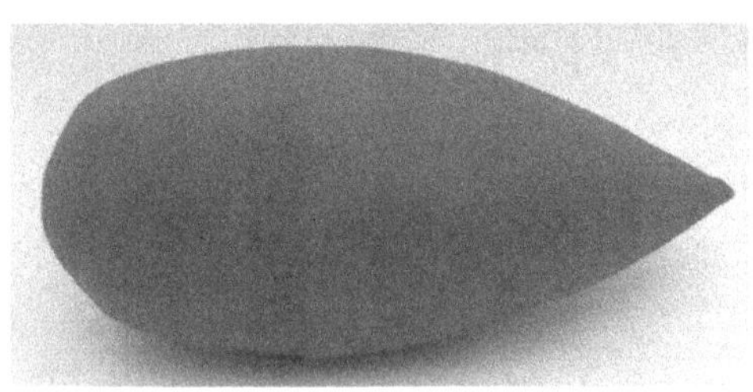

Pointer and Curved Pointer

Once Ovoid pointed so suddenly that she changed her name to Pointer.

(Option: Make up a story and form for a Long Pointer)

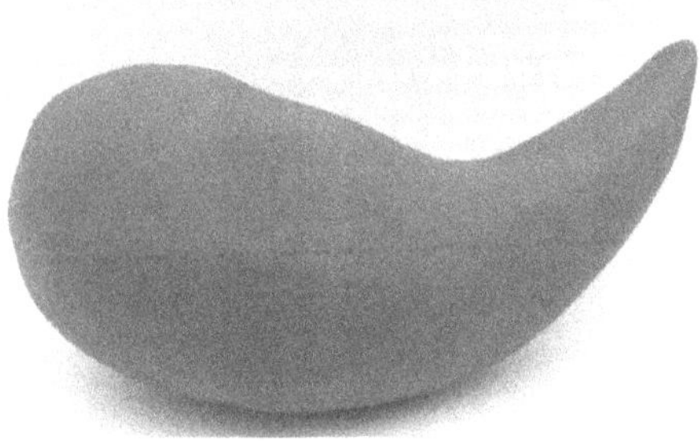

One day Pointer admired Sphere's roundness so much that she bent herself a bit into Curved Pointer.

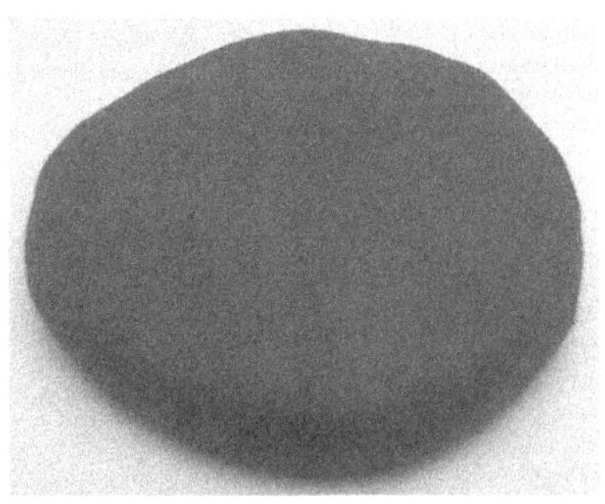

Magic Mirror (Flatness)

One day Sphere lay down to sleep on the earth feeling ever so tired and heavy. When she awoke she was still round but had become a flat Magic Mirror. Look into her and see the forms of all the world mirrored in her! I see a___________ ! (bumpy form, hollow form, bird, etc.)

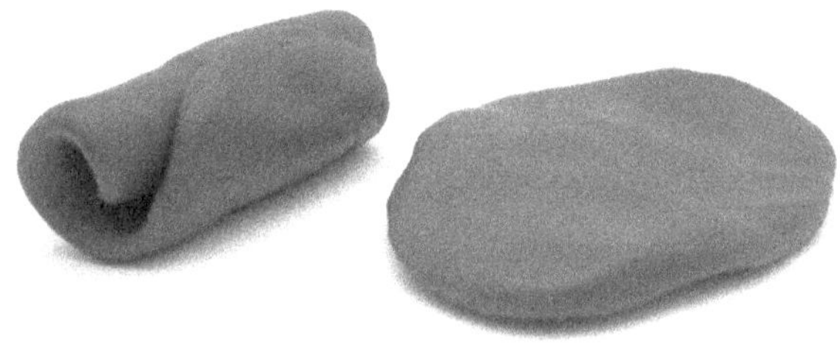

Roll Up and Oval Mirror

Two Twin Spheres flattened into two oval mirrors. One was tired and rolled up into a sleeping Roll Up.

Press spheres into a flat ovals. Roll one up.

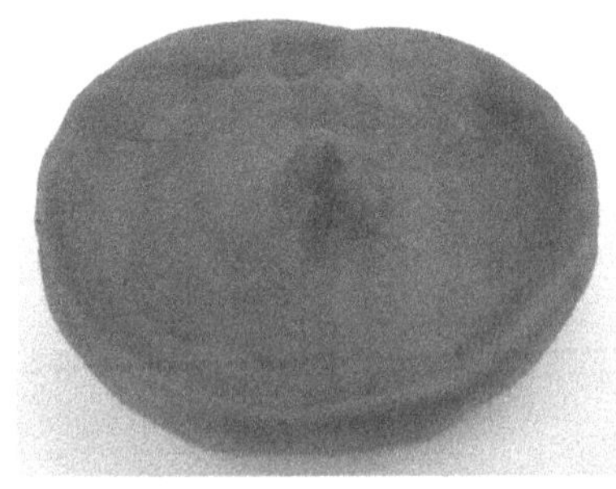

Center and Edge

Sphere spread out flat one day leaving a bump in the middle. Her edges turned up!

Widen out and flatten a sphere leaving a center bump. Curl up the outer edges of the circle edge.

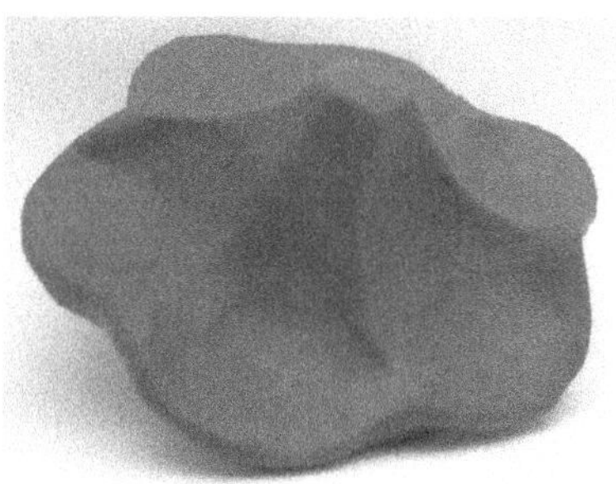

Raying from the Center

Sphere flattened and widened into six hollows leaving a bump in the middle.

Widen and flatten a sphere leaving a center bump. As you widen, make six hollows radiating out from the center.

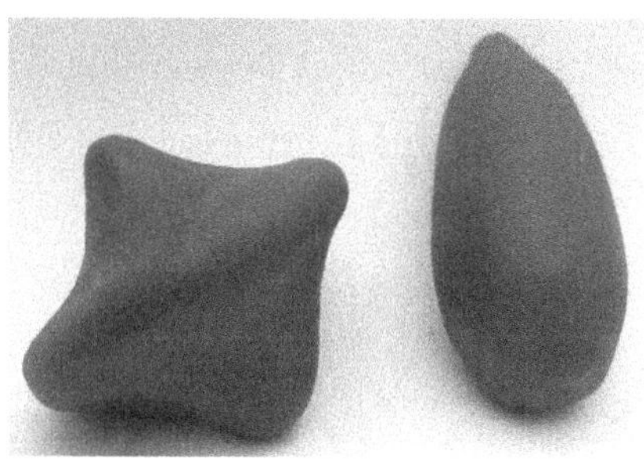

Widening and Pointing

One Sphere started to flatten and widen his sides and left a rounded middle and round points on his top and bottom. Another Sphere stretched out from one of her sides into a sharp point.

Press the sides of a sphere down and out into a disk-like middle but leave top and bottom center bumps. Pull one side of a sphere out into a narrowing point.

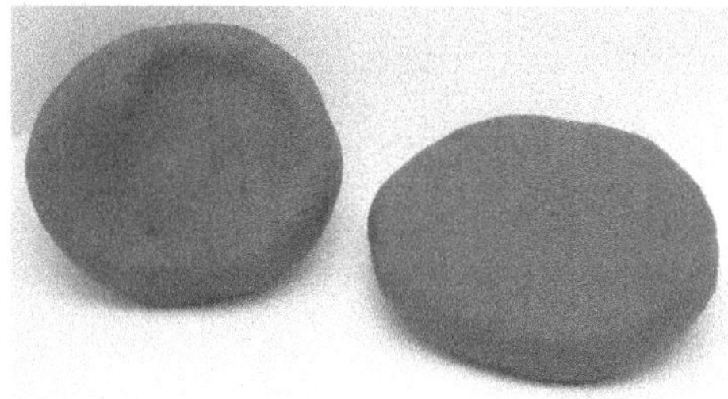

Flat and Curved

Two twin Spheres sank down to the ground: one became Flat; the other become almost flat but kept a curve on an edge and was called Curved.

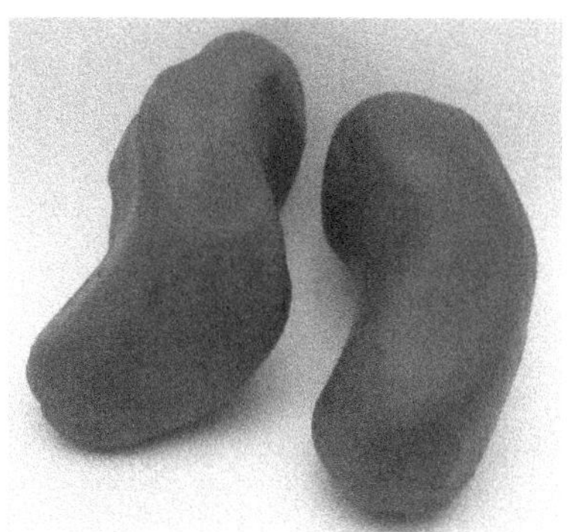

Curled Up Beside Each Other

Two Spheres stretched out on the cold ground and kept each other warm.

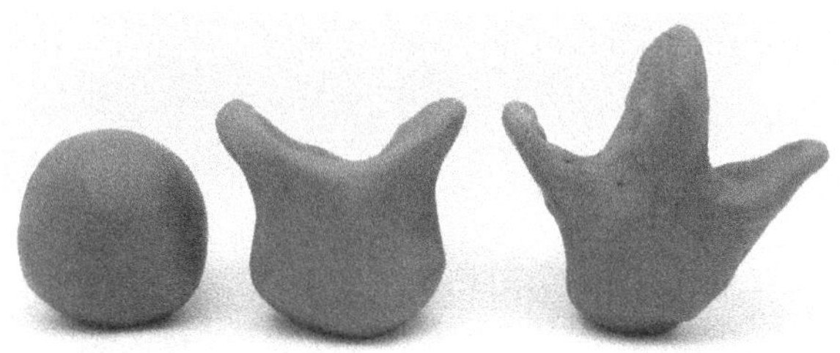

One Two Three!

Three spheres sat in a row. The second one shouted, "I feel like a Two today!" The third exclaimed, " I feel like a three!" To which the first sadly replied, "I feel no different—just One and the same."

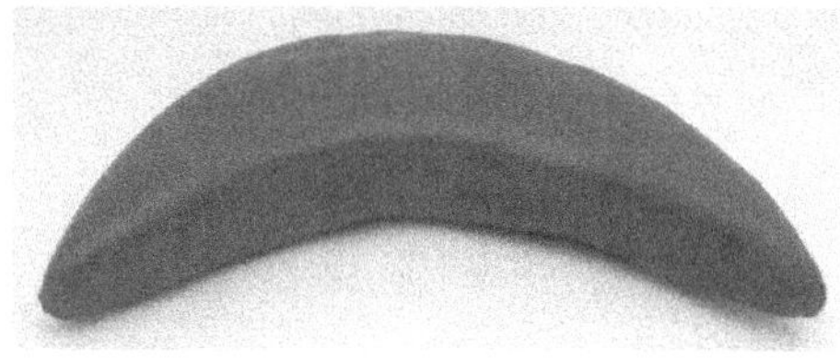

Crescent

Double Pointer became curved and flat. Her new name was Crescent.

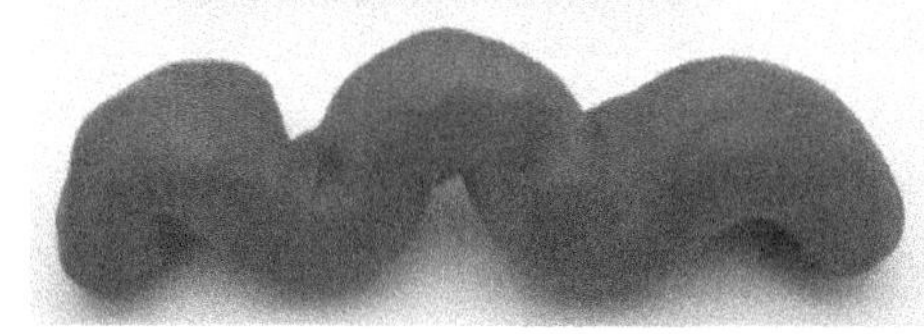

Wavy

One day Stretcher stretched out very, very long. Suddenly she felt a chill ripple in curves through her and she turned into Wavy.

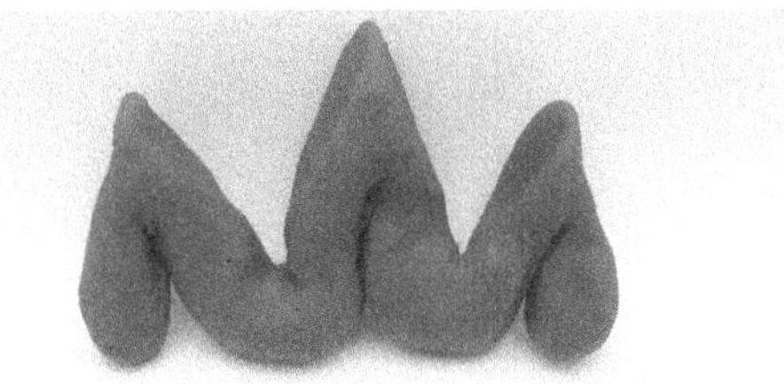

Zigzag

That night Stretcher felt even colder still and her back froze into a sharp zigzag!

The Wavy exercise story and exercise can immediately continue into the Zigzag incident in the same lesson or these two forms can be done in two separate lessons. A new Wavy is made and then angled.

Repeating, Running Forms

"Running" forms such as the preceding series of Wavy or Zigzag dynamically repeat the same simple element. They can be modeled individually or by groups of children. Imagine a whole class modeling a twelve foot meandering series of waves or of large bumps alternating with small bumps—in clay or on tables or in a sandbox.

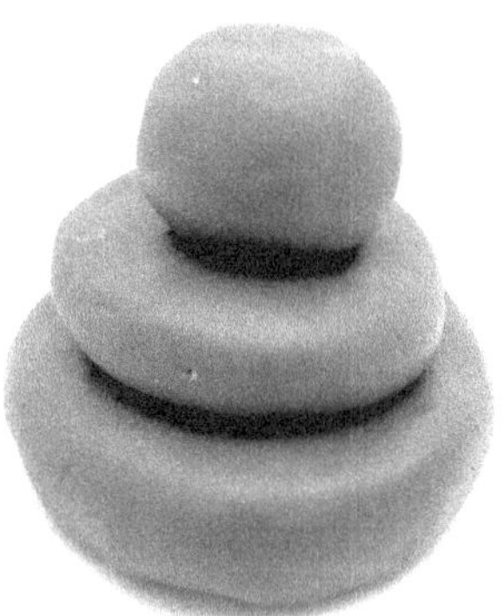

Sphere on Two Disks

1. Pull a small and a medium piece out of a sphere, leaving a large one.
2. Turn the three pieces into spheres.
3. Press the medium and large spheres into disks and place the medium on top of the large.
4. Place the small sphere on the very top.

Form Drawing: *A 2-D counterpart to this exercise is drawing concentric circles around a center point.*

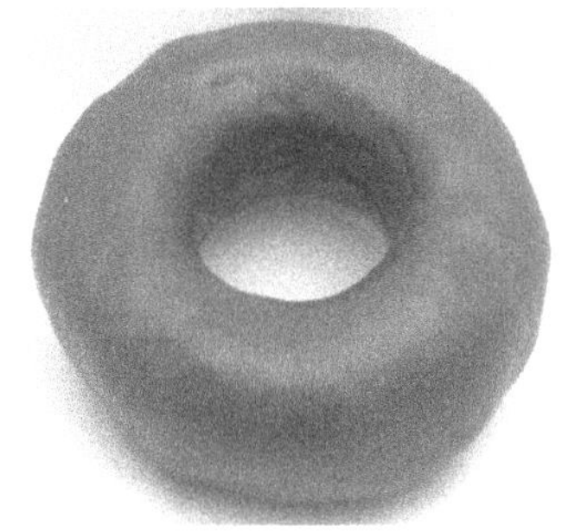

Magic Rescuing Ring

1. Press your thumb and pointer into opposite sides of a sphere until they almost touch.
2. Poke a hole through.
3. Round the edges of this ring.

Story: *There once was a prince who could only rescue the princess with a magic ring… (A powerful ring story will eclipse the donut association).*

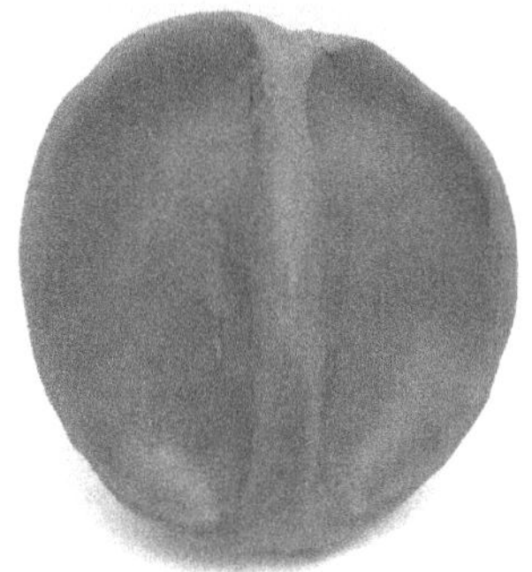

Straight and Curved Relief

1. Press thumbs into the sides of a sphere, leaving a ridge in between.
2. Make the center into a straight ridge.
3. Curve the two sides and lift them up into raised borders.

See Series Five: This form is pod-like.

Creating Thick Relief Forms in Groups

Most of the forms in Series One have been full, three-dimensional objects that can be held up in the hand and touched on all sides. It is also enjoyable to create forms in sand on a table or board or in a shallow box or tub. Such forms are like frontal faces with the backs or bases unseen, untouched and flat. Forms in relief are more abstract than forms in the round and are another wonderful way of exploring pure forms.

Sand Modeling

In two chapters in his book *Educating the Will*, Michael Howard describes how to create beautiful relief sculpture in sand or clay on tables. He shows examples of wavy and angular zig-zag-like forms. These are truly 3-D cousins of 2-D form drawing patterns. The worlds of form drawing and form modeling can inspire each other as you and the children learn the languages of 2-D and 3-D. Create a myriad of different forms for children by experimenting with different designs. Be playful! Make up your own!

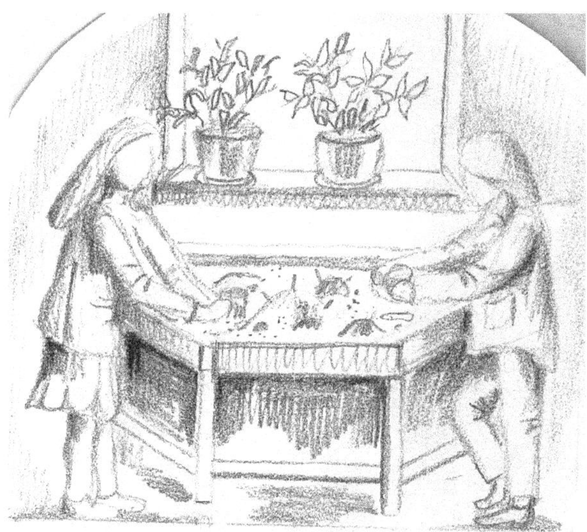

Sand Table

Have a sand table or boxes of sand readily available in the classroom so that children can make all kinds of forms in them—round mounds, hollows, cones, towers, meandering channels or ridges, etc. Sand must be moistened with a handy spray bottle before use.

More Basic Sculptural Modeling

For additional wonderful forms that can be added to the above exercises, see Hella Loewe's book *Basic Sculptural Modeling*: Sphere, Ovoid, Saddle Form, etc. It includes lots of hand awareness tips!

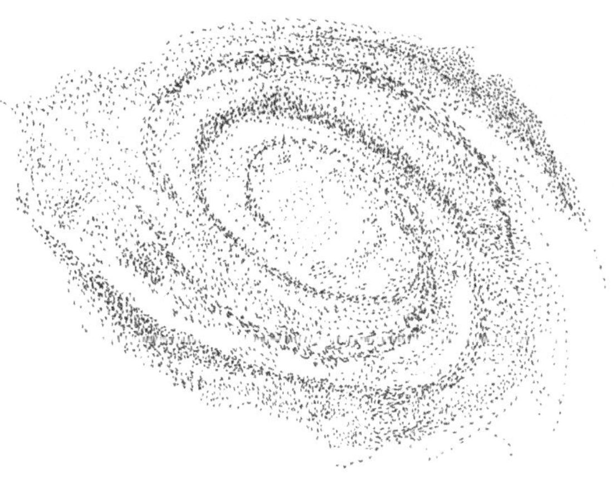

Learning How the World Is Made

The First Series strengthens perception of the most fundamental forms out of which nature and the universe are formed:

1. convexity, bulging, roundness, spherical, circle periphery and center; *Examples*: sun and moon, turtle eggs, eye ball
2. concavity, hollows, inner spaces, pockets, indentations; *Examples*: caves, nests, eye sockets,
3. flatness, straightness
4. stretching, extending; *Examples*: plant growth stemming, crystallization
5. curving; *Examples*: claws, rainbow
6. spirals, curling; *Examples*: galaxies, chambered nautilus, water vortexes, drying leaf
7. pointedness, sharpness, angularity
8. symmetry and asymmetry

All of these qualities come from different formative forces working in the world and in ourselves.

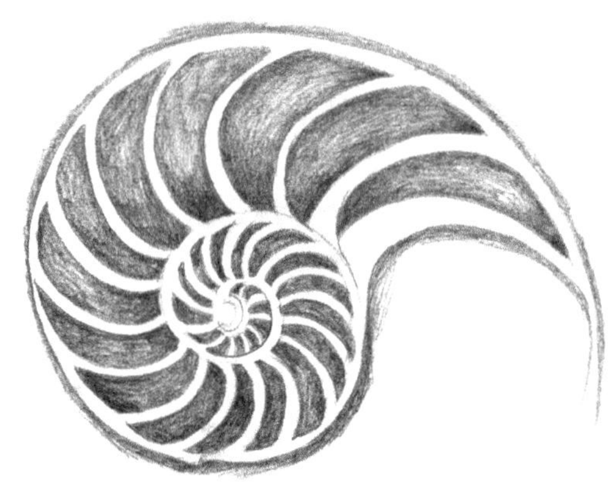

Practical Advice

Re-using and Storing Plasticine as Flat Magic Mirrors

It is very practical to store pieces in a flat shape for easy reuse. A thin flat mirror disk of plasticine (such as in the preceding Magic Mirror exercise) warms and softens very quickly in contrast to a thick solid lump. Energetic fingers can make it even thinner and inject new warmth into it. The disk can be held between warm palms for a few moments before shaping.

Daily Quick Form Exercises

To keep your children's sculptural capacities limber, have them keep two round Magic Mirrors in their desks in a sleeping bag (small zippered plastic bag) ready for spontaneous modeling in main lesson or at other lesson times. Children can take this kit out at a moment's notice for quick 5+ minute form exercises. This can happen on days when they do not have their weekly clay or beeswax modeling lesson. Quick daily exercises can go on for "runs" of several weeks; then give them a rest. Do this kind of activity whenever needed—Mondays after the weekend—to harmonize the class, much as form drawing is sometimes used.

Children automatically combine the two warmed disks into a sphere and await the word(s) of the day from your lips: "Ovoid!" or "Egg." Then a little later say "Bird!" and all hands take flight, making in five minutes, out of an egg form a rich array of bird forms that fly and then reverently curl back gently into a ball.

This large ball is then divided into two smaller ones which are flattened into two mirrors and placed back in the sleeping bag. Magic Mirrors hold the images of all the world in case you had not guessed—and so do Crystal Spheres. Use imaginative, winged words to generate warm anticipation!

Remember to make up spontaneous form stories as you go along

. . . Oh, even though Sphere was so beautiful and round, she was shy and kept to herself. Stretcher stretched out to her and showed her how to come outside and play together with others. . .

Feeling Forms: Pebble Exercise

Have a collection of smooth pebbles of varying shapes on hand. Pass them out periodically so that children can feel the forms in their hand with eyes closed. (Up through age 10.)

> *Think cosmically,*
> *Teach locally!*

Series Two: Form Stories

We have the whole world in our hands. The flexible threefold human hand is capable of making an infinite number of movements and forms. The tips of our fingers are like little heads with hard skullcaps on one side and are full of nerves and sensitivity on the other. The blind "see" with their fingers. The hollow heart of our palm is full of feeling and can be tickled! The bottom is strong and will-full with muscles which have pulled Thumb away from his four Sisters (or Brothers). Muscular Thumb opposes the four slender fingers. But thank goodness for that! That gives us our fine precision human grips! The space between our two moving hands is a creation space in which forms are born!

Flat Bottom Bump
Twosome
Lopsided Twosome
Very Long Spiral Pointer
Double Pointer
Deep Hollow
Double Hollow
Double Curve
Deep Double Curve
Two Meets Three
Brother and Sister
Triangular Hollow
Hollow Cone
Crouching Form
Widening and Narrowing
Two Harmony Friends
Three Friends
Mirror Forms
Pinching a Pentagon
Rising Spiral
Twin Hollows
Two Sides Separated
Ring Around a Ring

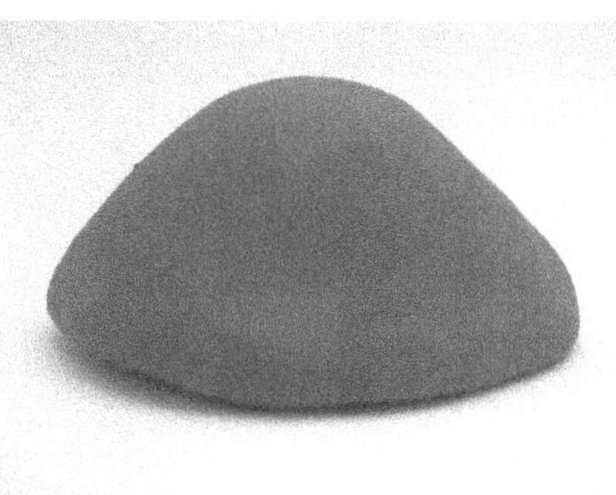

Flat Bottom Bump
Tired, Sphere sat down in one place for a long, long time. When she tried to get up, she found she could not roll. She felt so heavy and had become Flat Bottom Bump. Press down the sphere on the upturned palm of the left hand with the bunched fingers of the right hand.

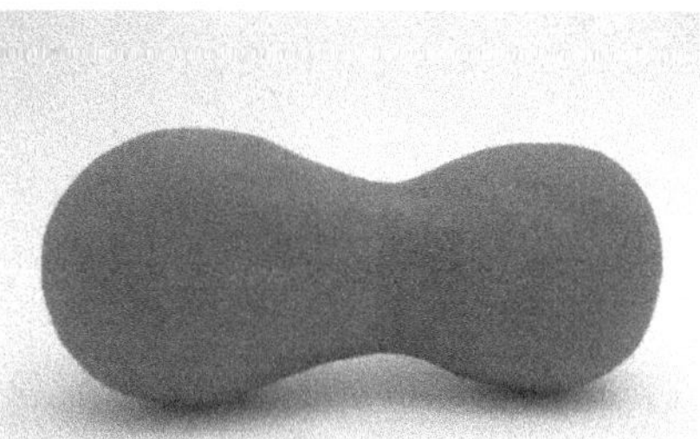

Twosome
One day Sphere was given such a big hug that she turned into Twosome (or two big

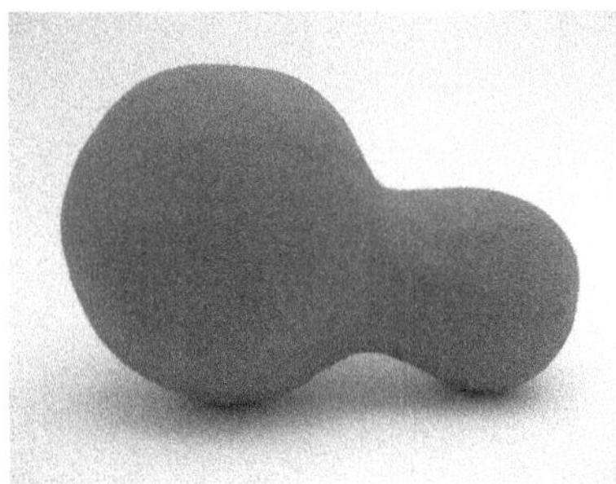

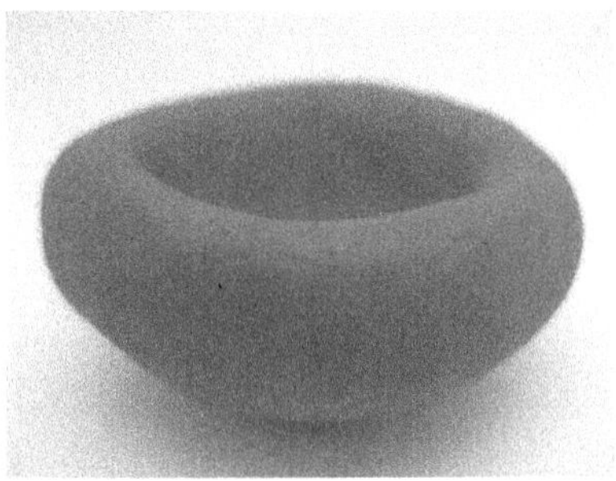

hugs into Threesome, etc.).

left and turned into Double Pointer.

Lopsided Twosome
Sphere was hugged on one side more than the other so that she became a Lopsided

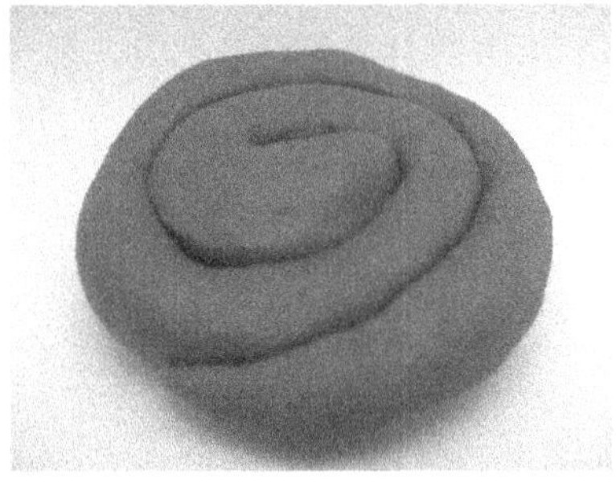

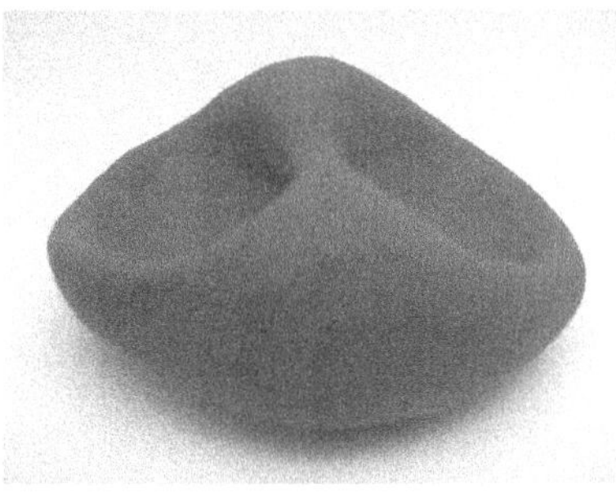

Twosome with a larger and a smaller side.

Very Long Spiral Pointer
Curved Long Pointer kept becoming longer and longer and curved inward to take a nap.

Deep Hollow
Sphere again felt Thumb pressing in and changed into Deep Hollow.

Double Hollow
Double Bump felt so tired one day that she collapsed into a Double Hollow.

  Make a double bump and press bumps into hollows.

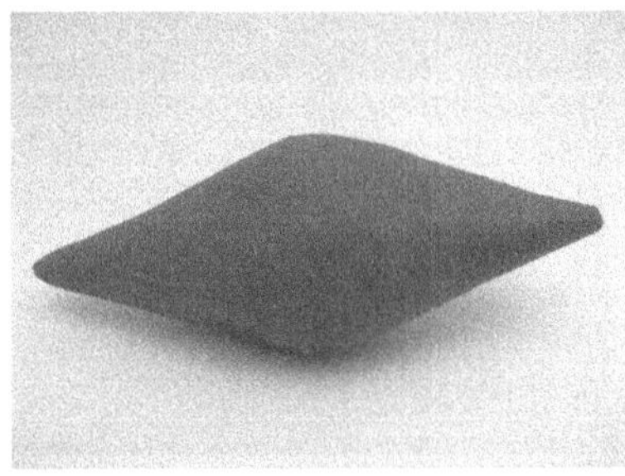

He became Very Long Spiral Pointer.

Double Pointer
Pointer pointed to his right and pointed to his

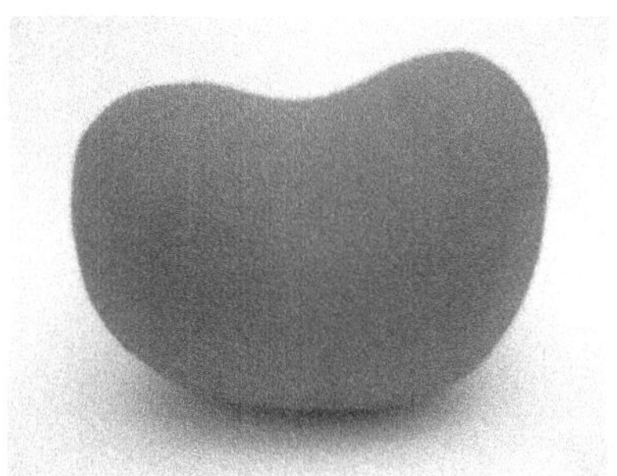

Double Curve

Hand Awareness: Look at the knuckles on the top of one of your hands. Do they remind you of Hand Hollow? Take your pointer finger and move down the hollow curve between two knuckles. Then in the same space trace the curve that goes up and then down but in the direction of the fingers (at right angles). Two kinds of curves come together in special Double Curve (like a saddle form). Demonstrate on your own hand.

Thumb pressed down on Sphere, rocked back and forth and became Double Curve.

Press into a sphere to make a double curve.

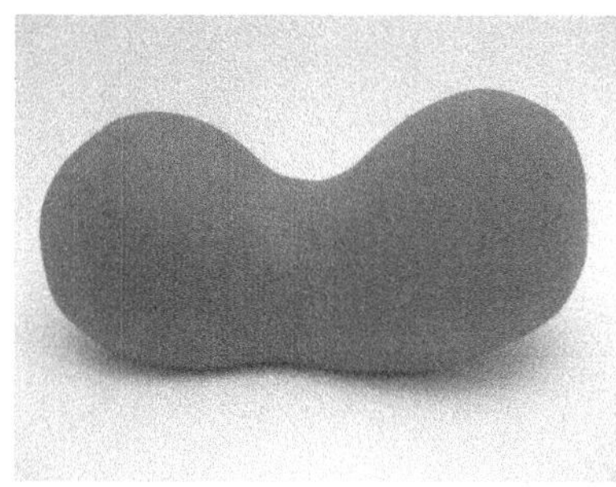

Deep Double Curve

Thumb pressed down even deeper and became Deep Double Curve. (In another exercise one can also emphasize the convex Double Bump.)

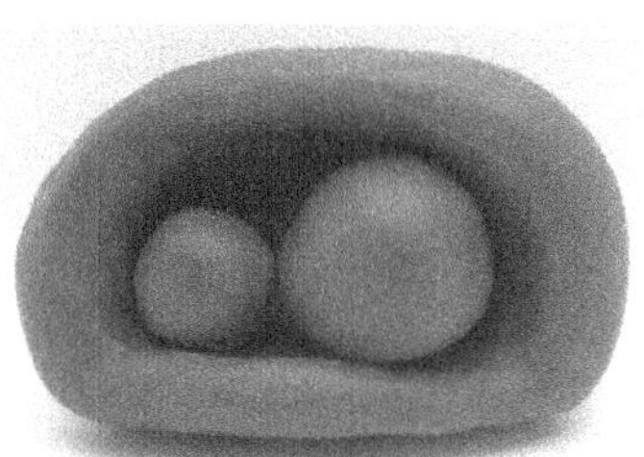

Brother and Sister Sphere in a Hollow

Brother and Sister Sphere hid in a hollow.

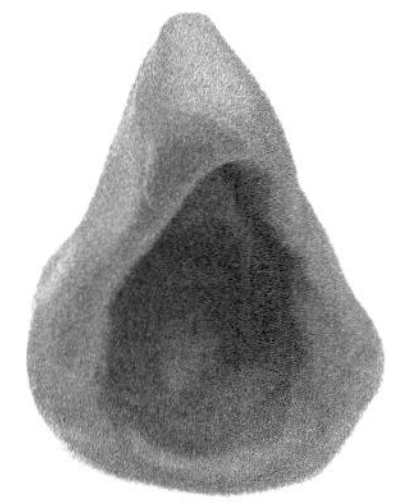

Triangular Hollow

Flatten a sphere's base and point its top. Press a hollow into it. Smooth the surface but leave a form rough and not perfectly geometric and triangular. Who do you imagine lives in there?

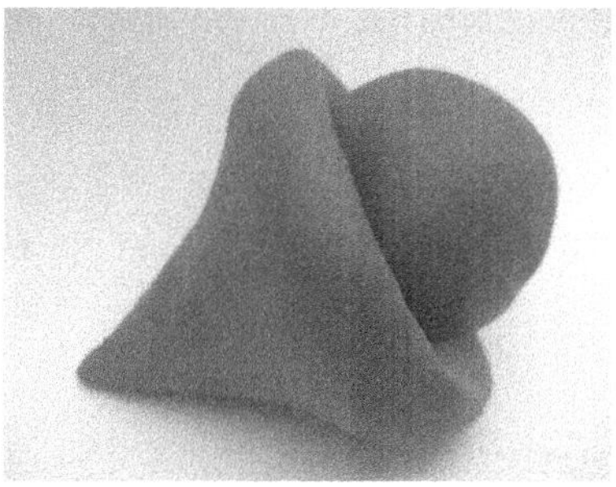

Hollow Cone (Opening and Closed)

Press into a sphere a hollow which opens to the world. Pull and close the other side into a point. Make a sphere that fits into the hollow of the cone—and now you make up a story for these forms!

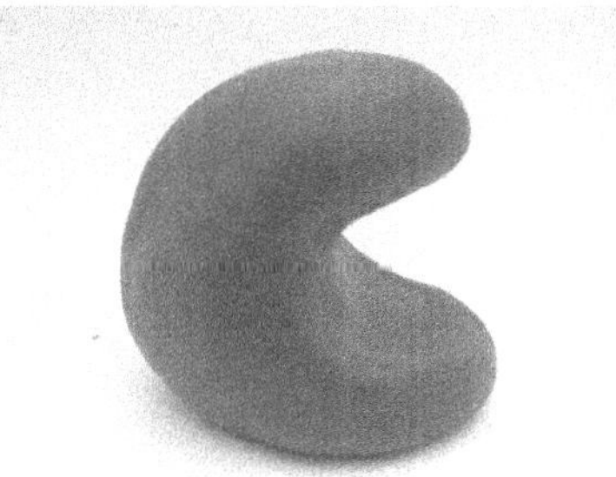

Crouching Form

Flatten a sphere's base, press a hollow into one side and create a curving back.

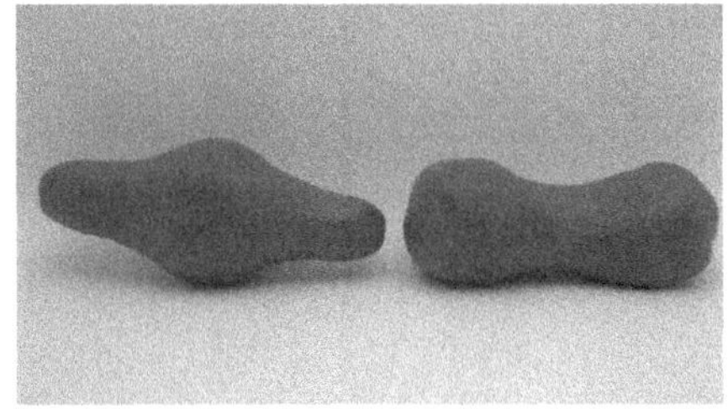

Widening and Narrowing

Make two equally sized spheres. Stretch one into a narrow elongated form and make its middle bulge and widen. Squeeze the middle of the second sphere and make it narrow in the middle.

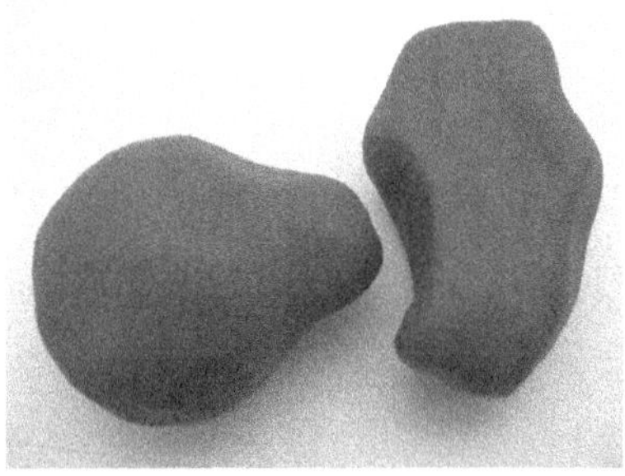

Two Harmony Friends

Two friends, who were shaped very differently, found that they got along in spite of their differences

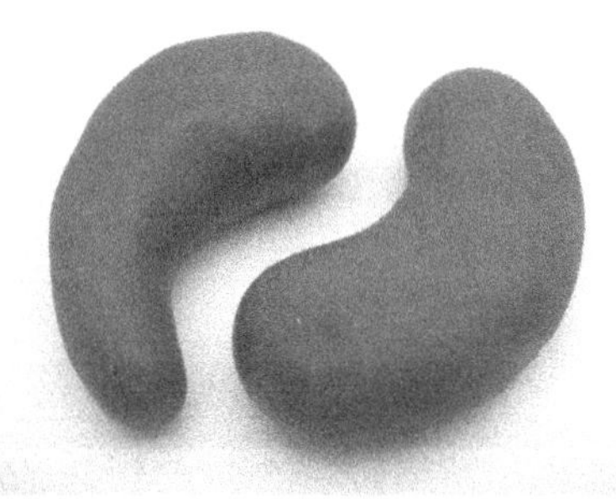

Another example of harmony friends

Forms are patterns placed into the nature of things. Transitory things are made in the image of the eternal Forms and are likenesses…

—Plato

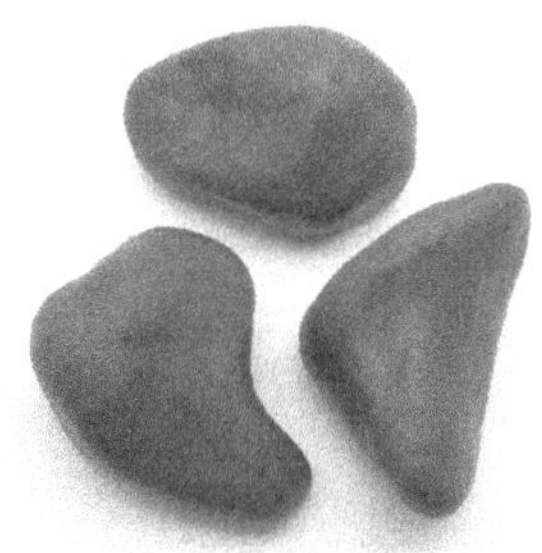

Three Friends Chatting

Form spheres into shapes that fit together and complement each other.

Mirror Forms: Challenge Form Modeling!

Challenge a child to make a relief form on the left and then recreate a symmetrical mirror form on the right just as in form drawing.

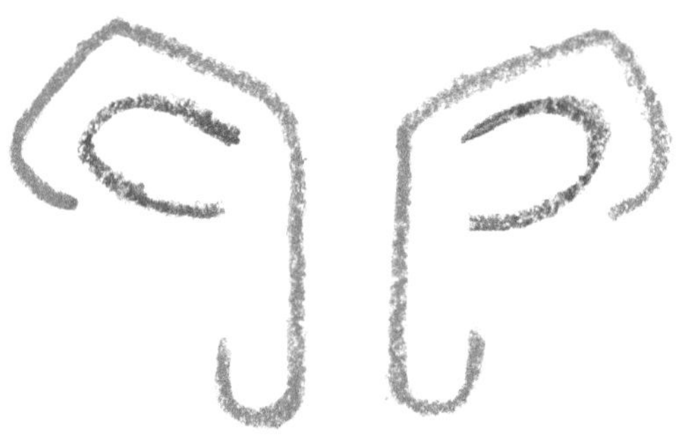

Linear 2-D form drawing

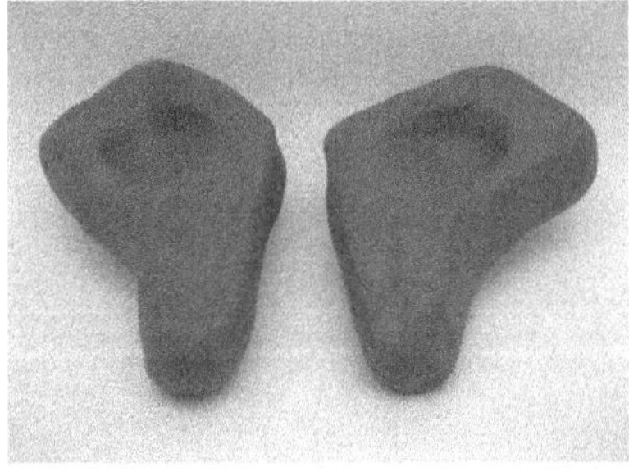

Comparable challenge form in 3-D

Hollow Angle looked in the mirror and what did she see?

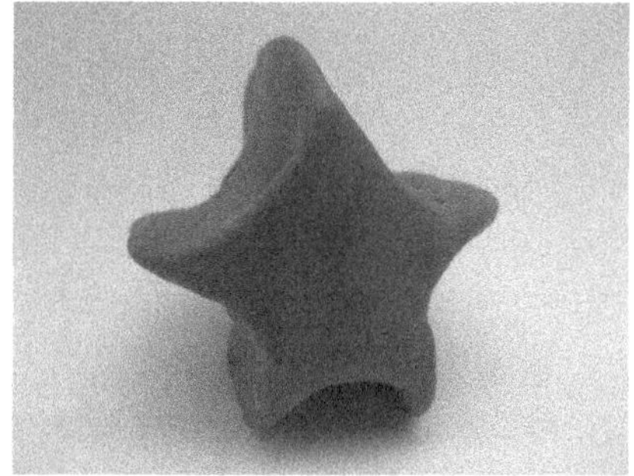

Pinching a Pentagon

Pinch a sphere on its sides to make a five-sided form—or six-sided hexagon.

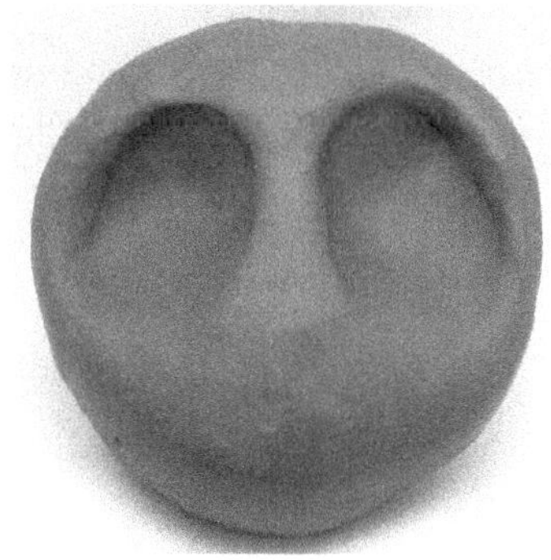

Twin Hollows Relief

1. Flatten a sphere into a thick disk.
2. Use the thumbs to press in two oval hollows with a strip in the center.
3. Refine and make uniform the hollows and inner and outer edges of the round form.

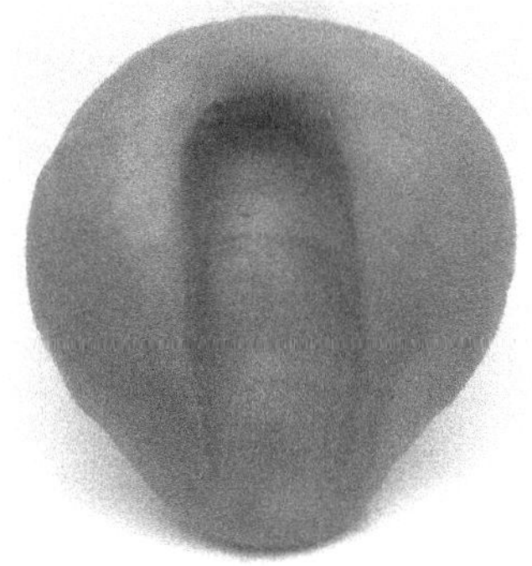

Two Sides Separated Relief

1. Flatten a sphere into a thick disk.
2. Use a pointer finger to press a crevice down the middle
3. Refine and make uniform the inner and outer edges.

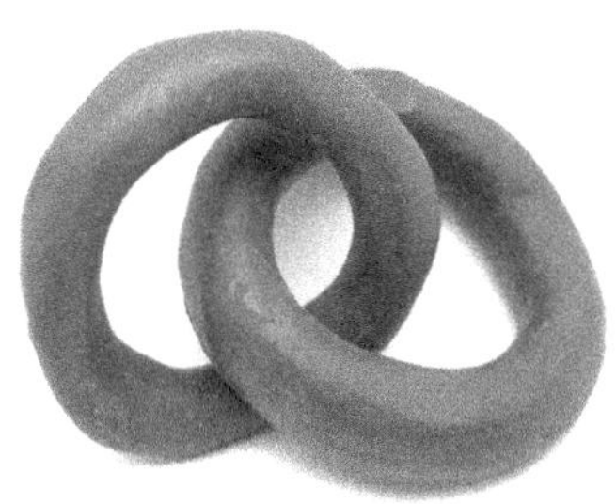

Rings Around a Ring

1. Make a 4-inch rope into a ring.
2. Loop a second one into the first and join it.
3. Options: (a) add more rings (b) partners make a chain (c) a whole class joins chain sections into a great circular chain on a large table.

Creating More Thick Relief Forms on Surfaces

Model new relief forms in clay or sand on a table or board or in a shallow box or tub. Be playful! Make up your own! Model more repeating forms. Work as partners or in larger groups.

More Basic Exercises

For more wonderful forms that can be added to the above exercises, see Hella Loewe's article and book: *Saddle Form, Right-left Symmetry, Asymmetry Forms, Two Saddle Planes*, etc.

Nature works as artist in shaping a child; the child herself in turn becomes a shaper of things. When the child does not have the opportunity to actively form things around her, her life forces and creative joy are lamed leading to a sluggish digestion and listlessness. If the natural energy for activity cannot express itself in a healthy manner, it bottles up in the body and becomes the cause of nervous restlessness.

—Caroline von Heydebrand

Practical Advice

The Transition from Anthropomorphic Form Stories to Simple Instructions
Form Stories speak the language of the 6-7-8-year-old imagination. They animate forms and make them magical and memorable. Adults will have to sense when the children become well-versed in the language of foundational forms and are ready to make the transition to simple instructions, usually at the end of Grade 2 or sometime in Grade 3. Some children may want to linger in the storied Land of Forms. In any case, a main mode of teaching continues to be the demonstration in front of them of the actual forming of pieces. Your hand movements speak the loudest accompanied briefly by some simple words describing actions and features.

Remember to RENDER!!!
Let the descriptions and pictures of forms inspire you to *render* them in particular directions in your own way. Fussy copying can be deadening. Do not reproduce too exactly what you see in the photos or what you read. From photos you anyway do not know what the forms look like in the back and have to use your imagination. The text explanations are only attempts to characterize some of the complex hand movements needed.

Exploration and Discovery
Let the playful wisdom of your hands (and heart) lead you. It may be that you begin a form and find your hands developing a new variation or a whole new form! Keep these discoveries for contemplation! The important thing is that you do not force the clay into copied constructions but allow hand and form to flow together organically in a process of gradual transformation. You can always take up a new lump of clay and try the original exercise again. If it still does not emerge, create whatever out of the moment and enjoy! Let the original exercise rest. You can come back to it later and see what happens. Or give it up! There are plenty of forms to explore. Keep the hands and *image*-ination playfully moving and exploring and inventing!

Series Three: Form Stories

Children around ages 9-10 start having a more intense inner awareness of self as well as a more acute outer awareness of the world (center and periphery). In addition to playful geometric shapes, forms in this Series include inner and outer spaces, qualities of light and heavy, expansion/ contraction, movement, relationships, etc. Gradually form stories can give way to simple yet interesting instructions with demonstration.

Widening and Narrowing
Threesome with Big Middle
Heart Shape
Equal-sided Triangle
Magic Square
Twist Sideways
Hollow Sphere
Spiraling Up
Narrow Spiral
Twister
Deepening Hollows
Hidden Space
Cube
Three Four Five Stretchers
Lifting and Sinking
Disks
Hiding in a Hollow
Long Hollow with Round
Nestling
Huddling in Friendship
Three Big Protect Little
Secret Huddle
Two Hug
Spiraling Up a Cone
Four Crevices—Four Triangles

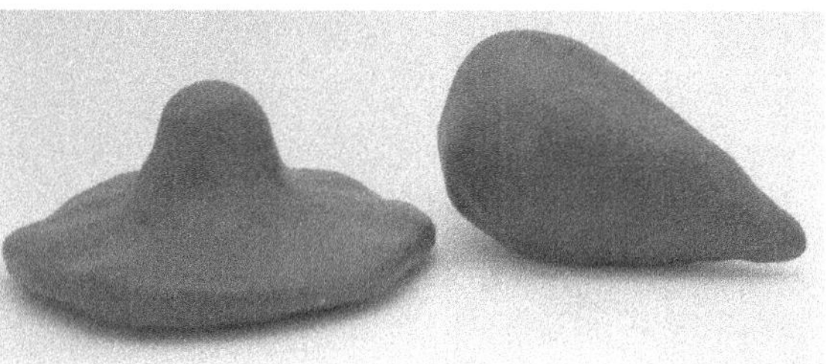

Widening and Narrowing
Press the sides of a sphere down and out into a disk but leave a center bump.
Pull one side of another sphere out and narrow it into a point (*"Do you remember Pointer in Grade 1?"*)

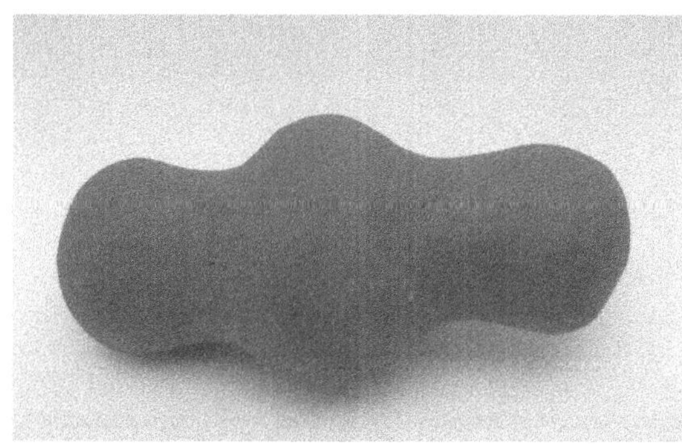

Threesome with Big Middle
Have a sphere bulge out to the sides into two smaller roundnesses.

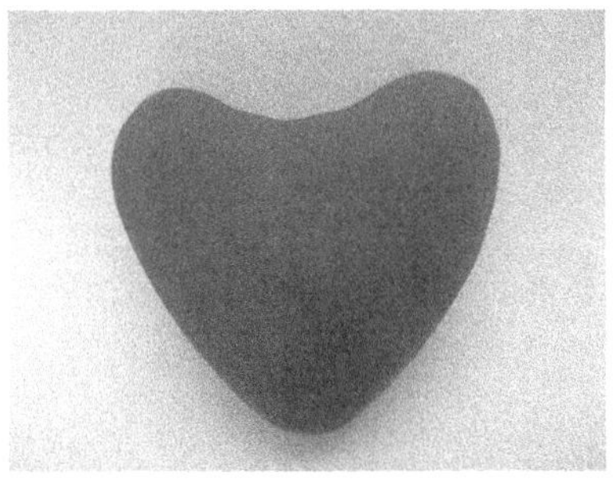

Heart Shape

Ovoid loved the world so much that she became Heart Shape.

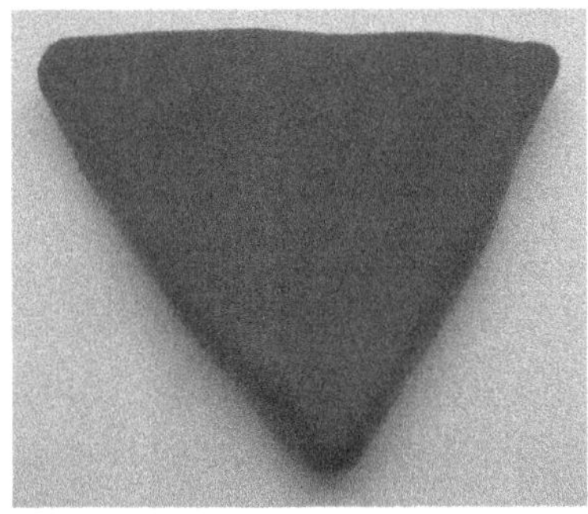

Equal-Sided Triangle

On some days Ovoid was out of sorts and kept to herself. She lost her heart-shape and softness. She was sharp with her friends. It was hard for them to be with her.

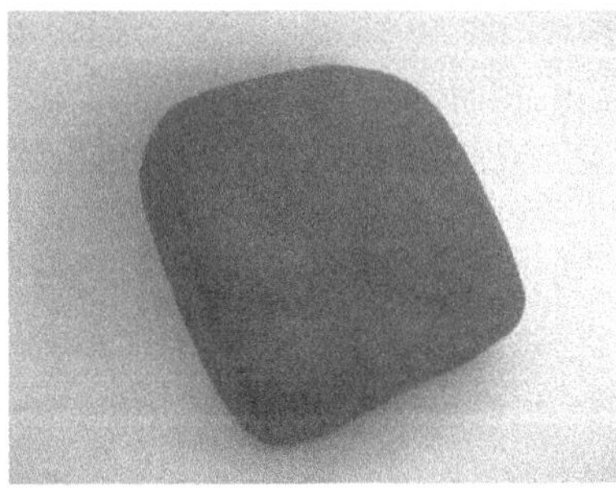

Magic Square

Round Magic Mirror bumped into the wall on the right, on the left, on the front and on the back, so that she turned into Magic Square.

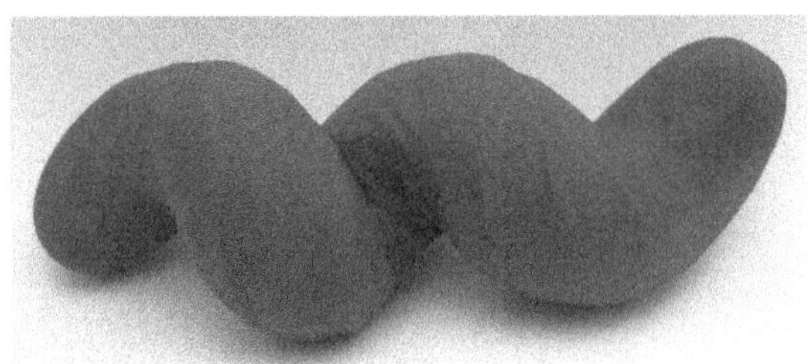

Twist Sideways

Lengthen Ovoid into a slender, straight form. See what happens to her surface when you twist her slowly from end to end.

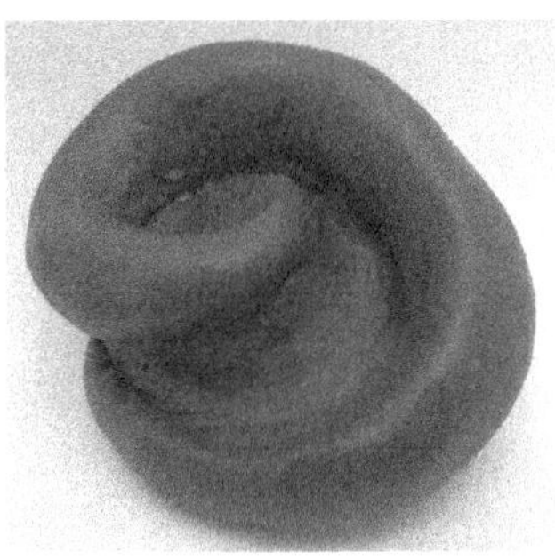

Spiraling Up

Challenge: Change most of a sphere into an upward spiral but keep a bottom base on which it can rest.

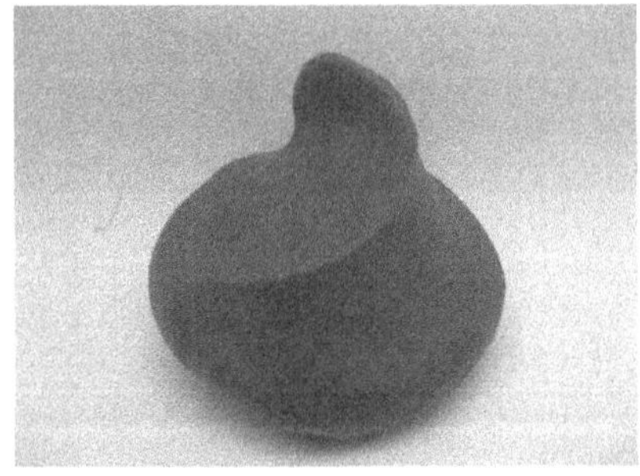

Narrow Spiral

Narrow Spiral rose joyfully up out of Magic Mirror!

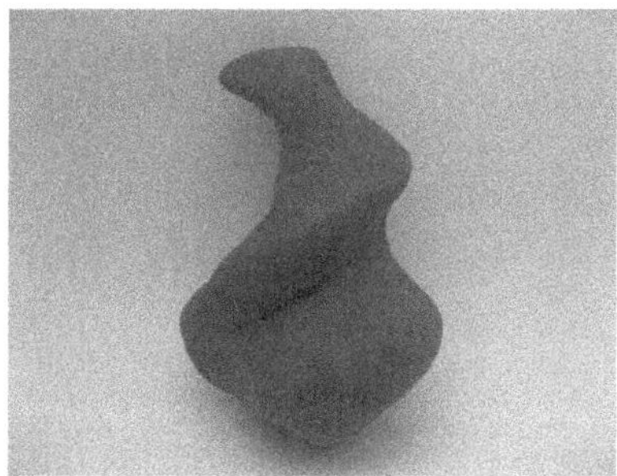

Twister

Stretcher twisted upward, round and round and became Twister.

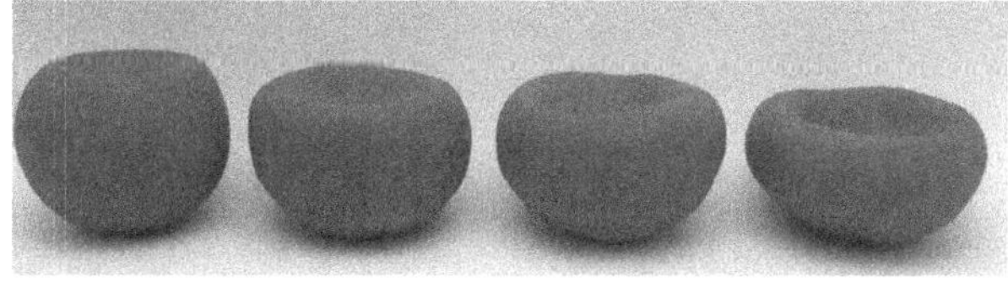

Deepening Hollows (Series)

Make 4 equal spheres. Slowly press hollows into the tops of spheres and watch how the inner space deepens.

Modeling forms that change incrementally in stages is an excellent individual or group exercise starting at age 9/10.

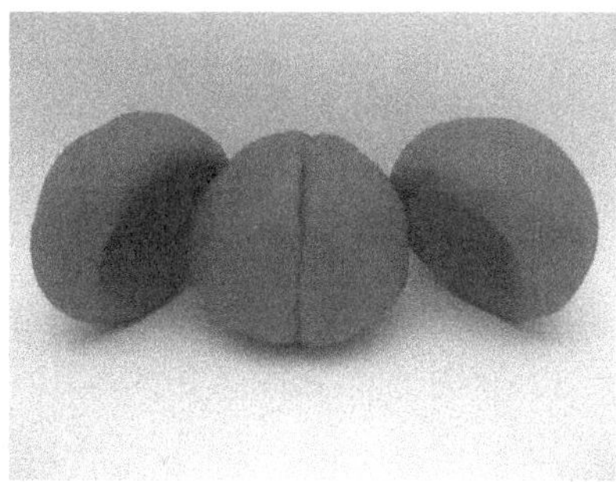

Hidden Space

Make two spheres into hollow half-spheres. Join them together. Smooth over the crack. Imagine how dark it is inside!

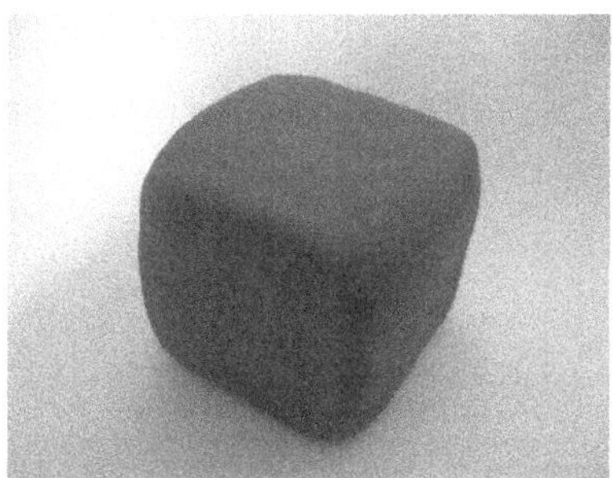

Cube

Sphere loved to be held up high above the ground. But one day she felt herself being pressed gently on the left, then on the right, on the top, on the bottom, in front, and in back! It kept happening from all sides until she turned into Cube! From having endless sides and floating, she now had only six sides and felt herself landing squarely on the earth —and she could no longer roll!

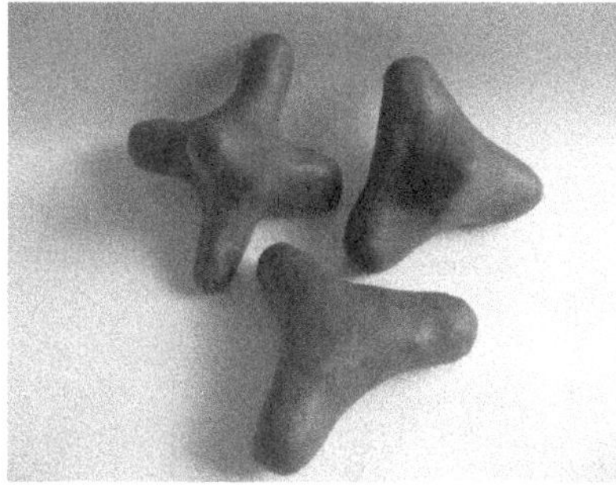

Three Four Five Stretchers

Stretch a sphere in three directions connected by a center hub. Variations: Four- and Five-Way Stretchers with perpendiculars.

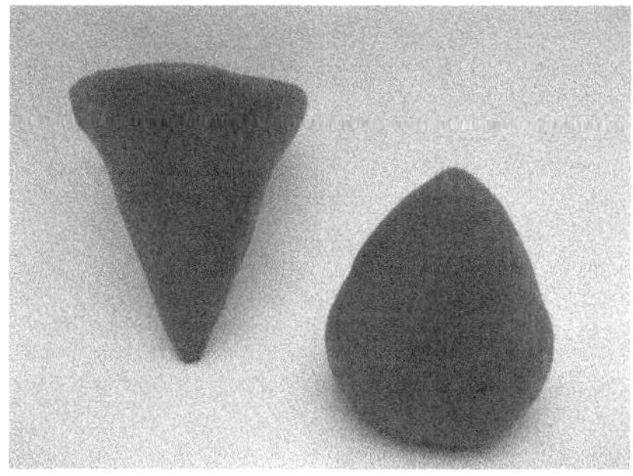

Lifting and Sinking (Light and Heavy)

One day Sphere felt her spirits lifted high, high, high. On the next day she sank into heaviness. Or simple instructions accompany a demonstration:

Pull the top bulk of a sphere up with one hand and simultaneously pull down its bottom into a point resulting in a cone shape. Hold them up next to each other and compare: "Which one looks lighter? Heavier?"

Note: Contrasting forms can depict verb actions (lift, sink) or qualities (light, heavy).

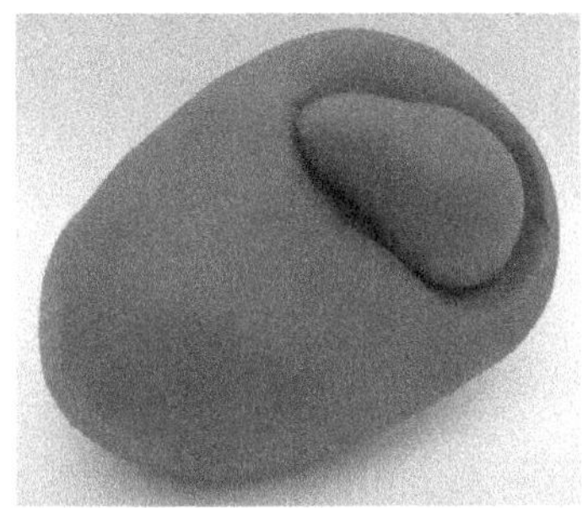

Nestling
A little form snuggles into a big one.

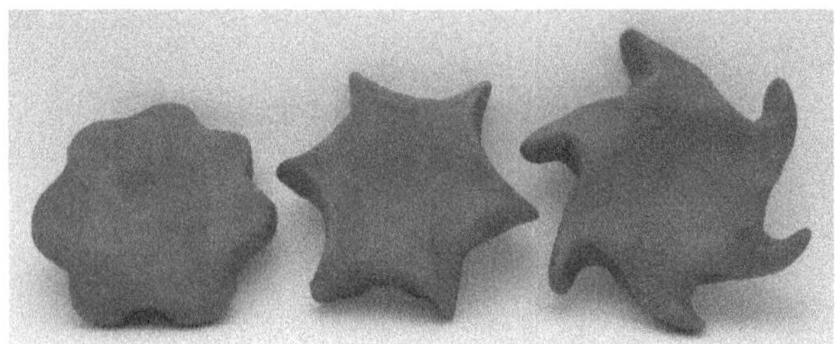

Disks Bulging, Indenting, Spinning
Flatten four spheres into four disks:
1. Leave one round (not shown)
2. Pull out and round bumps out on edges of the second.
3. Repeat #2 and pinch the curves into angled points.
4. Repeat #3 and bend and curve the points in one direction. *Which form is spinning?!*

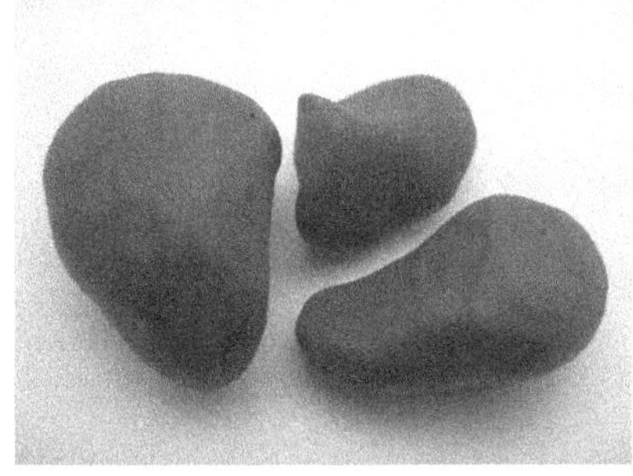

Huddling in Friendship
Three very different form friends got along in a harmonious group because their sides and edges matched!

Speak about how one form's sides and edges can be shaped to fit together with and complement another's.

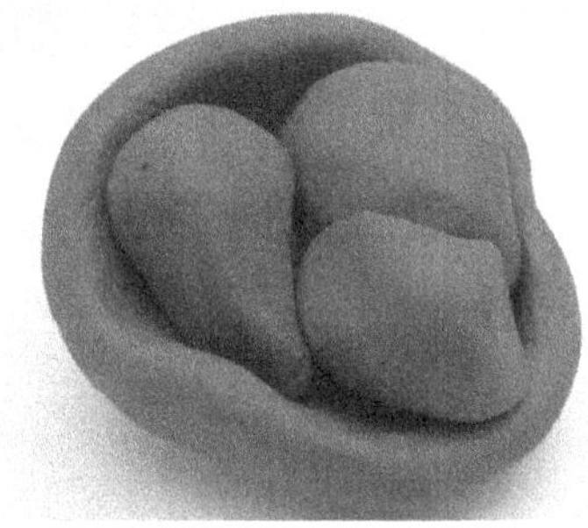

Hiding in a Hollow
Three very different form-friends hid in a hollow.

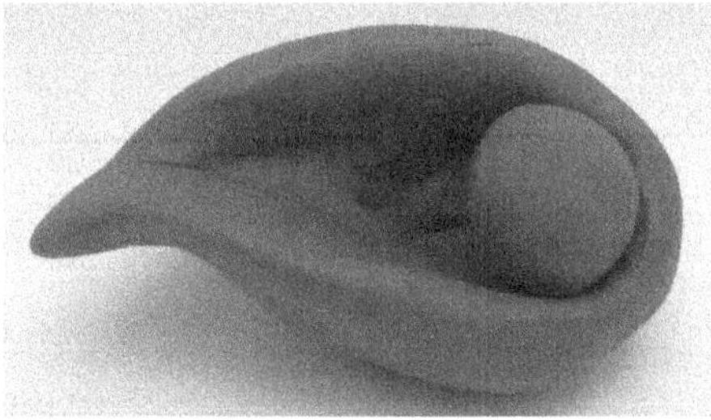

Long Hollow with Round
Stretch and hollow a sphere. Nestle a small sphere in the hollow.

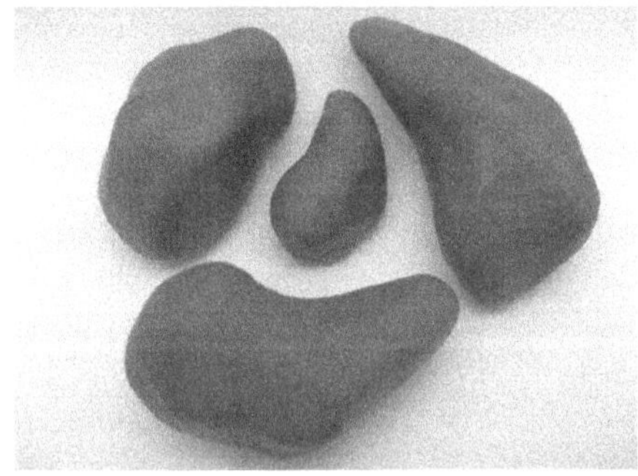

Three Big Protect Little
Little was being bullied.

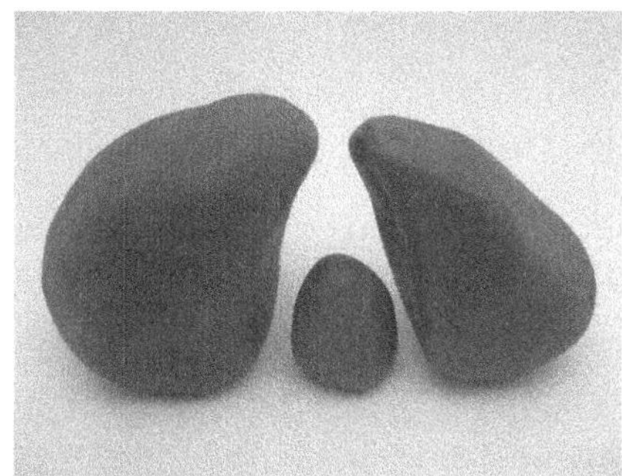

Secret Huddle

Two (or three) form friends huddled. They had a little secret between them. They did not let anyone join them and share their secret.

Or:

Form friends gathered together in a group and told each other secrets. When someone new came along, they invited her in.

(With all their edges sculpturally complementing each other, concave to convex and vice versa.)

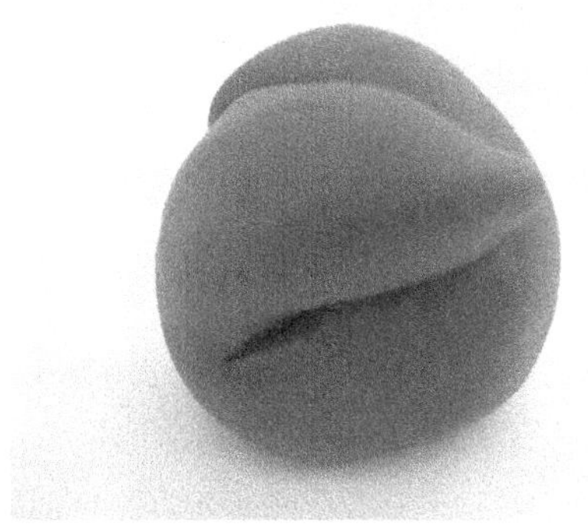

Two Hug

Pull the top of a sphere into two elongations and bend them toward each other in an embrace. *Two form friends hug after a quarrel.*

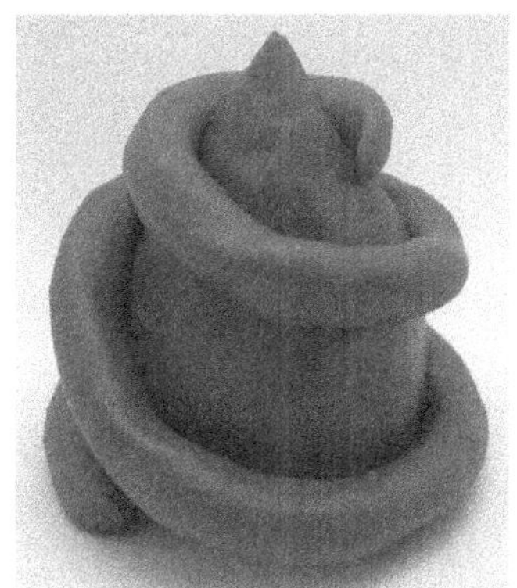

Spiraling Up a Cone

1. Pull the top of a sphere into a cone shape coming to a point (apex).
2. Make the sides of the cone straight.
3. Flatten the base.
4. Optional: Wind a long rope up and around the cone in a spiral.

Creating More Thick Relief Forms on Surfaces

Model new relief forms in clay or sand on a table or board or in a shallow box or tub. Be playful! Make up your own! Model symmetry forms like the one below or more repeating forms. Work as partners or in larger groups.

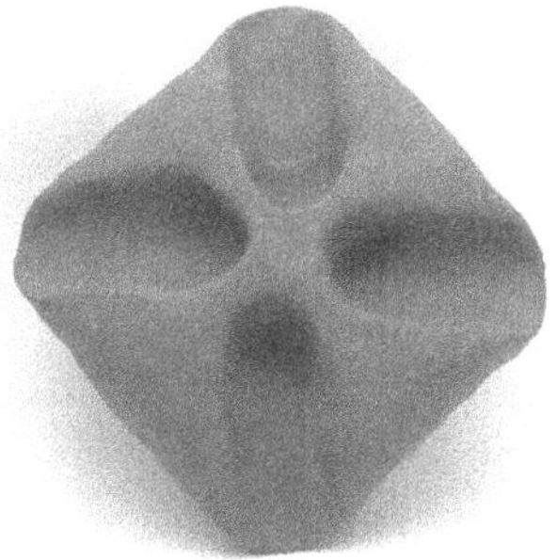

Four Crevices—Four Triangles—Relief

1. Flatten a sphere into a thick disk.
2. Use the pointer fingers to press in four long hollows in a cross form and leaving a center.
3. Make the four outer edges straight.
4. Refine and make uniform the inner edges of the four triangular forms.

Hand Awareness: This exercise gives prominence to the pointer finger. Forming straightness and regular sides is geometric and more "intellectual."

More "Challenge Forms"

Two or three children work in a group to create three to fourfold forms in a modeling medium (clay, sand, etc.) For example, one child makes a beginning form and the others in the group make mirror images of it so that a large radial form results from the repeated element. Children take quick turns or work on the emerging combined form.

Hella Loewe's Basic Sculptural Modeling

Supplement this Series with Frau Loewe's wonderful exercises for grade 3.

The Proteus Exercise
This general exercise should be regularly repeated as a fundamental experience or warm-up to modeling lessons.

In a beautiful way sculptural modeling enlivens all four of the child's lower senses… The sense of sight is strongly de-emphasized. It is wonderful at times even to model blindfolded. The sense of touch becomes more active as the hand continuously feels the surfaces and bumps. With our mobile hands, the sense of movement perceives all these surfaces, contours and angles. The sense of balance is active in weighing and aiming for an artistic unity and balance even when a piece does not involve symmetry. All sculptural modeling is a living organic process of creating… The sense of life is intensively involved in sculptural activity.

—Willi Aeppli, *The Care and Development of the Senses*

Series Four: Gestures

Exercises may suit a particular age because they artistically reflect how children are changing cognitively, emotionally and physically. In this Series, changing the dreamy, rounded wholeness of a sphere to the six directions of a sharp-edged, flat cube is a metaphor for children waking up intellectually to a more defined experience of reality. Children's hands become larger and more dexterous. They are able to handle larger pieces with a base standing "on the earth," i.e. on a table rather than cradled up between two hands. The children themselves are coming down onto the earth.

Double Twist
Weaving Figure-Eight
Meandering
Hollowed Sphere to Ring
Hollow Front and Back
Sphere to Cube
Full to Flat
Fractioned
Roll Over
Sharp Curving
Soft Curving
Entrance between Two Hollows
Full of Life and Drying Out
Big Protect a Little One
Lying, Crouching, Standing
Vertical and Horizontal
Stretching Out
Turning
Alert
Darting
Gobbling
Sleeping and Waking
Three Hollows—Three Spokes

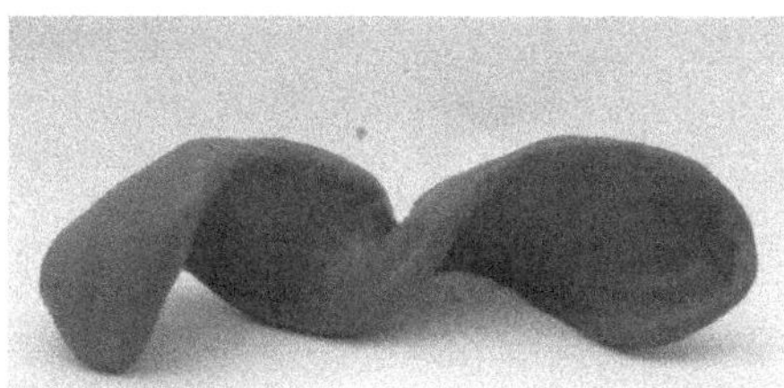

Double Twist
Flatten a sphere into a long strip and curl it. Also curl up inside edges (concave space) leaving outside surfaces convex. Works nicely in plasticine but clay handled gently is also suitable.

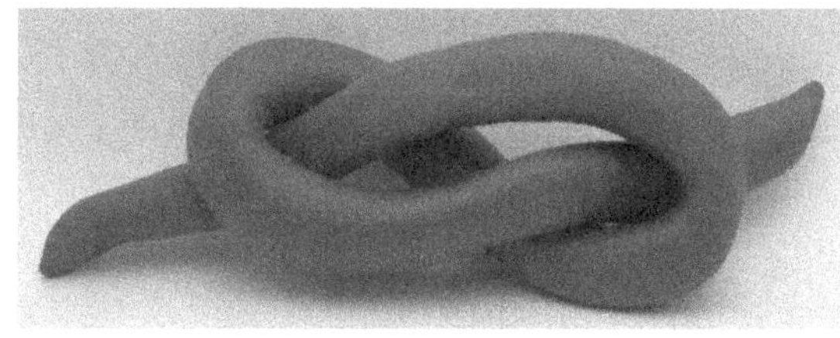

Weaving Figure-Eight
Form a long rope-like piece and wind it in and out and into an eight form. Works nicely in plasticine but clay handled gently is also suitable.

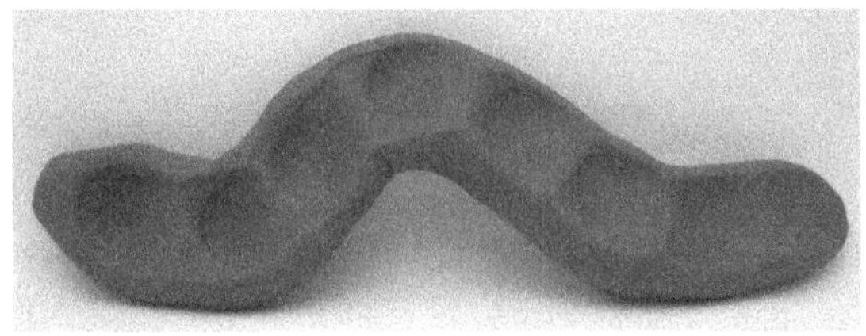

Meandering

When finding the most inviting way over and through the earth, water *meanders* back and forth, swinging between left and right. It depends on what it meets. Rivers and streams teach us the meandering form.

Design a long meandering form with a stylized wave-like pattern in it. Another exercise would be to model a more realistic winding river form in geography. The photo above shows only a section of what can also be a large group project on one long form on plywood on a table.

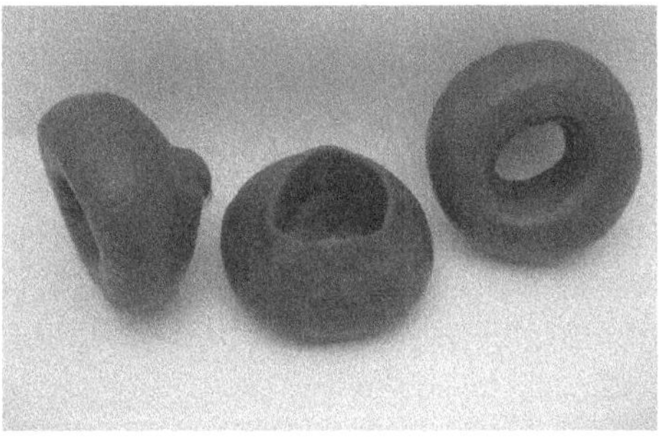

Hollowed Sphere to Ring

Press a hole through a sphere and smooth out its back edges. Call this exercise the "ring" form so that the name "donut" does not become stuck to it.

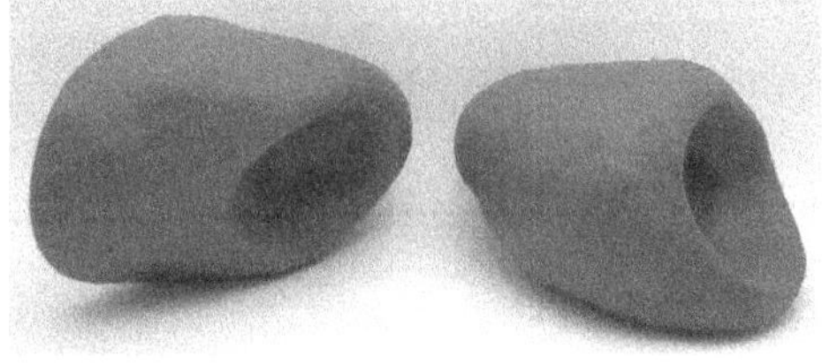

Hollow Front and Back

Press a hollow into the end of an ovoid. Diagonally on its opposite side press another hollow. Explore shaping out the result into more interesting, non-regular forms.

Nature produces the most amazing varieties of shapes, patterns, and rhythms… Observation enlarges the sculptor's vision. But merely to copy nature is no better than copying anything else. It is what the artist makes of his observations by giving expression to his personal vision and from his study of the laws of balance, rhythm, construction, growth, the attractionand repulsion of gravity—it is how heapplies this to all of his work that is important…I am trying to add to people's understanding of life andnature, to help them to open their eyes and to be sensitive. Nature is inexhaustible.

—Henry Moore, British sculptor

Sphere into Cube (Rounding and Edging) and /or Cube into Sphere

One piece transforming through three stages: Start flattening two opposite sides of a sphere. Do the same on the other two pairs of sides. Keep moving from side to side so that they are gradually transitioning to flatness and rounded edges are becoming sharper by pinching them. A cube can also be rounded back into a sphere. Dreamier children tend to leave their edges more rounded.

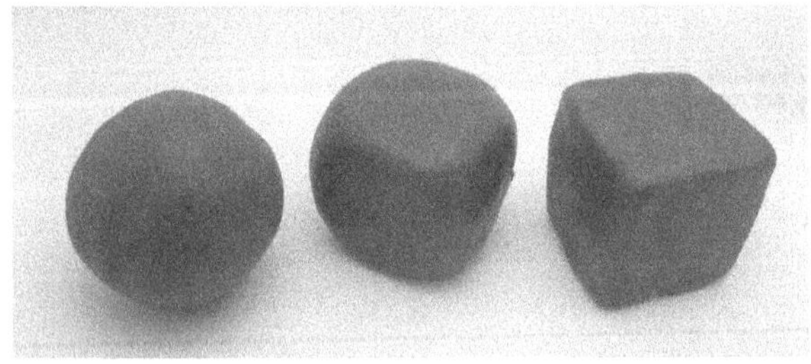

Three contrasting forms side by side: Make three equal spheres. Turn two into a rounded cube in transition and a sharper-edged cube.

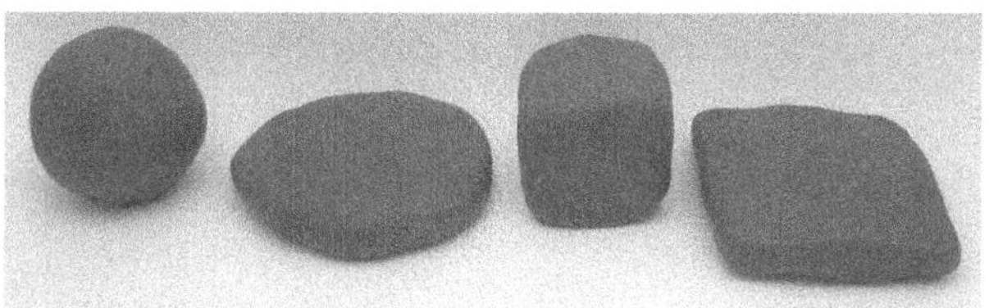

Full to Flat

Make four spheres.

1. Leave one as a sphere.
2. Flatten the second into a disk.
3. Press the third into a cube.
4. Repeat #3 and flatten the cube into a square of slight thickness.

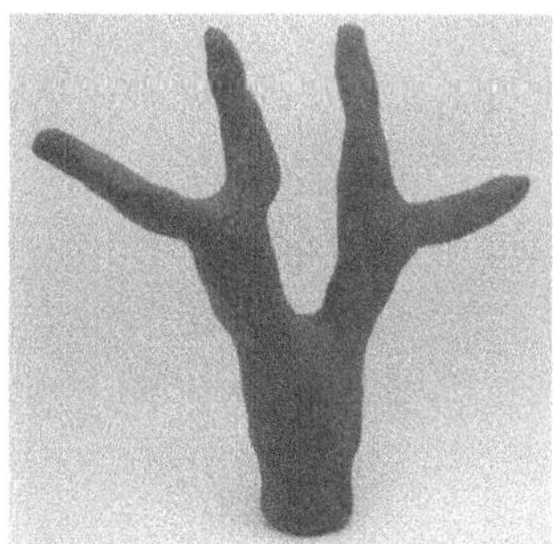

Fractioned

Fashion a sphere into a long upright, "trunk-like" cylinder and divide its upper part first into two and then each of these two into two making four. One breaks or "fractures"or "fractions," into two and then into four. (The Roman word for "broken into" or "divided into" parts is *fractus*. Example: a *fractured* bone.)

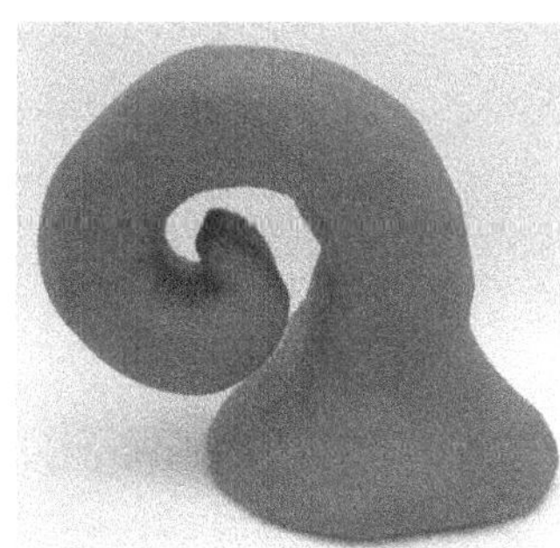

Roll Over

Press a sphere onto a flat surface so it has a flat base. Raise up the top part into a form that rolls forward and rolls over. It creates an arch, a spiral, and an inner space!

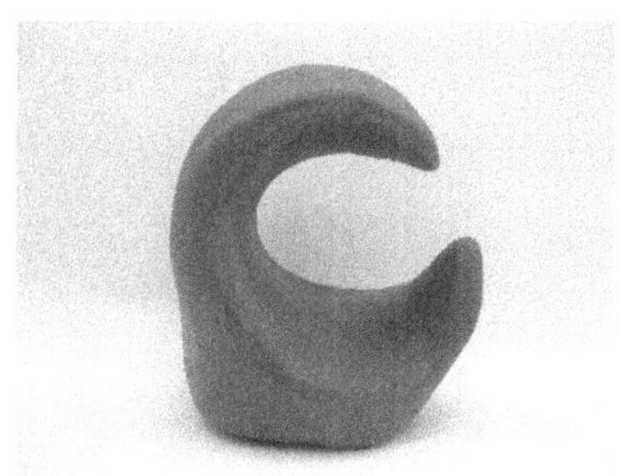

Sharp Curving

Hollow a sphere so that a sharp, pointed curve remains at the top and curls over a large round space. It faces a small curling form rising up from the base.

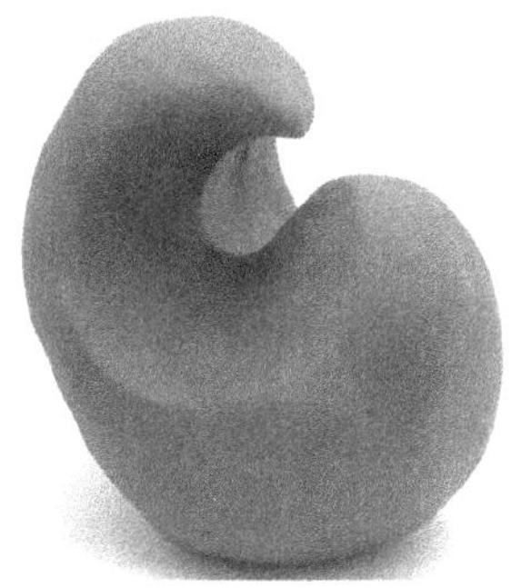

Soft Curving

Hollow a sphere so that a curve remains at the top and curls over a small round space. It faces a rounded, stubby curve form rising up from the base. Compare its quality with Sharp Curving above.

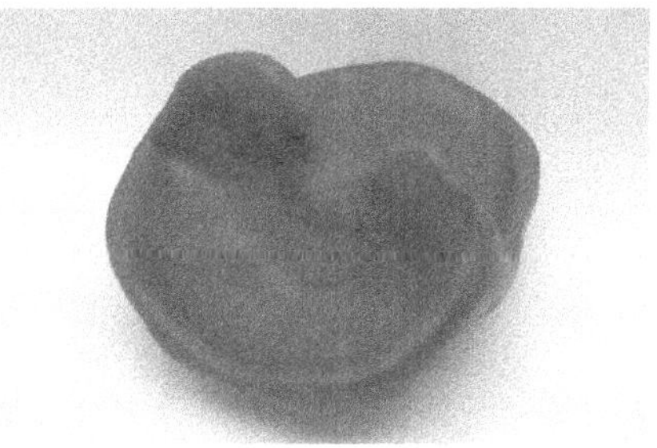

Entrance between Two Hollows

Press a hollow onto opposite sides of a sphere leaving a ridge in between. Make an opening in the ridge between the two.

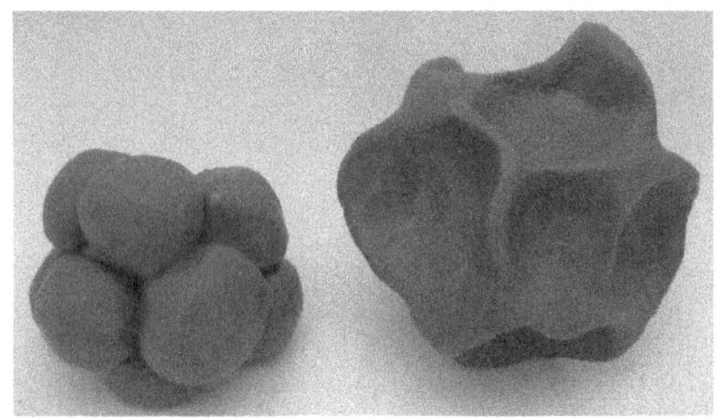

Full of Life and Drying Out

Make several little spheres and press them together in a thickening, bulbous mass (left). Make a second form like the first. Then press in each small globe so that it has a hollowed look (right). Compare their different qualities.

Big Protect Little

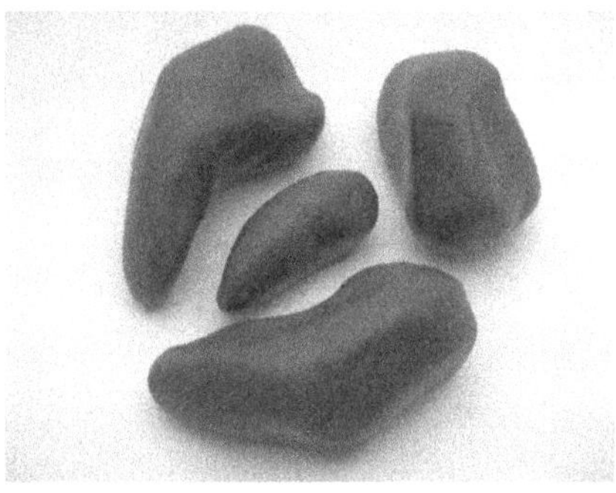

Form spheres into large shapes that fit around and complement one or more smaller ones.

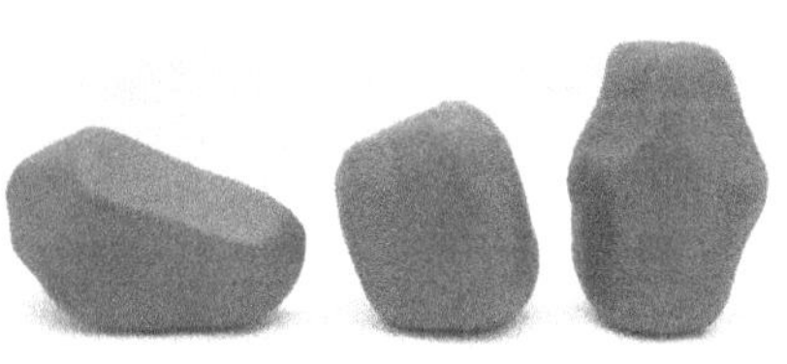

Lying, Crouching, Standing

Turn three equal spheres into horizontal, middle and vertical forms.

Gestures

Modeling pure forms helps the children develop an objective feeling for gestures and movement. This special sense is a valuable asset, particularly when they are studying and modeling forms of the natural organic world such as animals. Children artistically educated in this way come to sense the living dynamics of a creature's body and do not stop short at only its static conceptual structure. Their perception is able to sensitively and actively "slip into" and "grasp from within" the living movement and form-making processes that contribute to creating a living animal's final body shape. The absorbing process of hands-on, heart-warming engagement, in effect, teaches the mind as well as the senses to deeply "reach into" and "grasp" the forming of the world as a matter of healthy habit. It nurtures what can be called a "feeling-willing," that is, a feeling-doing in addition to just looking and thinking.

Gestures captured as pure forms can be modeled as a first step. In the process, the children sense what animal wants to emerge out of that movement. This stimulates and strengthens the imagination. The following exercises capture typical gestures.

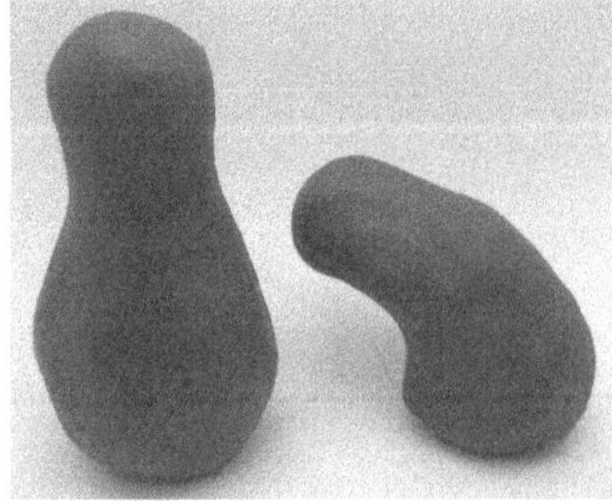

Vertical and Horizontal

1. Shape an ovoid into small above and large roundness below it and place it upright on the table. This pure basic form can be articulated into a detailed human form in other lessons.

2. Shape another ovoid so that a main body has a part protruding horizontally out to the side. This pure basic form can turn into many animals.

The two can be gesturally related to each other as archetypal upright human and horizontal animal shapes.

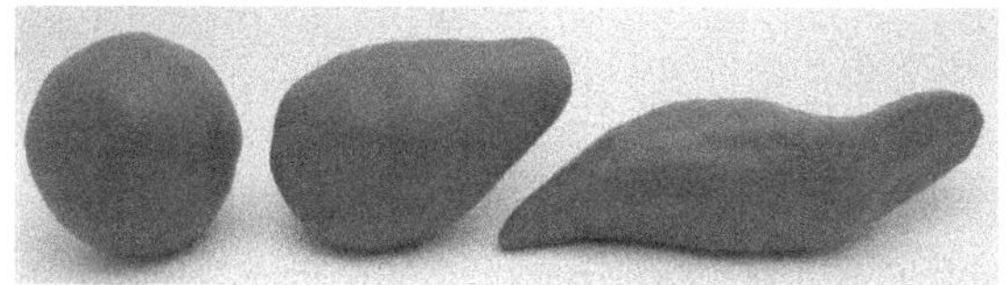

Stretching Out

Make three spheres. Stretch the second partially out and the third fully out into the surroundings. This shows the gesture of desiring and seeking.

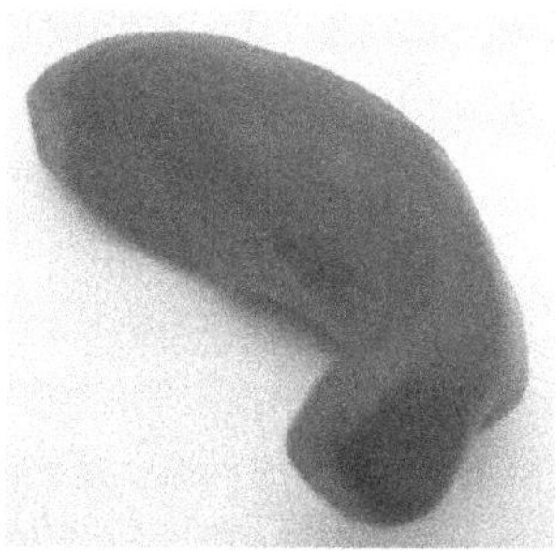

Turning

Elongate a sphere into an oblong main mass with a smaller one sticking out and making a turning gesture. *Comment*: This and others are not any animals but pure shapes meant to capture gestures such as turning. This exercise can call to mind any number of animals in motion. Such gestures that capture forms can be preludes to then changing the pure form into an articulated subject.

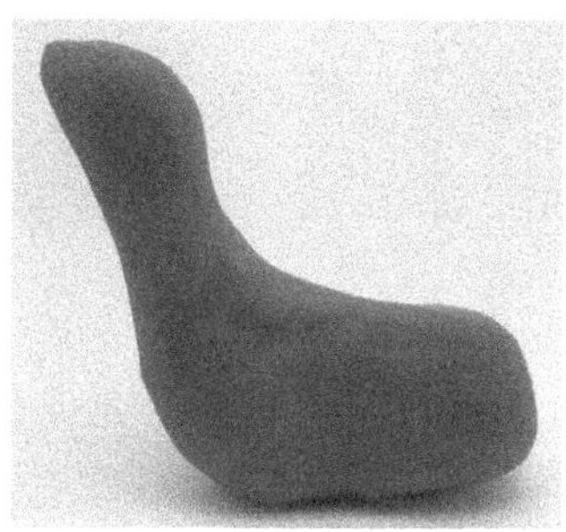

Alert

Elongate a sphere stretching out and up in wakefulness and alertness.

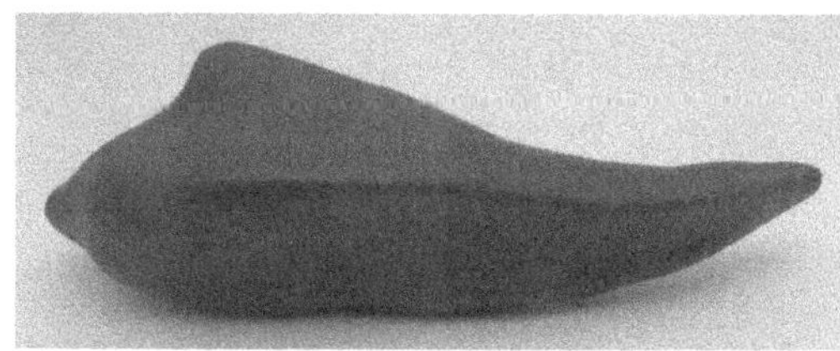

Darting

Elongate a sphere from a thicker to a thinner pointed part and streamline ridges to show darting (to the left in the photo). *Note*: This shows movement and is not a fish, which can be modeled at another time after this in animal studies.

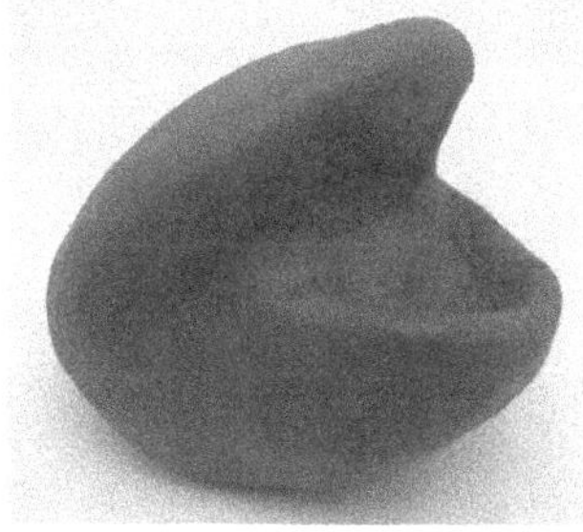

Gobbling

Split a sphere into an opening ready to gobble up! *Comment*: This is not a frog catching a fly but the (humorous) gesture of opening to devour!

Other Gestures: wrestling or fighting form, slithering, rising, falling, tipping, rolling, etc.

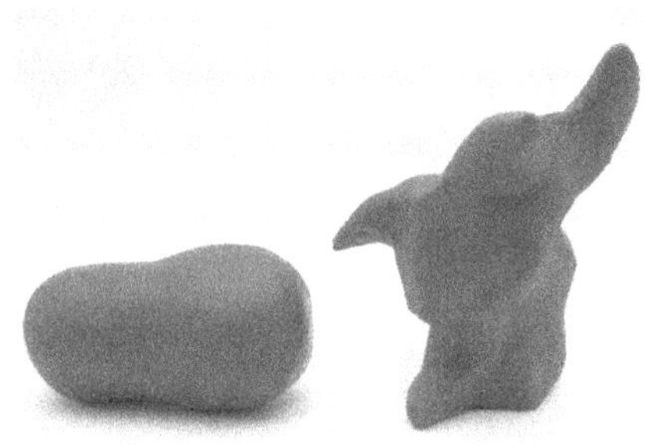

Sleeping and Waking

Give an oval a slight waist, round the ends and lay it on the table. Set a similar oval upright beside it and press it down so that a flat base results. Pull and press it into angular and pointed branches. Shape this "waking" piece on a table.

The sculptor shapes forms which the eye sees but weakly… It is a direct transfer of the sense of touch into the sense of sight that the sculptor serves. The sculptor attempts to release into gesture the static form which is otherwise solely an object of the one-sided perspective of the eye.

—Rudolf Steiner

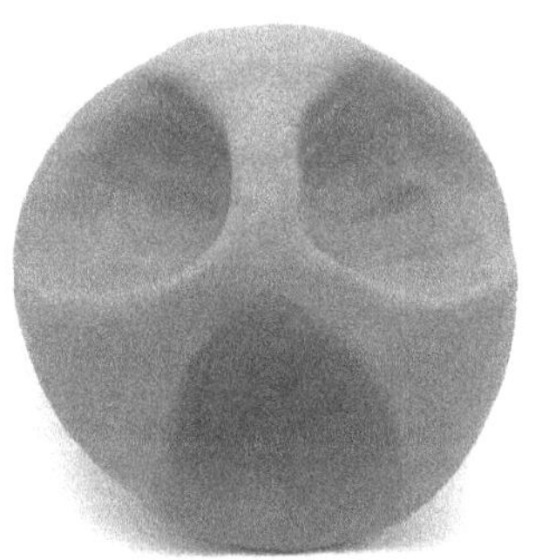

Three Hollows / Three Spokes

1. Flatten a sphere into a thick disk.
2. Use the thumbs to press in three rounded hollows in a pinwheel form and leaving a center.
3. Refine and make uniform the inner edges of the three curved spoke forms which are wide on the outside and narrow toward the center.

More Human Development: Coming Down to Earth

Around the age of 9–10, children can suddenly be aware of the world as separate from themselves and develop a growing sense of visual perspective, mass, weight, volume and the directions of space. (See Steiner and Piaget.)

Growing up is actually a growing down to earth and into the body including into more skillful hands—an incarnation process (from Latin "into the flesh"!). Children's hands become larger and more dexterous and can handle larger pieces of clay, an ideally malleable medium. (Large pieces in plasticine or beeswax are costly and impracticable.) Pieces can be given a flat "earth" base and modeled standing mainly on the table or desk. This is a metaphor for a new threshold of awakening of the children on the earth as individuals. Pieces now stand as separated entities "out there" in space on their own. Prior to this stage, many pieces, as described in the first three Series, have been smaller and could be cradled intimately in the creative womb of the hands up by the chest and heart.

The last two forms "Sleeping and Waking" show two different modes and transition. The waking form is an example of a four-inch (or higher) piece modeled like a statue on its flat base. The sleeping form, in contrast, can be held up and shaped in the hands.

*Remember to regularly practice the **Proteus Exercise** at the beginning of this sourcebook.*

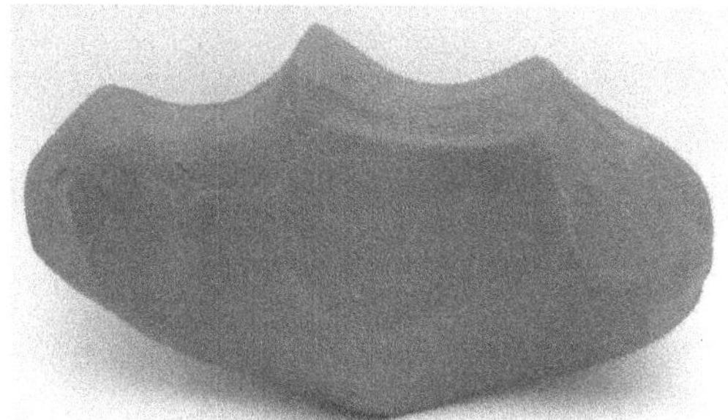

Hand Shape Awareness

Periodically remember the remarkable shape, movements, and forming ability of the threefold
human hand: fingers, palm, muscular lower part, round pads and hollows. Squeezing clay in
one hand creates knuckle-like shapes which are saddle-like double curves.

Series Five: Plant-like

The plant selflessly takes in earth materials, air, light and warmth and sculpturally models them into wonderful combinations of round, flat, and hollow shapes. In the heart of childhood, the growing plant can be the great teacher of form-making for young, growing minds. Series Five contains plant-like motifs that can be adapted in exercises for a whole range of ages.

Folding Oval
Curves and Points
Curling Edge
Pod-Like Seed-like
Bud-like Spiraling
Branching
Opening
Four Curved Edges
Hollow Cone and Enclosing Cross
Three Hold One
Three Round on Three Flat
3-Fold 4-Fold Hollows
Contracting Expanding
Spiraling Up
Mistletoe-like
Coming Together Falling Apart
Hive-like
Curved Side by Side
Ionic Spirals
Disk in Crescent
Labyrinth
Pyramidal Form
Mistletoe-like

Nature-like Forms

In Series One through Four, exercises keep for the most part to a pure form language and avoid giving the shapes a realistic, representational "thing" name. For example, sphere is used instead of "ball" and ovoid instead of egg. If a form reminds a student of some "thing," she can verbalize it and offer a concept, "It looks just like an egg." Pure forms after all are meant to stimulate the imagination and thinking! In form modeling the instructor, however, does well to stay within the realm of language of pure forms to promote form-thinking.

As thinking and self-awareness develop during ages 11–12 and up (grades 5–8 and high school) one can more reflectively and intellectually explain that in form modeling we are not copying nature's actual forms, but joining nature in developing and exploring certain motifs that lend themselves creatively to all kinds of variation. In Series Five through Eight and beyond, exercises will involve terminology that refers to forms nature herself may be working with: leaf-like, crystal-like, organ-like, bone-like forms, etc.

Do you seek the highest, the greatest?
The plant can be your teacher.
—Friedrich Schiller, Dramatist

Plant-like Forms

The experience of being out in the garden, fields and forests penetrates us deeply. It is not surprising that out of our sculpting hands there often emerge unexpected motifs reminiscent of plant forms. None of the following exercises are copies of plants or their parts, but are plant-like form-making and remind us of plants.

A shape is a mobile, changing, and passing phenomenon. The knowledge of shapes is one of transformation. Metamorphosis is the key to all the kingdoms of nature.

—Johanne Wolfgang von Goethet

Plant-like Motifs

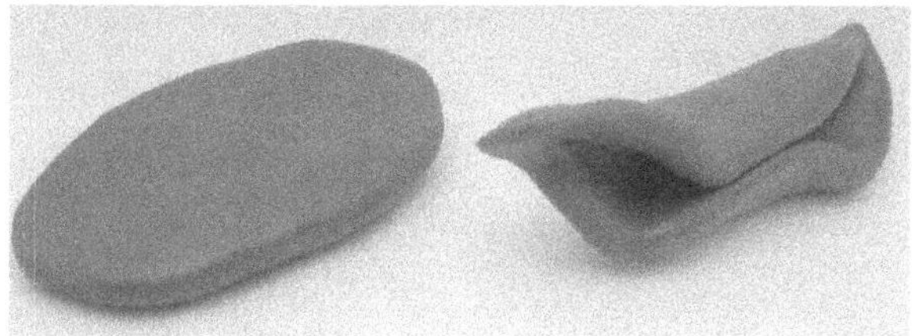

Folding Ovals

Flatten an ovoid shape into an elongated oval flat piece. Fold over, leaving different slightly open and pointed ends. This leaf-like form lends itself to many variations.

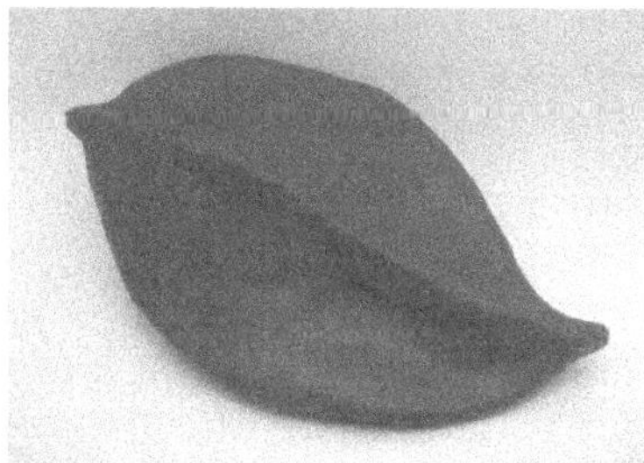

Curves and Points

Flatten and curve the sides of a long pointed piece leaving a middle ridge and two points. (This is a thin form and is done very nicely in plasticine or beeswax).

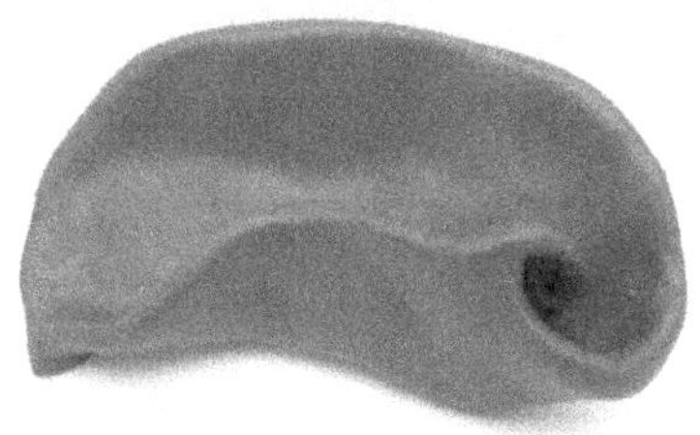

Curling Edge

A gentle curl forms on the edge of a flat form.

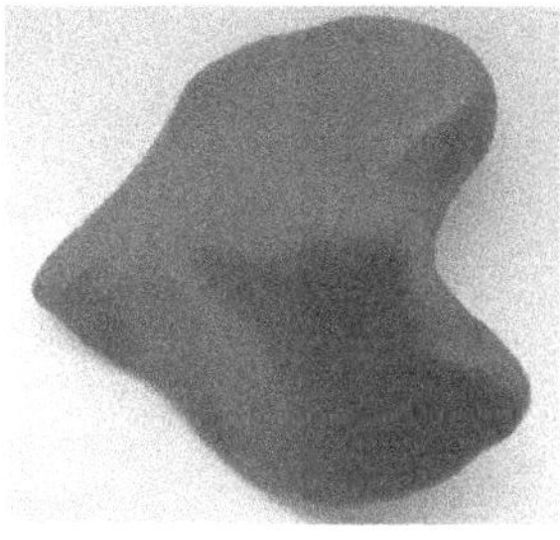

Pod-Like, Seed-like

Invent others.

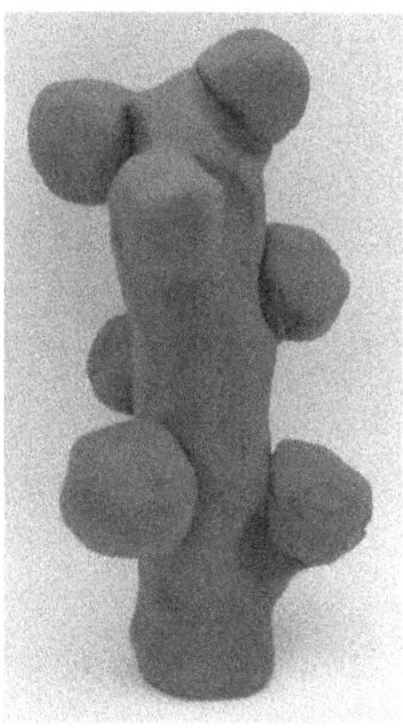

Bud-like Spiraling

Stand a cylinder shape upright on its flat base. Pull out bumps in a spiral along its sides. Make several small bud-like spheres and augment the bumps by sticking the spheres onto the bumps. This form exercise simulates the form experience of budding around and up an axis (*phyllotaxis*) and of Brussells sprouts!

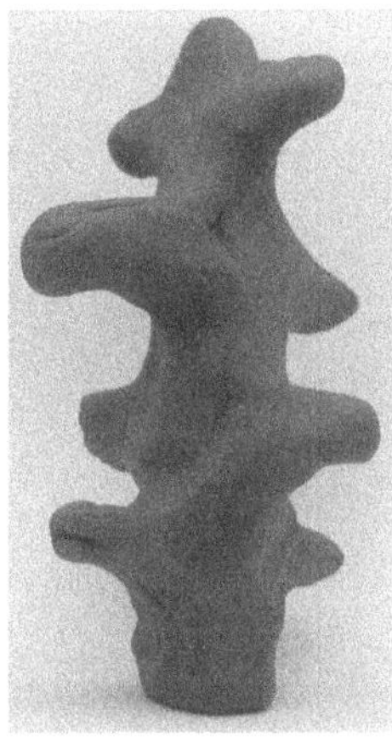

Branching

Stand a cylinder shape upright by flattening its base. Pull out stubby branching forms.

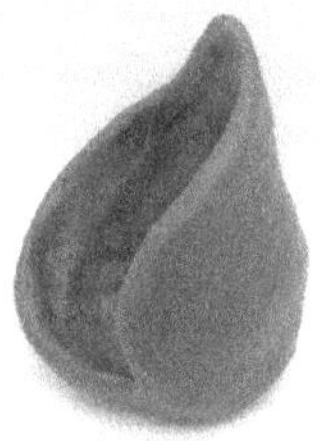

Opening

Flatten a sphere into an elongated oval piece. Wrap sides around an inner space and a flattened base. Bring sides to a common point at the top.

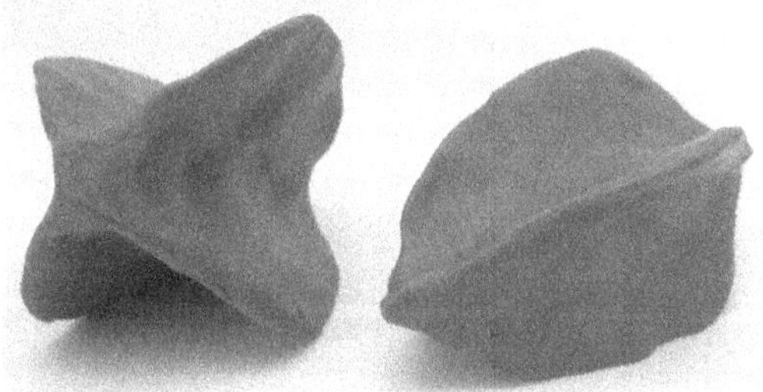

Four Curved Edges

Pinch an ovoid into sharp edges raying out.
  Variation: Point one end

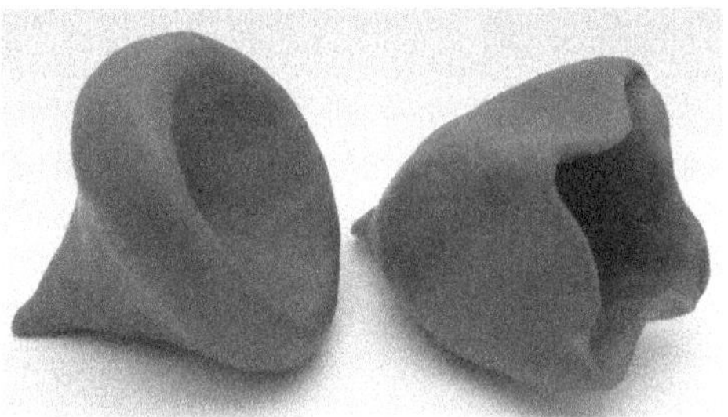

Hollow Cone and Enclosing Cross

Press a hollow into a sphere and pull out a pointed end opposite. Thin the edges of the rounded hollow and fold four sides inward to partially enclose the hollow space but with a cross-like opening. These can be done separately or as one changing form

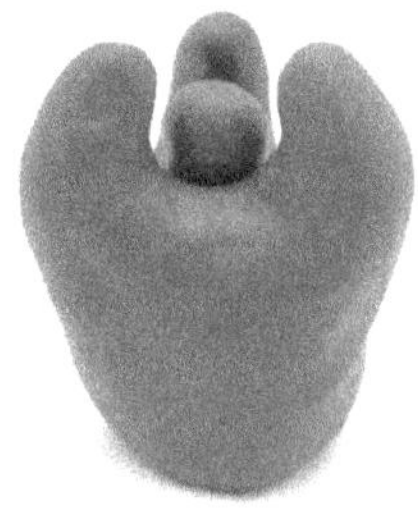

Three Hold One

A very small sphere separates from a large sphere which develops three embracing peaks standing on a base. The small sphere nestles in between them.

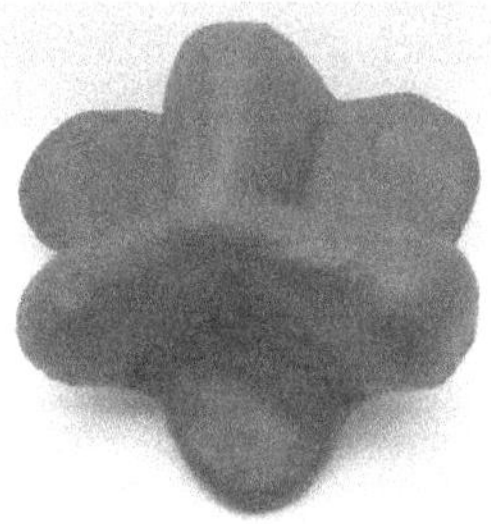

Three Round on Three Flat

Press a sphere down into three flattened, rounded corners. Shape three rounded rays.

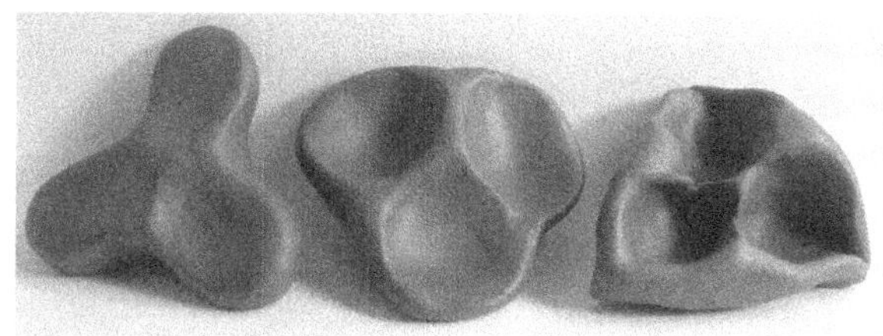

Threefold Hollows and Fourfold Hollows

1. Press and pull out a sphere into three flat hollows (left form).
2. *Variation* (middle): deeper rounder hollows.
3. *Variation* (right): Curl up the edges and deepen even more; bring the ends to points.

Steps 1 to 3 can be done separately or as one changing form.

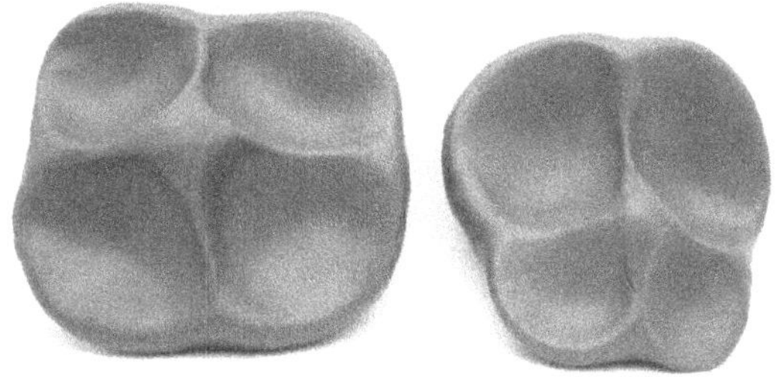

Fourfold: Similar process as threefold hollows.

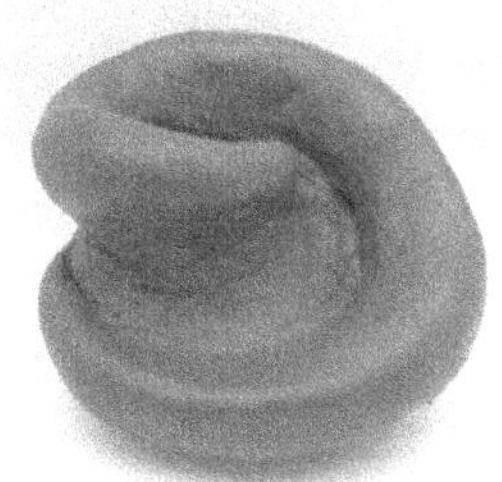

Spiraling Up

A sphere twists up into another variation of the spiral. Plant leaves spiral up in phyllotaxis.

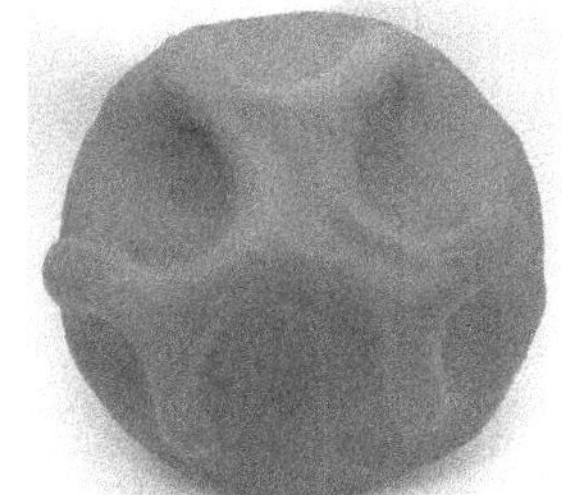

Mistletoe-like Relief

1. Flatten a sphere into a thick disk.
2. Press into the edges three crescent-shaped indentations and form twin seeding-like lobes with a stem toward the center.
3. Repeat in the two other branches creating a three-fold figure with a triangular center.
4. Flatten the spaces in between the branches into a round base.
5. Slope the branches down from the center in a slight curve.
6. Refine and make uniform all surfaces and edges.

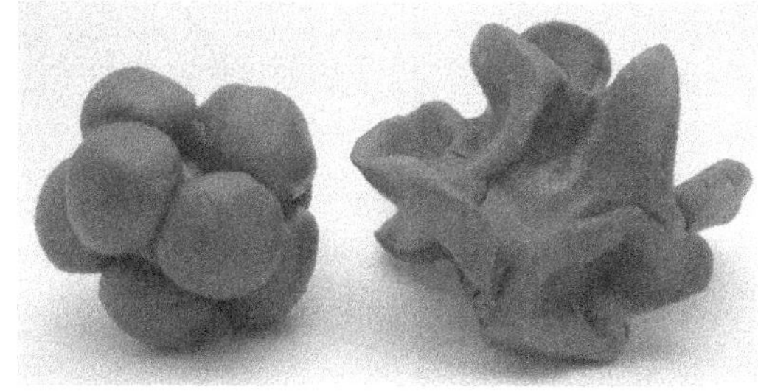

Coming Together and Falling Apart (Dissolving Decaying)

Make several little spheres and press them together in a thickening, multi-bulbous mass. Pull a sphere apart from all sides. Discuss and compare the form qualities of each.

The [sculptural] modeler is . . . the human maker whose activity arises from an imagination of water . . . Water thinking "runs through" the forms of the leaf, the flower, then flows into the forms of the fruit and seed. With our exact imagination we enter into the leaf shapes and move between them, through their sequence of growth . . . In Water thinking, we learn to "dwell" imaginatively in the form of living beings . . .

—Nigel Hoffman, biologist

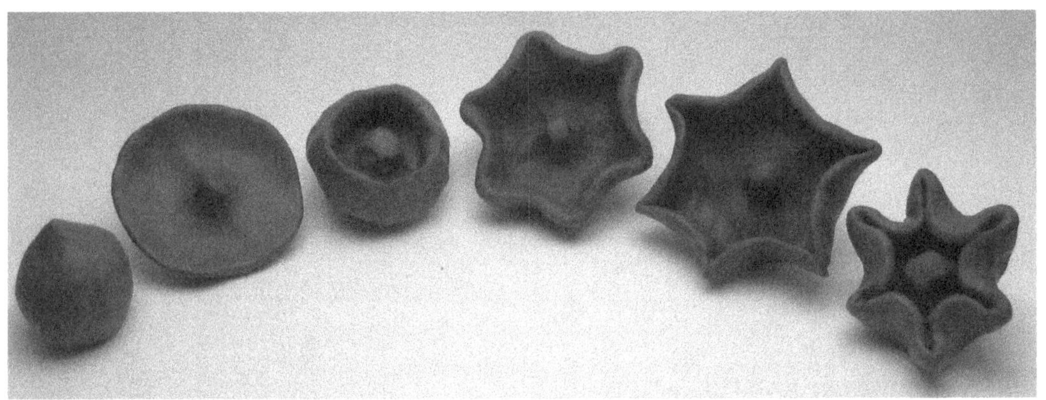

Contracting and Expanding

Set up six spheres of equal size in a row.

1. Pull the top of the first into a curved point (bulb-like contraction). Flatten the base slightly.
2. With the second, repeat #1 above. Then flatten into disk around a raised point and with an upturned circular edge (expansion).
3. Repeat #2 and lift the sides of the surrounding disk up and in toward a raised center point (contraction).
4. Repeat #2 and lift the sides up into a circular edge and indent with six curves and six rounded points (expansion).
5. Repeat #4 and make the curved points into sharper angular points (still expansion but with points contracting).
6. Repeat #4 and fold in the six sides so that six looping points tighten around the center (contraction but with points softening in roundness!).

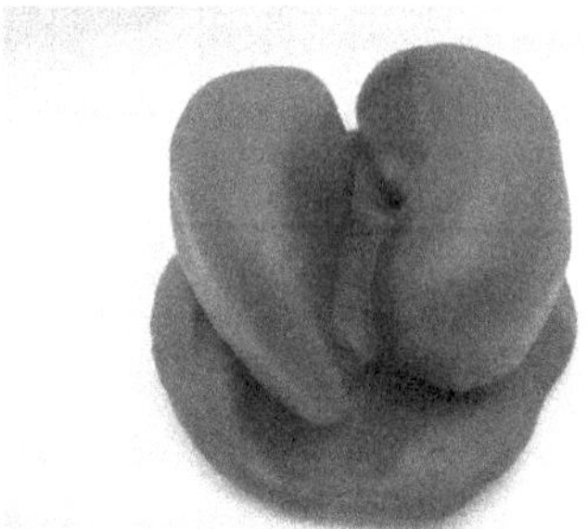

Curved Side by Side

On a rough base shape two figures relating to each other.

> *[Rodin's daughter] brought the shell of a small snail she had found in the gravel . . . He took it in his hand, smiled, admired it, examined it and said suddenly: "It is a question for me, that is for the sculptor par excellence, of seeing or studying. . . the plastic surfaces. The character of these, whether they are rough or smooth, shiny or dull (not in color but in character!). This little snail recalls the greatest works of Greek art: it has the same simplicity, the same smoothness, the same inner radiance, the same cheerful and festive sort of surface…*
>
> *—Rilke, poet and Rodin's personal secretary*

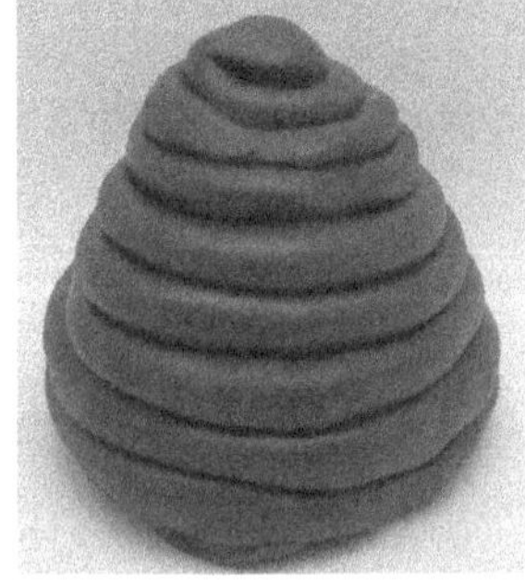

Hive-like

Make a very long strand and wind it up into a narrowing coil form with a little plug at the top.

Ancient History Motifs

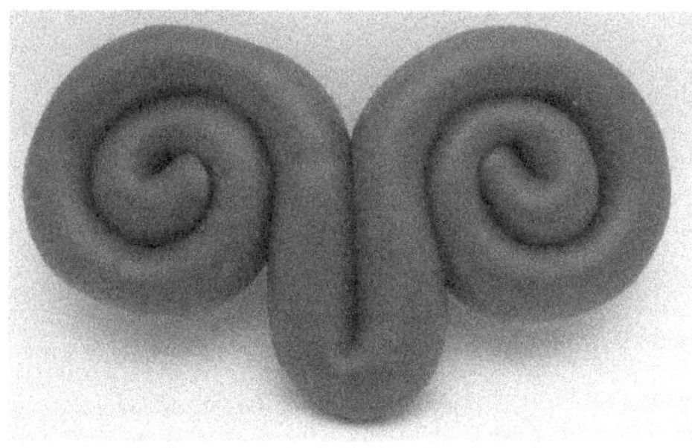

Ionic Spirals

Symmetrical double spirals decorated the top of Ionic temple pillars and also symbolized rams' horns and the power of thinking.

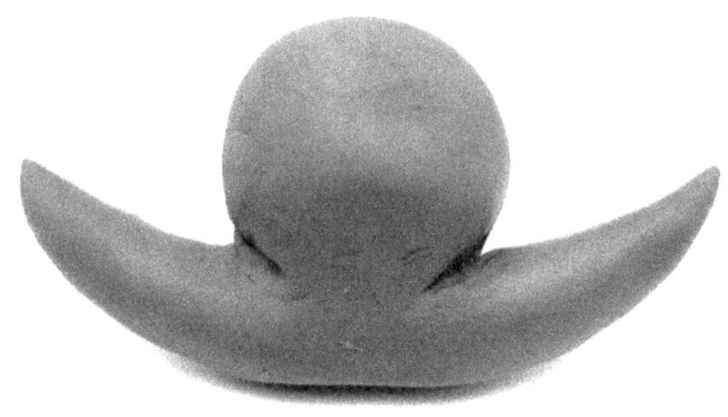

Disk in Crescent

The convex sun disk held in the concave crescent crowned certain Egyptian gods.

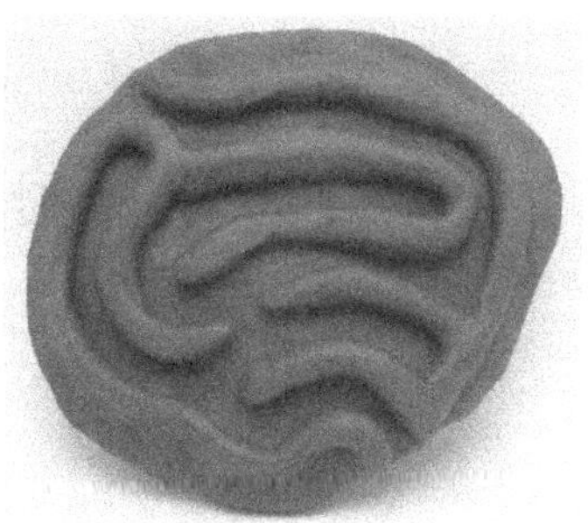

Design your Own Maze! (Labyrinth)

Explore and play around with different maze designs. They lend themselves to small individual formats or to large group projects if you have a lot of clay. One simple way to lay one out is to make a flat base and press long strands onto it, demarcating pathways.

Note: A maze has an entry, an exit, and a winding path between them with lots of misleading dead ends! A cousin of the maze is called a labyrinth which is technically supposed to have one path leading to a center and not out of an exit. (See Chartres Cathedral labyrinth.)

Question: Was the Minotaur's "labyrinth" actually a maze, since Theseus, the hero of the Greek legend, finds his way out of an exit with the help of Ariadne's thread?!

Option: Design a real labyrinth too! Endless possibilities!

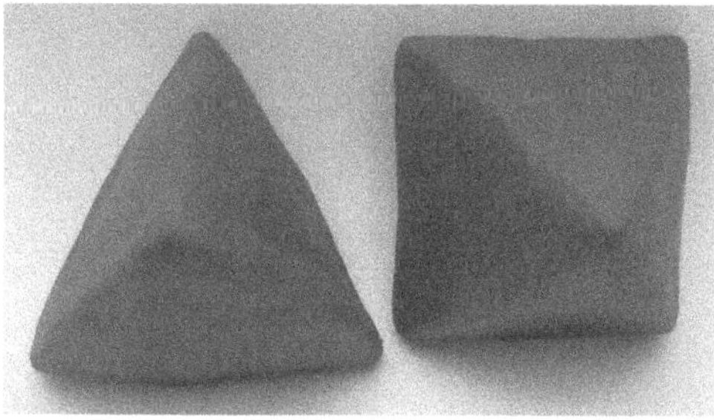

Pyramid Form Compared to a Tetrahedron

Model a sphere into a pyramidal form.

How many sides does it have?

What shape are they? In Series Six you will do its cousin, the tetrahedron. What is the difference between the two?

Series Six: Geometric

Older students can retain their imaginative powers and at the same time enjoy exercising new faculties in clear reasoning and astute observation. Geometric forms, proportions and relationships in architectural motifs and nature patterns stimulate budding capacities of discernment.

Tetrahedron Compared
Tetrahedron Moves
Arches
Entries
Spanning
Three Weaving
Raised Concavity
Rounded Bottom Rises to Top
Rounded Pointed Straightness
Hexagon
Parallel Shifting
Shell-like
Concave Spiral
Convex Spiral
Upright Convex to Through-Holes
River Bed-like
Building a Landscape
Space Between
Hollows Wrapping
Wrap Around
Front and Back

Geometric-Architectural

Tetrahedron Compared to a Pyramid Form
In Series Five you modeled a pyramidal form. How is its cousin the tetrahedron different? Shape a tetrahedron from a sphere.

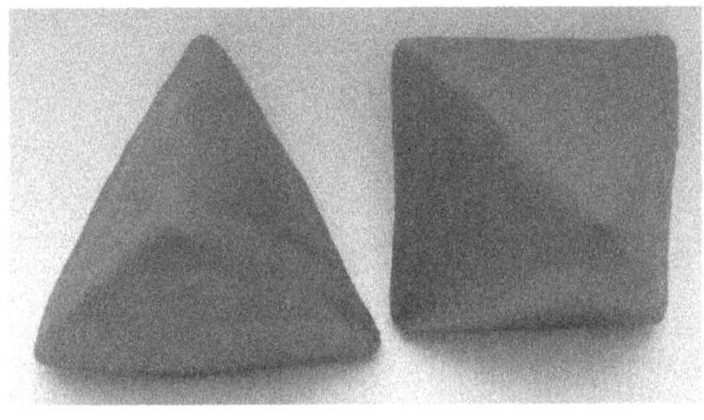

Options: Repeat a pyramidal form to experience the difference.

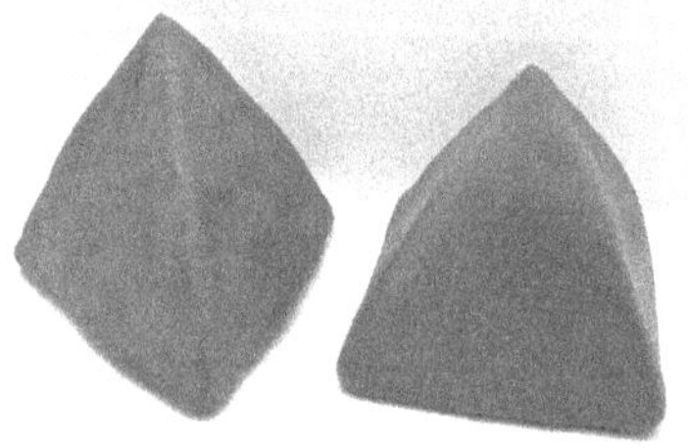

Since one of these is the pyramid, where is the sphinx? (There is room for humor in modeling. See next page.)

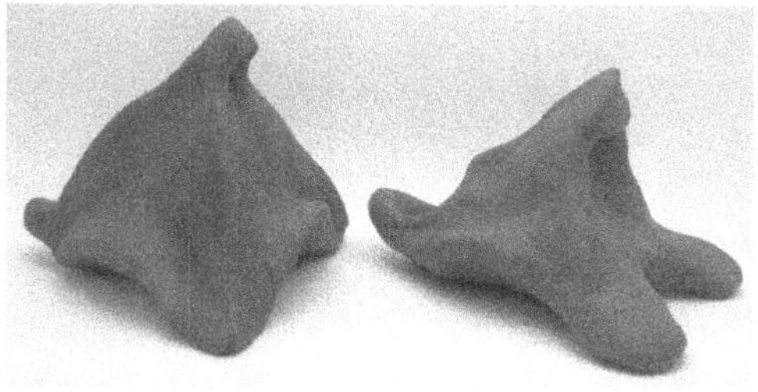

Tetrahedron Moves Forward (after Elsner)
Tetrahedron, immovable cousin of the rigid square-based Pyramid, felt restless and started stretching forward. Behold, she emerged as a_____________?! and stood guard over the Great Pyramid for thousands of years.

Or: In the Tetrahedron, immovable cousin of the rigid square-based Pyramid, is hidden a mysterious figure. Behold how she emerges.

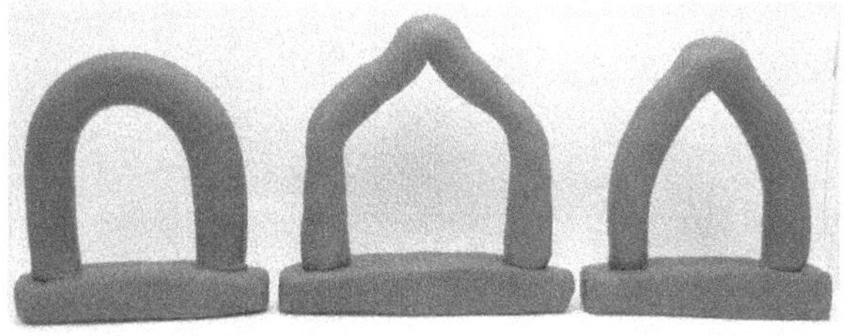

Arches: Roman, Islamic, Gothic Space
Capture the architectural differences in the historical development of arch forms. Emphasis in this form exercise is placed solely on the shape of the inner space created and on comparing the subtle curves and points.

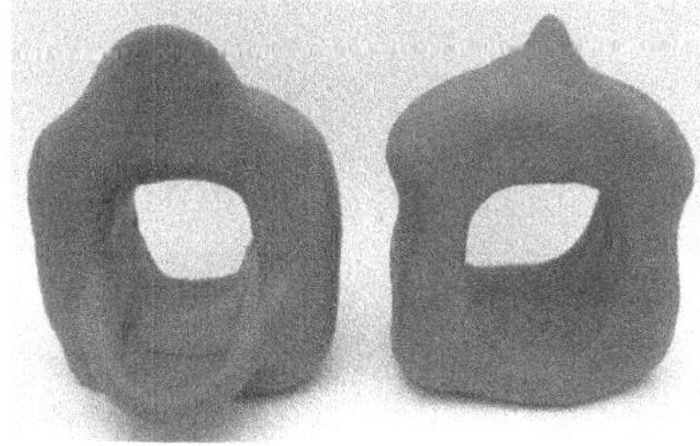

Entries
Design different entry forms.

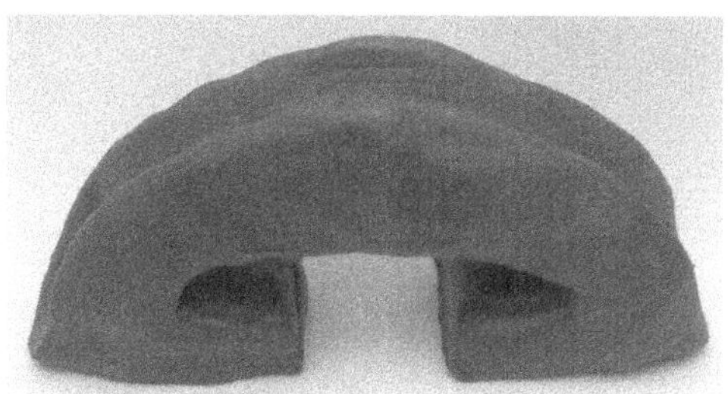

Spanning
Design different bridge-like forms that create and span over a space underneath.

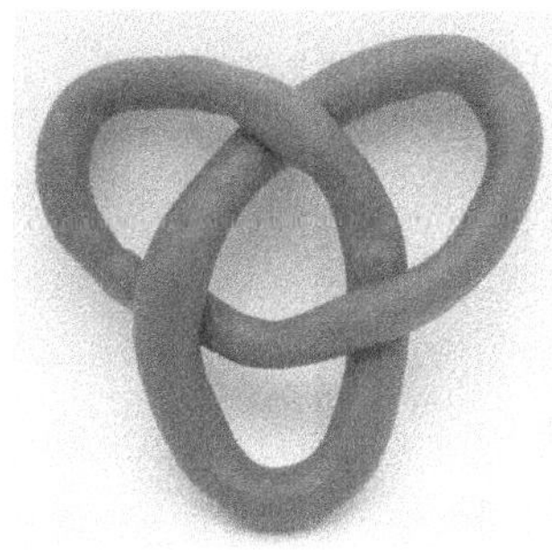

Weaving Three (Celtic Design)
Weave a long strand alternating over and under. Join the ends. Instead of clay, using plasticine for Celtic woven forms is less tricky and brittle, but both materials work. Strands in plasticine can also be disassembled and reused in other similar exercises. Develop other designs.

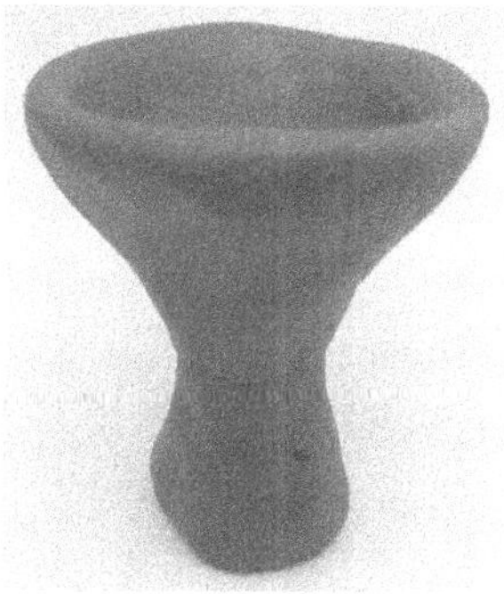

Raised Concavity
Raise up a vessel-like space on a base.
   Option: Form different shapes and add details to goblet-like or vase-like designs.

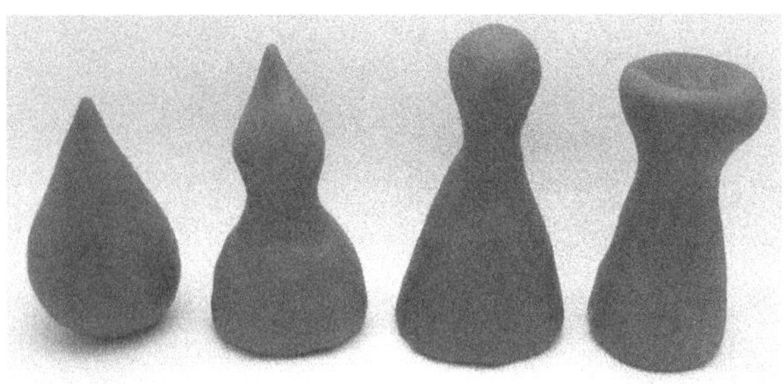

Roundedness Rises to Top

Make four equal spheres. Bases flatten as each form rises. Tops transform from pointed to convex and concave.

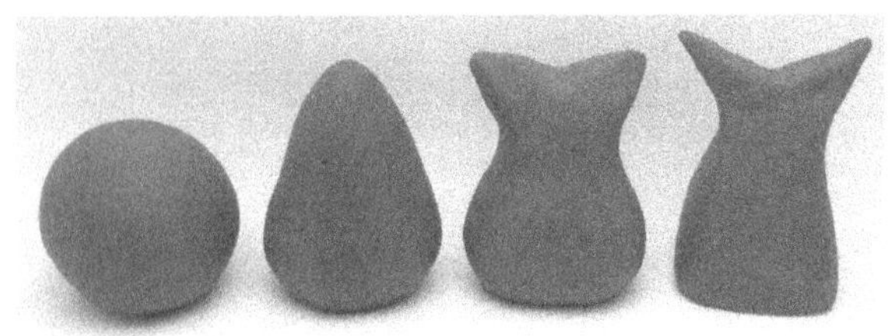

Rounded Pointed Straightness

Make four equal spheres.

Bring:

1. pointedness into the second sphere;
2. twofoldness into the top and more flatness into the base of the third;
3. sharp angularity into the top and complete flatness into the base of the fourth.

"God geometrizes"–this expression is attributed to Plato; "creative Nature 'imaginates' (imaginiert), she thinks in images"– this saying is one of Steiner's . . . In the final analysis, there is no difference since the geometrizing God of Plato sculpturally models (plastiziert) Nature just as a geometrician forms his ideal constructions: through His creative Phantasie, His Power of Imagination (Imaginationskraft). Whether we observe the shape of a plant or human being, we are always looking at a revelation of "imagining" Nature.

—Lorenzo Ravagli

Nature-like

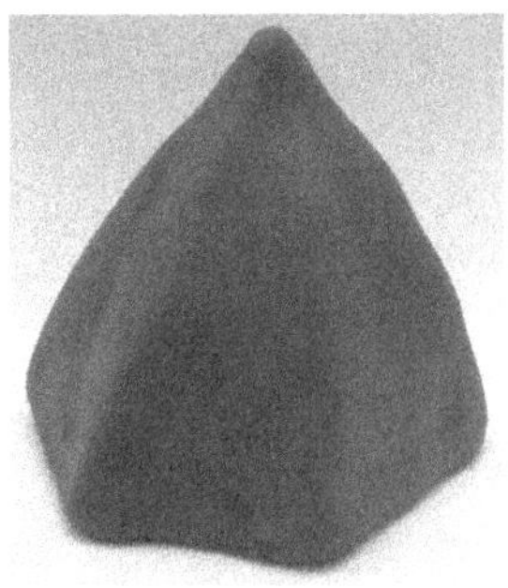

Hexagon

Drop a sphere onto a flat surface so that it begins to form a flat base. Press it on six sides, forming a point and a six-sided base.

It is not easy to achieve sharp edges.

This exercise can also be done as part of the study of mineralogy and the quartz crystal by adding a six-side shaft topped by the form above. The dome-like form can also be related to architecture.

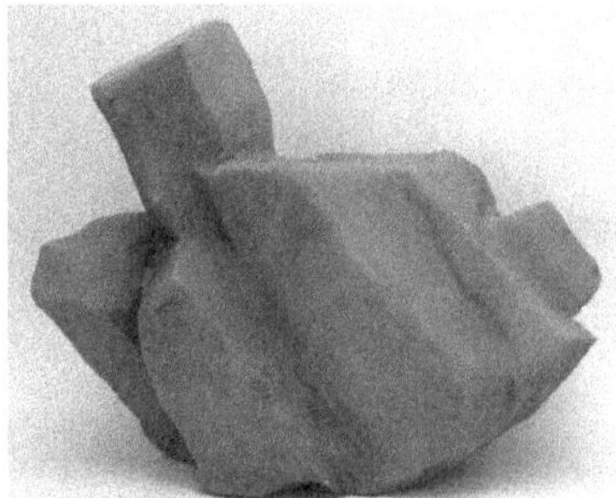

Parallel Shifting

Form diagonal linear rock-like layers.

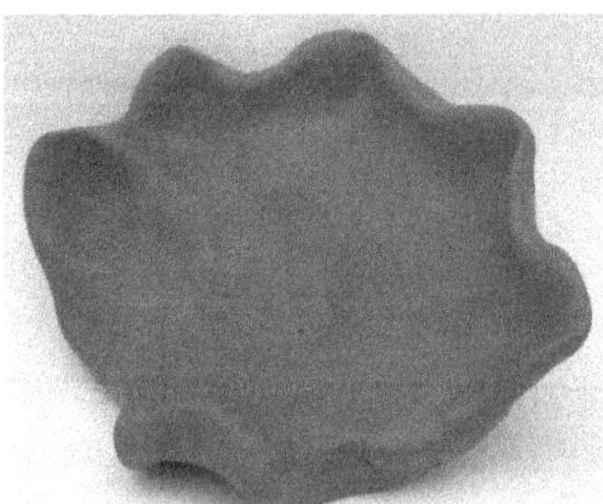

Shell-like

Design your own shell-like forms.

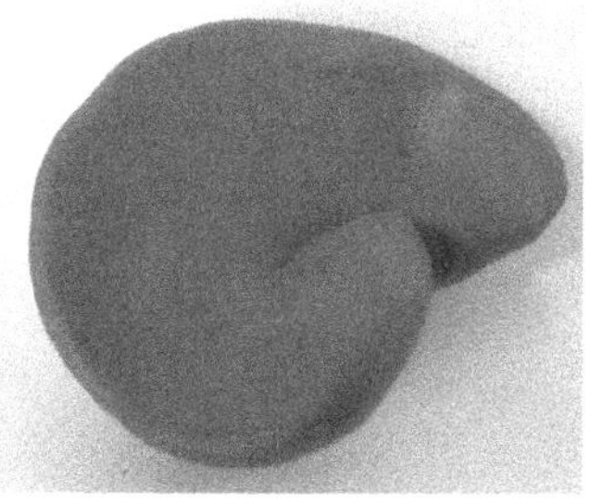

Concave Spiral

Flatten a sphere down into a subtle concave spiral.

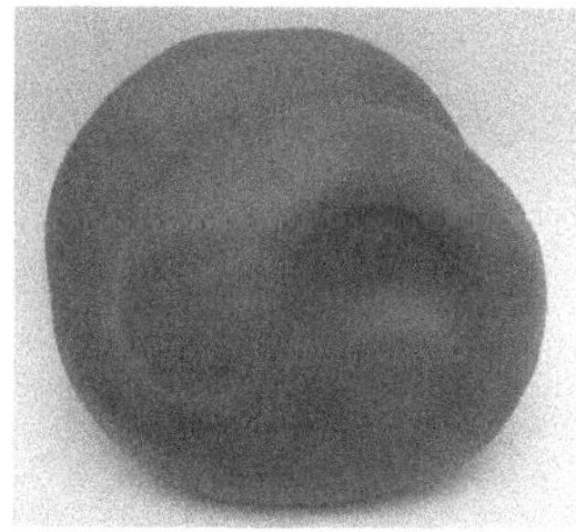

Convex Spiral

Press down into a sphere so that a raised, round-headed spiral comes up from one side into the middle and surrounds a hollow. The round base should be flattened in the process.

Tumbled

Exercise: You are a stone tumbling in a mountain stream. What form will you take on?

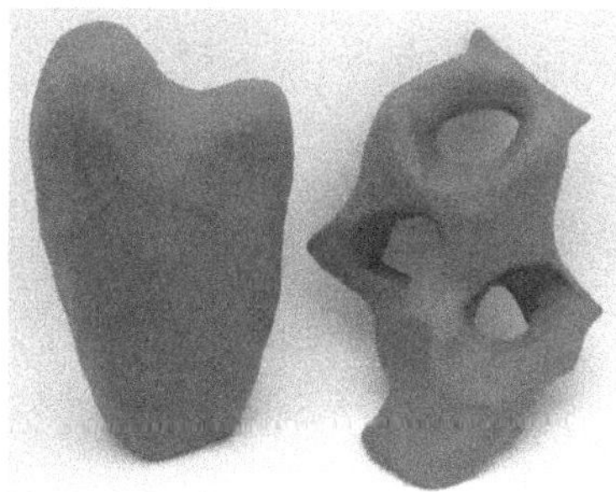

Upright Convex to Through-Holes

Shape two rising, slightly widening uprights.
1. At top, give the first form two round-nesses of different heights.
2. Repeat #1 and bring extreme concavities into a very different second form so that holes appear through it. The form also becomes more angular, flat and pointed in places.

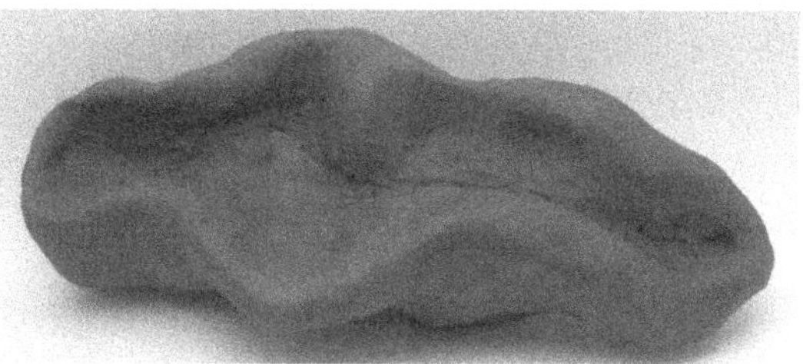

River Bed-like

Lengthen a sphere into a long, thin cylinder.

Indent it with a meandering groove of varying curves and depths.

Option: Relate to geology or geography lessons. This exercise can be done by groups forming a clay river bed on a long table or large piece of plywood. Students' hands are acting like streaming water sculpting out a river bed. This is the concave opposite of doing the same raising up convex mountain-like forms.

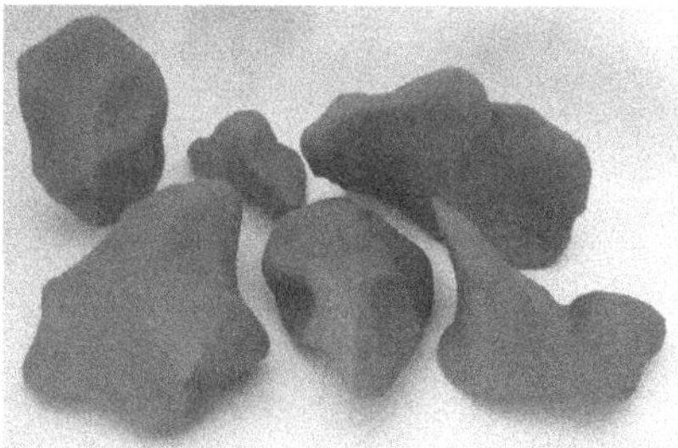

Building a Landscape

Make a half dozen or so varied forms like those above and unify them into a landscape (below).

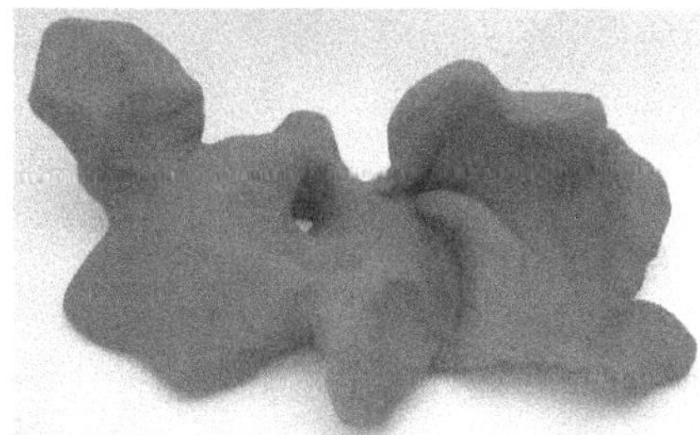

Topography is the study and 3-D mapping of the sculptural face of the earth. (Greek *topos*=place, *graphein*=carve or write.) Topology is the mathematical study of elastic geometric forms involving such properties as twistings and stretchings that are connected and continuous. Many of the pure forms in this book are of this nature and are a hands-on experience of advanced mathematics!

Relationships

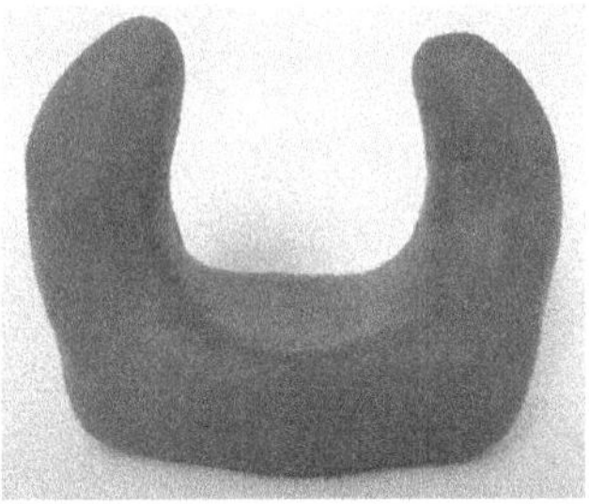

Space Between

Press a middle space into a sphere.

Make the overall narrow and curve two symmetrical sides upward and bending toward each other—ever conscious of the space between.

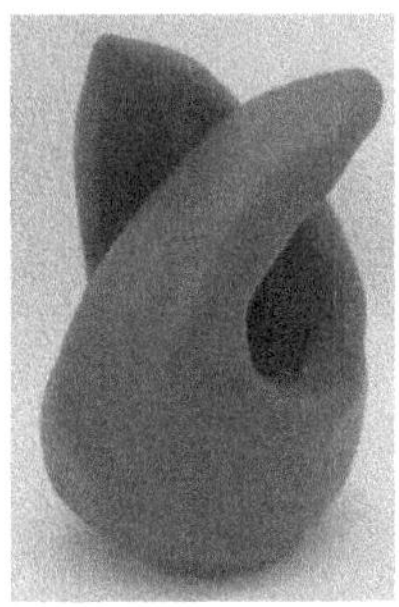

Wrap Around

Pull the top of a sphere into two flat elongations with a space between them. Leave the base rounded. Wrap the two partially around each other.

Variation: Completely wrap them around each other.

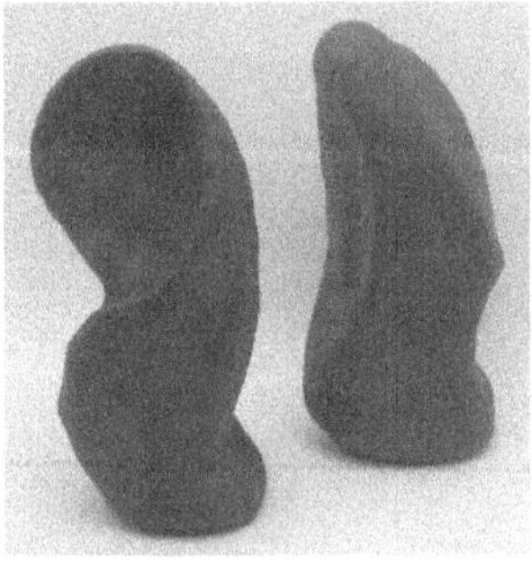

Front and Back

Shape two upright figures. Make the first with one side open and with the sympathetic gesture of "inviting into" an inner soul space (concave); the other closed with "turning its back" and antipathetically pushing away (convex).

The Social Proteus Exercise
Spontaneous Discovery of Pure Forms with Others

Proteus, born in the surging sea as son of Poseidon, possessed the power to change shape at will and to take on the guise of many shapes. He was able to create forms together with other beings—exciting forms of the future and never seen before!

In addition to developing sculptural capacities individually, students, as they mature, can also enjoy and benefit from working responsibly together with others on one piece of modeling. In the curriculum, this may take the form, for example, of making an adobe village (grade 3), a cave habitat for which each student makes a single bear (grade 4), a beeswax topographical map of North America (grade 5), a Roman coliseum (grade 6), three figures dancing in a round (grade 7) or connected bones in the skeleton (grade 8).

"Social-group" modeling can also be applied to the Proteus Exercise highlighted at the beginning of the Series. Below, the exercise is adapted for two or three partners developing one pure form.

Two, three or more people developing multiple pieces

- Each modeler shapes a sphere and then begins to bring out features of a spontaneous pure form—either seen by the others or not.
- Switching: After a set number of minutes, each passes her form to the next person to develop further.
- Pieces circulate a number of times until the decision is made to stop.
- Pieces are displayed in a circle on a table to view them as a collective effort and unity.
- Think of your own variations.

Modify the above according to what works best for you.

Again, what is presented are starter, "seed" ideas. Develop your own ideas.

The aim of the *Social Proteus Exercise* is to educate the capacity to collaboratively discover free forms without a lot of preconception—or discussion! Participants become open and flexible in the process of having their own individual work changed by others. Social excitement is added to the artistic excitement of discovering new forms.

Series Seven: Changing Bodies

Adolescence is a Renaissance and a birth of something new. The human being remodels her body and soul to accommodate the rapidly incoming individual spirit. A main theme is METAMORPHOSIS and trans-FORM-ation through many states of body and mind and the excitement of contrasts and differences. New and deeper soul space is being developed inside the human being as well as new relationships to what and who is outside.

Budding Opening
Inner Spaces
Bulging Flattening Hollowing
Straight to Curved
Rising Hollows
Bottom, Middle, Top Heavy
Rounded and Angular Landscape
Lung-like
Saddle Forms
Convex/Concave Mirroring
Figure-Eight Twist
Weaving S-Form
Flaming Up and Water Worn
Raised Inner Space
Flight
Octahedron
Hull

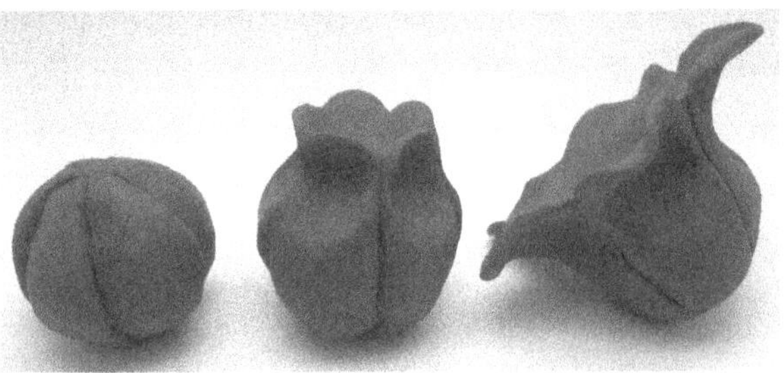

Budding Opening

1. Make three equal spheres with five or six vertical grooves down the sides of each.
2. On the second form, turn up the tops of each section between the grooves; indent and turn the resulting flaps out very slightly.
3. Extend and curve the flaps outward; indent them more deeply.

Human Development

In puberty young people feel like buds packed with new energy for imminent growth and change.

In modeling, an exercise of a closed "bud-like" form contrasted with one slightly opening can capture this threshold moment.

The final open form projects the future. This exercise can also be combined with creative writing. See two examples of the first sentences of "Wish, Wonder, and Surprise" compositions in the box to the left.

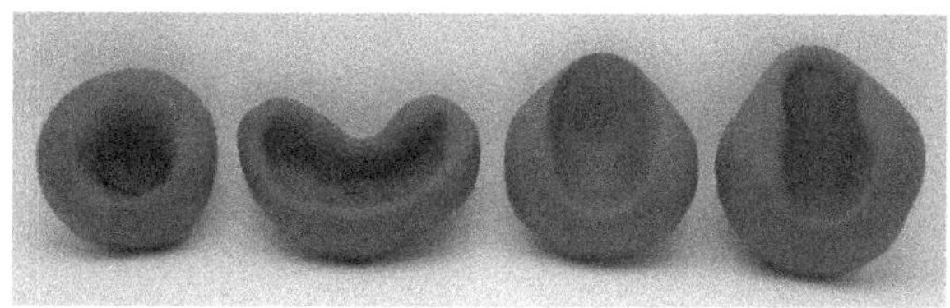

Inner Space Changes

Make four equal spheres, each with a differently shaped inner space.

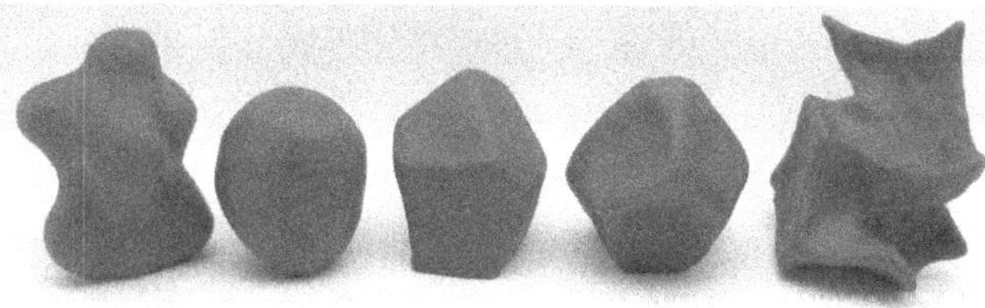

Bulging Flattening Hollowing

Make equal spheres for each of the five stages of transformation. *Option*: done over three days.

1. Turn sphere #1 into an upright ovoid. Pull out bulges and deepen the spaces between them so they stick out more. Round them. (Day 1)
2. Repeat #1 and press its bumps into slightly convex sides. (Day 2)
3. Repeat #2 and completely flatten its sides with exact adjoining edges. (Day 2)
4. Repeat #3 and hollow sides with defined edges and points. (Day 2)
5. Repeat #4 and deeply hollow its sides so that sharp edges and points protrude dramatically. (Day 3)

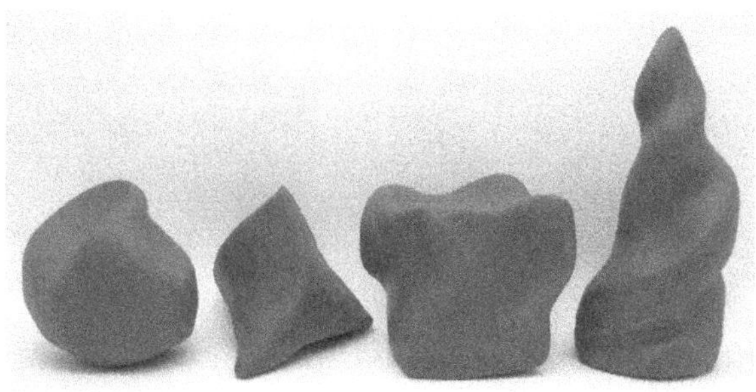

Straight to Curved

Four solids were tired of being so regular so they started moving and bringing some curving and twisting into their lives! Believe it or not, these begin as a regular sphere, tetrahedron, cube and cone! *Option*: Do the first two and second two on the same days.

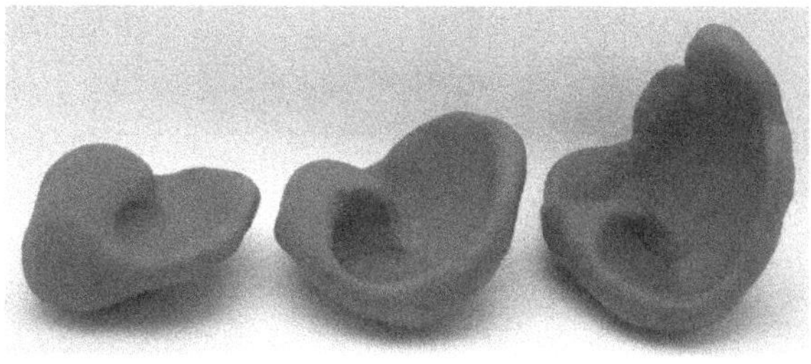

Rising Hollow

Make three ovoids.

1. Press the lower part of an ovoid into a hollow leaving a rounded, curling bulge at the other end. (Day 1)
2. Repeat but with a larger hollow space rising up and a thinning bulge. (Day 1)
3. Repeat with the hollow even larger and vertical and with a very small shrunken bulge. (Day 2)

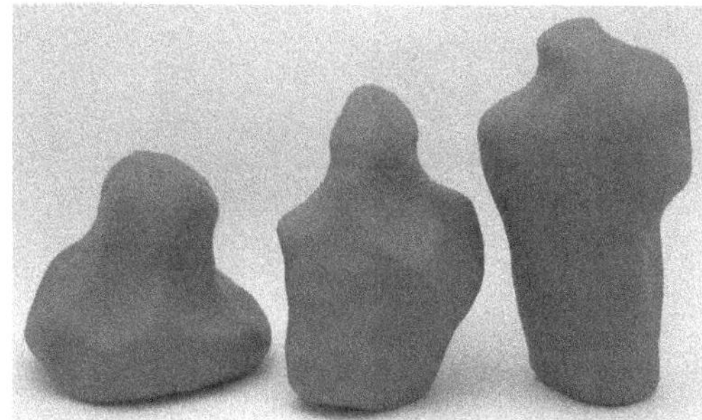

Bottom Heavy, Middle Heavy, Top Heavy

Make three equal spheres. Emphasize the bottom, mid-section and top masses.

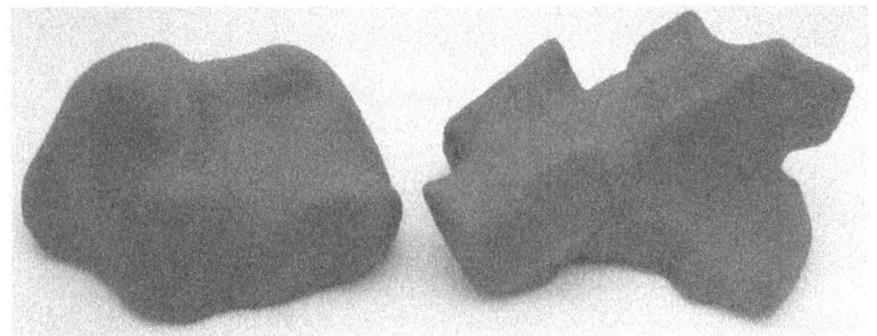

Rounded and Angular Landscape

Flatten two horizontal ovoids on one side to make flat bases. Model a rounded landscape and then an angular and pointed one.

Option: Turn the first into the second.

Physiological Organ-Like Forms

An artistic awareness of the marvelous *organ*-ic forms of the human body is particularly important for teenagers. For example, they can model the forms of asymmetrical lung-like forms below, symmetrical kidney shapes, brain-like convolutions, etc.

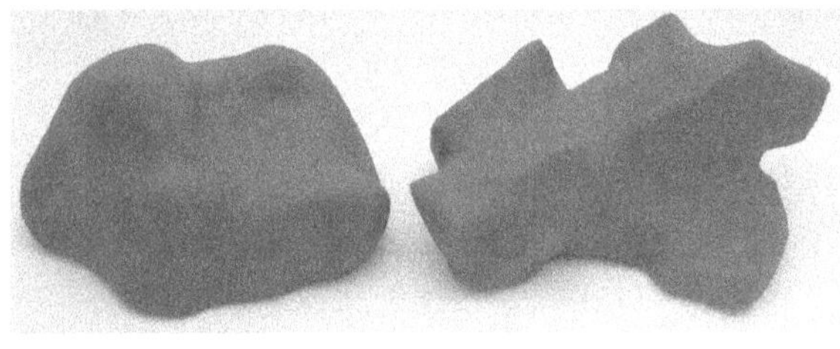

Lung-like (Asymmetry)

Divide a sphere into a u-shape with two connected sides and a curved space in between. Sever the two sides and shape three-lobed and two-lobed forms in asymmetric balance with each other.

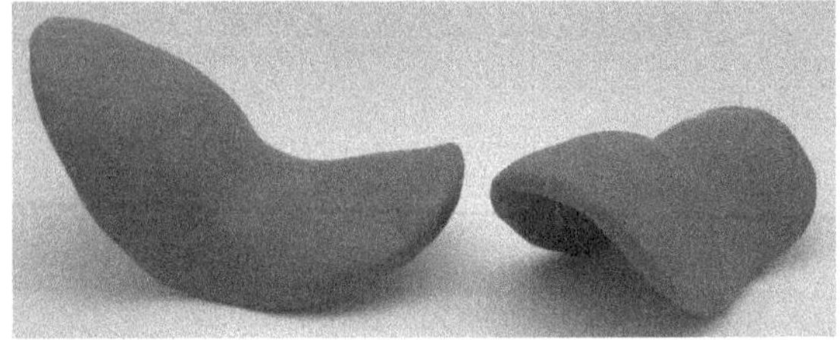

Saddle Curves

Flatten spheres into flat ovals and bend them into double curves. There are many variations to explore. The human body is covered with double curves. Look at your knuckles and nose!

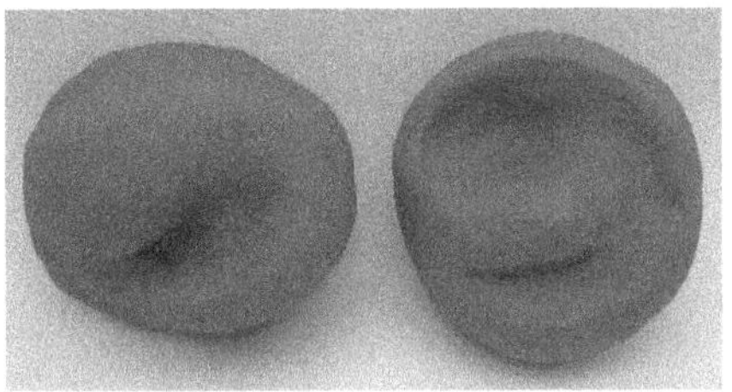

Convex Concave Mirroring

Make two equal hemispheres, then create a convex form in one of the hemispheres. Mirror its negative concave opposite in the other.

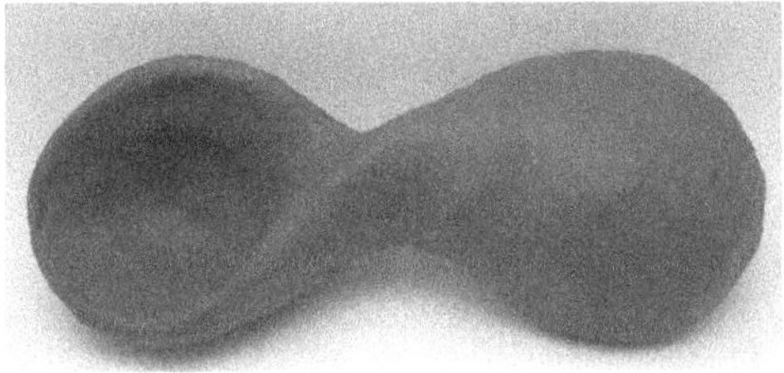

Figure-Eight Twist

Elongate an ovoid and narrow it in the middle so two spherical ends result. On the same side, press concavities into the spheres.

Then twist this figure-eight form so that the concavities move to opposite sides. Smooth middle diagonals so that one side transitions spirally from one side to the other. Refine the edges of the concavities. Life is full of twists and turns!

> *When we study forms, especially organic ones, nowhere do we find permanence, nowhere rest or completion. Everything is in ceaseless flow. For in nature no sooner has something formed than it is immediately transformed. If we wish to achieve a living perception of nature, we must strive to keep ourselves as mobile and flexible as the examples she herself provides.*
>
> —Goethe

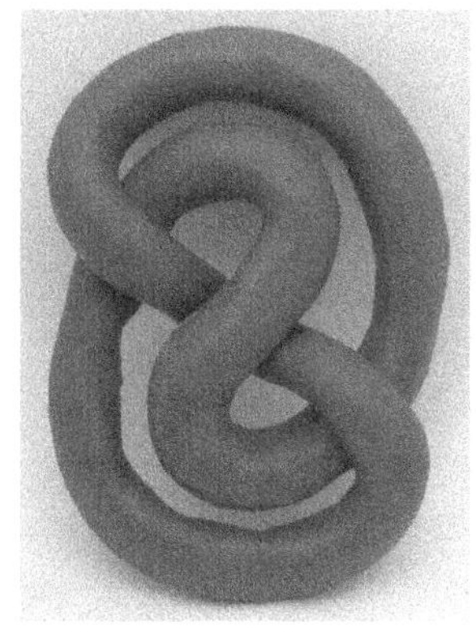

Weaving S-Form

Weave a long strand alternating over and under. Join the ends. It gets complicated inside.

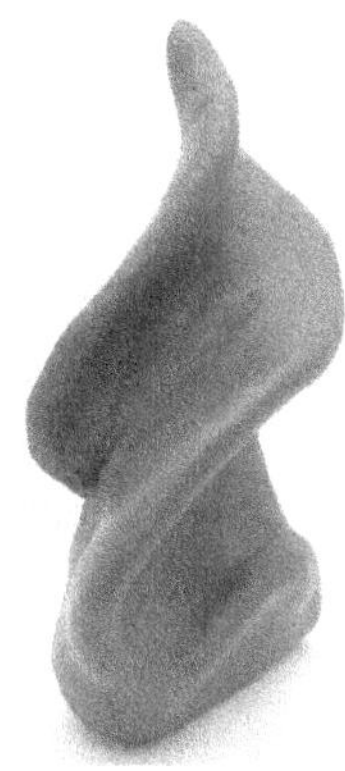

Flaming Up and Water Worn

Two forms are modeled side by side to experience the contrasting gestures of flame-like verticality (above) and water-like horizontality (below).

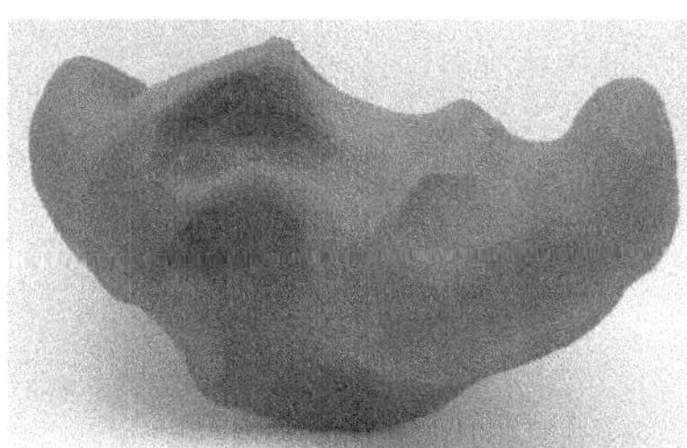

Water Worn

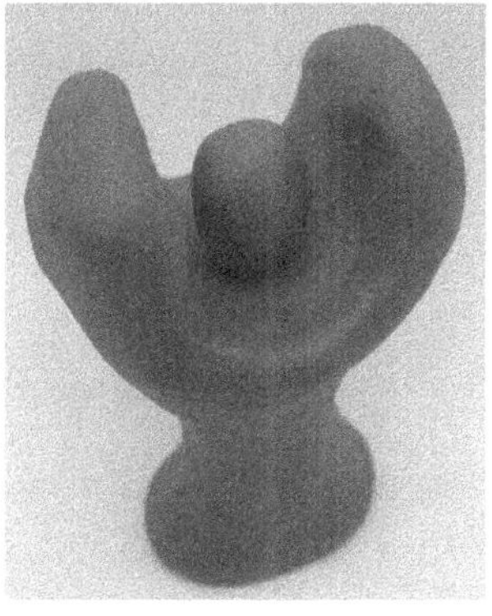

Raised Inner Space

Divide the top of a cylinder into two embracing sides with an ovoid or other small form protected within.

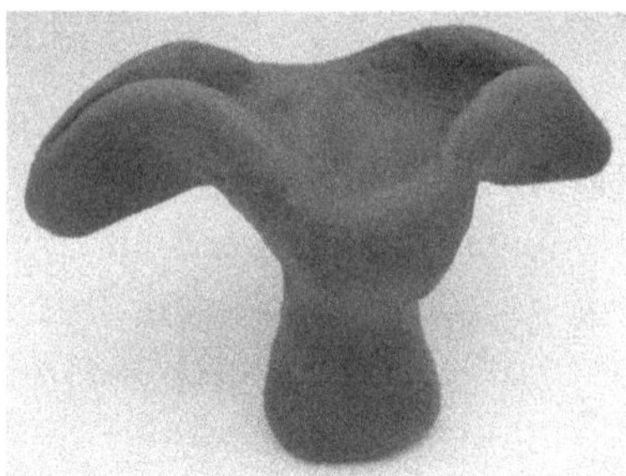

Flight

Make a non-representational form that expresses "flight or flying" but is not a making of a bird's wings. The example above is only meant to inspire individual explorations of design, although some may want to render the example.

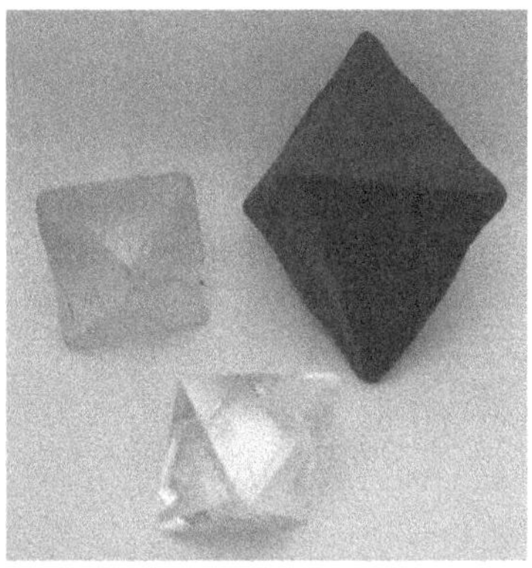

Octahedron

Add this third Platonic Form to your growing collection (cube, tetrahedron).
Do its top and bottom remind you of another familiar form?

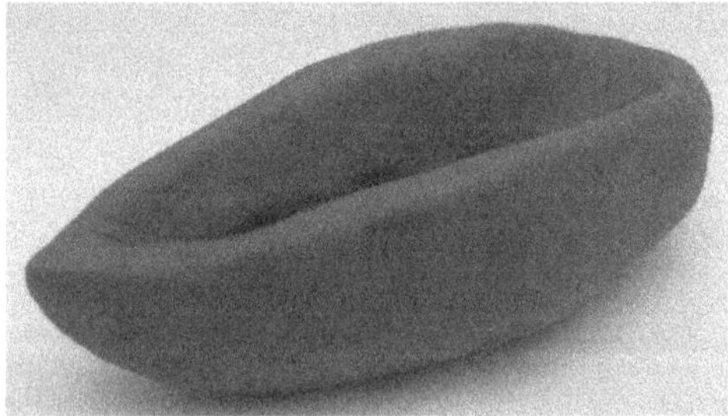

Design a Hull Shape

Design and make a model of a hull-like form of your choice. Lengthen and hollow out an ovoid. The shape in the photo is very simple. More complicated ship-like hulls can be tackled, for example, galleons in connection with the explorers. You yourself should explore and elaborate forms. See what you come up with!

Series Eight: Anatomical

Adolescence is a revolution of body, soul and spirit. The uprightness of the emerging individual is tested by the pressures of contemporary life. Challenges come in many shapes and call for healthy discernment, form and freedom. There are innumerable possible themes, some of which are: the anatomy of the human skeleton and senses, water forms and practical design.

Uprights
Pushing Forward
Welcoming Embracing
Three Piggybacking
Rising Piggyback
Two-Lobe Concavity
Sphere into Concavity
Twisting
Mirror Blades
Hearing's Dancing Leg
Hearing Sharp Sound
Torso-Like
Smile and Frown
Holder
Vase Design
Car Design
Eights Within Eights
Hip-like Twisting
Giving and Receiving
Three Impressings
Convex Falling into Concave
Form Circle

The dignity of the human being is given into your hands. It sinks with you. With you it will lift itself upright.

–Friedrich Schiller

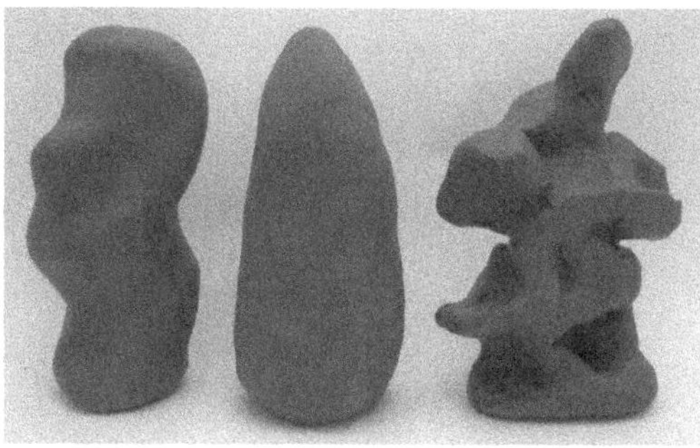

Uprights Synthesized and Analyzed: Convexity, Blended Balance, Concavity

Analysis: Shape three neutral uprights like the middle form. Develop rounded features on one like the one on the left and hollowed features on another like the right one.

Challenge: Create a balanced form in the middle that has mixed qualities of convexity and concavity. (Not yet developed in the photo to the right)

Synthesis: Build up each form with little pieces of material. The first upright rises up and surrounds itself in rounded forms. The second upright rises up and covers itself with hollowed features. A third form rises and shapes itself between the other two.

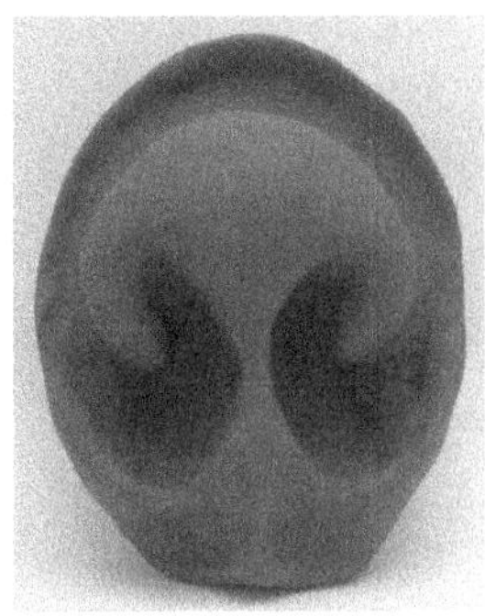

Pushing Forward

Into an ovoid lying on its side, press two facing hollows into its middle leaving a ridge in between and creating two curved, "arm-like" extensions. Round the overarching bulbous top so that an edge forms below it and sweeps around to join with the first hollow spaces. This form can be connected with water flowforms and jellyfish propulsion in other lessons (see Schwenk's *Sensitive Chaos* on water flow patterns). *How are our noses formed? In water?*

Anatomy-Like Forms

The Skeleton as Teacher of Sculpture

An artistic awareness of the marvelous forms of the changing human body is particularly important for teenagers. The skeleton, for example, at this stage of human development is changing significantly and is a veritable treasure trove of fascinating organic forms. In anatomy studies, students render the forms of femurs, vertebrae, skull, and other bones by observing real specimens.

In addition, they can, through pure form modeling, also freely and playfully create their own organically evolving sequences inspired by nature. Form features can be extracted that stand alone as striking examples of sculpture.

Examples such as the following "Embracing" and "Piggyback" sequences can be shown. Students then design their own nuanced shapes based on the form language they observe in a particular exercise. They are asked to keep to a similar organic look and not digress into unrelated fantastic forms. The imagination is thus empowered to objectively create all kinds of variations on a theme and artistically continue the dynamic form creating of nature!

The Human Spine

The human spine is an intriguing "running," repeating sequence of extraordinary sculptural forms. As a vertebral column, it holds us firmly upright in our unique human verticality and yet has subtle curves and flexibility—straight and curved, firm and flexible combined! For an excellent reference on possible eighth grade anatomy lessons, see von Mackensen's *Uprightness, Weight and Balance* (vertebral column, hip, foot, mechanics, etc.)

For class discussion: *What does it mean to be "spineless" or "have no backbone"?*

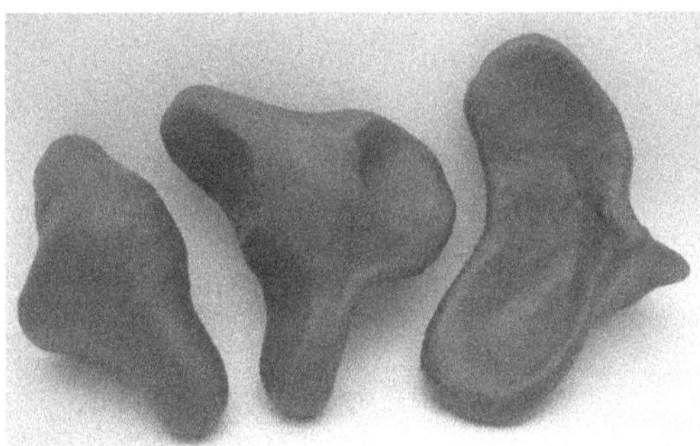

Welcoming Embracing Forms

Make three equal spheres and shape them into three forms that relate to and complement each other in a sequence which shows steps of increasing concave openness. In this example, the middle figure extends a welcoming opening gesture to the front one and is touched and embraced by the very open back one. The middle form "piggybacks" on the back one. See next photo.

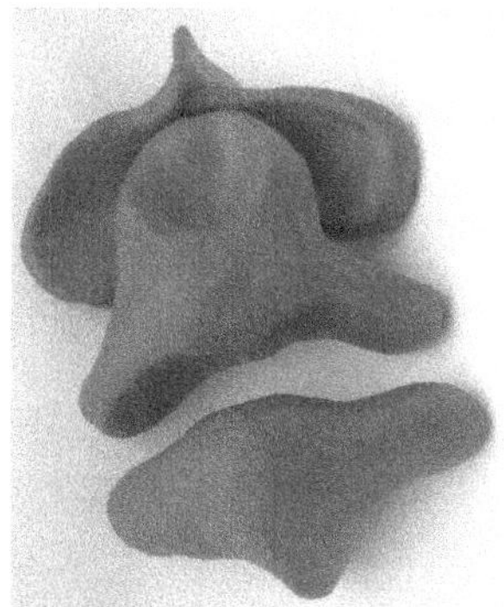

Embracing forms joined

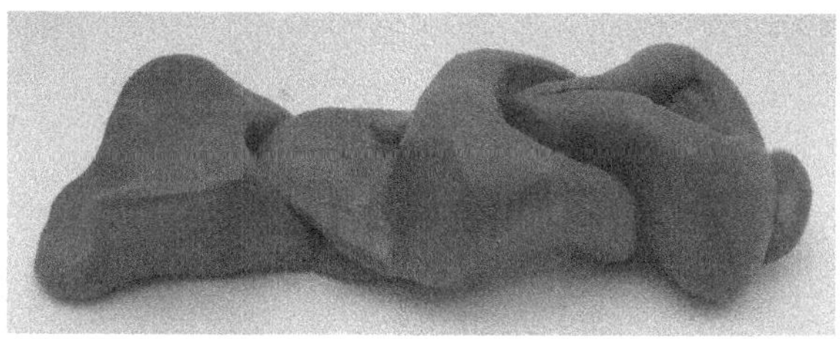

Three Piggybacking Forms

As you shape your forms to complement and fit each other, experiment with different shapes. Keep moving forms into/onto each other and then separating them for adjustment until you achieve an aesthetic fit.

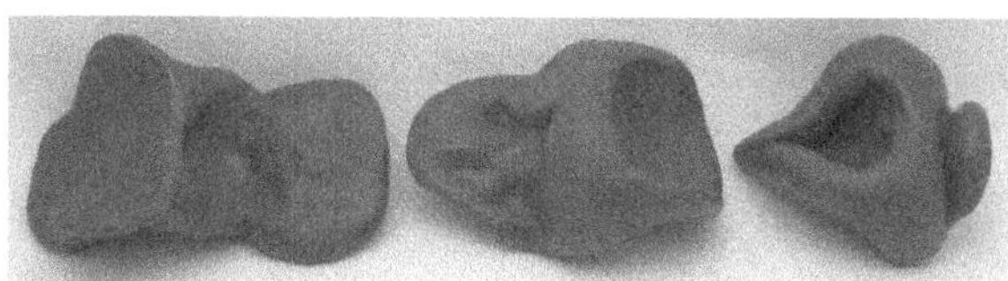

Make separately and then join

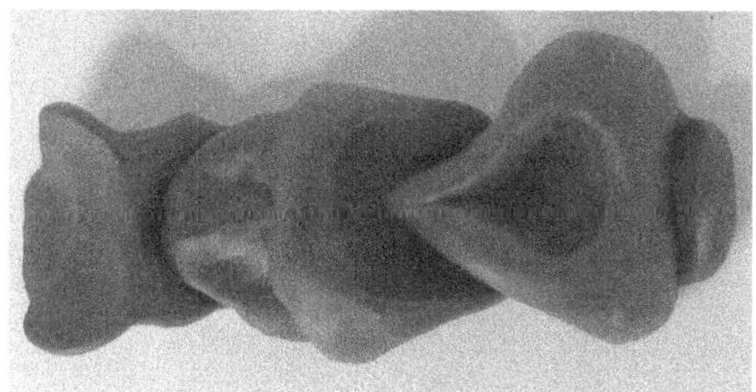

view from above

Rising Piggyback

Equal spheres can be hollowed and thinned in rising succession.

Or start with differently sized spheres for a similar effect.

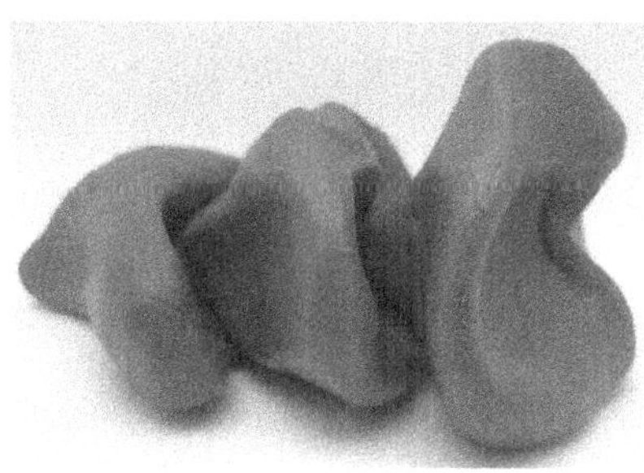

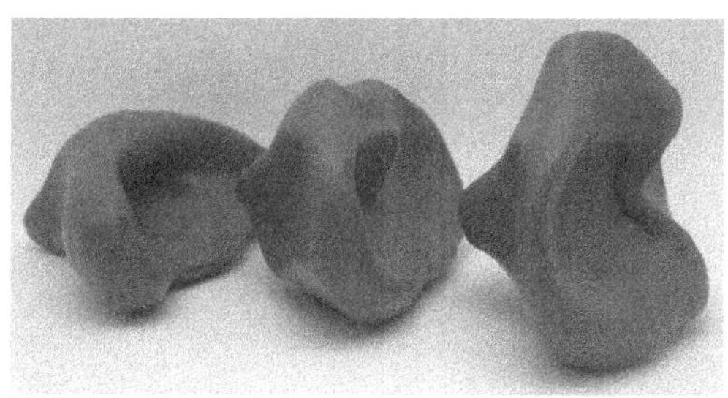

Make separately before joining

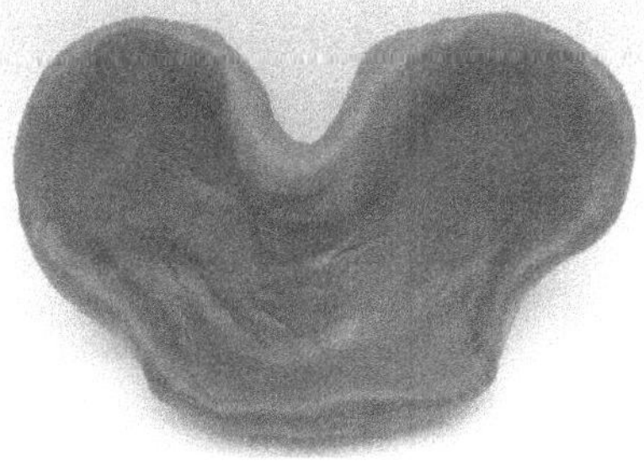

Two-Lobe Concavity

Press into a sphere with your two thumbs and hollow out two branched concavities (basin-like, pelvic bone-like).

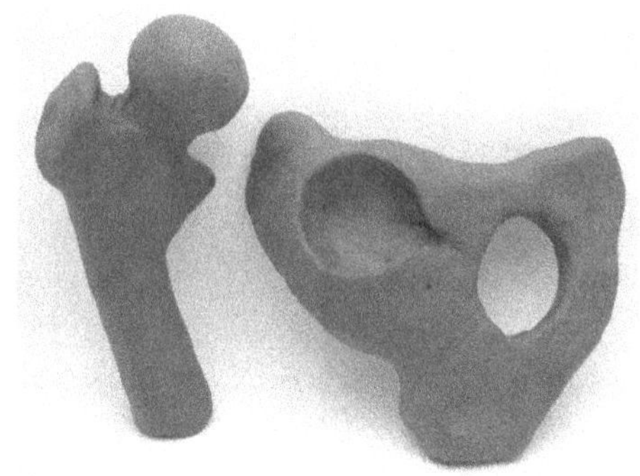

Sphere into Concavity

Shown above are partial extracts of the femur form and part of the pelvic bone. On the outside of the lower half of the pelvic bone (shown right above) is a quintessential concavity (socket) into which fits the sphere (ball on top of the femur left). Model the two figures separately as two contrasting yet very much related pieces of organic sculpture.

What do these forms remind you of?

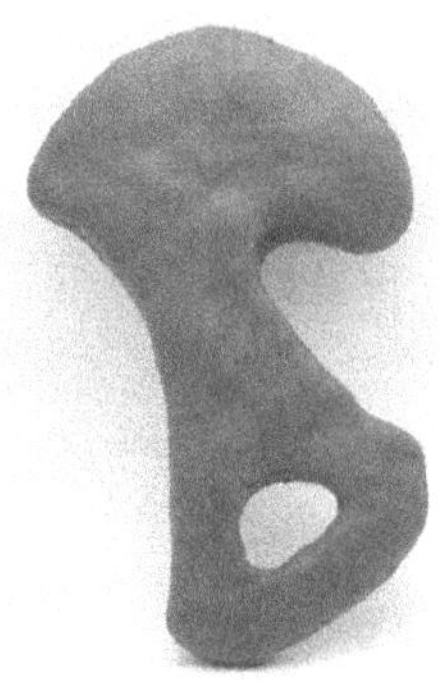

Twisting

Shown above is an abstracted part of a simplified pelvic bone. Model the form above first as a flat piece. Then turn the upper part to the left and at a right angle to the bottom part so that the connector in between twists. This gives an idea of the elegant curvature of this basin-like structure and the miracle of nature's "engineering."

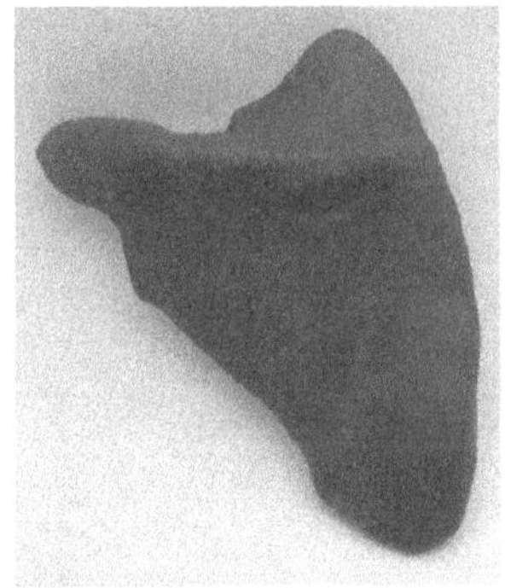

Mirror Blades

Model a simplified form of the left human shoulder blade. Make its mirror form on the right. Does this pair of forms look like our stunted or clipped wings?

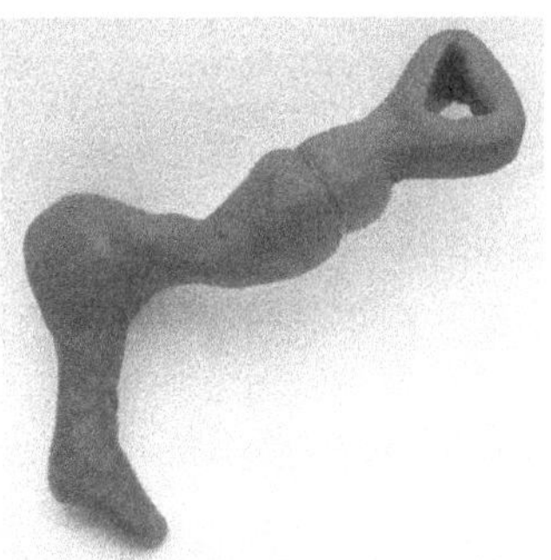

Hearing's Dancing Leg

Hearing can be imagined as the dancing of a limb-like form within our ear. The foot-like malleus on the left end of the figure above dances on the eardrum below it (not shown). It is connected to the knee-like incus in the middle which in turn is attached to the stapes at the right end.

> *Within your inner ear . . . you have a transformed . . . limb . . . The stapes . . . appears . . . as a metamorphosis of a human thigh-bone. And the [other] little bone, the incus, appears as a transformed kneecap. Finally, that part which passes from the incus to the drum, the malleus, appears as a metamorphosis of the lower part of the leg with a foot.*
>
> *—Rudolf Steiner*

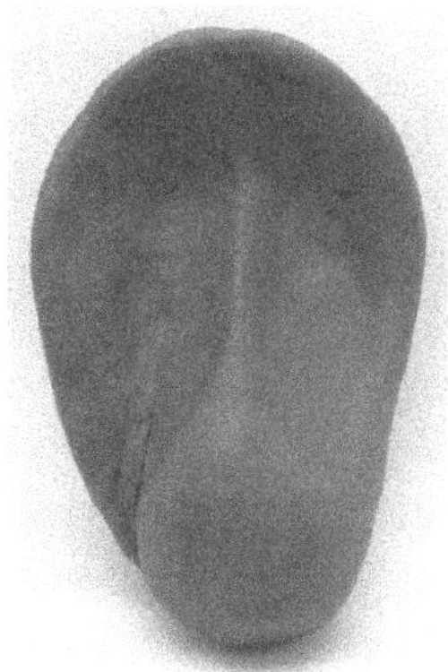

Hearing a Sharp Sound

Reshape an ovoid so that the wider, rounder end becomes concave. Make the opposite side narrower and bulbous with a ridge pointing upward into the concavity. The left side sweeps around asymmetrically to touch the underside of the convexity. This is a subtle ear-like form, so refer to photo!

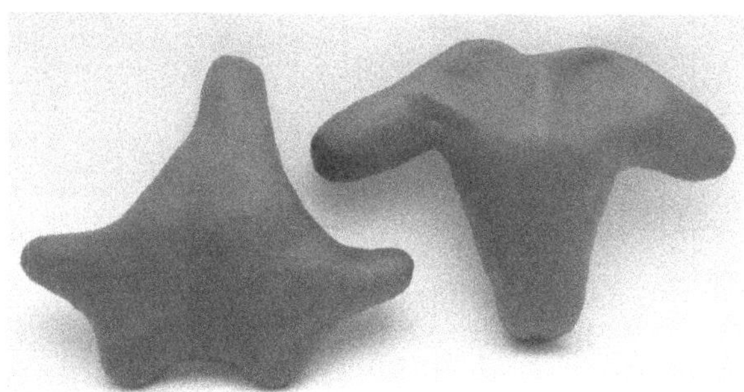

Torso-Like

Flatten spheres and play with torso-like forms. (Avoid turning them into realistic human torsos!)

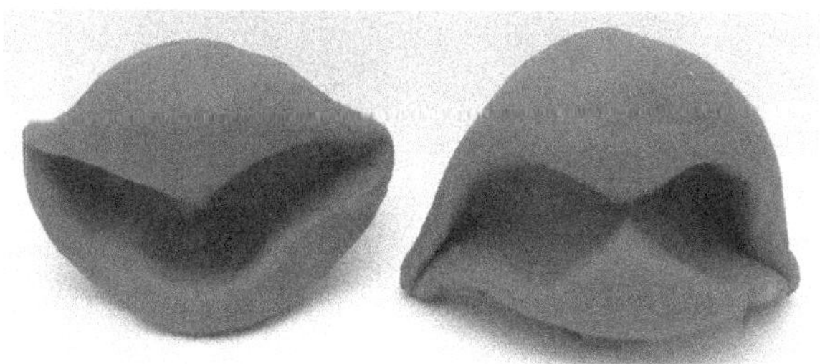

Smile and Frown

Shape mouth-like form gestures that express different moods.

Practical Design Forms

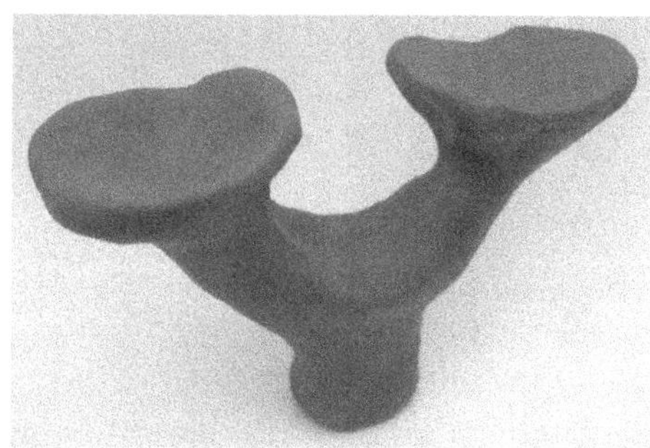

Holder Design

Split the upper part of an elongated ovoid into two branches and flatten the ends into two horizontal, slightly concave forms.

This is not yet a candleholder but could be developed into one in another lesson. Interesting forms can serve the practical.

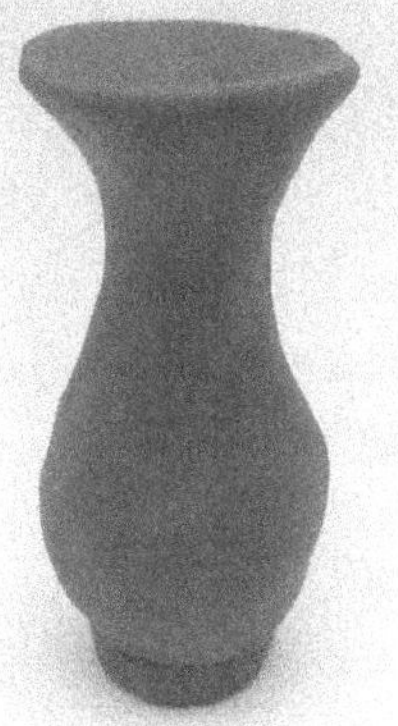

Vase-like Design

Design different vase-like shapes. This is a good exercise for students who do not have access to more complicated pottery other than making simple unfired coiled pots. It can also be useful to those who want to explore different vase forms before going to the wheel.

> *[A sculptural] work . . . may be a penetration into reality . . . The provision of pleasant shapes and colors in a pleasing combination [is] not a decoration to life, but an expression of the significance of life, a stimulation to greater effort in living.*
>
> *—Henry Moore*

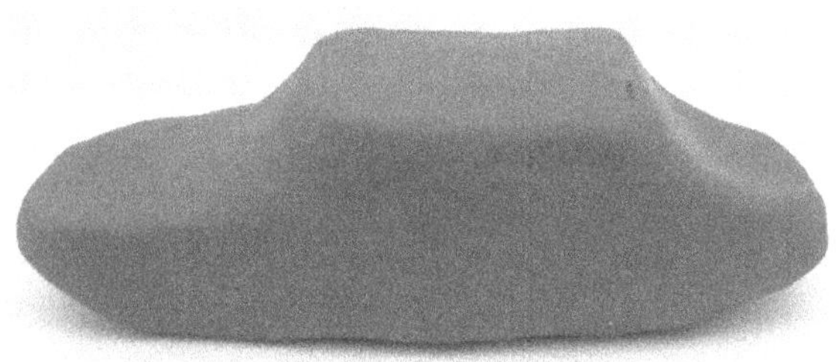

Car Design

Design a new car body model.

Note: New car models are literally models.

Car designs are developed by sculpturally hand modeling quarter-sized or even full-sized models in clay or plasticine. Computer modeling programs have been found to be insufficient to create car forms in the same way.

Eights Within an Eight!

Weave a strand over and under. Attach the ends.

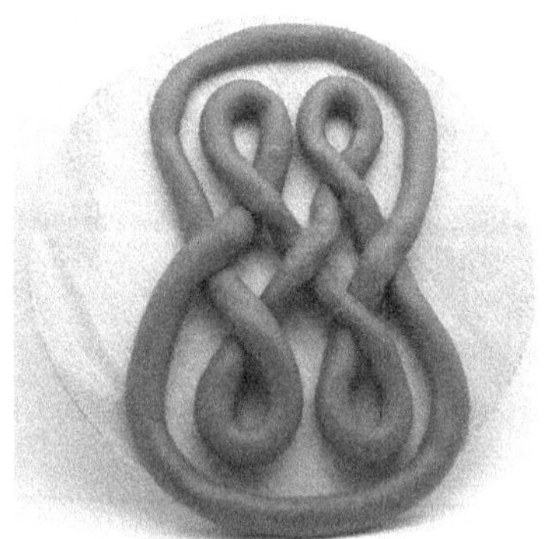

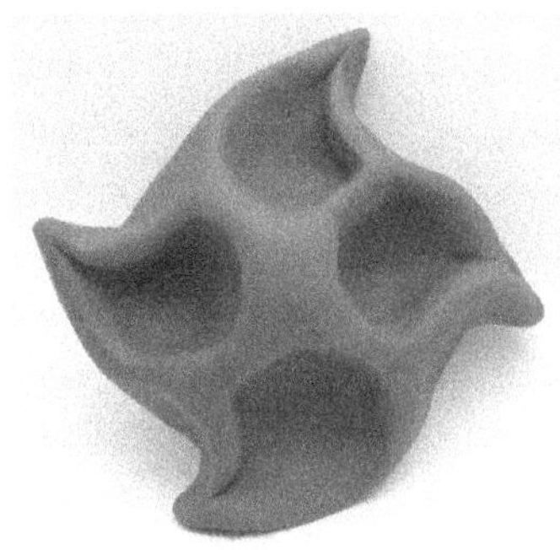

Twirling

Press four or more hollows down into a sphere leaving a nob in the middle. Pull out points and bend them in the same direction.

Miscellaneous

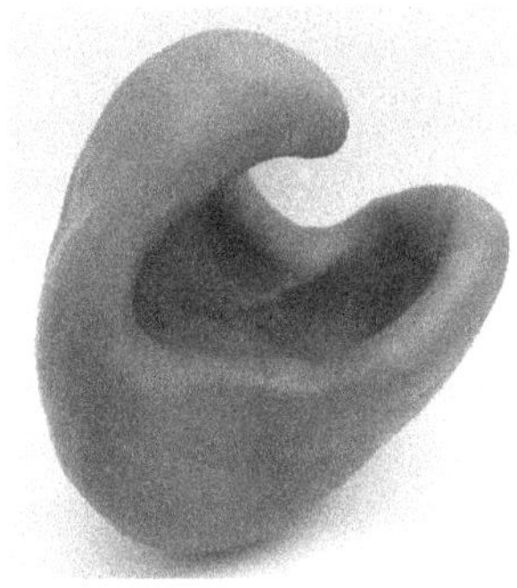

Giving and Receiving

A convex side bends downward in the gesture of giving while a concave side is opening ready to receive.

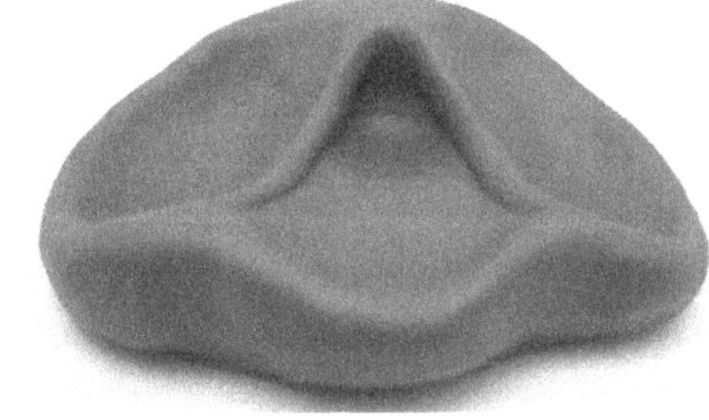

Three Impressings

Make a slightly concave disk with one edge higher at the back. Press three interesting spaces into the basin. The center space protrudes forward.

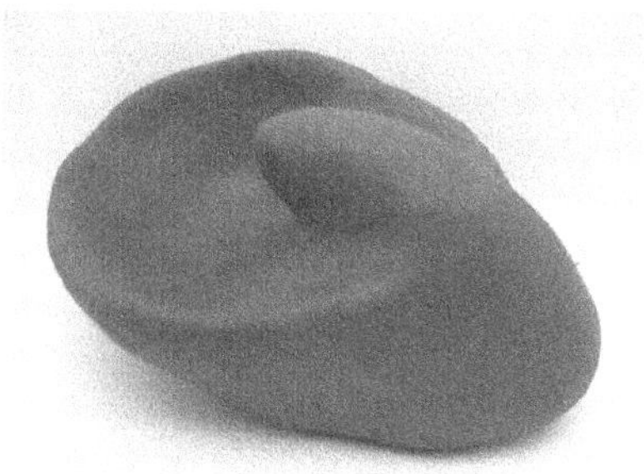

Convex Falling into Concave

Into an ovoid lying on its side, hollow a concave end so that a middle ridge arises at the other end. One end arches up "convexly" toward the other.

Geometry: The Platonic Forms

It is an amazing fact that there are only five regular three-dimensional geometric forms in the universe. Children can already model the cube from third grade on and the tetrahedron and octahedron from fifth and sixth grade on. Then, in grade eight and high school, students can model all five as a series and transform one into the other. As Michael Howard points out,

> "The Platonic geometric forms or solids can have an important place in seventh or eighth grade and again in ninth grade. Often these geometric forms are drawn on paper, cut out and assembled. This is an excellent "thinking with will" exercise. In addition, the Platonic solids can be made in a feeling-will manner by modeling them in clay. A tetrahedron modeled in clay may lack the precision of a constructed one, but the inner and outer activity of adjusting the clay on all sides to achieve the required symmetry is invaluable. The juxtaposition between the geometry of the forms modeled in an organic process allows the students to develop objective clarity that is not mechanistic but intuitive… Furthermore, whereas the constructed solids are made as separate forms, in clay they are transformed from one form into another in a lawful and ordered manner."

(*Educating the Will,* pp. 119-121)

Swain Pratt, high school teacher, adds further:

> "Of the infinite number of possible polyhedrons (three-dimensional figures formed of plane polygonal faces) only five are regular—meaning that all the faces of each are congruent regular polygons. These five are known as the Platonic solids because of their significance in Plato's cosmic scheme.

> Three of the five are formed of equilateral triangles: the tetrahedron with four faces, the octahedron with eight, and the icosahedron with twenty. One, the familiar cube, hexahedron, has six square faces. The fifth, the dodecahedron, is formed of twelve congruent regular pentagons. The only reason five are possible will become apparent upon careful consideration of the number of degrees in each angle of the equilateral triangle (60°), the square (90°) and the regular pentagon (108°): the number of each size angle you can fit together to coincide at one point without any overlapping of sides, and the fact that the common point must be raised out of the plane in order to form the necessary polyhedra angles of the solid."

Plato associates the Five Forms with the elements.

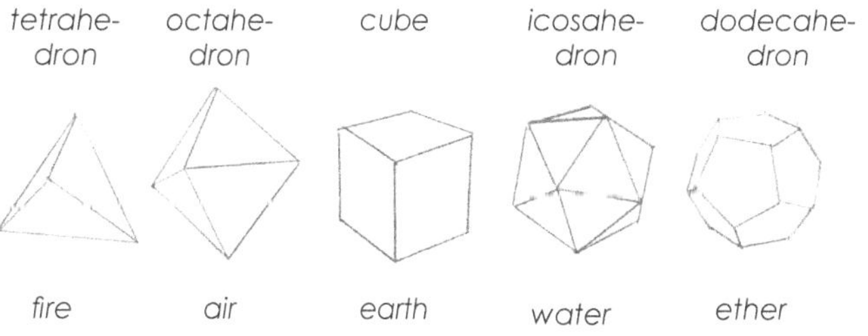

The full sculptural development of these forms is described by Michael Howard and illustrated in *Series Nine: the Transformations of the Five Platonic Solids.*

*Remember to regularly practice the **Proteus Exercise** at the beginning of this sourcebook.*

Series Nine

Transformations of the Five Platonic Solids
By Michael Howard
Illustrations by Elizabeth Auer

THE PLATONIC SOLIDS are often made as paper constructions. They can also be made in clay. The finished forms in paper construction are usually quite beautiful. As educators we must consider not only the finished results but the pedagogical experience. In other words, we must ask: What faculties are exercised using a constructive technique compared with that of modeling? Both are equally valid, but the constructive approach exercises analytical thinking and skill, while modeling engages an intuitive thinking and organic formative capacity. The one is head and hand, the other head, heart and hand. The one process creates physical form directly from an archetype, while the other process brings the archetype to physical expression through a sculptural process involving living formative forces within us.

In addition to these considerations, modeling the Platonic Solids in clay makes it possible to transform one solid into the other. In this manner the students experience not only the lawful beauty of the individual forms but of the magical order that allows one solid to metamorphose into another. Just at puberty, when we begin to question the objective validity of external authority (suspecting that it is merely a subjective construct of adult tyranny), the transformation of the Platonic Solids offers a powerful experience of an objective lawfulness that transcends any whims of the mere mortal teacher. They also reveal that the world is not limited to a static fixed order but is permeated by a living and mobile order.

1. Transformation from a Ball into a Tetrahedron

- Form a ball of clay that fits the space created when your two hands are cupped and just touching each other.

- Place the ball in your open, flat right hand. Position your open and flat left hand with the palm facing down so that it is both parallel and at a right angle to your right hand (*see Figure 1a*).

- Press the ball with both hands so that instead of making a curve they create two right angles. The 2" x 2" surfaces thus created by your hands will form the four surfaces of the tetrahedron (*Figure 1b*).

Without necessarily having ever seen or heard of a tetrahedron, this beginning is enough for the students to visualize the ideal archetype. The students can be helped to recognize the various elements which they need to bring out fully: four flat and equilateral triangular surfaces (*tetra* = four), four corners created through the intersection of three flat surfaces, and six straight edges formed through the intersection of two flat surfaces. In addition, it is important that they are helped to see the form elements that do not belong, such as convex and concave curves, in order to change them to the elements that do belong. The primary orientation that will enable the students to see the right relationship of all the elements is from above.

- In the beginning rotate the form quite frequently to the four different surfaces so that from above one can check that the emerging corner at the top is in the middle of the equilateral triangular base (*Figure 1c, top*).

2. Transformation from a Tetrahedron into an Octahedron

Students can be challenged to try to imagine which of the remaining four Platonic Solids could arise from the tetrahedron and by what orderly process.

Usually someone will see that in pressing down carefully on each of the four corners will create four new triangular surfaces (*Figure 2a*). The four new surfaces added to the four original surfaces suggests the octahedron. While this is correct, it is good to direct the students attention to the changed shape of the original surfaces—they are no longer triangles, but irregular hexagons, which as the triangles continue to enlarge will eventually become regular hexagons (*Figure 2b*). This is an important half-way point which it is essential to insist the students get right before continuing. The hexagons become irregular again before finally becoming the triangles that produce the octahedron.

- Only press on the corners when they are at the top so that they can be seen to be parallel to the base. Do not make the new triangles too large before rotating to another corner. Try to keep all the new triangles about the same size, always looking for the smallest to enlarge, so as not to lose the symmetry.

- Through the first half of the transformation, it is natural to see the form as a truncated tetrahedron with the corners cut off. After the half-way point, the student can be helped to see the emerging octahedron by looking where the corners will appear. With one of the new triangles on the top and parallel to the base, there are three corners visible. Positioning themselves directly facing one corner, students will see that each corner should be in the middle of a square with two edges parallel to each other and the base, while the other two edges are parallel to each other but perpendicular to the base (*Figure 2c*).

- The octahedron has eight equilateral triangular sides, six corners, and twelve edges.

3. Transformation of an Octahedron into a Cube

Based on the same transformative principle, students will easily recognize that the six corners of the octahedron, when pressed will create the six square surfaces needed for the cube. Again this is correct, but they should be cautioned not to be lulled by such a predictable outcome for there are challenges along the way—one surprise in particular can lead to confusion, if not a chaotic result. The challenge is not to get a cube any old way—anybody can do that—but to get the cube through the proper intermediate forms. The care and control developed in the first transformation must be sustained all the more.

- Carefully press on the top three corners to create squares no larger than one inch to a side. Invert the form to do the same on the other three corners. Again the eight original triangles will become hexagons. As a first of three primary steps, the students should be required to form the six new squares so that they create eight regular hexagons before going further (*Figure 3a*).

- At this point the squares should be large enough so that from now on the piece is set down on the square surfaces and not the triangles. This encourages one to press only on the square surface on the top, checking that it is parallel to the base. Furthermore, it becomes easier to see the relationship of the square surfaces to ensure that they are appropriately parallel or at right angle to each other. This orientation enables one to see the emerging second inter-mediate form where the squares will eventually touch corner to corner (*Figure 3b*).

- • This is an important intermediate form to examine with the students. They will see the cube–only the eight triangles create the impression that it is a cube with the corners cut off. So close and yet so far! What is not right? The six squares should touch edge to edge, not corner to corner. But how to get this?

- • Stay faithful to the process–keep pressing on the squares. Any resistance to doing this does not come from the clay but from the corners touching corners which give the impression of being rigid and fixed. In fact, if we continue pressing on the squares but now two surfaces at the same time, say the top and one side, the surfaces will interpenetrate so that the corner becomes an edge. When

this is done to all four corners of the top square, the square will no longer be a square, but an octagon.

- Rotate in turn the other five squares to the top in order to do the same and thereby have six regular octagons (*Figure 3c*). This is the third essential intermediate form. It now becomes clear that the new edges that create the octagons are in fact the edges that will allow the squares to touch edge to edge and thus form the cube.

- The cube or hexahedron has six square surfaces, eight corners and twelve edges.

4. Transformation of a Cube into an Icosahedron

Here the transformation of the whole sequence falls out of the perfect process we have seen thus far.

- Once again one begins by pressing on the eight corners to produce eight triangles. The alert student will realize that if they continue in this way they will only succeed in reversing the process back to the octahedron. We have eight triangles, but we need twenty. Where can we get twelve more triangles? Again the mobile of mind will see the possibility of getting two triangles from each of the six squares: $2 \times 6 = 12 + 8 = 20$. But how to get those twelve triangles?

In a much less elegant manner than was possible to this point, one must redistribute the clay so as to build up a ridge in the middle of each square, thus bending each surface to become two surfaces. In the process, one must adjust the triangles from right angle to equilateral. The other main factor is to get the ridges aligned in the right directions–each one should be perpendicular to the ridge on the adjoining square (*Figure 4a*).

- Ultimate success depends on seeing as soon as possible that twelve corners are emerging, each of which is formed through the intersection of five triangles. In other words, each emerging corner should appear to be in the middle of a pentagon in the same way we saw in earlier forms a corner in the middle of triangles or squares (*Figure 4 b*).

- The icosahedron has twenty equilateral triangles, twelve corners, and thirty edges.

5. Transformation of an Icosahedron into a Dodecahedron

Conceptually, this final transformation is straight forward. Clearly we can press on the twelve corners of the icosahedron to produce the twelve pentagonal surfaces that belong to the dodecahedron (*Figure 5a*). However, it will now also be easier to anticipate that in doing so the original twenty triangles will become twenty hexagons. Here lies the rub–to avoid a royal mess by confusing any of the twelve pentagons (five-sided) with any of the twenty hexagons (six-sided) (*Figure 5b*). It is purely a matter of patience and discipline. At this point working on a larger scale is easier than a smaller scale–this is actually true for the whole process. The only additional surprise and challenge is that the twelve pentagons will at the final stage become ten-sided surfaces (as the squares became eight-sided to become the cube) in order that the pentagons touch side to side instead of corner to corner. Consider yourself a Master of the Platonic Solids if you avoid muddling the twelve surfaces with the twenty triangles and thereby arrive at the dodecahedron in the right manner!

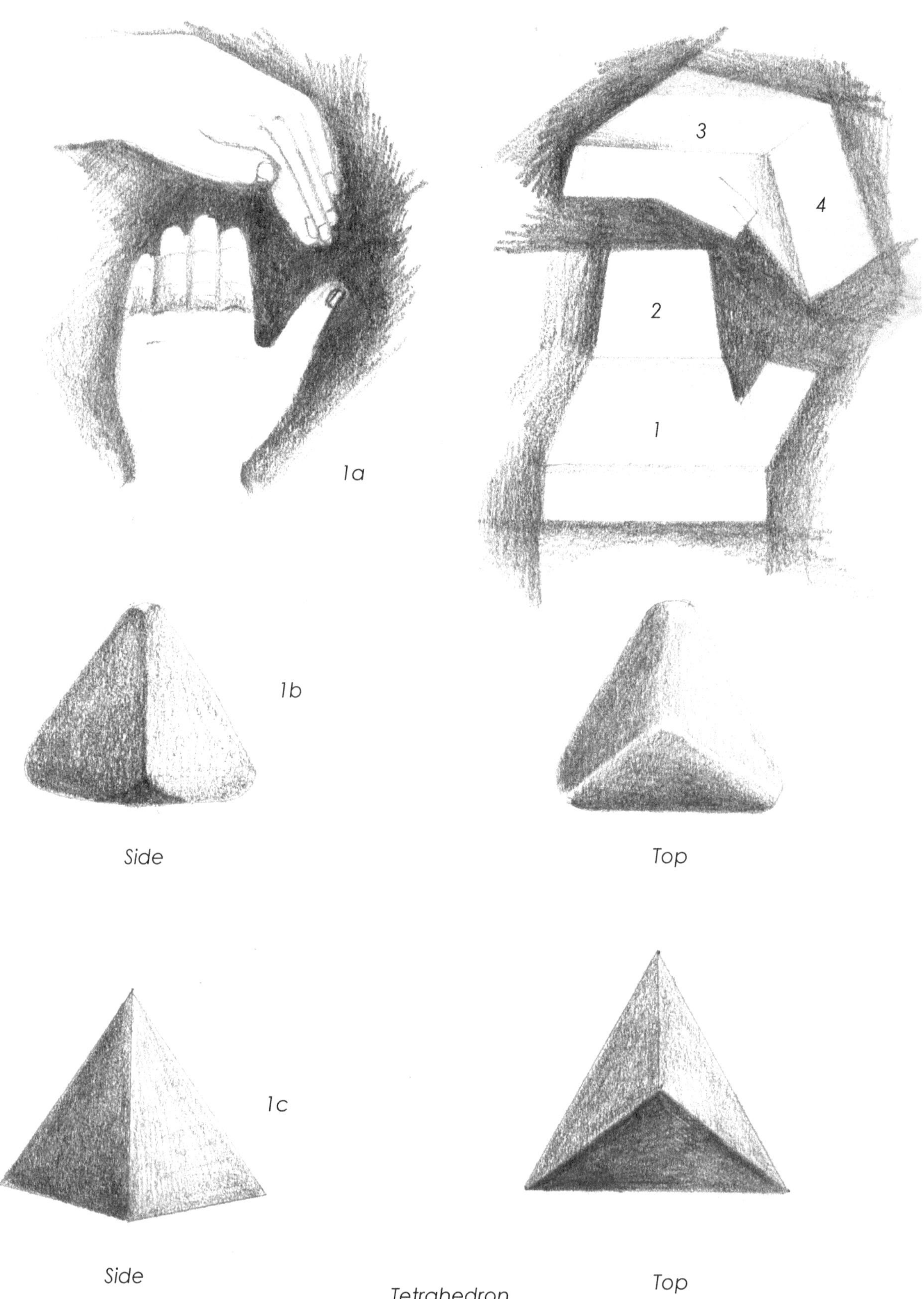
1a
1b
Side
Top
1c
Side
Top
3
4
2
1
Tetrahedron

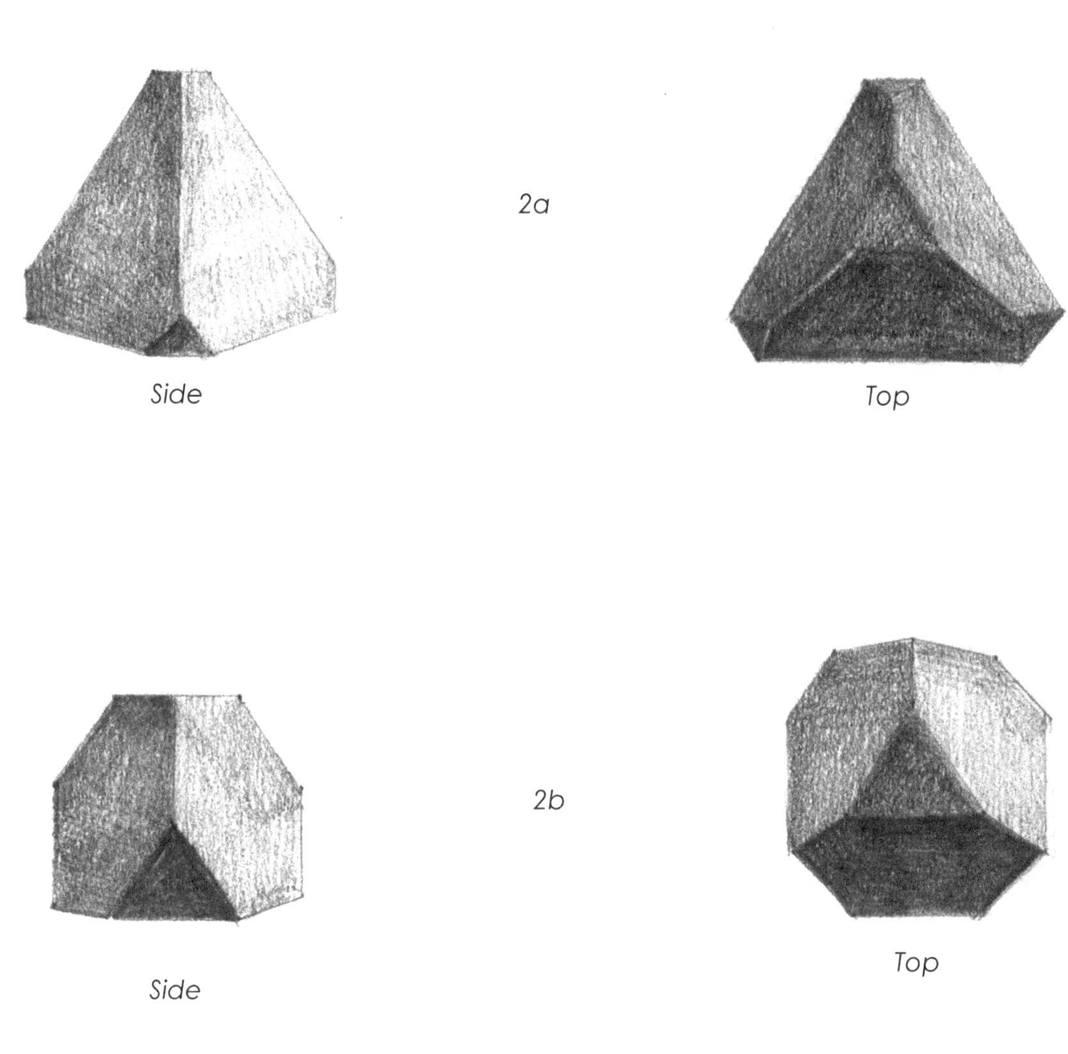

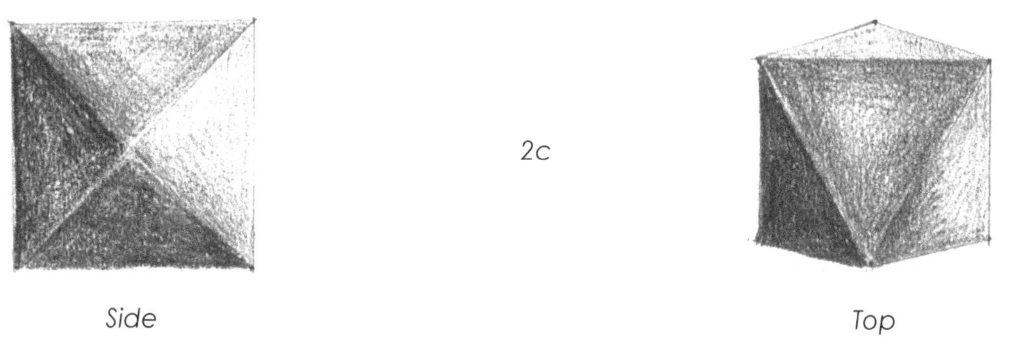

Octahedron

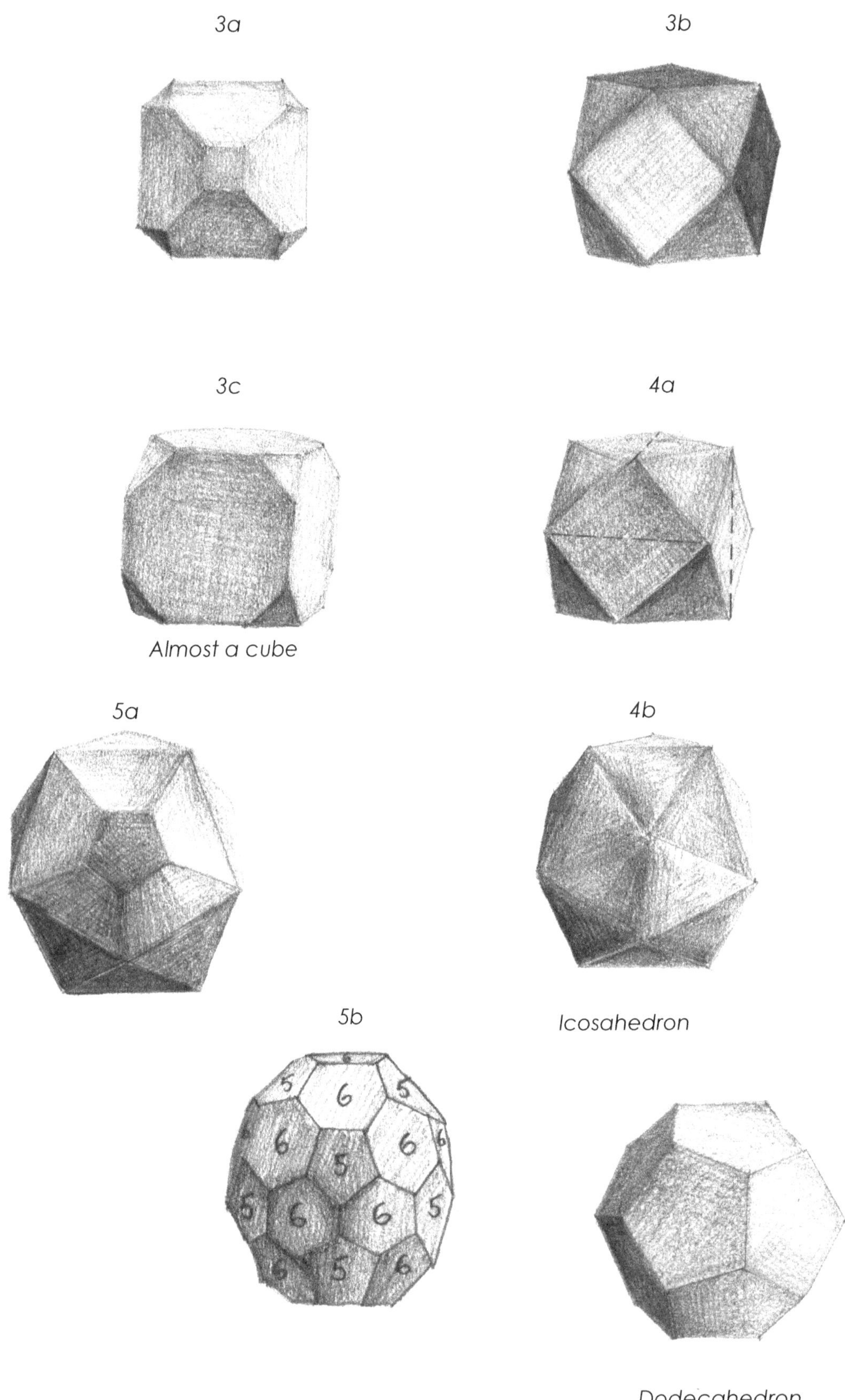

3a
3b
3c
4a
Almost a cube
5a
4b
5b
Icosahedron
Dodecahedron

Series Ten
Embryogenesis: A Sculptural Approach

Sphere
Spiral
Two-, Four-, Eight-Divisions
Morula
Blastula
Nest
Leaf Disk
Neurula: Seedling
Serpent-like
Mammal-like
Emerging Human

Embryogenesis

The forms of the embryo in the first two months before the full human figure emerges are some of the most wondrous and fascinating sculptures in the universe. They constitute an otherworldly series of organic, archetypal shapes from which we can learn. They help us to experience how the invisible spirit makes itself visible, how the macrocosm becomes microcosm through what biologists call "embryogenesis." (For anthroposophical insights and more details on the subject, see Part II: *The Archetypal Forms of Embryogenesis*).

In the course of this grand metamorphosis, these universal forms gradually begin to magically *suggest* plant, animal, and finally human form gestures and contours. These mysterious shapes can stimulate the imaginations of adolescents and adults in a powerful, artistic way.

Modeling as a hands-on art is particularly suitable for exploring the embryo. The space between our two cupped hands is a creation space, a womb space in which forms are birthed out of movement and flow.

Earliest Embryo Forms in 12 Steps (plus a nest)

The embryo itself is a flowform in motion created out of universal forces. The figures that follow are selected from the sequence of the first eight weeks or two months of physical human development (the "embryo" stage before the so-called "fetal" stage of the last seven months). Making this sequence of forms "hands-on," albeit in equally sized and unproportional solid forms, is an artistic aid to experiencing and ultimately imagining the embryo as a *living,* growing, moving "river," as the poet Novalis characterized the human being. (After all, the embryo at this stage is in reality over 95% streaming water and very minuscule!)

The following forms follow a simplified *"imaginative–sculptural–artistic"* approach, in thirteen major steps. The author is a modeler-sculptor-educator and not an expert embryologist. I recommend that you who are interested in studying the incredible complexity of the subject, consult Jaap van der Wal's website "Embryo-in-Motion" (www.embryo.nl). It is a treasure trove of wisdom and information as are his superb dynamic workshops (also on DVD). Very helpful are Jaap's moving animations of the sequence. Also, see my ending Bibliography on the subject to find other experts (Breme, Weihs, König, and others).

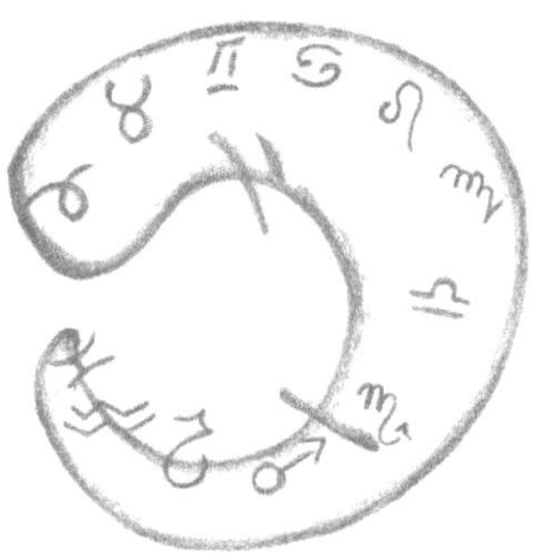

Formed by twelve forces

To feel . . . a sphere in space is to feel the self, the I Am, the ego . . .
> —Rudolf Steiner

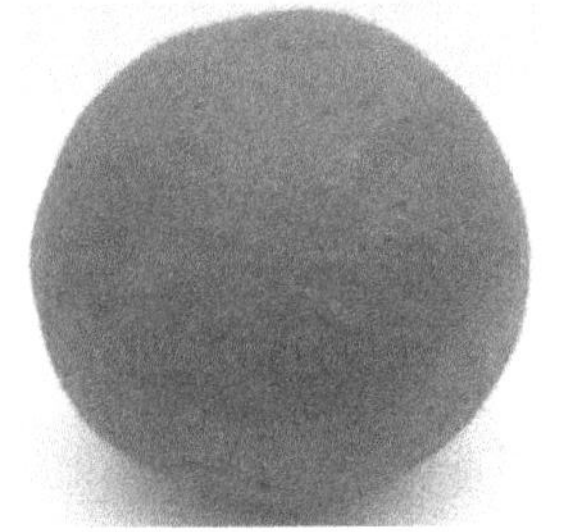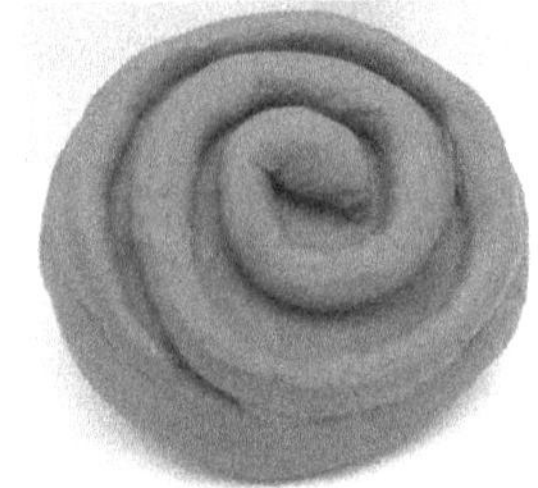

Forms 1–2: Sphere and Spiral
(First Week)

The shining ovum sphere has received into itself the shining, spiraling, silica-laden sperm. Its thin linear filament is modeled separately in a simplified, practical, symbolic format. The sphere is both a whole universe, a macrocosm, and at the same time the microcosm, the forming temple of a self about to incarnate and dwell in it. The spiral is another universal form of life (helix), motion and change. Both ovum and sperm are so minuscule as to still exist in a one-dimensional world of point and line respectively.

Forms 3–6: Morula: Geometric Divisions into 2, 4, 8, 16
(First Week)

Make four spheres and divide them into composite forms of little spheres (2, 4, 8, 16). The mathematical cleavage is like a *mineral* crystallization process of similarly sized but not exactly equal globules. The sixteen-cell form at three days is what biologists call the *morula*, Latin for "mulberry" (form on the far right below). Steiner described the beginning of the universe as being in a mulberry shape made up of warmth globules.

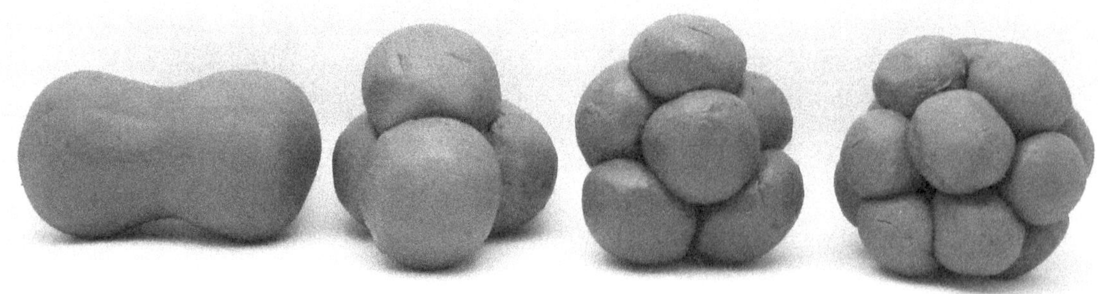

Form 7: Plant-like Blastula Form: Sphere of Leaf-like Planes in a Concave Nest

(Second Week)

Begin with a sphere again. Make many tiny separate spheres and flatten each into round planar forms between the tips of your fingers and stick them onto the surface of the sphere.

The round cells making up the morula flatten out into **leaf-like** cells and gravitate to the periphery. The interior is filled with a gelatinous liquid, represented here by the solid clay interior sphere—a world surrounded by a diaphanous husk of leaf-like cells. Biologists call this new little world the *blastula* (from the Greek "to bud, to grow"). It is also reminiscent of an **eyeball** filled with vitreous humor or a grape filled with juice.

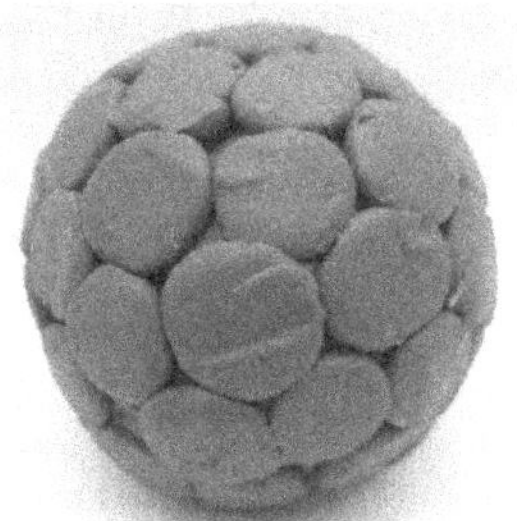

Blastula

Nesting

The blastula indents and im-*plants* itself like a seed bulb in the mother's uterine wall. Its round convexity pushes and fits into a receiving maternal concavity, the two archetypal forms of sculpture: curving and pushing outward and giving way inwardly, receiving, hollowing nature's egg fitting into the nest. The hollow is mother, vessel, formation of inner space in which soul, sensitivity and feeling find a new home.

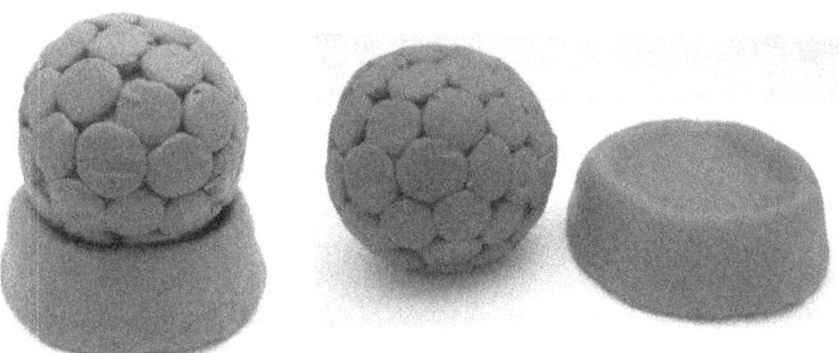

Blastula in and next to uterine nest

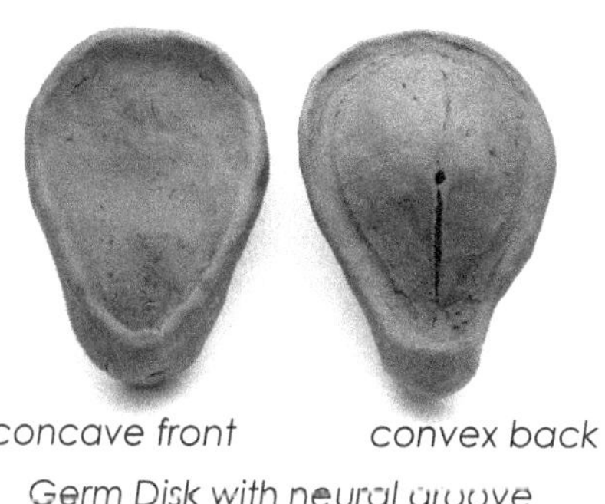

concave front   convex back

Germ Disk with neural groove

Form 8-9: Leaf-like Germ Disk

(Third Week: 15-18 days)

Unseen within the little fluid blastula universe, an arching membrane wall is developing, separating fluid inside from fluid outside. In this bed, a round sleeping *leaf-like* disk suddenly appears as if out of nothing!

Should we call her Diskula?! The tissue thickens, lengthens and becomes the physical germ of the future human body.

Fashion a "pear-shaped" leaf form with a slightly curved concave front and shallow convex back. Make the narrow end more pointed and curve it slightly toward the hollow side. (This is complicated to describe so follow the photo as best you can!)

A surprising pit appears and a vertical axis line (*primitive streak turning into a neural groove*)—the site of a future spine—mysteriously appears down the midline of the germinal disk—the letter i or I—and sets all kinds of wondrous sculptural contortions and foldings into motion. The beginnings of all future organ systems (called primordia) are mapped out and laid down. The leaf-like plant form is transitioning, undergoing "animalizing" as the soul enters and takes hold of the plant-like body. (Latin *anima* = soul which humans have in common with anima-ls, "soulimals!") With a pointed clay tool or pencil point, poke a hole (primitive pit) down from which you inscribe the neural groove as shown.

Geometry of the Embryo
The *point*-like ovum sphere, chaoticized by the entry of the *linear* sperm, expands into the blastula form emphasizing a surface of *flat planar* cells outside. The planar surface forces then focus in the interior where the *planar* germ disk appears where yolk sac (earth) and amnion (heaven) touch in a flat circular intersection. The burgeoning and sculpting vegetative-etheric life forces thrive on surfaces as well as in liquid. The thin tiny being has yet to expand into three-dimensional space.

Form 9: Neurula Seedling-like
(Third Week: 18-21 days)
The rapid transverse folding and almost chaotic rearrangement of cells in week 3 results in the flat, circular, leaf-like germ disk turning itself into a new straight, longitudinal cylindrical *seedling-like figure with two seed-leaf-like* protuberances at its top. (See below.) The embryo thickens still further and transitions from a flat two-dimensional plane to three-dimensional space with a top/bottom, back/front and right/left bilateral symmetry.

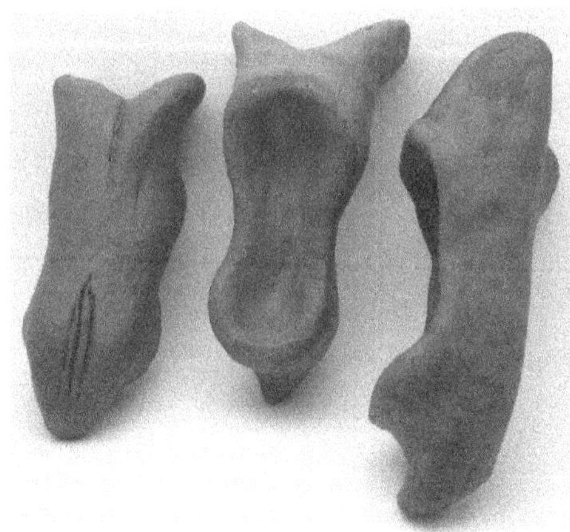

Stalk-like thickening: Back, Front, Side

Enclosed inner space and surface has been created to house the incarnating soul with its ego spirit center and supporting organ systems. According to Steiner's research, during the end of week 3 (days 18-21), the individuality (spirit ego-soul) starts to enter the embryo body, hence the dramatic changes during this time. (See the chapter on *The Archetypal Forms of Embryogenesis* in the second half of this sourcebook.)

Form 10: Serpent-like Gesture: From Straight to Curved
(Fourth Week through Seventh Week)
What has become a relatively straight form then dramatically curves into a "serpent-like" form and outwardly bends and curls in an *"animal-like"* gesture. The embryo body turns inward and grows fuller to further articulate the inner soul space needed now to grow the organ systems. (These systems were already laid down as primordia in week 3, in which "soulification" or "animalization" began).

With the head resting on it, the chest bulges with an enormous protruding heart—the first organ to appear out of the blood flow and the only one to mysteriously develop outside of the main body. It gradually moves inside! *"The origin of the **heart** marks a turnaround of the dynamics of the embryo [which] **become more like that of an animal** . . . an inner world is formed over against the outer world."* (van der Wal)

Arms and then legs bud out—"landing-on-earth gear"—and reach toward the world. This water being still has an animalic tail and fish gill-like ripples at the neck (not shown in the figure). Just as the blastula is eye-like, the entire embryonic body at this point is "ear-like" in shape (Poppelbaum) as if listening to the "silent music" of the cosmos for further sculptural instructions. The curved concave crescent-moon form indicates the continued growth of inner space and organs as the foundation for future sentience and consciousness.

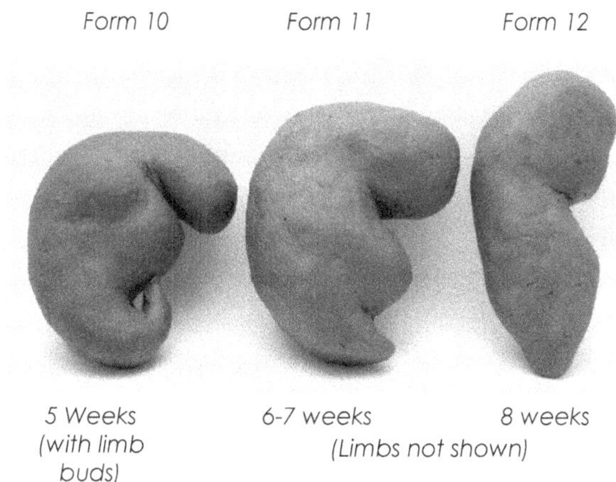

Form 11: Mammal-like: From Curved to More Angular

(Sixth through Seventh Weeks)

After bending and folding, the embryo then starts to unfold. The head raises itself and swells to be proportionally large in a *mammal-like* gesture (bison-like?)

Note: In the last two Forms 11 and 12 shown above, *only the gestalt of the head/ torso* are modeled to keep the gesture of central form within the realm of the suggestive and emerging toward the "human looking." The lengthening limbs are tight against the main body and are left to the imagination for sculptural purposes As soon as limbs are added, the figure becomes a kind of floppy doll and the spell of the unfamiliar is broken. See last photo of the fetal form which can be modeled as a second part later in connection with the human anatomy of months three through nine

Form 12: Emerging Human: Rounding and Straightening

(Week 8 onwards)

The gestalt of head/torso finally unfolds markedly and emerges into the *"human-looking."* The head lifts itself still further and becomes rounder and more dome-like because of the expanding brain. The back *straightens* out of the crescent-like curvature of the animal-like exterior of weeks five through seven (Forms 10-11). Unfolding, stretching and straightening are again the signature of the human ego at work and anticipate the characteristic upright posture of later human development (standing at age 1 year).

Summary

To grow and articulate its inner organs, the form goes from straightness in Weeks 3-4 through concave curvature (organ growth and articulation) in weeks 5-7 and then to straightness again from week 8 on: Form 12.

To achieve human stature, the organism passes through intermediate stages of mineral-like, plant-like and animal-like gestures in which folding and curving inward creates concave organ soul space—an inner world. Concavity and hollowing inwardly are a signature of the soul-astral principle working into the body; convexity, of the life-etheric body pushing outward; and straightness, of the ego.

The interweaving activities and expressions of four "signature notes" (**P**hysical, **E**theric, **A**stral and "**I**" principles) are musical. These notes (PEAI) appear and repeat thematically throughout this 2 month "fugue-like process." As Karl König points out: *"These images call for truly **imaginative thinking**. [This] does not mean to give rein to fantasy, but to look until suddenly one begins to hear, to perceive from the form and the structure, **what the gestalt has to say, to sing, to tell**"* (König, 1968).

(For more on the musical embryo, see the chapter in Part II, Archetypal Forms of Embryogenesis)

End of the TwoMonth Embryo Sequence

The first two months represented in the preceding series constitute the stage of the strange, otherworldly and wondrous forms of the so-called "*embryo.*" The last seven months in the womb are those of the familiar, recognizably human-looking form of the

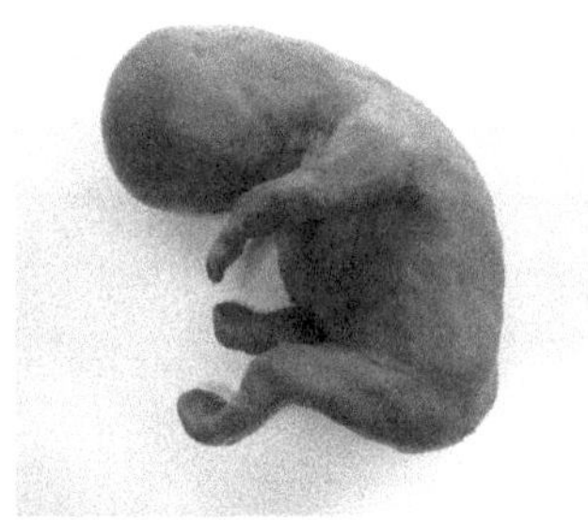

"fetus" (from the Latin: "fruit"). One can choose to add limbs and extend the sequence of forms beyond the examples illustrated to complete the picture to birth.

Fetus Stage: Months Three through nine can be added as a second phase sequence (anatomy)

Sources:

For an expanded sculptural/drawing approach with more exercises for the embryonic membranes, see Christian Breme's *Embryology Experienced through Modeling in Clay: A Path of Exercises in Seven Stages* (distributed in the US by Waldorf Publications). See also a fuller bibliography on Embryology in the back of this book.

Embryogenesis in Thirteen Cosmic Forms

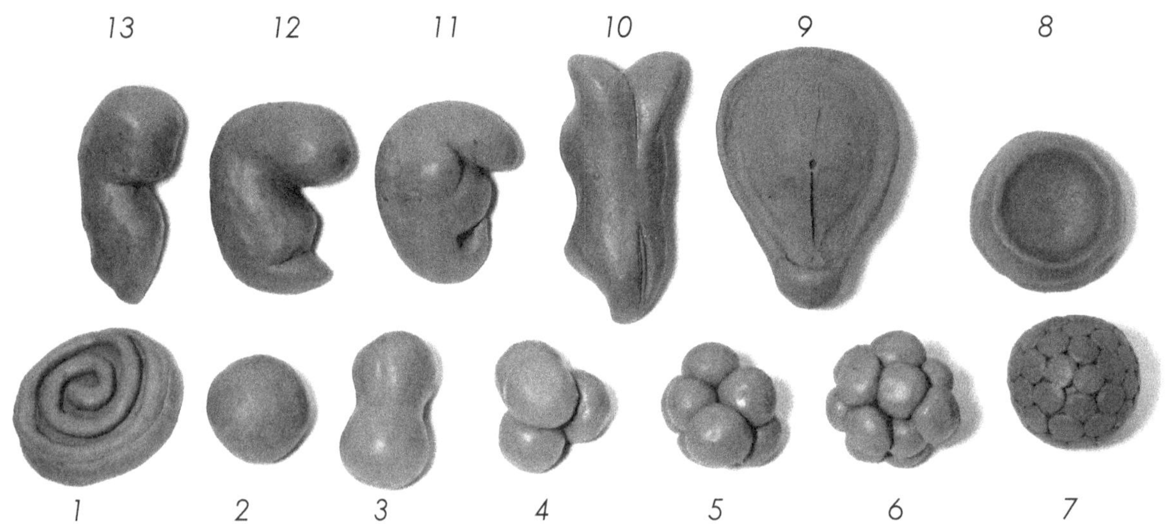

Phase 2: TOP ROW (left to right) MICROCOSM (Body Center): 13. emerging human; 12. Animal-like gestures: "mammal-like; 11. "serpent-like" with limb buds;10. Seedling Neurula (back); 9. Leaf Disk Back; 8. Uterine Nest

Phase 1: BOTTOM ROW (left to right) MACROCOSM (Sheaths of periphery): 1. Paternal spiraling; 2. Ovum; 3. 4. 5. Cleavage 2x, 4x, 8x; 6. Morula 16x; 7. Blastula

I have again and again grown like grass;
I have experienced seven hundred and seventy moulds.
I died from minerality and became vegetable;
And from vegetativeness I died and became animal.
I died from animality and became human.
Then why fear disappearance through death?
Next time I shall die
Bringing forth wings and feathers like angels:
After that soaring higher than angels –
What you cannot imagine, I shall be that.

–Rumi

Series Eleven: Nature Forms

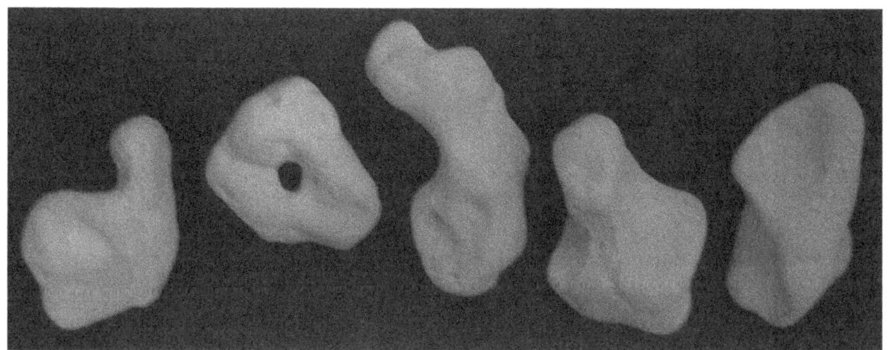

Natures' Inspiration

Nature's language of forms is a great source of inspiration for sculptural modeling. The dynamics of different shapes and features work on and in us. We then take certain aspects a step further into new forms of expression.

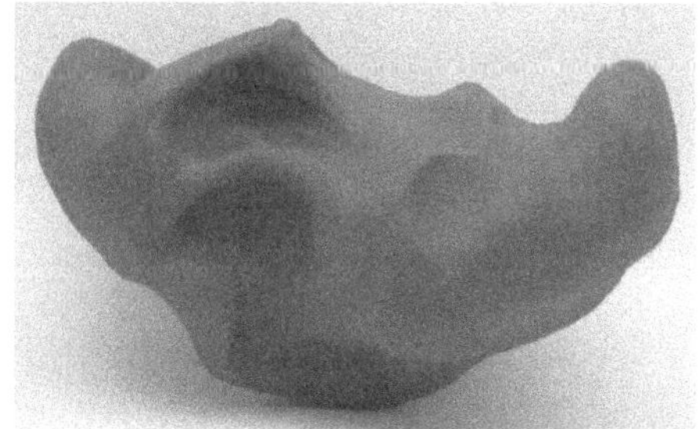

Water Worn: Inspired by rock worn away by water.

The following are some simple examples that stimulate the impulse to observe and be inspired by nature's works of sculptural art.

Sea-Sculpted Stones

The water-shaping of waves continuously washes and tumbles stones creating sea-sculptures on the shore:

- Gulf of Mexico tumble-washed stones (above)
- A piece of the coast of Maine worn by water (below)

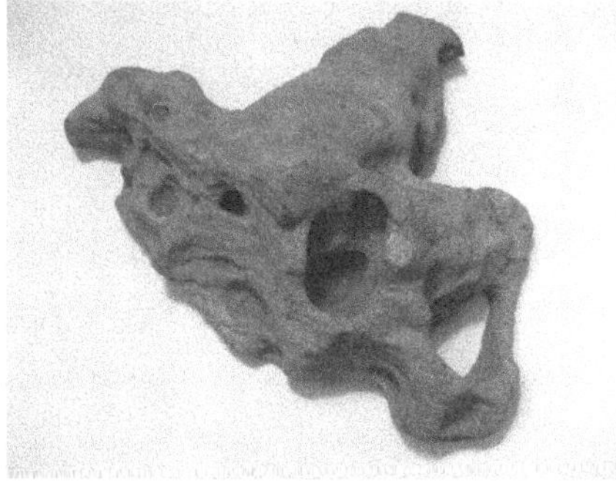

- Atlantic tumble-rounded stones (below)

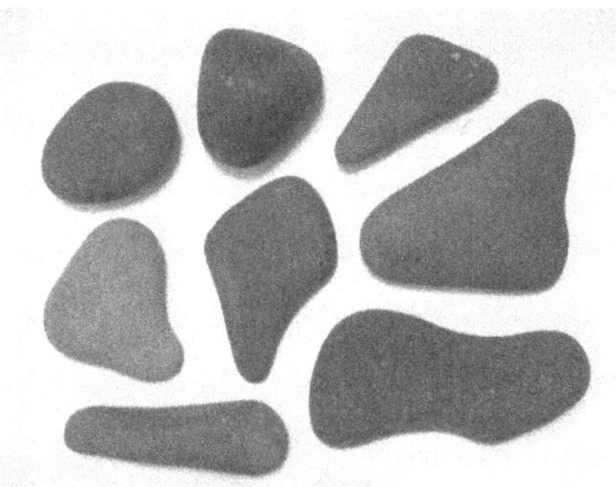

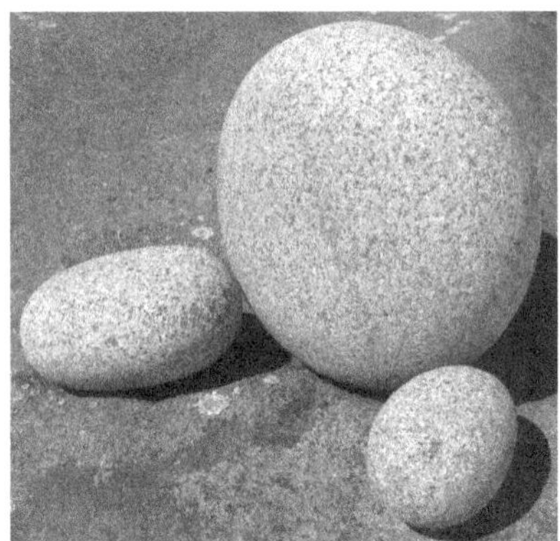

Sea-rounded pink granite stones

Exercise: *You are a stone tumbling in a mountain stream. What form will you take on?*

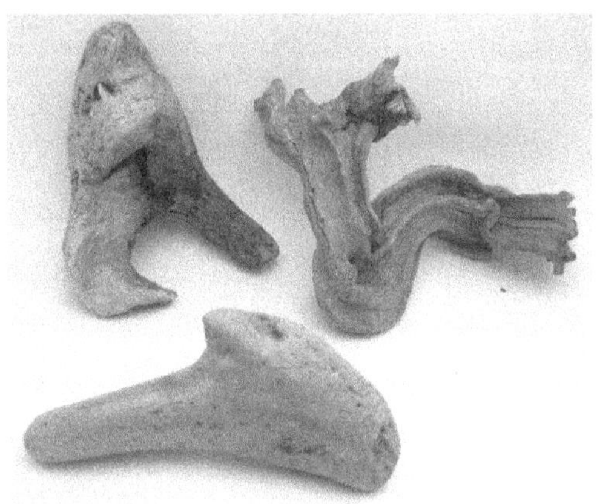

Driftwood
The sea as sculptor loves to shape wood.

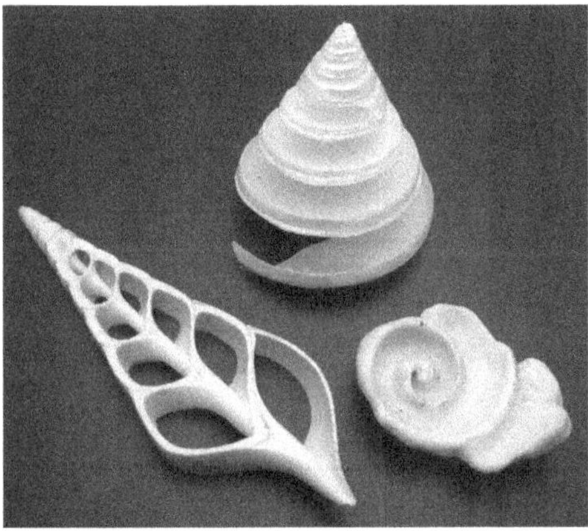

Spirals
Shells and their fragments are a sea treasure of variations of this primary geometric motif of life.

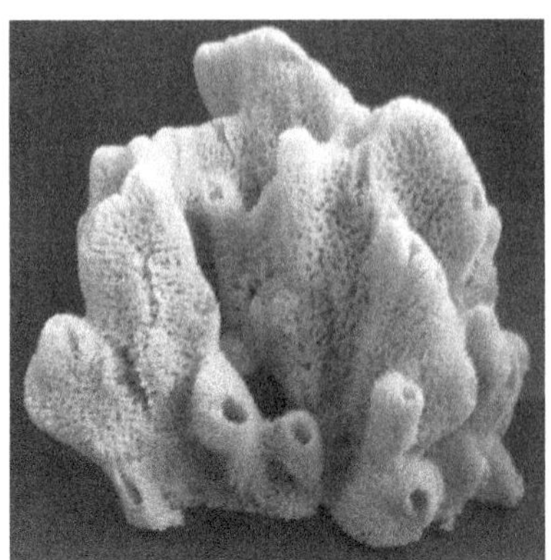

Sponges
These come in all kinds of wonderful sculptural shapes.

> *Many of the movements and forms we . . . [see] in water reappear as body and movement in the lower water animals . . . jellyfish . . . sea-stars, sea urchins, snails and many shells. 'The resting state originates in movement.' (Novalis, Aphorism) There is no doubt that our body is a molded river.*
>
> —Theodor Schwenk

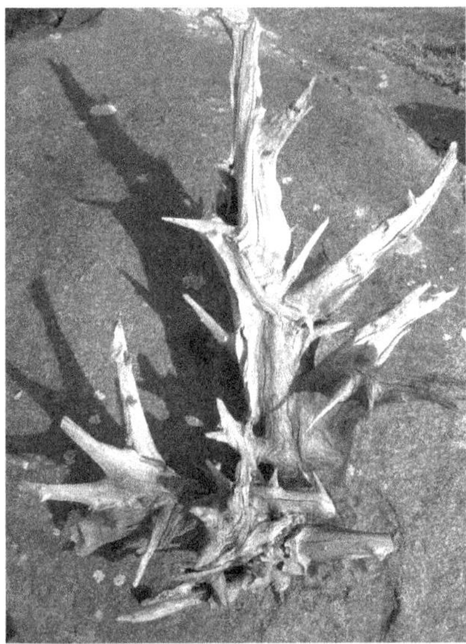

My First Tree Stump
When I was ten years old and roaming the back woods, I came across my first upturned, dried-out root stump. It was a marvelous work of nature sculpture. I sawed it loose and dragged it home for display. Above is a recent acquisition from our back wetlands.

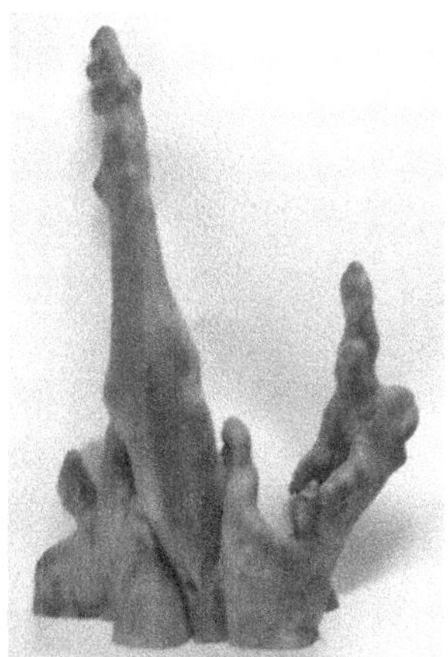

Cypress Root

This section turned downside up has the interesting combination of pointed rays with rounded flowing surface features.

> [In sculpture] what you depict you create not through mere imitation of a model, but by immersing yourself into the forces out of which nature herself has formed and created. . .
>
> —Rudolf Steiner

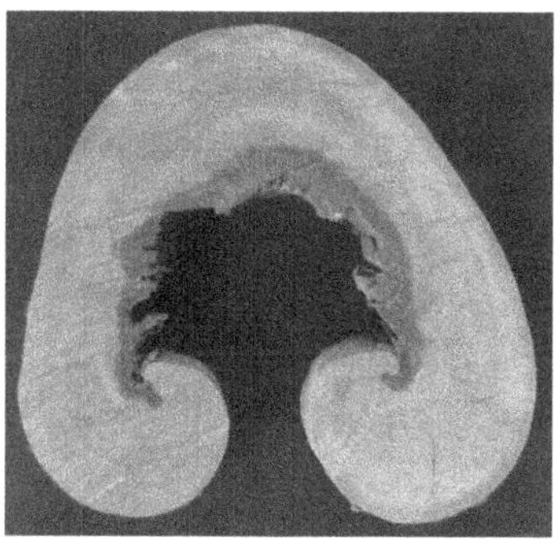

Hollowed Cedar (cross-section)

Something invaded this tree when it was young. It grew in spirals around the intrusive element and created a special inner space (concavity).

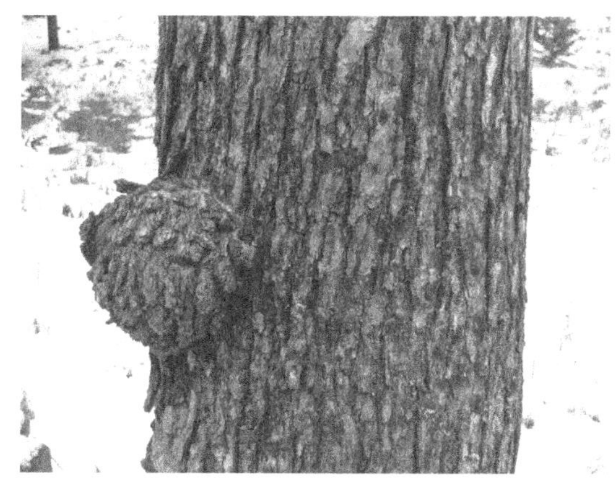

Burl Burgeoning

In contrast to the cedar, a burl burst forth from a maple tree (convexity).

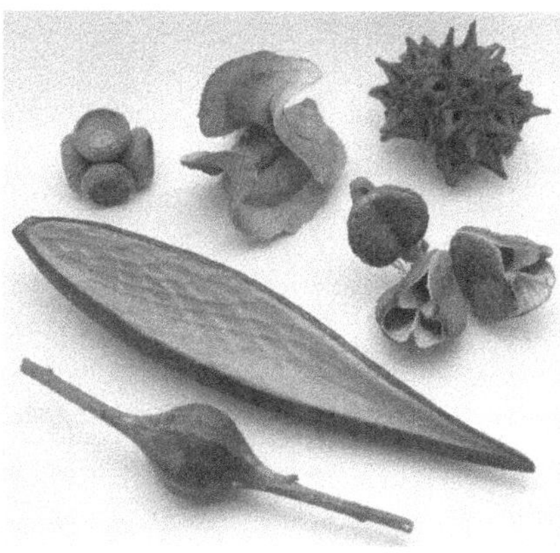

Plant Pods and Husks

There are all kinds of botanical vessels: round, curled, long, pointed, spiked. Some are quite exotic. Which one is the Australian pine cone below or the durian fruit cut in half?

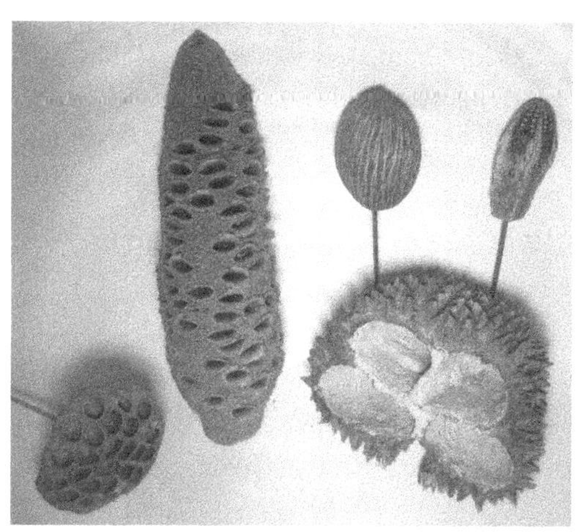

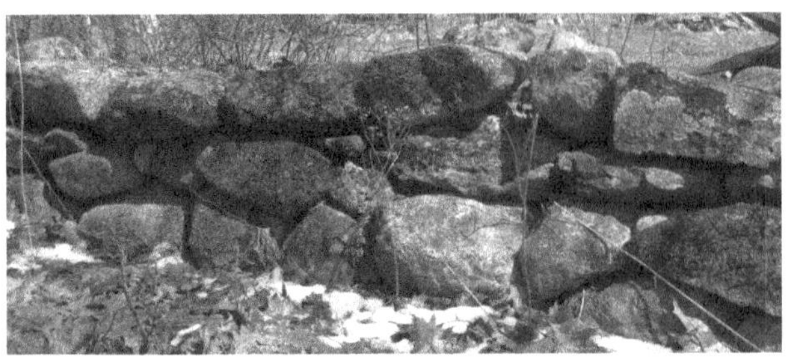

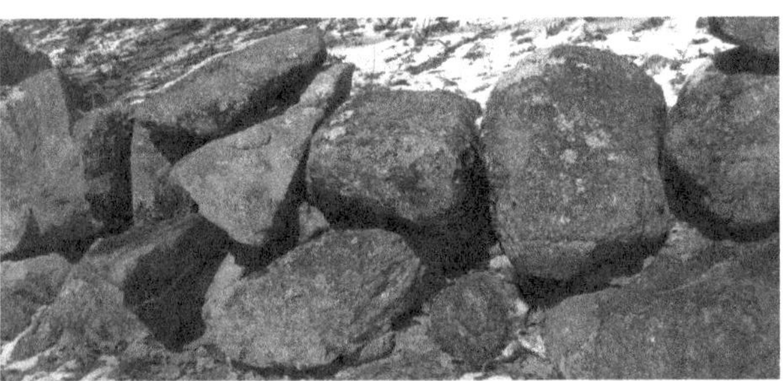

New England Stonewalls as Teachers of Form

I have been building "dry" stonewalls—dry meaning "without cement"—since my teens in Connecticut. Practicing this art has educated my sense of form immensely. All different shapes and sizes have passed through my hands. I have helped countless tons of New England stones to find the places in which they were meant to be in walls—at least for a few decades or centuries at least.

I learned that *every stone has its place.* You just have to be open to what the rocks tell you.

The wall in the photo above is on our New Hampshire land and was built by a farmer in the 1800's with draft horses to pull huge, unwieldy stones out of the field. At the top of the next column is a photo of a section of wall by A. A. (1980s).

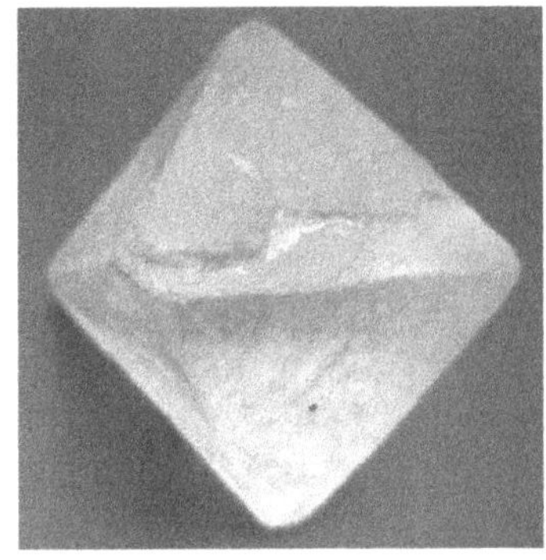

Calcite Octahedron
Many crystal forms to learn from.

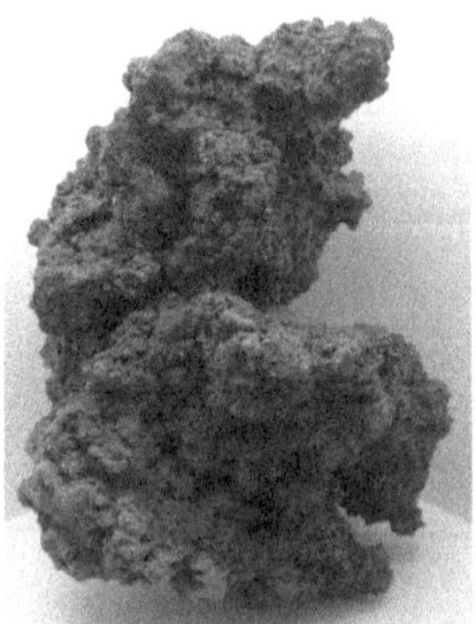

Volcano Ash
The majestic cone of Mount Aetna spews forth all kinds of shapes.

Other possible formations to look for:

* Ice
* Limestone caves
* Coral and sponge formations
* Clouds
* Wind and water erosion
* Geological wonders: Google "rock formation wonders"

Collections of Photos

Andreas Feiniger, *Roots of Art*

Ernst Haeckel, *Art Forms in Nature*

Karl Blossfeldt, *Art Forms in the Plant World*

Series Twelve: Sculpture

Inspired by the Pure Form Sculpture of Others

Sculptures are the embodiments of motifs, gestures, qualities and ideas that can inspire and stimulate our own form-making. There are innumerable examples in modern art of non-representational art to study and learn from. These pieces are called "abstract" not because they are divorced from real life, but because they "abstract" and capture dynamic aspects of reality—some more effectively than others.

For instance, Brancusi's "Bird in Space" (figure below) in my experience does not embody a "thing," a "bird." Rather this sculpture captures the "soaring upwards" of a bird on the wing in the simplest and purest of forms.

Other modern sculptors whose works may especially nourish the pure form imagination, are Henry Moore, Jean Arp, Barbara Hepworth, Alexander Archipenko, and Jacques Lipchitz. (See also Alberto Alberto Giacometti, Morice Lipsi, Etienne Beothy, Hans Schleeh, Alberto Viani, Helen Philips, Olga Jancic, Erik Thommasen, Raoul Hague, and Etienne-Martin).

Artists inspired by Steiner's impulse in sculpture include Michael Howard, Raoul Ratnowsky, Manfred Welzel, Gertraud Goodwin, Annete Boos, and Stephan Guber. (*For Waldorf teachers and others interested, see Part II: Learning from Steiner's Goetheanum Forms*).

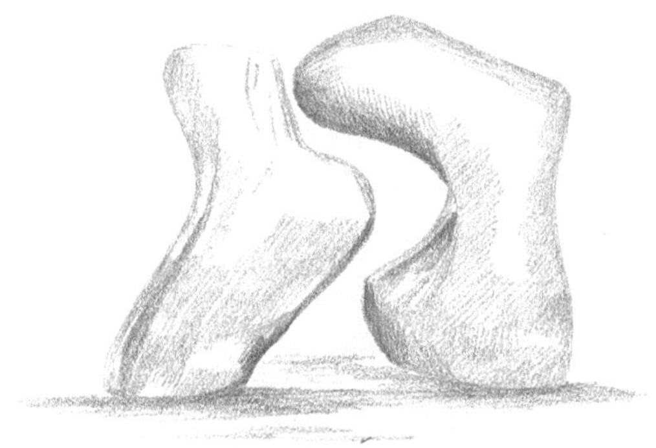

Sculpture by Henry Moore

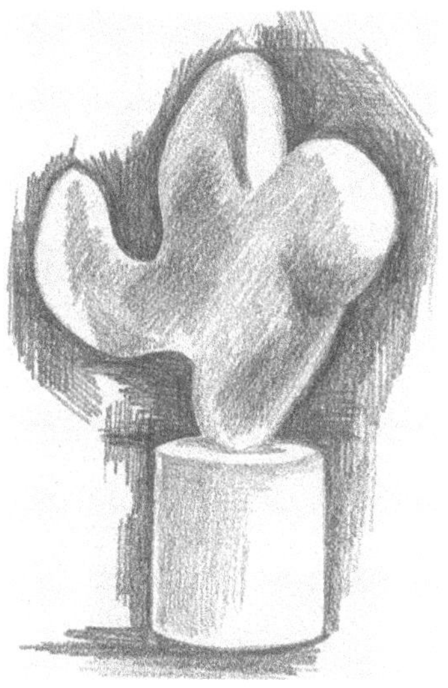

Biomorphic sculpture by Jean Arp

Middle and High School Hand Appreciation Exercises

- Observe, study and describe how people gesture with their hands.
- Study, draw, and model hands depicted in master paintings, drawings, and sculptures.
- Provide students in grades 7-12 with photos of the interesting hands of famous and unknown people. Ask them to describe the character, gestures, meaning and emotions they project. (I have collected over two hundred postcards of hands. They are a very popular item frequently to be found on card racks!)

Series Thirteen:
Words, Poetry, and Forms

A Sculpture Worth a Thousand Words?
Sculptures have been known to inspire poetic verse. The poet Rilke, for example, composed poems capturing his experience of particular works such those of Rodin and of the ancient Greeks.

Interestingly, the word poetry is derived from the Greek word *"poiein,"* meaning "to make or create." Poets and sculptors are both creators of images, conjured up in words and sculptural form respectively.

Examples of Poetic Descriptions of Forms
Doing this exercise with sculptures that distinctly represent something, start with a determined theme. Working with a more abstract, pure sculptural form–even if has a name–leaves more room for the imagination and a wider range of associations. In both cases, a reader of your poem should be able to read its lines and connect them with visible aspects of the sculptures image and forms. This exercise calls for "disciplined, objective imagination" rather than "wild fantasy" which may leave readers obscurely in the dark.

The first two sculptures are carried over from Series Twelve and are pure forms to contemplate, although the first piece has been named.

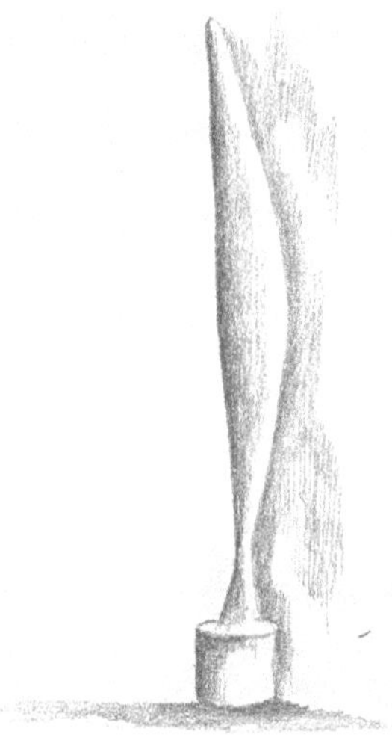

SOARING

Soaring high
I feel all that is below fading
Lightening, thinning.
Gravity no longer holds me,
I shoot towards the sun,
A ray from earth,
Never to return.

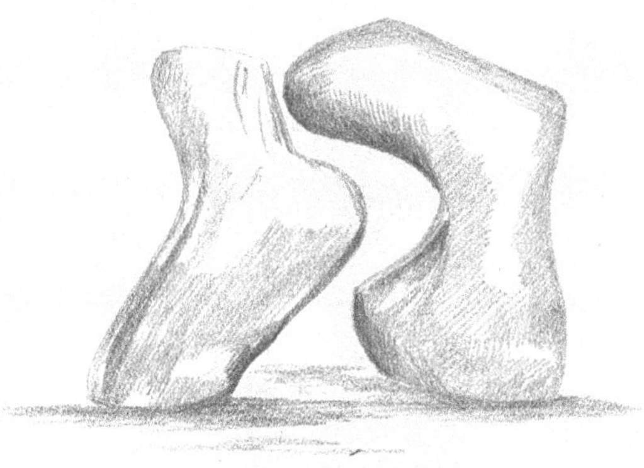
Sculptor and title intentionally withheld

THE SECRET

She bursts with a secret to tell.
Her friend bends low to listen.
No one around can hear.
Whispering fills the space
Between them.
The space is forever changed.

Ernst Barlach
The following is a "representative" sculpture. It has a very strong gesture which lends itself to verbal description.

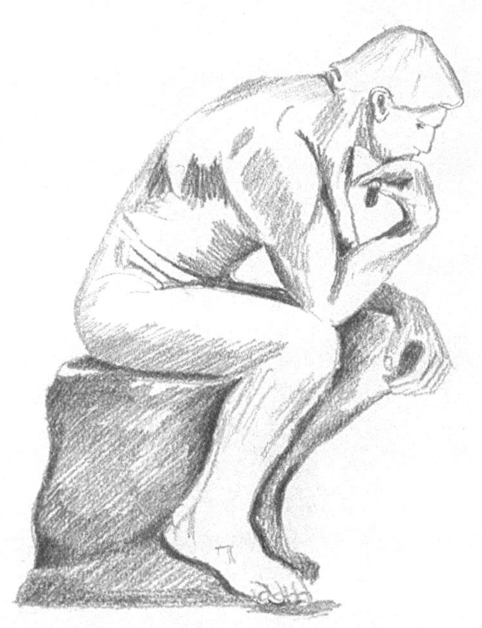
Sculpture title withheld

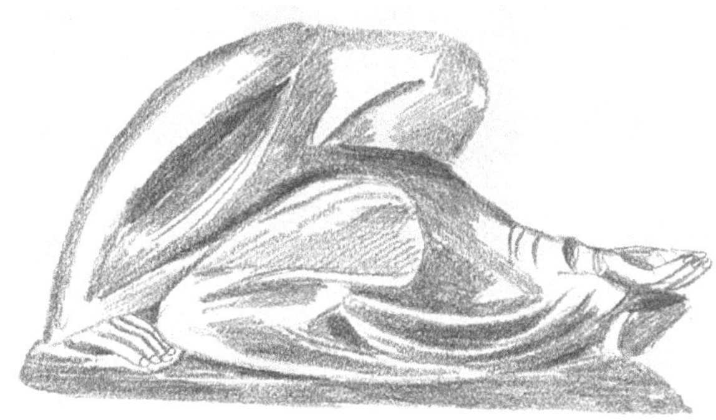
Sculpture title withheld

LIFE AND HOPE

Laid low,
She bows to life's blow,
Sinking into herself.
Her hand turns upward.
Its humble openness
Fills with hope.

Other sculptors and their works to explore
Non-representational:
    Hepworth
    Archipenko
    Lipchitz
Representational:
    Giacometti
    Michelangelo
    Greek Cycladic figures

Simple Pure Forms

It was a real pleasure to compose "form stories" for younger children in the first three series of this sourcebook rather than merely describing how to make them.

In the examples below, I have taken the simplest of these same forms again and turned them onto "Form Poems" for teenagers and adults.

Round to Long

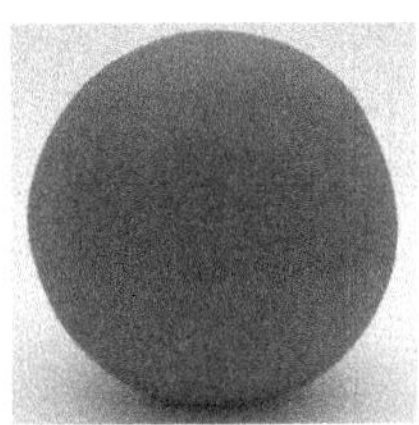

To be true to her nature.
Sphere, the most universal of forms,
Hovers high aloft,
Always circling and moving
a heavenly body.
She has only an inner and outer,
No up or down, no right or left,
No base to rest on the ground.
Only one scant point to touch down on,
But only if she wants.
Stretching forth ever so gently,

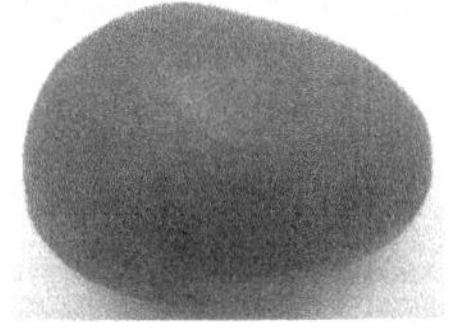

Ovoid is born,
Ready to reach out into life,
Still half round, but pointing
Toward adventure.

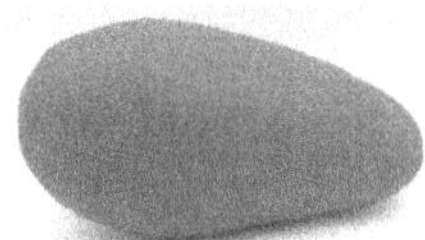

Extending further and further
Seeking experience.

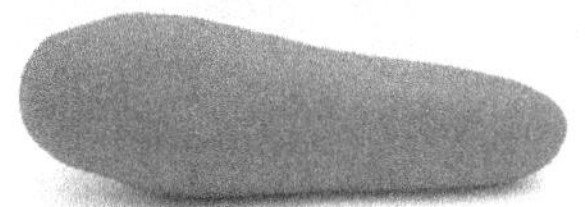

Roundness fades,
As Long emerges and lengthens,
To connect with the world,
No longer hovering.

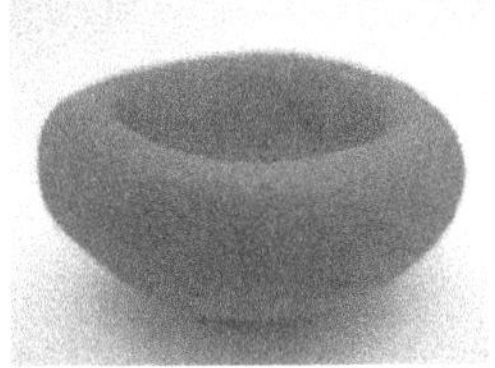

Birth of Hollow

Sphere is pressed and impressed
More and more by the world outside.
Hollow is born.
Roundness gives way
To the space
Growing within.

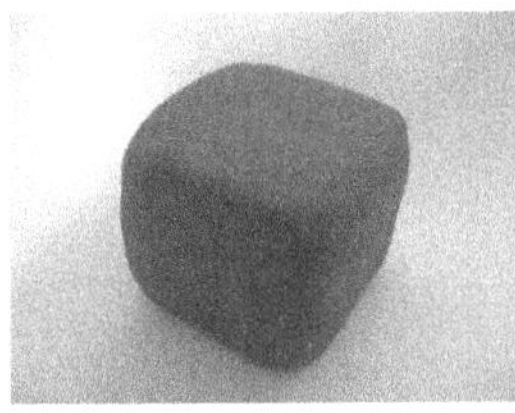

Square Straight Flat

Hello, I am Square Straight.
I thought I was great,
Until I met Curvy Surface.
I lost my nerve
And introduced myself as "Flat."
But there she sat
Unimpressed and cool.
I walked away—
straightaway—a fool.

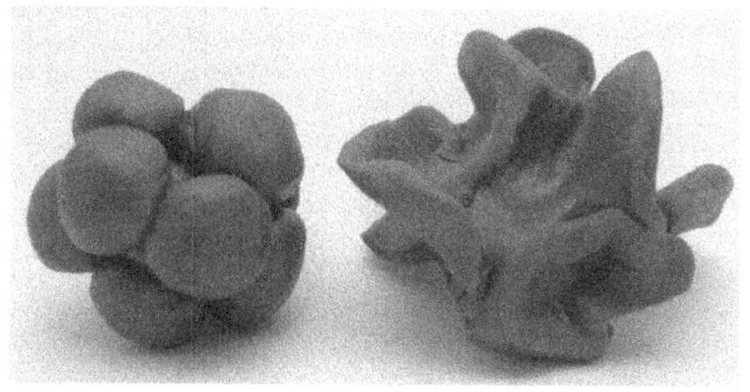

Coming Together and Falling Apart

Bursting outward with life and energy.
Roundnesses join and fill with sap.
Weathered and worn by dry winds,
Sides collapse inward
Into a chaos of hollow spaces,
All falls apart.

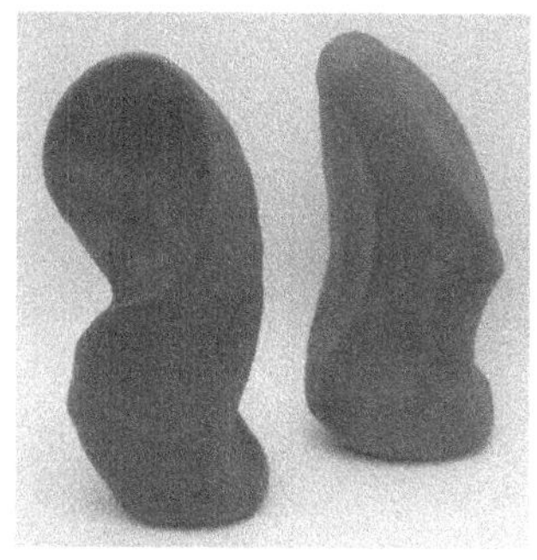

Front and Back

Open countenance welcomes
And invites all to look within.
Thoughts and feelings are shared.
Back turned,
Cutting off conversation.
What has been said to offend?

Interesting Perspectives on Formation: Writing, Speech, Eurythmy and Music

In the beginning was the word
and the word was full of life and light
and became form.

Mouth-Hands Speak Words and Forms

Hands speak in signing, writing and modeling. They are shaped like mouths—children make mouth shadows on the walls with them.

We sometimes put a pencil as tongue in our mouth-hand and it speaks words onto paper: *"s-p-h-e-r-e."* These "written" figures are sculptural formations albeit very flat ones in graphite.

In modeling, instead of putting a graphite pencil in our "talking hand," we insert another medium for expression: a lump of clay. Our hand speaks "sphere" but this time not as flat symbols but as full three-dimensional sculptural poetry.

Words as Vibrating Air Sculptures Laden with Meaning

Interestingly, when we speak words and sounds we actually form invisible air sculptures in our outgoing breath. Instead of clay, we use the air as a movable, vibrating sculptural medium to express meaning. Each sound and word makes it own sculptural configuration. This phenomenon has been demonstrated by researcher Johanna Zinke. She has systematically photographed the breath formations of alphabet letter sounds and syllables exhaled in trails of smoke. Her wonderful study is called *Luftlautformen sichtbar machen* (air alphabet sound forms made visible).

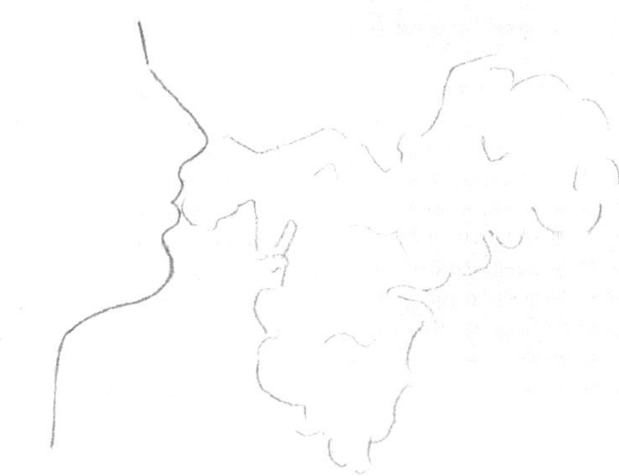

The sculptural form created in smoke by the consonant "T"(followed by a slight "ha" for breath).

In eurythmy, the whole body is used to create moving sculptural formations in space and combined with music and speech formation.

Music and Sculptural Formation

Music itself is a "sculpture-maker," as demonstrated in Chladni form experiments. They show visibly how sounds produce forms in matter. The most recent theory in physics is that all formations in the universe are created by the harmonic vibrations of countless subatomic energy "strings." The cosmos is imagined as a huge symphony creating everything we see. (See Chapter: Form-Giving Forces)

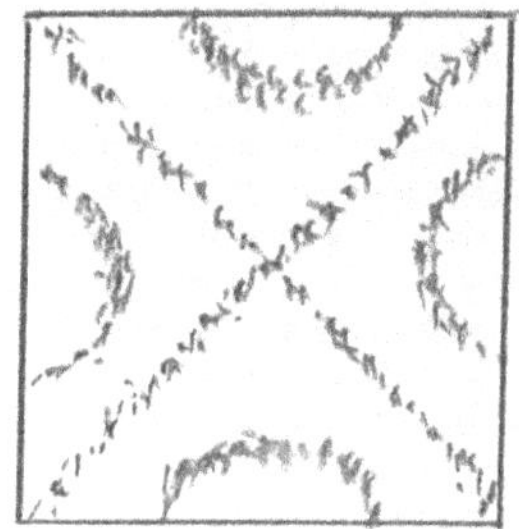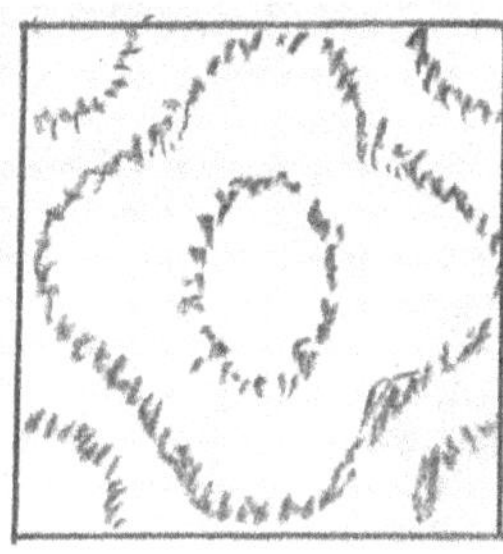

Chladni Forms

Basic Pure Forms Born Out of the Hand

Excerpts from the Groundbreaking Action Research
of Class Teacher Hella Loewe

In 2000, Waldorf class teacher Hella Loewe published a report of her pioneering clay modeling of pure forms with her class, a challenging mixed-age group of 36 children in grades 1-4. In 2004, she developed her work further into a handbook called Basic Sculptural Modeling: Developing the Will by Working with Pure Forms in the First Three Grade *(English version: Waldorf Publications, 2006). Before the book could be published, I drafted an English translation of her 2000 report entitled "Modeling in the Early Grades: An Action Research Report on Classroom Practice." I include excerpts here to encourage teachers and artists to acquire her fully developed text of exercises, which also includes excellent, very clear photos.*

On Developing the Will into the Future through the Art of Modeling

"I would like to designate the pedagogical stream that activates and strengthens the will forces of children as the 'stream of the future' (*Zukunftsstrom*) in the plastic-sculptural realm. In contrast to this, we can speak of a stream that the children bring with them, the 'stream of the past' that becomes visible in the illustrative drawings and paintings of children and in the little representational figures they model. This stream gradually exhausts itself. It is important that we clearly distinguish the underlying character of the different artistic activities we teach the children."

Hands-On Conversations about the Hand

"In interacting with first graders, I learned how essential it is to conduct such conversations– particularly in this case the discussion of the hands. The manner in which Rudolf Steiner introduces the exercise in 'skillfulness with the hands' (*Handgeschicklichkeit*) inspired me to create suitable verbal introductions to modeling lessons with my first graders. Later on, I found comparable age-appropriate words for them when they grew into second, third, and fourth graders. I thereby wanted *to make my children increasingly aware of how their hands were a unique gift and how the different parts of their hands could be used for artistic modeling* (*Gestalten*). In modeling, for instance, we use both of our hands fully whereas, as a rule, we use only three fingers in drawing to hold a crayon and in painting a brush.

"When we ourselves model, we experience how the hollow of the hand, the inner part of both hands, becomes warm and stimulated in a special way. Furthermore, our entire sense organism is finely enlivened; above all, the will senses—touch, life, movement, and balance—are activated and 'nourished.' Through this artistic activity, the life processes are ensouled and stimulated, particularly the breathing and warmth processes."

Clay Modeling in a First Grade: A Concrete Example

"The classrooms for both of our first grades are situated on the first floor of the so-called 'Old Villa' in which the Kraherwald Waldorf School in Stuttgart had its beginnings fifty-two years ago. It is the end of January—a Monday morning around 7:30 am. Outside it is dark; a cold wind blows around the building. Inside the classroom, the teacher has prepared everything in anticipation of receiving the multitude of children: 21 boys and 18 girls. They have been specially entrusted into her care as an experienced Waldorf class teacher, who has guided two other groups through the Waldorf Curriculum before.

"The children noisily stomp up the wide, old, wooden steps and quickly enter the classroom to be greeted by their teacher. Immediately, individual children are asking: 'Oh, are we going to model clay again today?' 'Can I pass out the clay?' 'Ah, modeling clay is much more beautiful than painting!' Joyful sounds fill the room. The children seat themselves amazingly quickly on their chairs, which are set up at their desks rather than in the usual beginning morning circle. (This is how they would also usually begin a painting session in main lesson time). Even the wildest and loudest boys find their places—after they have quickly had a 'little fight' before entering through the door.

"A joyful readiness pervades our little class community. The teacher gives a sign and all the children stand and fold their hands before reciting the morning verse: 'The sun with loving light makes bright for me the day,' resounds powerfully and trustingly out into the world. And, when next a song is sung by all, the sun actually rises and shines into the classroom. An ideal picture? Can such a scenario exist today in a first grade class of 40 children? The magic medium for these happy, cooperative children, lies on a table in front of the blackboard. It is hidden under wet cloths. The outlines of at least 40 little hills can be seen: fine, light colored clay in small portions to appropriately fit first grade hands.

"The teacher appoints helpers to gently lay out painting boards and a lump of clay on each. There is no shortage of volunteers! The children wait in great anticipation of finally starting. This is a real test of patience; the beautiful, wet clay is right in front of their noses and is so tempting! It wants to be held in their hands! However, there is a golden rule that all are learning to heed and practice: only pick up the clay when every classmate has been given a piece and only when the teacher takes up hers. That is the sign for beginning.

"At last—a joyous sigh of relief is heard! Let's first test out how our clay feels today, dear children!" The children imitate their teacher by putting the clay to their cheeks and feeling how cold it is. 'Now take a little chunk from your clay and lay it aside. Then we want to 'feel through' and 'touch through' the rest of the clay—piece by piece—finely with our fingertips and thus prepare it for our work. Whoever finds a little stone or hair in the clay should put it aside." Immediately, the children eagerly and quietly set to work. One of the most important golden rules is 'The mouth is silent while the hands work!' It becomes apparent how justified and fitting this is to the occasion when a palpable feeling of wellbeing spreads through the classroom. After the children have carefully 'felt through' their clay, their teacher shows them how to hold it in two hands –with the exception of the little piece that was previously put aside. They press the mass together in such a way that they embrace it crosswise with the hands. The teacher travels around to check that every child–according to his or her hand size–can grasp the clay appropriately. This means that the fingers of the right and left hand do not touch anymore.

"The children sit upright in their chairs, which have a marked distance from their desks. Their feet are placed with entire soles on the floor. The teacher stands in the front of the class and begins to form the clay at the same time as the children. All hold the clay at the height of their hearts and, alternating from one hand to the other, turn it, press it forcefully, form it and thus slowly make it round. The teacher watches out that shoulders and elbows remain relaxed. In most cases matters take care of themselves because most children flexibly move their arms and elbows 'like wings.' As soon as a child presses his elbows against his body and tries to model, he or she cannot breathe or work as freely. When everything is going well, the children tend to 'slip into' the movements of the teacher, which is characteristic of this age group.

"The teacher accompanies the work with only a few words, for example: 'I move the clay back and forth between both hands. I form it in the hollows of my hands.'(Previously, she had shown them how their hands form cup-like curves).

'I round the clay as I turn it again and again. My thumb wanders over the form, touches the rough spots and presses and makes them smooth; it pushes a little clay in any holes and evens them out.' Then she works further.

"Meanwhile, the pieces of clay in the hands of most children have been rounded into harmonious forms. (It can happen that a child–even after repeated practice–is not able to shape his or her clay into a round form; in this case it should be determined what extra help is needed). The teacher now lets the children model with their eyes shut for a time. They feel the roundness with the hollow of the hand, use the sense of touch to guide them in pressing and evening out rough spots; this activity also activates the feeling powers of the fingertips. And this means that the eyes have a rest as well as the mouth. Most children are amenable to this kind of activity. After this phase of turning more inward, the children are asked to open their eyes again, to lay their form on one of their hand surfaces and hold up high for all to see the beautiful form that has arisen. The teacher goes around the classroom to look at the individual works. She expresses praise and wonder and gives advice here and there for improvements. And perhaps she points to two or three works which have been very successfully rounded. This can stimulate the children to work further with renewed interest on smoothing remaining rough spots. Then the moment has come when the children can again hold the clay, on which they have worked for 20-25 minutes, to their cheeks. At the same time they also do the same with the little piece they originally set aside. The astonishment is always great: how warm the rounded form on which they have worked is and how cold the untransformed piece! The children naturally report this remarkable fact to each other.

"At the end of the lesson, the children carefully scratch the beginning initials of their first names in the form and place them on the painting board in front of them. It is time to give the hands a rest! Four industrious helpers go quietly around to carefully collect the forms and lay them on the boards on the desk of the teacher. There they will be covered and preserved with wet cloths until the next day. Watch out, this can be critical moment! Remember, there are all those other little pieces of clay lying on the desks in front of the children. This means that they also have to be quickly collected and brought to container with an airtight lid. Clay, after all, is not a toy, but our working material that we will need next time to continue! The boards are cleared away quickly and the desks are wiped by other helpers. In front of the blackboard stand four buckets, each on a chair; hand towels hang on the chair backs. The children take turns washing themselves. Their hands are covered with a thin layer of dry white clay and are not really dirty. As long as the teacher keeps all the children in sight during this clean up break, everything goes well as it does on painting days.

"Following each modeling lesson, I see with pleasure how my children developed healthy, ruddy cheeks; even the delicate, pale ones appeared rosy and stimulated. It proved especially fruitful and economical to follow the modeling immediately with language arts work: for example, to have a detailed conversation about a fairy tale told the day before; or during writing blocks periods, to have the children recite words with particular sounds and rhymes. Oh, how their speech gushed forth in such a good way! After a lively practice of language for about 20 minutes, there were about 25 minutes for the teacher to tell a new story. In this manner, main lesson could be rounded off to the satisfaction of all and ended in a beautiful mood."

Practice of a Series of Sculptural Modeling Exercises with Children in Grades 1–4: Description of Method

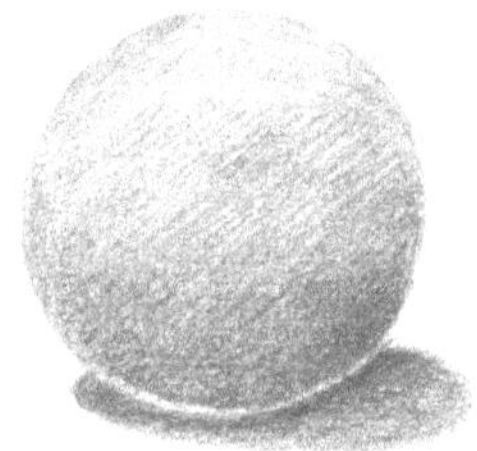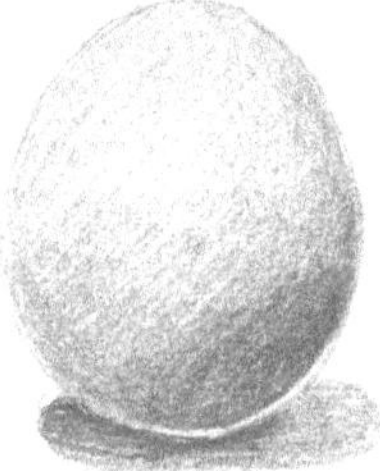

1. First Transformation: From the Sphere to the Ovoid (See above)

"After I had practiced several times with the children making as harmonious and round a form as possible, we were able to try our first transformation. A basic principle still underlay the method: no preconceived goals were prescribed! Through repetitive practice, almost all the children had become so skillful that within fifteen minutes they completed a round, centered form as a first stage towards the next step.

"'Put your form down for a moment and watch what I show you: we all have between our single, moving fingers and our sensitive feeling palm a middle part which connects the two (the middle hand bones). Feel it with the fingertips of your other hand! Under your pointer finger and your little fingers are little cushions, almost like cats' paws. Under the middle and the ring fingers it is flatter in comparison. This entire middle area is very strong and you can use it for good work and forming. I now take my round form between my two hands like this and press and carefully stretch it with this middle part so that I slowly keep turning it in the same direction. I press, stretch and turn, press, stretch and turn. Now you try to stretch your form as I have shown you!' After a time during which I have continued to make the described motions with my form, I make the children aware of something else: 'Now as we pause, we see that our round form has become long. When we place it upright on our hand, we can say that it has a top and a base.'

"Demonstrating in front of the children is the method! Follow this with working together, pausing, observing, giving short instructions, and having a time of modeling and touching with eyes closed. Then open the eyes again and follow the form with more conscious touching and beholding—'with the will emerging through the eyes' [*mit dem durch das Auge gehenden Willen*] (Rudolf Steiner, *Practical Advice to Teachers*, Lecture I, p. 21 (1988 English edition). When individual children recognize the form and call out, 'It's an egg!' this does not contradict the method. The children have simply at the end of the exercise added an appropriate concept, which is thoroughly justified.

"This form is practiced at least three times. The children learn how best to turn their forms rhythmically and evenly

around a middle axis and to simultaneously stretch it. When they sit up quite straight in their chairs, a stream of forces flows from the spine over the shoulder blades into the shoulders and arms right into the hands. 'The creation of forms is the active working of forces' [*Formbildung ist Kräftewirkung*] (Rudolf Steiner, *Ways to a New Style in Architecture*, June 26, 1914)."

2. Second Transformation: First Hollowing with the Thumb

"If progress with the exercises is satisfactory, I show the children how a new third form can arise out of those we have practiced. We round the clay again and stretch and shape the round form into an oval one. I ask the children to lay their pieces down on the boards. Again I direct their attention to their hands. 'You now know how we round the clay with the hollows of our hands and with the help of our thumbs. You have learned how to stretch the clay with the powerful middle part of our hands and to turn it in a particular direction so that a beautiful ovoid form arises.

"Now we have on every hand a wonderful friend whom we do not know so well. With its help we can do something that we have not yet tried. This is the strong, somewhat rounded ball at the bottom of the thumb whom will call 'thumb ball.' Check what it feels like! Now I lay my oval form flat on my left hand. With the thumb ball of my right hand I press gently at first and then more and more firmly into the form and make a hollow space—not down the long part of the form nor right across its middle but slanting across it like this The thumb ball nestles quite naturally in the ovoid. Do as I show you!'

"I demonstrate to the children how the thumb and its ball move back and forth in the hollow space that has arisen. This motion is a kind of rocking through which I widen and deepen the shallow indentation in relationship to the total from. Now the stage has been reached to model beautiful transitions between the slight inward curvature and those surfaces that curve outwards."

"The thumb is again a very suitable helper. So that the children develop a feeling for the new form as a whole, I have them lay it in the 'bowl' shape created by holding their two cupped hands next to each other. Their thumbs and the rest of their hands embrace and explore it through touch. (See above) In this way they are able to smooth out the form further—as I show them—and give it a final shape."

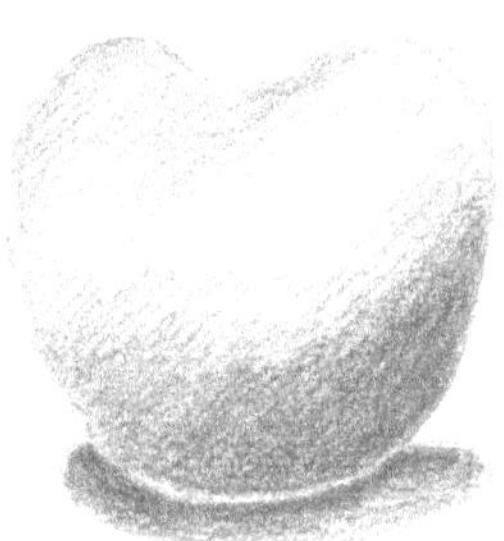

3. Third Transformation: From the Sphere to Modeling Right-Left Symmetry (See above)

"In second grade form drawing, some of the forms that the children practice involve mirror symmetry. They draw on the paper a vertical axis in the middle, a figure to its left and then a mirror image of that figure to the right; in the third grade the challenge of a horizontal axis is added and create four quadrants in which to make such figures. These exercises are based on the development of 7-8 year olds, who are most secure in grasping the axial symmetry of a form when the axis is in the plane of symmetry of their own bodies. This shows us how intimately the grasp of symmetry hangs together with the perception of one's own balance.... I carried this experience over into the three-dimensional sculptural realm with children of this age group.

"The round form is very centered upon itself. It hovers in a balance between inner and outer space, as it grew out of the rhythmical movement of the two concave hands, the hollows of the hands (*Hohlhände*). The children practice making a first indentation in the recumbent ovoid form, whereby above and below, right and left are still treated freely and not emphasized. The essential point is to experience and form the surface as it curves inward toward a center.

"The next step calls for a more conscious grasp of right and left in consonance with above and below. Again starting with the round form I direct the children to do the following.

"I place the round form on my left hand. The place where it touches my hand I call the 'base.' Now I put the rounded pad at the end of my right thumb on the opposite side, which I call the top. I press a slight little rounded groove into the top with my thumb pad so that two sides of equal size are formed, a right one and a left one. With the round ends of the thumbs I widen and deepen this hollow space—also using the rocking movement, which we practiced before. 'Now you do what I have just done!'

"Then it is time to stimulate the children into action using different hand grips, touching and feeling the right-left symmetry and finally to model the form in balanced proportions. It is helpful after a while to embrace the form with both hands in such a way that the wrists touch below… and the fingers nestle into the hollow above–without clawing into it!

"Now the child can smooth out any remaining uneven areas with the fingertips, continuously acting out of a feeling of inner balance. Following this, we turn the form 180 degrees around the vertical axis so that we can observe and form: the right-left symmetry from another perspective. It is worthwhile doing this several times. Also with this form it is a matter of creating beautiful, plastic transitions between those surfaces curving inward and those curving outward. Sharp edges should be avoided! Towards the end of the process I let the children lay the form once again in a reversed position on one hand, that is, the upper, differentiated part on the hand surface. They thereby can feel with the other hand that, what was the bottom half of the form, has retained its roundness and that the transformations only happened in the upper half.

"This form should be practiced several times and always be looked at and contemplated the next day so that the children ever more consciously assimilate this spatial right-left symmetry form, which depicts the first differentiation of the spherical form …The children show us that repetitive practice of an artistic activity does not have to deteriorate into a boring routine. They sense and like this state of regular absorption and engagement. I emphasize different aspects each time: sometimes I will, for example, put special emphasis on the form being beautifully full and not skinny with edges. Another time I might stress that the surface should be done especially carefully. In this way, the children over time become ever more skillful and self-sufficient in their handling of the clay. The form language is inscribed in their body. We teachers must provide the opportunity for this language to find expression through malleable material, in this case clay."

4. Fourth Transformation: The Larger and the Smaller Side

"Prepared to this degree, the children are ready the next time to joyfully engage themselves in a lively transformation of the right-left symmetry that was last practiced. First, they practice it once again just as they did previously. Then one can say to the children: 'You have shaped your form so evenly and finely into a right side and a left side. But it seems as if it is sleeping; mine is also sleeping. Therefore, I want to wake it up with my warm hands. Watch how I do it! Is something already stirring within? One side stretches itself and wants to grow upwards out of the roundness. With the hollow of the hand I help it and carefully shift some of the clay upwards from the bottom half of the form so that the form outwardly remains round. Up until now, the other side has been dreaming, but it now starts after a while to stretch itself a little. And how it is astonished to see its opposite side so grown up! Does it want to become so large? No, it would rather wait a little while in peace and I allow it to have its way. Now, all of you also wake up your forms. Then a little later: 'Let our hands touch the place between the larger and the smaller sides and try to form a beautiful, gentle bridging path (*Übergang*=transition). Also we want to finely shape the path from the bottom half of the form to the upper half…." Before and after, it is important that the children are able while they model to orient themselves to my movements and hand positions (grips), not only during the time I introduce the new exercise."

5. Fifth Transformation: From the Sphere to Threefold-Symmetry

"Every class teacher has the experience that exercises in visual arts with children—be they form drawing, watercolor painting or beeswax crayons or even modeling—are most successful when he or she works with the motif, form, or colors actively the night before and sleeps on these experiences. I would like to specially point out that the next form I am about to describe is not an easy one for the children. The teacher needs to be sure of each particular positioning of the hands (grip) and certain in the choice of words to stimulate the children in their own efforts.

"First of all, the round form is modeled and placed on the board. Then the following instructions are given: 'Dear children, today you must follow very attentively and exactly with your eyes what my hands are going to show you! I take the round form like this in the hollows of both hands so that both thumbs lie next to each other…Holding it in this way, I press powerfully into the clay with the upper parts of my thumbs. I then loosen my cupped hands somewhat and open my thumbs, which still lie on the top of the round form, so that a big 'A' is formed.

The two thumb tips stay close to each other while the other parts of the thumbs each ray out as legs of the letter 'A.' In this position, I press the 'A' forcefully into the clay. 'Now you try this too together with me as I once again go through the different hand positions.'

"This effort results in two hollows on the outer rim of which some clay has swollen out and in an elevation … These markings should help us bring into being a regular threefoldness of the upper half of the form (I was striving for a threefold symmetry like that which the children know in form drawing). I say to the children something like this: 'You see how in this part it presses and shifts upwards, the clay arches up, round itself, grows out of the form. On the other side, however, it is still resting, it sleeps, nothing stirs. But look now at the right and the left, it pushes out from the inside. Clay swells upwards and allows our hands to form it and round it.

"The thumb notices and feels what has pushed in such a lively way up out of the darkness into the light. It evens out the distances between the three little curved swellings (*Wölbungen*). The hollows of the hands nestle against the sides of the form. We lay both thumbs and one of the middle fingers each in one of the hollows that have arisen between the three swellings…As we slowly turn the form around the upright axis in one direction, stopping, forming, evening out and turning it still further, we grasp it always in new ways with the three fingers. In this process the thumb wanders over and feels the swellings and shifts here and there some clay from the outside of the form to make the swellings fuller. It wanders over the paths, which lie between them, arrives in the gently curved place in the middle and turns back from there. In this way the thumb carefully forms the paths which lead here and there on the form. The form becomes more and more beautiful.

"After we have worked together in this way for a while, we turn the form with the hollows of the hands around the vertical axis and press the sides of the upper half carefully from the outside and repeat turning and pressing. This should help us to hold the three swellings beautifully together for they should not spread out too widely. When we lay the form upside down on one hand, we see that the base has remained round and we have only transformed and threefolded the upper half. After this, it is a matter of checking with the sense of touch the transition between the upper and lower halves and to even out any small dents, cracks or bumps…Finally, the thumb goes wandering once again over the whole form and completes it. For this task I needed thirty, at most thirty-five, minutes exclusively for modeling and then time for cleaning up."

Transition from Third to Fourth Grade

"In the method described thus far, I was working with students in the first through third grades and between the ages of 7-9. The children were eager and content in their activity, which met their needs at this stage of development. Teachers who observe their children with love, wakefulness, and understanding notice a change in every individual that happens at the end of third and beginning of fourth grade, earlier with some

and later with others. Every child experiences between the ninth and tenth birthday that significant 'turning point in life,' which we call in Waldorf pedagogy the 'Rubicon.' The child, who up to this point has not differentiated herself in her feeling from the world, now develops the need 'to inwardly become a human being, a self-contained individuality and to confront the world' (Rudolf Steiner, *Soul Economy and Waldorf Education*, January 1, 1922)."

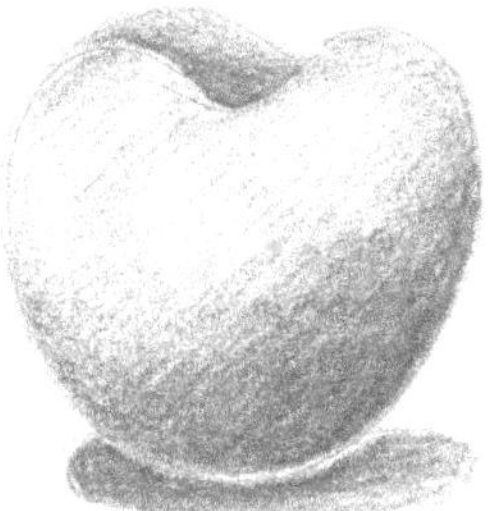

6. A Surface to Stand On: The Form Is Brought to Earth

"In this stage of development, I took up once again the regular threefold form in modeling (Fifth Transformation). This form, like all the others derived from the sphere, was modeled by the children as though floating quite close to the heart region and retained unchanged its fully round bottom (except for the ovoid). Now it became a matter of changing this hovering state of balance, bringing it to 'earthify' (*erden*), and of releasing the form with which the child felt so closely connected up to this point.

"I therefore asked the children of the fourth grade to hold their threefold form between the hands in such a way that the unaltered roundness pointed downwards. 'You begin now with the powerful middle part of your hand—the middle hand bones—to stretch the base of your form downwards just as we have already practiced earlier with the oval. You turn your form slowly around the vertical axis and thereby you press it, turn it and press it again. So you gradually stretch it. You no longer change anything at the top of the form.'

"After the students work on this a while and their forms have become clearly slimmer towards the bottom, I make a new request of them: 'Now place your form firmly and upright in front of you! Then kneel in front of your desk and look at it exactly and from all sides.' By placing it firmly upright, the form acquires a flat surface on which to stand. The slenderness towards the bottom gives it a certain lightness. Unlike the previous forms which have to lie down on round bottoms, the new form by standing acquires a relationship to the surrounding space . . . The children experience this with joy and satisfaction. In a discussion the next day this experience plays the most important role."

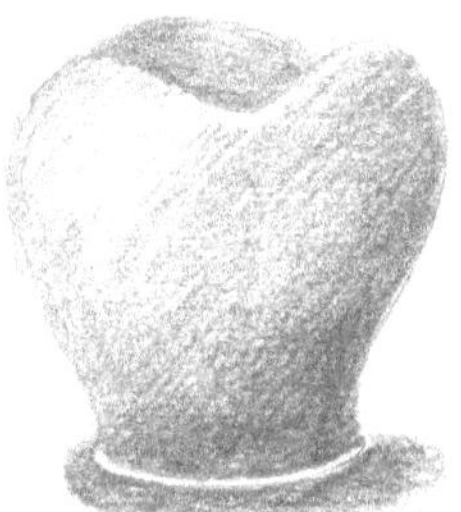

7. Refinement of the Surface to Stand On: The Form Receives a Foot (not shown)

"In the next practice session I allow the children to model another form that had three parts above and was again derived from the sphere. I give them the choice of forming the three swellings at the top either of equal sizes (symmetrical) or of different sizes (asymmetrical). I remind them of the right-left symmetry form, which we had transformed by making a smaller and larger side. After this, I let them make their forms slimmer at the bottom and even more so this time. The children only have to be careful not to have the form lose its fullness at the top. The form is again firmly planted on the desk as it was last time and carefully scrutinized from all sides. It came out in this observation that 'it would be beautiful if the form still had a little more lightness to it.'

"Thereupon I show the children how to bring out a little protruding edge scarcely one centimeter wide. The effect of this special touch is astonishing. The form stands upright and firm on the base, but appears lighter and more charming than before. It stands there as an expression of a long journey of practice; and it embodies the feeling and movement of the children congealed (*geronnen*) into form along this way."

How I Came to Have My First Grade Model with Clay

"The fact that my students came to regularly and naturally model in addition to the typical activities of painting and form drawing did not come about casually. I will give a brief history:

"When in the summer of 1986 I took on a new class for the second time in my career as Waldorf class teacher, it became quickly apparent that there was a confluence of tremendous gifts in this group as well as the influences of different ethnic groups, languages and religions. Amongst them was a group of markedly aggressive and often inconsiderate boys. The behavior of these boys lacking in social skills made difficult and even disrupted meaningful activities in the rhythmical circle part of the main lesson. There were also crisis situations at recess times. The usual pedagogical measures for such remedial situations did not help sufficiently. I could not and would not allow this situation to go on for long. With great urgency I asked myself how I could help channel into meaningful activity this pent-up aggressiveness, which expressed itself particularly in the children's hands. They were using their hands to push, hit, hurt and choke each other, all obvious symptoms of fear and insecurity.

"As I wrestled for a solution to this problem over Christmas vacation, an inspiration finally came to me: I knew I had to find a compact, earthly material for my children's hands to manipulate: rich earthen clay it had to be! I also realized that I had to do sculptural modeling not only with the aggressive children, but with the entire class. I had the hope that this would not only resolve the pent-up aggressiveness but might also be of benefit to the whole group. I would develop exercises that were generally artistic and therapeutic, which would be good for the entire class.

"Following this decision, I began to ponder how I could responsibly introduce this innovation into the curriculum and justify it to my colleagues. Why? Because

at that time to model cold, wet clay in the first grade of a Waldorf school was totally unusual. It was deemed—and perhaps is still today—as something damaging to the health of young children. Therefore, I consulted a former professor of the Seminar for Waldorf Education in Stuttgart, Germany, who had been my beloved instructor in the methodology of form drawing and painting. Hildegard Berthold-Andrae encouraged me strongly to do what I felt was right for my children and what life circumstances were demanding, rather than follow tradition. She subsequently followed my 'pioneer work' with great pedagogical interest. Also thanks to her initiative at the beginning of my work with the children, a small group of colleagues came together, who were prepared to become involved in pedagogical research on the theme of modeling in the early grades. The efforts of this group were energized by Winfried Schmidt and Peter Schiefer, both of whom teach arts today as professors in the Seminar . . . We were able to meet only a few times over the course of three years. However, it was possible in this period due to our intensive efforts together, to break ground in developing a method of modeling for the younger grades that sensibly took into account Rudolf Steiner's indications for this subject.

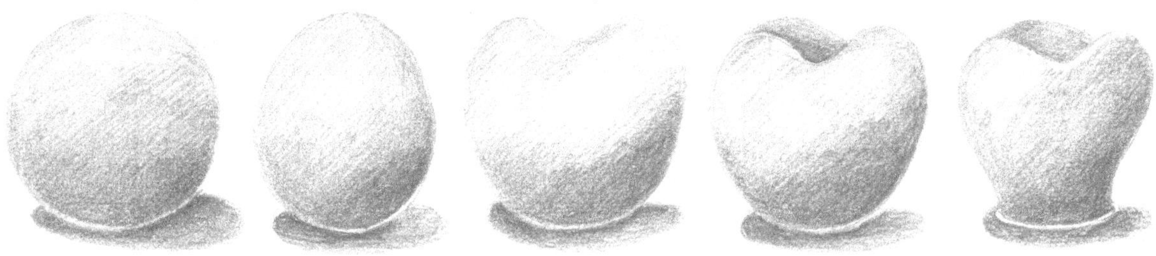

"In each session together, we looked at the practical experiences I was having with my children and related them to our considerations. We were looking for simple, clear forms that could nestle nicely in the hands of small children. In accordance with what we felt was age- appropriate, we avoided formations with sharp edges, points, deep, inner cavities and bone-like forms. In this process we discovered forms that were straight forward, clear shapes. One could characterize these forms as predominantly 'cosmic' and universal in nature. Our approach excluded exercises in relief or in building up or constructing pieces on a set baseboard. In this way, we developed the series of forms that are described and pictured in this article as examples of the work. Not all of the forms developed in our group or with my students are represented here.

"I would like to take the opportunity to express my gratitude to Hildegard Berthold-Andrae, Peter Schiefer and Winfried Schmidt for their fruitful collaboration with me! I am also thankful to the faculty of my school, which allowed me the freedom to go this new way with my students and which accompanied my work with well-meaning and positive criticism, particularly in its initial phases. This support manifested itself particularly when all colleagues modeled several forms with me in two of our faculty meetings. I must also report on my class, which was the inspiring impulse for initiating this collaborative pedagogical research: Through regular modeling between the autumn and spring (see also Steiner, *The Cycle of the Year as a Breathing Process of the Earth*, April 7, 1923), artistic and sculptural capacities were indeed powerfully strengthened in my group; I maintained a weekly painting lesson, whenever possible, and gave form drawing in block units. Regular modeling had an incredible harmonizing influence on the class community as a whole. Over the course of time the especially aggressive children found a better and better relationship to the will activity of the modeling lessons I directed and learned to bridle their own wills through this experience."

Power Source of the Arts

"With this report, I hope and wish to encourage class teachers as well as parents to model with their children in the lower grades! Today, in a time when the computer is finding its way into so many children's rooms and lives, it is more urgently necessary than ever to enliven and sensitize their hands. The modeling of basic universal forms, as I have suggested, is a means to activate special human capacities.

"The computer as a learning tool appears to continue its victorious campaign march; computer games, which hold such a powerful fascination for children, are hard to forbid. This means that our youngsters often gaze for hours at electronic screens and strain and exhaust their eyes in an unhealthy one-sided way. It also means that their fingertips quickly and skillfully move over the keyboard and click the mouse, but the hand as a whole with its manifold, creative possibilities is not used to the fullest. Furthermore, not only the eyes and hands are adversely limited in the typical interaction with the computer, but, in fact, the entire human being in body and soul suffers to a considerable degree a reduction in sense perception, life processes and mobility.

In the face of the trend toward more and more interaction with the virtual, lifeless world of electronics, we would do well to provide our children with the powerful resources of arts such as modeling. Artistic experiences allow young human beings to encounter and understand processes of transformation integral to the world of the living. Through the arts, we give our children the possibility to sensitize, refine and expand their perceptual abilities and to learn to know and use their hands as remarkable tools in the service of enhanced creative activity."

An Adult's Experience of Hella Loewe's Forms
Hella Loewe's modeling exercises also help grown ups to experience not only organic archetypal forms but also the primal shaping power of their own hands. I recommend that adults work with them meditatively. Here are some of my own reflections:

Sphere: Our readily cupped hands naturally embrace and surround a globe of earthen clay and feel "met" by its moist smoothness.

Ovoid: Through stretching a sphere into a universal "egg" shape, we experience the turning and pulling powers of our hands working together.

Saddle form: Through exerting the muscularity of the full thumb, we experience this unique opposing finger's special versatility and will-fulness.

Mirror Symmetry Form: The mirror symmetry form shaped between two upright hands in front of the chest is an experience of a heart-like shape in the heart-like space of the facing cupped hands. The hand rhythms of making forms in this position echoes the rhythms of the heart close by.

Asymmetry Form: The mirror symmetry form above also echoes in miniature the two-sided symmetry of our whole body. Following this with an asymmetrical form proves to be an experience of the dominance of one side. As a right handed person, I made the right side higher.

Threefold Form: This exercise emphasizes the specialized shaping power of the two thumbs working together with a middle finger. The making of this threefold form is an experience of single fingers im-pressing, shaping and grasping.

On the Earth: Setting the threefold form on the table is an experience of landing on the ground and being separate from one's creation and the world.

Elongation: Stretching the form downward onto a flattened base is a further coming down to earth.

Foot: Adding this feature at the bottom gives the form a real "footing" and standing on the earth and mirrors the child's own development and soul separation at 9-10.

The sequence of forms is not only a profound encounter with organic archetypal forms and our own hands but also one getting to know our own hands as instruments of the spirit. I highly recommend that they be used in adult education as in the classroom.

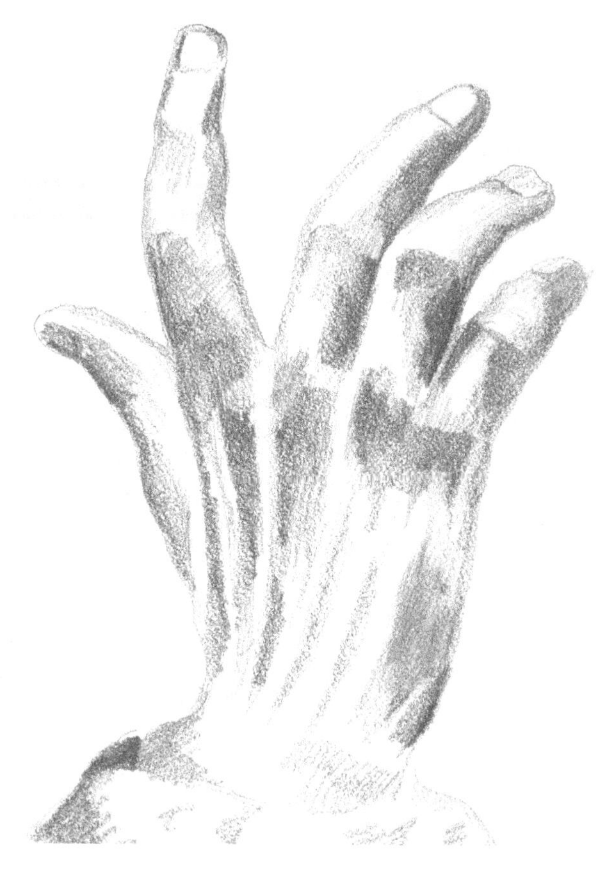

PART II
PONDERING

*Sculpture should always at first sight have some obscurities,
and further meanings. People should want to
go on looking and thinking . . .*
—Henry Moore

Qualities of Form
By Michael Howard

Selections from the Introduction to *Art as Spiritual Activity: Rudolf Steiner's Contribution to the Visual Arts*, Hudson, NY: Anthroposphic Press, 1998, pp. 12-34

The chapters in this Part II Pondering section are intended to enhance an understanding of the significance of the the sculptural forming of matter for developing human beings. With growing awareness of this process, modeling and sculpting activity becomes ever more meaningful, enjoyable, and educative.

What Is Form ?

We see, in Figure 1, a quantity of material substance, in this case, a patch of ink. As a drawing, it fills an area that is more readily measured than its physical weight. However, if this and any of the subsequent drawings we shall be looking at are seen as the silhouette of a quantity of clay, then its weight is also measurable.

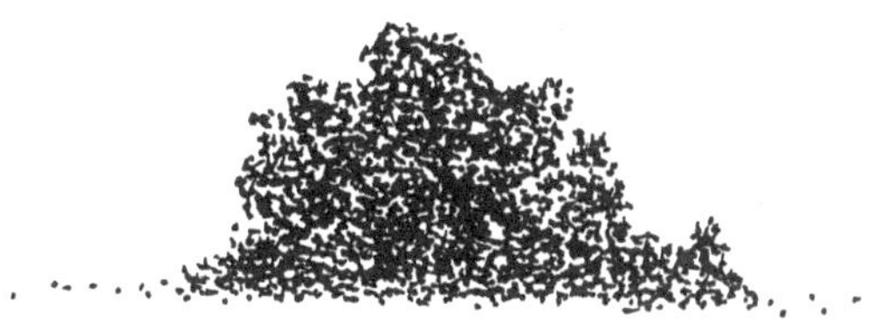

Figure 1: Amorphous mass

In either case, as a two-dimensional drawing or as a three-dimensional sculpture, the quantitative attributes of volume and weight that an object possesses are self-evident to our experience. With every sense impression, we encounter matter but in a diversity of forms. Although form is a commonplace phenomenon, we must be clear about its meaning. For example, does the above patch of ink (Figure 1) have form?

When I put this question to my students, very few doubt that it has form. When asked to justify their claim, they point to the fact that it occupies space, has volume and, in particular, that it has a boundary. If these are the defining attributes of form, then we must agree that such a drawing or sculpture has form.

The Distinction between Form and Matter

However understandable, this commonly held view of form poses a difficulty. It makes no distinction between form and matter, they become one and the same thing. Matter always has volume, occupies space, and at some point ends, thus creating a boundary. Does matter by definition have form, or are there conditions in which matter is without form?

Until recently we could say matter is formless when it exhibits no apparent order or is, in other words, in a state of chaos. Today, chaos is a major subject of scientific research, the fruits of which indicate that order may be found where it had previously eluded our awareness and that our recognizing it may simply depend upon our developing more refined capacities of perception and thinking. The unveiling of such hidden order within apparent chaos, rather than blurring the distinction between form and matter, actually helps clarify it. When we perceive form in a material substance, whether microscopic or macroscopic, an ordering principle may be recognized behind it; conversely, wherever an ordering agent is active, form is created. Form always points back to an ordering principle; an ordering principle always results in form.

With the aid of ever more refined instruments, modern science has been able to recognize ever more subtle manifestations of order within matter itself. We can say that material substances, because of their lawful properties, possess order and, in that sense, inherent form. This is a matter of practical experience for a sculptor when modeling clay in contrast to carving various woods or stones: each material must be worked according to its inherent properties. But no matter how much a sculptor cultivates a sensitivity for the lawful nature of the material, he or she would not equate "the natural form of the material" with "giving form to the material." The driving force for an artist who has a full appreciation for his or her material is to give form where there is none or at least to transform the material from one form into another. In this sense, Figure 1 (especially as a mass of clay) represents the raw, unformed material that awaits our forming activity. In forming matter, however, we enter a world of great mystery. How does matter acquire form? What are the sources of order that give birth to form? [. . .]

The full scope of our inquiry into the nature of form leads us beyond the specialized concerns of sculpture or philosophy, for it touches upon the heart of our common humanity. For example: What is the relationship between sculptural forms and social forms? [. . .]

If we take the view that Figure 1, in spite of its having volume and boundary, is unformed matter, then we can ask, what must happen for it to acquire form?

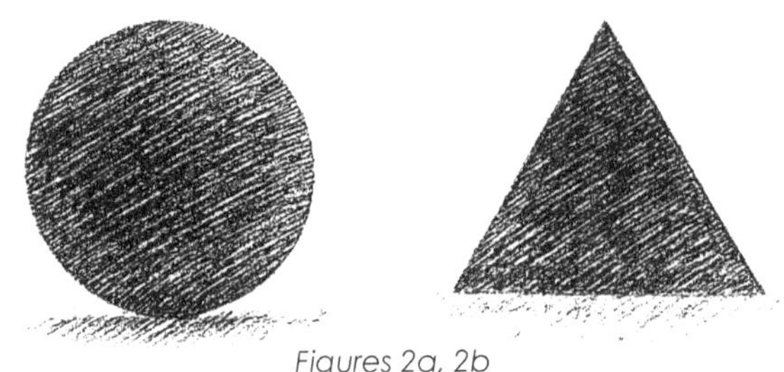

Figures 2a, 2b

In Figure 1, we may have tried to find something recognizable to which we could have given a name—perhaps a face or animal. Even if we did give it a name, we could not claim for certain that the maker of those marks intended such a face or animal. We would have to admit that we might be imposing the idea upon it. When in a playful mood we see something in a cloud, we know we are only projecting our own mental pictures onto the random configuration of the cloud. Similarly, with all natural and manufactured forms we can learn to discern when a concept inherently belongs to it or not.

Formed Matter

With Figure 2, however, we find a significant difference. From the first instant our vision falls on these figures, we can hardly avoid thinking "circle" and "triangle" or, as silhouettes, "ball" and "pyramid." There is no question that they have form; they are quantities of ink or clay organized by an idea. In fact, the material substance is all but forgotten, relative to the power the idea holds over our attention. How do we read an idea from formed matter?

The Elements of Form

Figure 2a is a surface with a particular convex curve that remains constant and thereby returns on itself. In contrast, Figure 2b is a surface with three straight lines, or planes, intersecting as three sharp angles. In addition, Form 2a is widest in the middle, tapering to a single point both at the top and bottom. Form 2b is widest at the very bottom and tapers to a point at the top. Both forms are symmetrical. Particular configurations constitute the various forms:

curved / angular

wide / narrow

symmetry / asymmetry

We make such distinctions so automatically that we are usually unconscious of the process. With familiar forms such as these, we effortlessly and subconsciously search through our field of mental pictures to find the appropriate concept, such as "ball" and "pyramid."

Even the simplest of forms are composed of these more fundamental elements of form. As viewers, we look, however subconsciously, for such elements in order to make sense of what is otherwise a blur of sense impressions. What elements of form are before us? How do they combine to make a form? Is it a familiar form?

No existing natural or manufactured form, nor any possible form yet to be created in the future, can exist outside these form elements. No painting can employ a color outside the spectrum created by the infinite shades and combinations of red, yellow, and blue. We have tremendous, seemingly limitless freedom in the forms and colors we can make, but these are all within a given reality that we did not create.

Form as Idea

The above examples demonstrate that matter is organized into form through the presence of a particular constellation of ideal form elements.

Curvature-angularity, wideness-narrowness, symmetry-asymmetry are some of the ideal elements from which all conceivable forms are composed. They are the alphabet by which the ideal world of ideas expresses itself in natural or human-made forms. The world of ideas, from the simple to the complex, is therefore one source by which matter is organized into a form. But idea, as we normally understand it, is not the only force that orders and gives form to matter.

Like and Dislike

In the presence of every sense phenomenon and, in particular, works of art, we not only think, but also feel. We feel some degree of like or dislike, pleasure or displeasure. If the ball and pyramid illustrated in Figure 2 were presented to us as objects made of the same material, and we were invited to keep only one, how would we choose? Very likely our choice would be based on the relative degree of like or dislike we feel for their respective forms. Such feelings of sympathy (attraction) and antipathy (repulsion) are active not only toward finished forms but also with respect to something we are forming. In this case, we can observe within ourselves the play of like and dislike influencing what we change or keep of our form. This is the most elementary way in which feelings act as an organizing principle to form matter.

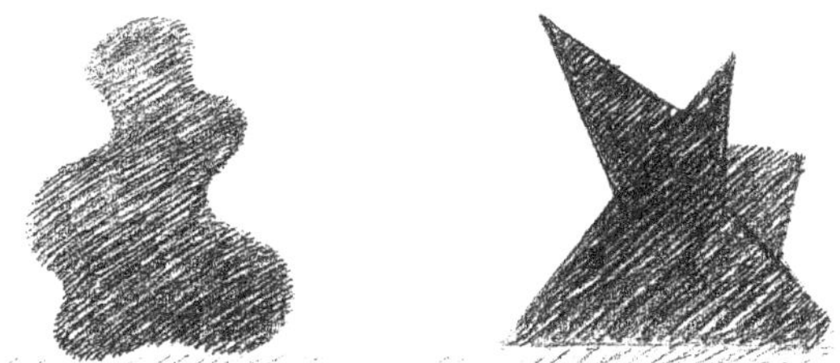

Figures 3a and 3b

With forms such as 3a and 3b, it may not be so easy for us to give them a name as we could with a ball or pyramid, but it is very likely that we feel some sympathy and/or antipathy for them. Some people may be drawn to the curved form; others, the angular. Most of us tend to accept as a given the apparent subjectivity of our feelings.

It is not uncommon for us to identify with our feelings to such a degree that we can feel personally threatened by someone who feels differently. We are inclined to treat our own sympathies and antipathies as objective facts while we often regard the feelings of others as subjective. Sometimes we can be so enamored by the vitality of our feelings that we empower them with primordial significance. At other times, we can feel overwhelmed and wary of feelings just because of their power and intensity. Clearly, feelings are a central aspect of being human.

Likewise, it is generally understood that feelings are a central force in generating works of art; some artists seem to work predominantly out of feelings, while others are more active with ideas. Thoughts and feelings are the ordering principles of forming activity, as intentions, values, sympathies, and antipathies. This has been the case throughout the history of art, but in this century, the quality of thoughts and feelings has assumed particular significance [. . .]

Artistic Perception as Soul-Spirit Perception

Artistic perception is not seership of spiritual realities and beings in the direct and most developed sense. However, the arts are not merely symbolic languages or signposts capable only of pointing to spiritual realities. Artistic perception as described here is an actual, if only elementary, form of soul and spirit perception. Steiner makes it clear that the path of art is not the only way—but a most important one—by which a modern person, fully engaged in the world of the physical senses, can become more self-aware as a being of soul and spirit. Our soul-spirit nature originates in soul and spiritual worlds, as does every facet of physical existence. The physical and spiritual are not two irreconcilable worlds, but complementary realities. We must not think, however, that the physical and spiritual are homogeneous; in order to be clear about their interrelationship, we need greater exactness in distinguishing the one from the other.

Qualities of Form

Let us examine the way artistic perception applies to sculptural form.

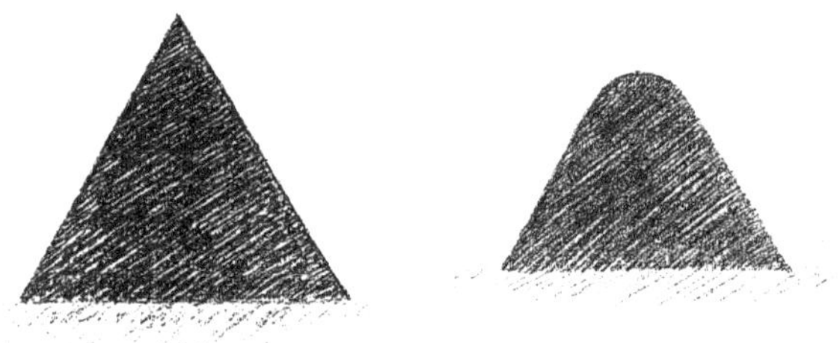

Figures 4a, 4b

In Figure 4a, we have the silhouette of a pyramid or cone, which if we imagine it made of moist clay, can be rounded at the top to produce 4b. The idea of an angular point transformed into a convex curve is the principle that changes the one form into the other. We can also ask, "Does this change in form evoke a corresponding change in our feeling experience?"

If we actually made such a change in the form, it would be unusual if it did not stimulate a corresponding change in our feelings (e.g.,"I liked it the way it was"). If we ask someone who likes the changed form, and another who dislikes it, to explain why, we are likely to get similar explanations from each. The one might say, "I like the relaxing softness I feel from the rounding; the sharp point feels too hard and rigid." The other might say, "I like the strength and wakeful clarity of the pyramid; rounding the point makes it too soft and weak." The two observers might use different words to describe their sympathy or antipathy, but in both cases they speak about a feeling of softening when the point is rounded, in contrast to a hardening when made into a point again.

To speak of a change in form as a change in the quality of softness or hardness is comparable to our description of color as warm or cool. Just as the warmth of a color is not physical, the softening or hardening we refer to has nothing to do with the softness or hardness of the physical clay. The translation of these qualities into like or dislike is our natural and subconscious habit. However, attending to the objective qualities of form or color, at the very least, opens an additional dimension of experience. This new dimension soon enhances our sense of relationship to the rest of the world. Any sense of estrangement we may feel toward nature or other people is largely related to our limited capacity to know the other—including plants, animals, and all natural processes—from within, as if we are the other or the other is ourself.

Moral Qualities

As a young man, Steiner was chief editor of Goethe's writings on natural science. Goethe's work with color and the natural sciences played a major role in the evolution of Steiner's lifelong effort to demonstrate the spiritual foundations of the natural world and human life. Goethe prepared the way for perceiving the spiritual within the physical through a particular method of color observation described in his *Theory of Color*. There he coins the term moral qualities to characterize the objective qualities he experienced in color. Unfortunately, in English the word moral has a different connotation. In Goethe's usage it has nothing to do with good or bad but simply refers to the non-physical and, in that sense, spiritual properties of color (the inner warmth of coolness).

This mode of observation that Goethe and, subsequently, Steiner developed is the same activity I am calling artistic perception, insofar as that observation attends to the "moral" or spiritual qualities of sense phenomena. We shall clarify the "moral" or spiritual qualities of graphic and sculptural forms through the sequence of forms below.

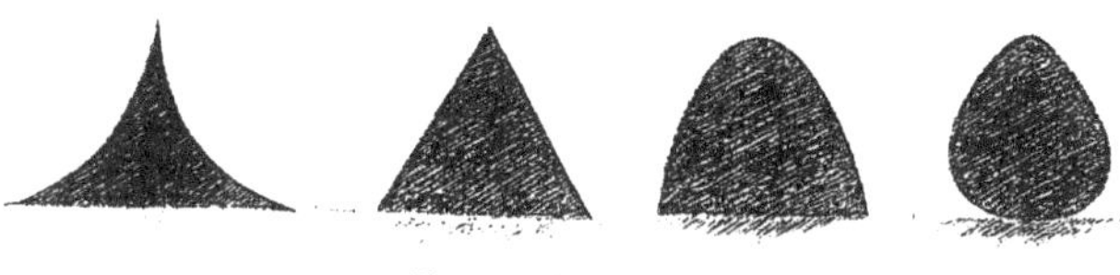

Figures 5a,b, c, d

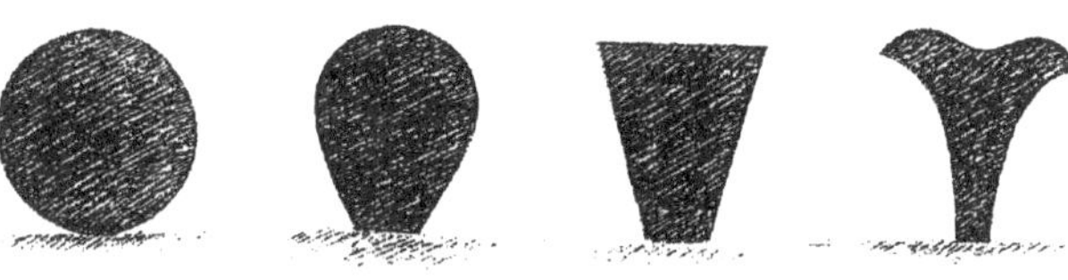

Figures 5e,f, g, h

The Spiritual Qualities of Form

When we first look at the forms in Figure 5, we naturally try to make sense of them by trying to name them. We recognize Figure 5b as the silhouette of a cone or pyramid and 5e as a sphere or ball. Whatever names we give to each of these forms we are able, in addition, to recognize an ordered relationship in the sequence as a whole.

Forms 5a, b, and c are all widest at their bases and narrowest at their tops. Forms 5f, g, and h are the opposite, widest toward their tops and narrowest at their bases. While forms 5c and 5f are quite different as to where they are wide and narrow, both are composed entirely of convex curved surfaces. Likewise, forms 5b and 5g are straight surfaces, and 5a and 5h are concave surfaces. Therefore, the similarities and differences between these forms can be described in relation to five attributes:

1. the distribution of mass—the widest part is at the top, middle, or bottom of the form

2. the surfaces are straight or curved

3. the surfaces are convex or concave

4. all are symmetrical instead of asymmetrical

5. their relative height and width remain equal

Such an analysis of the various elements of these forms is possible through the activity of our thinking. What do we experience when we enter into them with our feeling—feeling which transcends like and dislike?

Let us look at forms 5c, 5d, and 5e. If we begin with the ball, form 5e, imagining it made of moist clay, we can carefully redistribute the clay so as gradually to lower the widest part from the middle toward the bottom until the widest part reaches the base. In this case, 5e is the first form and 5c the final form. Form 5d represents only one of the many forms that would arise through the orderly transition from 5e to 5c. What do we experience through this simple transformation?

Form as Object

First, we experience that forms are not unrelated to each other as our everyday experience of thousands of discrete objects would suggest. We distinguish a car, a tree, and a person largely by their different forms. Because these forms are visible to us through a material substance, we equate form with "objectness"; our experience of form as object leads us to equate form with the static and fixed. Yet, when we make a series of forms all in the same material, such as a lump of clay, we can more easily see that the form is independent of the material; the material is constant while the form changes. The material substance serves to make the nonphysical forms and interrelationships of forms visible to our sense-bound consciousness, but at a price. The material veils the living, dynamic nature of form by making it appear fixed and dead. [. . .]

The forms of Figure 5 are a sculptural equivalent to the spectrum of colors. As with color, this series embodies a spectrum of qualities. Both the individual forms and the series as a whole derive their inherent order from the world of ideas, on the one hand, and the world of qualities, on the other. In this sense, form is a language of ideal qualities,

The Language of Form

This language of form is not symbolic or metaphoric. If we look at the transition from the ball 5e to forms 5d and 5c, we experience something more than a change in ideas. There is a change in our feeling experience. We feel 5d giving in to the weight of gravity, drooping, or sagging. Relative to the ball, it is less buoyant. When the widest part of the form reaches the base as in 5c, there is less buoyancy when compared to 5d. As the widest part moves from the middle toward the ground, there is a sense of succumbing gradually to weight. In 5c we feel this process come to rest. The form may have lost much of its buoyancy, but it has gained stability; it is grounded. With forms such as these, it is natural to associate them with known outer objects.

Figure 5d may remind us of various buds or seeds, 5c of a beehive or gumdrop. However, what is less natural but, ultimately, of greater relevance to the arts, is to ask, "When do we feel like these forms?" At first we may feel uncertain about how to relate to this question, but with time we may recognize qualities in these forms that are familiar to our experience. For example, as a natural part of our daily rhythm, we feel more buoyant and energetic at certain times and more sluggish and heavy at others. Different people experience varying degrees of buoyancy and heaviness. Whatever our individual differences, buoyancy and weight form the parameters of one dimension of our experience. In fact, we must distinguish three different kinds of buoyancy/heaviness. There is the heaviness of eating too much, or gaining body weight. That is different from the heaviness of being tired or sick, as compared to the buoyancy of healthy vitality. Sadness brings with it yet another source of heaviness, contrasted to the buoyancy of joy.

Until this century, when a sculptor wished to create a sculpture expressing inner qualities, such as tranquility or anguish, there was no recourse but to create the external human form in a gesture corresponding to the appropriate inner experience. The simple forms of Figure 5, however, open a new possibility. Now we can create forms with no intended resemblance to any outer form, but that mirror directly the qualities of inner life. As we have seen with color, the elements of form also embody qualities belonging to our inner life. *The dynamic language of form is the language of the human spirit…*

Sculpture as Formative Forces Made Visible

In regard to the visual arts, Steiner suggests we cannot fully understand their potential in human life as long as we perceive them to be merely outer physical mediums. Steiner speaks of the relationship of art to the spiritual, not in general, but in quite specific ways. For example, if we return to sculpture, it is possible to consider that the material substance of the clay is only one of two realities—the form being the second reality. The form of a sculpture is made visible to our senses and our consciousness through the material substance. The distinction we have made between the form of a sculpture and its material substance Steiner attributes to two separate realities. The material substance of a sculpture belongs to physical reality; the qualities of its form belong to the world of etheric formative forces. The etheric is the world of softening, expanding, buoy-ing-up that counteracts the hardening, contracting, and weighing down tendency of the purely physical. These are the forces that organize and, thereby, give form to matter. Both natural (living) forms and sculptural forms are nothing less than etheric formative forces made visible through the material substance they penetrate and, thereby, organize.

For sculptors, the outer form of a human being must be the result of cosmic forces and inner forces. [. . .] Visual artists are steered away from imitating the physical human form, which in itself is only an imitation of the body of formative forces. [. . .]

What we are shaping is the ether body; we are filling it out only with matter, so to speak.

When we develop the right feeling for beauty, this means that we are properly fitted to our etheric body, the body of formative forces. [. . .] However, we cannot be human beings in the true sense of the word if we have no feeling for beauty, because to have a sense of beauty is to awaken to the etheric body. To have no sense of beauty is to disregard, or remain asleep to, the etheric body.

The Language of Form

From Round to Pointed in Nature

When we look at the shape of a thriving maple tree in midsummer, it appears clothed in a green mantle of burgeoning life. Its boughs have the gesture of a rounded green wholeness billowing upwards, a living fullness nourished by rising juice.

Seeing the same tree months later in mid-winter, we are struck by its separate exposed branches spiking starkly outwards like frozen rays. The tree stands naked in the cold air, creaking stiffly as if in a rigor mortis.

Picking a fresh apple in summer and holding it in our hand, we feel its roundness and living juices bursting beneath its skin. One bite confirms what we sense, as fluid squirts into our mouth and out onto our lips. With a knife we cut the apple not in the usual way from stem to bottom but from side to side—the Waldorf way!—to reveal a pointed star in the middle. What mystery is this? Five spiked rays surrounded by all that juicy flesh and life? Furthermore, the little inedible star in the middle is husk-like with its hollow air spaces filled with little dark, stone-like seeds (which have arsenic in them!).

What is Mother Nature trying to tell us with this contrast of rounded life-filled "juicy-ness" and hollow, "death-like" spiky-ness? We look further at other things in nature:

- The daffodil begins in the earth as a juicy roundness and ends in petal-pointed star. So many plants end in flower stars. And some have luscious round leaves low down on the stem but as leaves spiral up the stem they become more pointed and simplified, especially at the top.

- The fresh green rounded cone oozes resin at the top of the pine. Later it ripens, open to the air and dries out into a spiral sequence of woody, pointed petals. (Cut a dried cone across and see).

- A juicy round tree trunk is sawed cleanly and smoothly across; its round stump dries out and cracks: a star opens up in the middle to the air.

- A tree trunk is sawed cleanly and smoothly across; its round stump dries out and cracks: a star opens up in the middle to the air.

- The human being begins as an ovum sphere but then as a first grader can stretch out wide into a five- pointed star!

Nature is communicating one of her "open secrets" to us in her tendencies. What language is this?

Nature's Language of Convex and Concave: Bulging and Hollowing

Given the complexity of organic forms in Nature, how do we begin to "read" her language, gestures and tendencies? Here are some thoughts and observations to explore and ponder:

Convex forms in organisms often appear to be the result of life growing and expanding from within outwards and sustained by water and liquids. Etheric forces are responsible for growing, bulging, burgeoning life and follow the streaming of fluids. Examples:

- Water, bearer of life, although it selflessly takes on all kinds of shapes, above all, to form in round raindrops and rounded waves.

- The round belly of the expectant mother is filled with a roundly compacted baby inside a round world of living waters ready to burst forth. The baby is born pink with life and with round chubby head, cheeks, belly arms and legs. She loves the rounded breast.

- Outside in mother nature there are round buds, fruits, berries, beaver houses, the back of the hand, human backs and bottoms, the earth, life-giving sun, all rounded forms.

Concave forms often appear to be related to the opposite. They result from processes of dying, aging, hollowing out, contracting, wilting, wrinkling, drying out, with air flowing into these concavities. Forces from outside predominate and penetrate and wear out the waning life forces of an organism. A tree lives out its life cycle and starts to die; air-filled hollows appear as woodpeckers and ants and fungi take their toll. Soul-astral forces live in the air and breath and carry sentience and consciousness into an organism. In human beings, increasing awareness and worry over the course of life wears us out: a round convex cheeked baby becomes a wrinkled elderly lady with concave hollowed cheeks. Other examples:

- hollows in a dying ant-infested tree pecked by woodpeckers

- the inside of a wilting, curling leaf

- the craters of the moon

- eye and nose sockets of a skull, outer

ears, etc.

Flatness and straightness are characteristic in nature of mineralized forms in which life forces are diminished or absent. Examples: crystals, rock layers, porcupine's spines, narwhale's tusk, cactus spines, thistle needles, etc.

Quotations from Dr. Armin Husemann's *Harmony of the Human Body* (Floris Books, 2003)

Husemann co-relates convex with the life etheric body and concave forms with the soul astral body:

- "The generative processes [of the etheric body] in the infant create the convex forms of the head, the cheeks, the back of the hands and the feet. In mid-life these shapes have stretched and in old age concave surfaces and wrinkle lines dominate…as the expression of degenerative forces [of the astral body]. The influence of increasingly concave surfaces from infancy to old age [happens] through the influence of the sensory and nervous systems." (20)

- "The length of time that we stay awake… increases in the course of our life…The sculptural transformation of the body becomes linked with the growing length of time that we remain awake during life: increasing sensory and nervous activity [created by the astral body] promotes the degenerative processes which gradually turn the convex forms [of our bodies] into concave ones. " (18)

- "Extension is the activity of the etheric body in the finished physical body which is the equivalent to the expansion it promoted during growth. [Example of extension: stretching out the fingers.] Flexing and bending are associated with contraction and the hollowing process caused by the astral body." (30)

- On Respiration (35), Husemann quotes Steiner: "We breath in with the astral body and we expel the air with the etheric body." (CW 283, The Inner Nature of Music)

On the in-breath our astral body, bearer of consciousness, presses into our inner space (concavity) and en-souls us. Our out-breath presses outward, the convex gesture of the etheric body. Anatomically, however, this may seem the opposite since inhaling expands our thorax and exhaling makes it contract.

Quotations from Michael Martin's *Living with Forms in Art and Nature (Mit Formen Leben in Kunst und Natur)*

Artist Michael Martin also "reads" roundness in nature as an expression of life forces, and-hollowness, of soul forces which create inner space, and harmony as a signature of the "I":

- "What are the formative forces? Those forces that create out of roundness stand closest to our experience; these are the etheric forces, which we know as growth forces in the plant. They unite everywhere with the element of that which is watery and streaming, flowing continually, shaping rhythmically. Things that resist these forces in running water [such as river stones] are transformed into round, convex forms… The archetypal manifestation of the spherical tendency when it comes to rest is the raindrop. (54, translations by A.A.)

- "The drying air consumes all growth. The air is creative in the hollowing out of substance, opening forms to space, and creating inner spaces. Through this

kind of formative force there arises the [concave, cup-like] blossom of plants. This force shapes a multitude of different hollow, concave forms." (55)

- "The sphere is the fundamental form into which the soul works, hollowing it out. The soul presses into and consumes the round form. The cause of this lies in the capacity of the soul to carry waking consciousness in the human being. Consciousness destroys the life forces of the etheric. The result is tiredness. If our day consciousness went on and on [uninterrupted by sleep], our physical health would degenerate." (56)

- "Round, convex forms are relatively easy to "read' in nature…It is more difficult to discern the [soul astral] forces shaping hollow, concave forms because they work from the periphery and produce a whole range of very different forms such as the star-like flower blossom cup (calyx), the dried out cones of conifers…; In animals and in humans they conceal themselves in the concave, pocket forms of organs. Still more challenging…is the human form as expression of the spirit I…We find the 'I' revealed not in any one form but in a harmony of forms…" (65)

Michael Martin has created a graphic series from circle to star below to help us "read" the transformation of convex to concave in nature. (19)

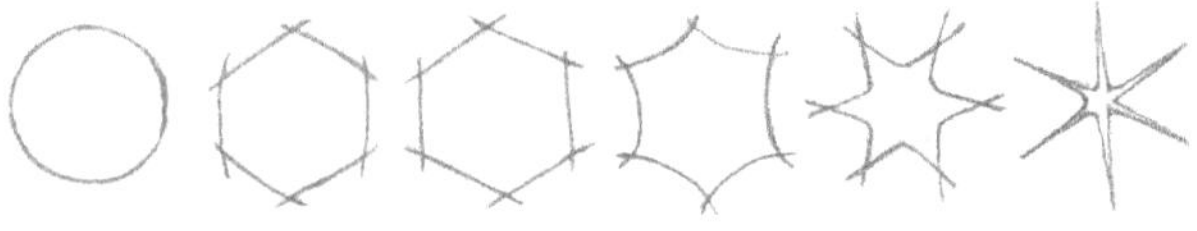

In his lectures on architectural forms (*Ways to a New Style of Architecture*, Lecture 3, London: RSP 1999, p.102), Steiner gave a related and simpler geometric depiction of the qualitative differences of inner and outer working forces. The middle form below has the soft, round quality of life-etheric forces of growth; the sharp form on the right, of hardening, dying, sclerotizing.

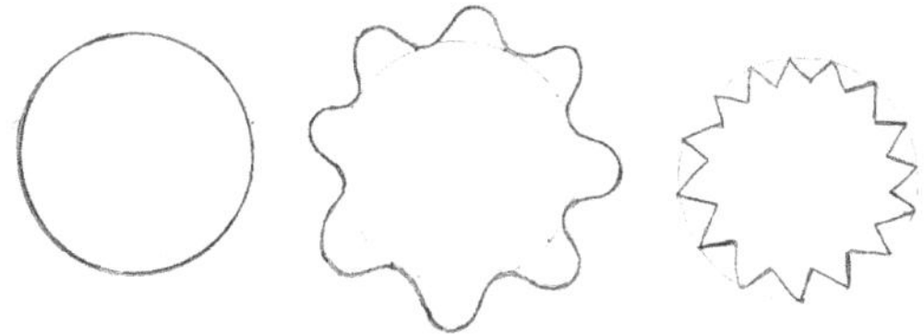

From Circle to Star

Imagine Michael Martin's two-dimensional diagram above as a three-dimensional form with round, flat and concave surfaces. The description below is my "reading" and interpretation of the form language I see playing out this transformational sequence.

Form #1. The sphere is full of life pressing outward into one continuous surface—or an infinity of sides?

#2. From all sides of the surroundings influences start to press in upon the sphere and counter its curving extension outward. Multiple, separately demarcated surfaces appear as blunted sides and "soft" corners. The form still has the quality of roundness; its inner forces are still stronger than the outside pressures.

#3. Outside pressures become equal to the life forces pressing outward, resulting in straight, flat sides and a very different, mineral-like quality.

#4. Outside influences are now so great that the form's whole surface consists of growing concavities with sharpening angular edges and points. Air is intruding into these hollows.

#5. Outside pressures penetrate very deeply and create a star-like figure.

#6. Extreme pressures have completely overwhelmed the original form's fullness of life and transformed it finally into an angular figure of pointed rays.

The life-filled sphere has gradually been changed into a radiant star. As they ripen and age, life forms become "star-ified" or "astralized"– penetrated by astral forces. "Astral body" means literally "star body, " carrier of forces from the periphery of the heavens. Imagining and studying this progression of forms can help to illuminate not only convex, flat and concave phenomena but also how in the process points and spikes, edges and lines arise at the same time. Also, you can use both the two-dimensional diagram as well as your three-dimensional imagination to help "read" forms in different ways. For example, when I see a dried curled leaf lying on the ground on its side, what may strike me first two-dimensionally is its curve into a C-form. When I take it up into my hand as a three-dimensional fullness, I see what appeared as a C- curve from the side is actually a narrow concave space and curved surface.

> *"To feel… a circle in a plane or a sphere in space is to feel the self, the ego… When even….a fragment of a sphere (Kugelschale) rouses in him a sense of independence in his own self, then he is learning to live in forms."*
>
> —*Rudolf Steiner*, Architecture as Synthesis of the Arts

The Sphere (*Die Kugel*)

Michael Martin's description provides us with a wonderful "meditation on a sphere":

"…Our hands are not formed out of flat surfaces. Indeed, on our entire body we do not find one single straight surface… If we want to choose and work on a form that corresponds to the quality of our human form, it must be round. When we behold the inside surfaces of our hands…[we see] that together they form a round bowl and lend themselves most naturally to forming a sphere out of clay!

"It is exciting to experience how the sphere arises out of unformed material within the form of our two hand surfaces. We continually turn the emerging form in their hollows; with careful touching we finely sense any irregular spots on the sphere's surface. And how odd: our eyes cannot immediately participate, because the hands conceal the clay in the process of sensitively surrounding it. Only after shaping the sphere for a time can we observe it at a distance and check if it has become uniformly round [and smooth]. The eye itself is a sphere and can perceive imperfections missed by the hands…

"And we can contemplate this unusual thought: what would happen to our sphere if it became the size of the sphere of the earth: its surface would appear as a straight plane losing its round, curved look…[Or contemplate the thought] that every sphere has one stable, resting point at its center whereas, in contrast, there are countless points running all over its one borderless (*grenzlose*) outer surface. While we entertain such thoughts, the clay sphere has become warm through and through and now has a dry skin. The sphere is completed!

"But how should we put such a form down? It has no base, no up, no right or left? Its sole relationship to space is 'inner' and 'outer.' Are spheres in some sense strangers on the earth in contrast to other objects that have a clear up and down? We come to the conclusion: a sphere has to float in space and continually move and circle around to be true to the nature of its form. That is what the planets and their moons do along their paths in the universe. And then the thought occurs to us that our hands with the mediating experience of the sphere also have a definite relationship to the cosmos, The clay

which has assisted us in having this encounter is merely the eroded product of feldspar stone that once lay in the earth. [With these thoughts in mind], let us feel united with heaven and earth through the form of the sphere…

"However, we are curious to see if spherical formations only belong to the cosmos or if they are be found on earth…Spider eggs are nearly exact spheres…there are many other egg forms…that are closely related to the sphere form: insects, salamanders, reptiles, fish, birds. Mammals and humans carry egg cells out of which spherical embryos develop. In plants we find the sphere in modified form in buds, fruits, seedpods, and blossom shapes.

"All these forms have in common is that they occur where germs of life (*Lebenskeime*) are preparing themselves to enter into the light of the world one day. They are forms in a resting state with their forces turned inward. Therefore, they require the protective sheath of the spherical. Actively creative within, their forces reveal themselves streaming in the watery element. This element brings forth in all fluids round, bubble-like forms and then dissolves them…

"The primal form of these living forces appears in the raindrop which is filled inside with rhythmical, never-resting movement. We again arrive at the sphere form that we started with…

"On the one hand, we behold the connection of forms of life with the form of the sphere. On the other hand, we see how the spherical form is not of this earth and does not fit into its three dimensions of space. This raises questions: Do the primary forces of life originate on earth? Or is the real source of life on earth to be sought in the realm of the sun, moon and planets?" (9-11)

Circle of Forms and Form Progressions

Artist and researcher Peter Elsner has wonderfully captured the world and language of form in his sumptuously illustrated book *Metamorphosis in Nature and Art: The Dynamic of Form in Plants, Animals and Human Beings (2010)*. This work charts "*an artistic path of practice for the development of morphological awareness.*" Elsner's lively, poetic descriptions help the reader to live into the fundamental form principles of art and nature:

Threefoldness: "In both nature and culture we encounter an endless variety of forms… All the different forms arise and are composed of three aspects, a trinity. These form elements are the convex, the level plane (*Ebene*) and concave." (26)

Polarity: "We find . . . polarity in the form circle. The convex surfaces work from within outward. Filled with substance, the convex form has a swelling, pushing, pressing gesture. The concave recedes from us, creating space. Here interior space is formed. In the form circle, the in-drawing and out-flowing formative forces stand in opposition." (38)

Convex: "The convex form arches toward us and makes an impression on us. A space composed of convex, arched surfaces, seems to be trying to overwhelm or even crush us. Convex sculptural forms have a germinal, seed-like and growing quality: they are filled with substance and work out strongly into their surroundings. Here we encounter soft substantiality, with little form. Convex shapes have a dreaming, sleeping quality." (27)

Level plane (flat, straight): "Where the level plane appears in several intersecting surfaces in a sculpture, a sharp edge arises at the intersections which, as form quality, has an attacking, wakening effect on the observer. The forms make a clear and ordered impression, their character is crystalline and they strike us as colder than does the convex form quality. Immovability and rigidity can emanate from forms configured from a level plane. On the other hand, if we stand in a very level, flat landscape, or gaze upon the calm surface of the sea, we gain a sense of great breadth, and a feeling of endlessness arises in our soul." (27)

Concave: "The concave form is the polarity to the convex, What pushes outward in the convex here delves inward. The concave absorbs and sucks in; it forms interior space and envelops or encompasses. Here too a sharp edge arises where several concave forms intersect. The sharp edges that arise mean the concave form has a strongly formative character in contrast to the more 'fleshed out' and formic nature of the convex. We can compare the concave to an experience of wide, empty space, just; the convex relates to space filled with substance. The empty, wide landscape of the far north can be intimidating and give us a sense of forsakenness. This feeling is intensified by the idea of an infinite expanse of cosmic space."

In Nature: "If we go to the equator we can find landscape forms there that have a strongly up-building or substance-forming character. In the burgeoning plant realm of the rainforest we meet this sprawling exuberant, growth-force principle. Toward the poles, the globe shows more of the space-forming principle, while toward the equator the substance-forming principle comes to the fore. In season cycles too, we encounter this phenomenon: the world strikes us as cold and empty in winter, as warm and full in summer. In fact the whole earthly and cosmic world reveals these primal polar principles of space and substance.

"In the natural world, convex and level plane surfaces can be more frequently seen than concave surfaces. The concave often appears in organic nature as space filled with substance —for instance in the human eye embedded in its orbit in the skull. In the pelvis and thorax we find similar examples of cavities filled with substance. Plant fruits are in this sense also filled 'bowls' while the new seeds develop. We more often find empty cavities when the organism dies, when they become visible to us. A walnut shell, an empty snail shell, a sea urchin shell, a cow's skull—all are spaces which life on filled and from which it has departed." (28)

Art is research.
—Peter Elsner

In a simple illustration, Elsner shows the primal geometrical script of the three sculptural gestures transforming into each other.

Form development between the full sphere and the hollow sphere (after Elsner).

"If convex, flat plane (*Ebene*) and concave are brought into a process of transformation,we obtain the developmental series which passes from the most extreme convex quality—the solid sphere—in stages to the level plane and from there to arrive eventually at the universal manifestation of the concave, the hollow sphere. Convex becomes level plane and level plane becomes concave. Modeled forms . . . connect with each other in a continuous movement from one pole to the other."(32)

In a photograph, he presents the same progression actualized artistically in clay models.

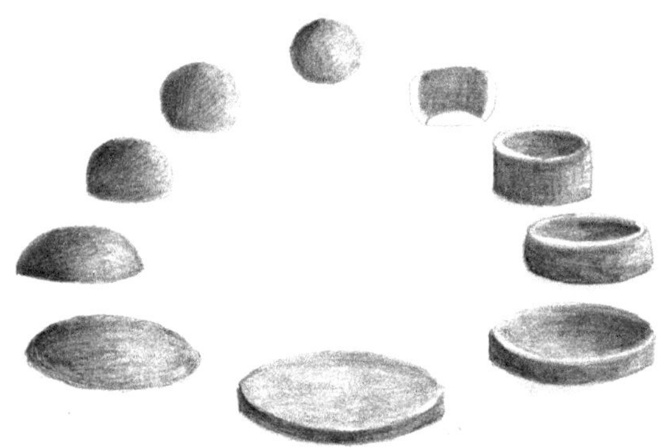

Form Circle Exercise in Clay: Convexity to flattening to concavity (after an Elsner photo)

Elsner illustrates a marvelous "form circle" (*Formenkreis*) of 12 sculptural sequences. Forms radiate out and differentiate in a progression from convexity to concavity.

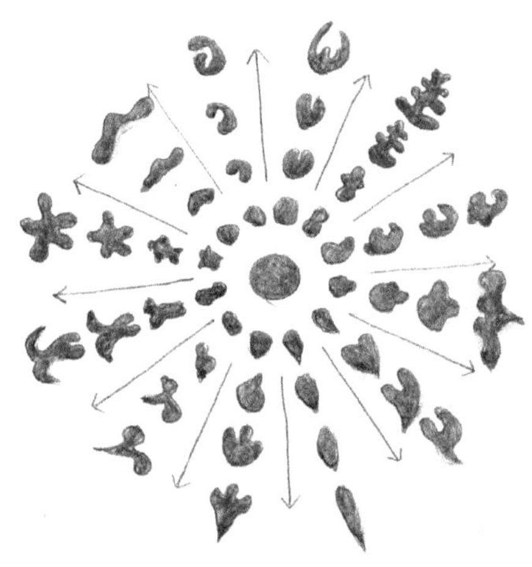

Circle of Form: From the Universal to the Particular (after Elsner)

Elsner includes numerous photos and descriptions of modeling exercises and sculptural works. He makes visible the living dynamics of a rich multiplicity of changing forms in a treasure trove of inspirations.

Into the Heart of Nature's Creative Dynamics

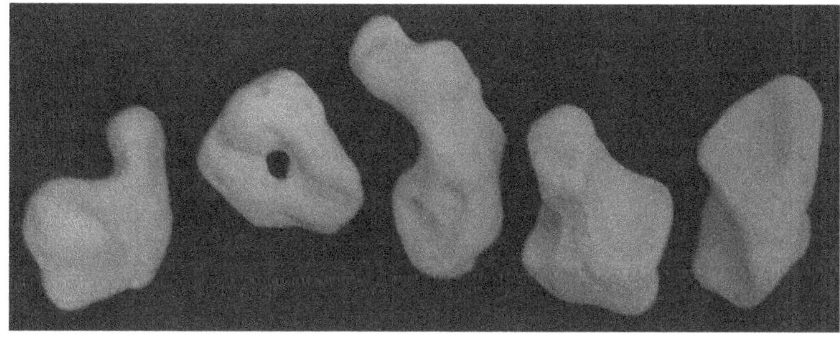

There are many more form-blind people than there are color blind.
—Henry Moore

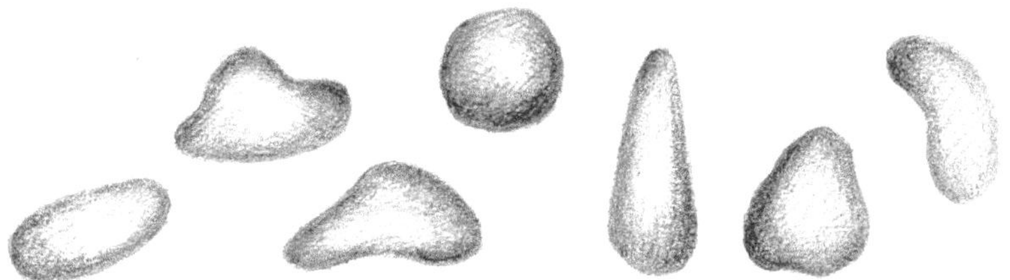

Why Model Pure Forms?

The practice of shaping pure "non-representational" forms enables children as well as adults to experience more fully what is actually going on dynamically in the on-going creation of the universe. Through Pure Form modeling we come to encounter and learn nature's fundamental and underlying language and alphabet of forms. We participate more deeply and perceptively in how Nature herself uses form processes and patterns to make the objects around us.

In observing the sea-washed stones above or an animal horn or whirlpool, for example, the attention of children, who have been active in creating many types of pure spiral forms, will naturally 'reach into" and connect with the spiraling action that forms such objects. This enhanced and active perception does not stop short at noticing the static conceptual structure alone, but it "slips into" and "grasps from within" the living movement and form-making processes that lead to a particular final shape. The moving process itself of hands-on, heart-warming engagement teaches the mind's eye to visualize changing stages of form as a living, dynamic process over time. This capacity of objective imagination is valuable for science as well as art and life!

Playful Explorations

For children (and adults!), to playfully discover "pure," non-representational forms in the hollows of their hands is a wonderful process and experience. They need not always model and represent specific "things" from the world. Students benefit immensely from learning to explore and "read" the whole new language of pure universal forms arising out of movements into roundness, concavity, flatness, angularity, etc. The infinite plasticity and space-creating motions of our miraculous human hands allow us to find and fashion all kinds of three-dimensional geometries and topologies. As organs of gesture and movement, our hands are supremely organized and attuned to the gestures and movements of nature.

When exercised regularly, such sculptural explorations profoundly educate the sense and feeling for form and its different qualities, especially in children in the very formative years. Children have the ability to imaginatively and directly experience them with fresh and open senses. Such experiences lay down fundamental capacities and neurophysiological dispositions for later life and connect the human being to the world as a rich energy source. Childhood and adolescence are a window of opportunity and "sensitive moment" for developing critical form-sensing faculties by enhancing particularly the senses of touch, movement, balance, life, and the co-ordination of sight-hand.

When we form something through artistic activity, we are formed and changed in the process and that spurs the developmental process.

—Henry Schaefer-Simmern, psychologist and therapist

Gesture and Dynamic Forming

As Wordsworth pointed out, children come "trailing glory" out of another dimension and arrive on earth full of spirit, wonder and readiness for *action*. Through inter*active* movement, they discover the forms of the world and learn to discern their meaningful gestures. Nature herself evolves through constant, pattern-making motion. Each of her forms is imbued with the movement that led to its creation and is inscribed in the signature of its gesture.

Ultimately, children as action beings take great joy in the ever-changing form making process and less in the aspect of producing and "having" a finalized piece of sculpture. Deciding when to stop modeling a piece is not always easy for children who may want to stay absorbed in the stream of action. Settling on a "final form" is an exercise of discipline that has to be learned along with a maturing aesthetic judgment—when to step back and behold what has been built up. An "end" product is movement frozen in time—movement that could have continued ad infinitum. Meaningful movement as gesture is captured in three-dimensional form just as in drawing it is made visible in two dimensions.

Modeling as a Primary Sense Experience

Touching and moving our hands in transforming and molding earth materials into new forms is one of the oldest human activities and at the foundation of creative human experience. We shape the world's materials and objects around us continually.

The main physical connections of most human beings to reality are through the senses of sight (light and color), self-movement, touch and hearing. In addition to hearing, the blind use, instead of sight, what is called haptic perception or *"moving touching"* to perceive forms. Touch is only the "boundary sensor" by which we know our body's limit and that there are other "out there beyond" ourselves that also have boundaries also. To know the shape of things, the blind, or blindfolded, need to add the sense of self-movement. Such "haptic perception" combines touching and exploratory hand/finger movements over surfaces and often holding an entire object in the hand. With this combination, people are able to sense the shape of objects without using their eyes. Children love to be blindfolded and guess the names of objects!

Our so-called "sense of form" therefore is mainly a combination of two to three senses working together: touch/movement or sight/eye movement (visual touching!) or sight/touch/movement. (See next chapter on *Enlivening the Senses* and the "haptic sense.)

The Waldorf Approach

To enliven the senses, Rudolf Steiner, the Austrian educator and inaugurator of the worldwide Waldorf education movement, intended hands-on sculptural modeling to be one of the three main artistic pillars of a visual arts curriculum along with drawing and painting. Furthermore, he purposely wanted young children to start creating *pure forms* in drawing as well as in modeling. This pure geometric form-making was to educate their primary "form feeling" and "form sense" in preparation for observing and experiencing more deeply and accurately how Nature herself uses form processes and patterns in the creation of the universe.

In the process of discovering new configurations of shape, children become aware of the transforming capabilities of their own *"spirit-permeated"* hands. Using the hands in modeling means not only that the eyes are guiding and assisting the hands, but also that the hands are teaching the eyes to really look actively into the world. The hands are organs of our will to action. They are our "doers" who transform the world. By working in mutual cooperation with the eyes the hands bring will power into our eyes and change passive seeing into a real looking at things and observing them properly.

Unmediated by brush, crayon, or other utensil, the primal human activity of modeling engages the whole hand and both hands working together and directly sensing and feeling the clay of the good earth. In so doing, it engages the whole child. Sculptural modeling as a "direct contact" art has a wonderful harmonizing effect on children—and grown-ups!

Today's students are calling out for the excitement and anticipation of exploring *new* forms and the deep and formative "hands-on" experiences that the art of sculptural modeling with clay uniquely pro-vides. They long to freely exercise the intel-ligence of their hands in earthly substance, to feel its challenging resistance and to see what emerges anew each time. Exerting their so-called "will-intelligence" (volitional) releases new energy and naturally charges the learning process with emotion and life. Exercising this magical fusion of feeling and will– a "feeling-will" –builds and promotes real and whole intelligence. More than ever before, our young people are showing us that they wish to be whole human beings of hand, heart and head. They do not just want to think ideas but feel and act on new ones!

En-*Live*-ning Our Senses:
A Mission of Modeling

This chapter assembles various perspectives and resources on modeling as an important means to develop healthy senses.

Being healthily connected with fully developed senses to nature and other human beings can mean that not only knowledge but also the world's abundant energy flows back into us and strengthens our body, soul and spirit.

Summary of this Chapter

Modeling as a primal human activity:

- Enlivens our senses, especially our four "foundational" ones.
- Activates and ensouls the seven life processes of our life body.
- Develops plasticity of mind, brain, and hand, a critical trait of the human spirit.
- Strengthens the will to be active and curious in life, to explore and discover.
- Builds and strengthens observational skills.
- "Bloodifies" and literally brings life to the learning process.
- Stimulates metabolism, blood circulation and warmth in which is seated our humanness and spirit-ego.
- Makes children more peaceful and their cheeks ruddy.
- Contributes to confidence in space and a sense of self and self-esteem.
- Provides a healthy balance to the artificial digital environment.
- Entails a whole-hand workout, i.e. holding fully a piece of the world, not just picking at it with fingers or brush or pencil.
- Involves articulate hand movements which translate into articulate speech and flexible thinking.
- Promotes healthy work habits that have an influence on and carry over to other situations and subject lessons.
- Helps develop the foundational senses of touch, life, movement and balance so that they metamorphose into higher senses for attentive listening, language and concept comprehension, and the social perception of others as individuals.
- Fosters in students a sense of the teacher's and parent's authority and thereby a child's "teachability."
- Develops the sense of judgment (aesthetic, moral and scientific).
- Brings us "in touch" with reality and ourselves.
- Brings balance into a civilization dominated by the eye.
- Reverses the historical evolution toward the devitalization of the senses and dry intellectualism.
- Preserves and restores the liveliness and freshness of sense perception which in young children is still saturated with life processes.
- Educates imag-ination (image-making), inspiration, and intuition
- Fosters a sense of beauty, truthfulness and goodness.
- Reconciles the age-old tension between Plato's eye and Aristotle's touch.

Modeling Enlivens Our Senses

In a chapter in my first sourcebook, I examine modeling from the perspective of each of the twelve senses identified by Steiner. (Today science has identified at least ten senses.)

Modeling, the quintessential direct-touch contact activity, turns out to be the great educator and vitalizer of most of the twelve, especially of what Steiner describes as our four foundational "body" or "will" senses: touch, life (wellness), self-movement, and balance. As Waldorf educator Aeppli points out:

> "All the four will-senses are wonderfully enlivened through modeling… [T]he significance of the sense of sight recedes greatly. It is indeed an excellent exercise to model without looking…The sense of touch is then all the more active…[W]ith our sense of movement we perceive all these surfaces, contours and angles…The plastic forms must be weighed up, balance must be constantly established in an artistic way, even if we do not strive for symmetry in a schematic way. A plastic work of art must have an inner balance, for only then does it grant to us, when looking at it, security and inner satisfaction. All plastic art is a creating, a working in an organic way, similar to the mode of working of the 'Urpflanze' [archetypal plant] in the spirit of Goethe. For this reason the sense of life also participates intensely in every plastic activity." (Aeppli, *The Care and Development of the Senses*, 52.)

The Seven Life Processes of the Etheric Body Pulse Through and Enliven the Senses

Steiner found that modeling as a gestalt-making art activates very strongly the life-etheric body because life itself is a sculptural modeler and consists of sculptural forces. Modeling thereby brings into play the etheric body's *life processes*, seven functions which pulse through the senses as a *breathing, warming, digesting, secreting, maintaining, growing, and generating*. These processes not only enliven each sense but also, interestingly, each relates to the modeling process itself in a special way: the rhythm of the shaping process corresponds to *breathing;* its energy-activating nature, to *warming,* building up a form to *nourishing,* its taking away to *secreting.* Finally, the last three coincide nicely: *maintaining* a form, *growing* a form, and *generating* a form —all kindred processes.

Through a *living* form of education as an art, the life processes can be *ensouled* just as the senses can be *vitalized.* Dr. Karl König summarizes,

> "[Rudolf Steiner]…has described how, if the sensory processes are only slightly enlivened and the life processes slightly ensouled, the result is aesthetic creation and aesthetic appreciation." (König, *A Living Physiology*, 94. See also Steiner's, *The Riddle of Humanity*, CW 170.)

Modeling as a Quintessential Activity of the Human Spirit-Ego Activating the Senses and Life Processes

In modeling, many factors synergistically converge to make it one of the most transformative and deep-reaching human activities:

- According to Steiner, our limbs, particularly our hands with their special flexible shape and plasticity, are the most uniquely human and spiritual part of us and a direct expression of the incarnating I Am, the human I-being, the ego, last member of our make-up to arrive in evolution. The plasticity of our hands, brains and minds and that of earth clay go beautifully together to bring form into matter.

- The plastic brain itself looks like clay.

- Our limbs as organs of the human spirit make up our motoric organism, which is one half of what Steiner calls our *"will-organization."*

- The other half is our metabolic organization which physiologically nourishes and energizes our will activity. Like the hands, our metabolism creatively re-shapes matter (breaks down nature's food, builds up our human form).

- The metabolic and motoric functions join and work in tandem to form the anatomical foundation of our will, our *"metabolic-limb system."* (Steiner's threefold model of the human being also includes a head-centered nerve-sense system and a chest-rhythmic middle system).

- Modeling with our hands significantly invigorates the "metabolic-limb" activity of the hands, arms and muscle systems connecting into the torso. It intensively stimulates blood circulation (warming) not only through muscles (self-movement proprioceptive sensors) and skin sensors (touch), but in fact throughout the ecosystem of our entire body.

- Our warm activated life-blood carries etheric-life sun energies from our metabolism through our heart into our hands (life sense).

- Our ego is strongly present in the warmth forces of the blood (temperature sense). The will activity of the ego in fact generates warmth which is at the core of being human.

- Our ego also manifests itself in the constant motoric balancing of our bilateral hands cooperatively shaping matter in a dynamic sculptural space between them (balance sense). The ego loves to live in the forces in this space "between."

- This balancing of hands and arms is intimately connected to our ego's holding us upright and in balance on a larger scale in the directions of space–up/down, right/left, and front/back. Modeling works on a small scale with these same directions expressed in the sides of every piece of sculpture. It strengthens our sense of being in space and gravity/levity which is part of our balance sense.

- The sense of balance (space, gravity-levity) also gives us a strong awareness of being in a physical body with its particular form. König describes this relationship: *"The sense of space opens the experience of the three directions of space for the human soul…In this way the soul experiences the* **gestalt, the form** *of its body."* (König, 2006, 247)

- When we model a sculptural gestalt, a form "out there" in front of us, we are artistically using and projecting our overall "in-our-body sense" and strengthening it along with our ego sense, uprightness, and confidence in space.

> *When we form something through artistic activity, we are formed and changed in the process and that spurs the developmental process.*
>
> —Henry Schaefer-Simmern

Bloodifying Learning: Hella Loewe's Pioneering Research and Work with Children

In short, one could say that modeling is an ideal activity for "bloodifying" (*verblüten*) and literally bringing life-blood to the learning process. Class teacher and researcher Hella Loewe found regular evidence of such an effect after each weekly clay modeling session when she saw *"with pleasure how my [early elementary grade] children developed healthy, ruddy cheeks; even the delicate, pale ones appeared rosy and stimulated."* (Loewe, 2000, "Modeling in the Early Grades: An Action Research Project Report on Classroom Practice," *Bund Lehrerrundbrief* Nr.70, A.A. translation, 96).

She also observed that modeling with an earthen medium was an organic means to educate the senses and enliven the life processes of her students. This activity brought an absorbing, calming element to her initially restless and aggressive urban students. It provided a balance to the overstimulation many experienced due to the influences of modern family life situations, and the considerable influences of the inorganic environment all around them, particularly the electronic media.

I recommend Hella Loewe's book not only for its powerful series of practical pure form clay exercises but also for her summary of pioneering research on how modeling affects the senses and *"**makes children more peaceful**."* She movingly describes how her boisterous class developed a *warm* enthusiasm for their regular weekly clay modeling lessons and was harmonized. The following are a few additional aspects of this excellently articulated and richly illustrated work for study and further research:

- Hella Loewe documents case studies including one indicating the *"stimulation of the metabolic processes"* by clay modeling. She calls on teachers and other researchers to make their own observations asking such questions as: *"Is it possible that the activity of the inner organs, for example, the intestinal peristaltic, is beneficially stimulated through clay modeling experiences? Is it possible that development and improvement in the metabolic-limb system might be brought about by the rhythmically impulse pushing, groping and forming movements of the modeling process? "* (Ibid.,p.93)

- She shows how modeling offers children a whole-hand workout. Her book is replete with hand awareness exercises, some of which are given at the beginning of this sourcebook. She compares the benefits of the intense touch-experience of modeling with the partial touch-experiences of knitting, painting and drawing.

- Articulate hand and finger movements are correlated with healthy speech development and more attentive listening skills.

- Special subject lessons right after modeling had *"improved work atmosphere."*

- The intense tactile engagement contributes to children's sense of self and self-worth.

Why Development of the Body Senses is Critical to Learning Capacities and Teachability

Below is a diagrammatic example of how the four body senses are the critical foundation for the four higher ones involving a child's mental and social functioning in relation to a teacher (or other adults).

> **Four Heathily Functioning Body Senses**
> **Support →**
> **Four Higher Cognitive-Social Senses**
> Example: Child sensing a Teacher:
> 1. Balance → **Hearing/** listening to the Teacher
> 2. Movement → **grasping her words**
> 3. Life → **grasping thoughts** behind her words
> 4. Touch → **sensing her ego-authority**

An incarnating child's secure and confident sense of balance in the body and the space around it is *organ*-izationally developed in the ear and semicircular canals which are spatially configured at right angles. The balance sense interconnects with and supports the hearing sense and the ability to listen accurately to the word sounds of a teacher's voice. The sense of self-movement (including gesture) supports the language sense which then grasps the teacher's words as words and not just sounds. Life sense energies are recruited and developed into mental processes that grasp the thoughts behind the words. The development of the sense of touch, which educates the perception of the boundaries of other objects and beings, *gradually* metamorphoses into the mental process of sensing the adult ego of the teacher, the I-being expressing and permeating the thoughts, words, sounds and gestures experienced. Only in adulthood does the human being have a well-developed ego-sense.

In childhood a sense for and respect of loving adult authority becomes the bud-like proto-form of a gestating ego-sense. The child develops a picture of the teacher and parent as ego-endowed beings and role models (Aeppli). The deep psychological need for adult authority and guidance becomes especially acute around age nine to ten. A child encounters his/her own I-being (Self) and experiences an increasing feeling of separateness as an individual. At this crucial moment, loving but firm adults as mature I-beings need to find ways to reassure and to embrace the child throughout this crisis. The major theme of the subjects and activities of the Waldorf curriculum and method (described later) for grades 3 and 4 becomes *reassurance*.

Sensory Disturbances and Damage

A child whose soul is not incarnating harmoniously into the interrelated hierarchy of bodily senses will not readily respond to a teacher's guidance due to incomplete and distorted perceptions of sound, meaning of words, and authority. Spatial disorientation, restlessness, being uncomfortable in a physical body, and oversensitivity interfere with attentive listening and becoming absorbed in a given task. Obsessive movement and the inability to come to rest (hyperactivity) can translate into disturbances not just in hearing but in understanding language and instructions. In such cases the self-movement organism cannot become an organ for the language sense.

Research is accumulating on the effects of modern lifestyles and, *electrified, mechanizing media* on the development of children and their senses still in the process of formation. It goes beyond the purpose of this sourcebook to enter into this important issue at length but I can briefly mention a few thoughts and examples and cite sources for further study.

The issue of the effect of content aside, staring for lengthy periods of time at plastic screens, irradiated by unhealthy electronic light (sight), with most of the body semi-paralyzed (self-movement and balance senses), has been connected to:

- hyperactivity (life sense)
- inability to focus (ego)
- irritability (touch-iness)
- mood swings (balance, equanimity)
- aggressive behavior
- diabetes
- obesity (life sense).

Exposure needs to be kept to age–appropriate levels. As educational philosopher John Dewey pointed out, *"We do not feed babies beefsteak."* (See Jerry Mander, *Four Arguments for the Elimination of Television*)

Screen images of phenomena in nature and of human beings speaking and carrying out activities are confusing illusions that capture our attention and fool us, especially young children. They appear to move but are not really doing so. Acoustically, they lack overtones and do not provide the full rich sound of real voices and live music. Behind the human images there is not the presence of real I-beings according to which children can form a sense of adult authority and ego-sense. In contrast, artistic *media* such as paper and wood (from plants), paints, clay, stone and metals (earth), tools (brushes, chisels, instruments) and the human body itself (dance and voice) are not virtual and fake and do not fool and confuse. In using them, it is we who actively engage in the creation of tangible images in such a way that we know that they go beyond the material and into the realm of imagination and metaphor. These media are not surrounded by electromagnetic fields. They are not mechanized and programmatically automated but promote flexible, rhythmical activity and initiative.

> *All the senses accomplish their functions by virtue of a more or less modified sense of touch.*
>
> —Jacob-Rodriguez Pereire

Touching as the Underlying Gesture of other Senses

Touch, the primary sense of sculptural modeling, is in many ways a general underlying archetype or gesture of most other senses which "touch" upon" and come into "con-*tact*" with different aspects of the world—con-**tact** from the Latin root *tactus,* to touch. Through smelling, tasting, seeing, warm/cold sensing, hearing, word-sensing, concept-sensing, and other-ego-sensing, the world is "touching" into me and I am touching it. At the same time, there is also will in these sense activities expressed in the gesture of "going out" to meet, grasp, and per*ceive* the world—Latin *percipere=to grasp through*.

Interestingly, Steiner at first developed a series of only ten distinct senses (1909-10) and did not include touch (or ego) but initially treated it as a universal capacity which played into the other senses. *"What is directly felt by the sense of touch can always be found in the domain of the first three senses…. For example a body that presses on me causes a change in position within my bodily make-up, and this change is perceived by means of my sense of life, … self-movement, or … balance."* (This quotation is found in Steiner's unfinished and, in his view, unsuccessful attempt to find a new language to capture how the seven life processes complex pulses through and vitalizes all the senses. This work is published with the title *Anthroposophy: A Fragment*, (1996) indicating that the understanding of the senses was central to Steiner's life-long research—a veritable quest for a new "sensosophy."

Haptic Perception: "Seeing" with Our Hands

Haptic perception (from the Greek, *hap-
tikos* meaning "able to take hold of") is the
capacity that combines touching an object,
exploring its surface with hand movements
and holding it in the hand. People are able
to readily sense the nature of an object without using their eyes. With haptic perception,
we can analyze and judge the character of
objects in a fundamental, primal way.

As stated earlier, touch alone does not
give us our complex "sense of form." Touch
is the "boundary sensor" by which we simultaneous experience our body's limit and
that there are other bodies bounded "out
there beyond" us and pressing against us
as resistances, "hard," "soft" etc. By adding the "sense of movement" to touch, we
feel "what's out there" as specific shape
with varied surfaces "rough," "smooth", etc.
The "sense of form" is for most people the

working together of our senses of sight
and self-movement (muscle sense). Sight
reaches out to give us light and color and
our eye muscles and sight very rapidly
"move around" and scan an object from a
distance to "grasp" its geometric form.

If we are blind, we reach out, not with
our eyes, but with our arms and hands,
using touch to "see." The "eyes" of our very
sensitive fingers and their "nerve-dense"
tips *move around* an object and literally
"grasp" its form both physically and mentally. Perceiving forms through "outreaching eye-touching" and/or through direct
"outreaching-hand-touching" are two of our
most fundamental, primal and vital bridges
to reality. The haptic mode actually begins
when we are touching, moving water beings
in the womb.

Blindness and the Sensing of Forms

As noted above, the blind use *"moving
touching"* instead of sight to perceive and
create forms. They most often have a highly
developed haptic perception. According
to Herbert Read, *"[congenitally blind chil-
dren] can mold the human figure with a high
degree of realism but with certain exaggerations or emphases…The general form of the
sculpture is built up from a multitude of tactile impressions."* One of the exaggerations
can be of the hands. Read shows a photo
of a clay figure with upstretched arms and
huge hands, indicating an enhanced sense

of their power and expanded capabilities. (Read, *The Art of Sculpture*, 1961, 30 with photo 37b *"Youth Imploring"*) The blind use the hands to "see."

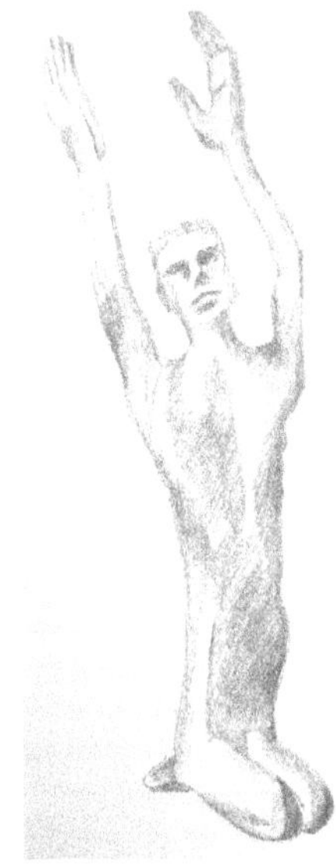

Clay figure by a blind person

Enlivening Soul and Spirit Senses

Modeling a three-dimensional "weighty," and resistant substance develops and strengthens our eye-hand coordination, active looking and sight, a middle "soul" sense, but, as Aeppli points out above, it does so with less emphasis on the eyes than the two other visual arts: two-dimensional, linear drawing and painting with colors. The less strenuous, fine motor movements involved in the latter employ the intermediary utensils of pencil or brush and are less physically vigorous. They work more on the head-nerve pole coupled with the rhythmic middle system of our feelings (feeling-thinking) rather than the metabolic-limb-will system as does modeling. Modeling emphasizes the feeling-will. (See Michael Howard's *Educating the Will.*)

Of the three other middle soul senses, modeling primarily enhances our sense of warmth and the different temperatures of materials. It also makes us aware of our human warmth which flows into and warms up a piece of clay. Will activity generates heat! Modeling does not develop a gourmet sense of taste nor a dog's acuity of smell!

As described above, the four higher mental, "spirit" senses metamorphose out of the four lower bodily ones which are intensively exercised by modeling. The higher senses play a crucial role in creating culture and in discerning/ judging the character of other human beings and our surroundings. (See next section on the faculty of judgment).

Our ego-sense—sensing another ego-being "out there"—is initially prepared on a basic level by touch-sensing, and by our body's encounters with the boundary of "me" and the "not-me" of the world of everyday objects. Modeling and feeling a clay object, a simple sphere, for example, provides both a sense of my physical boundaries as an I-being in a body and simultaneously the perception of a self-contained, well-formed object body with a center "out there" beyond my skin.

Interestingly, according to Steiner, this simplest and yet most universal of geometric shapes, the sphere, gives us more than just a sense of boundary and form. As he puts it, *"to feel. . . a sphere in space is to feel one's selfhood, to feel the ego . . . A fragment of a sphere rouses in [the human being] a sense of independence in his own self." (Architecture as a Synthesis of the Arts,* 1999, p.102*)*

One's experience of one's self and body-boundedness is the platform from which we then sense other such individual I-beings.

"Sense of Form" and "Sense of Judgment"

The senses work together in modeling. Touch and self-movement with or without sight combine to give us our complex *"sense of form.*" Steiner points out that it is the collaboration of our senses which ultimately creates the basis of our human capacity for discernment called our *"sense of judgment."* We can sensorily analyze the world in twelve different ways with our senses and connect them to make a judgment.

Our sense of judgment is seated in the non-material soul but has its physical instrument not only in mirroring function of the brain but also in the activity of the balancing, weighing and measuring forces of our hands and arms. *"We make our judgments…with our soul body, supported by our arms and hands."* (*Education for Adolescence*, 1996, p.33) *"The faculty of judgment is …essentially enhanced by this activity of the hands"* (Ibid.,p. 53). The upright human being with arms and up-facing cupped hands stretching out straight to the sides is an image of a weighing balance scale. Both grasping hands and grasping senses are *discerning/judging* organs of our active will, centered in the soul body, and integrated there along with our thinking and feeling.

Shaping and differentiating forms and "ideas" with the discerning hands in modeling material is an ideal sensory-motor activity, using multiple senses and supporting the development of judgment seated in the cortex, the most "human" part of the brain. (At the end of the chapter, see more on the Waldorf educational development of judgment: aesthetic, moral, and scientific.)

De-vitalization of the Senses

The intellectualism initiated by ancient Greek philosophers, particularly Aristotle (see later section on Plato vs Aristotle) has enabled human beings to think for themselves, independently of collective group norms and societal pressures. But this achievement has come at a price, as creative energies have been redirected for new evolutionary purposes. Humanity has become more mentally awake, more reflective and more taken up with outer sensory experience but paradoxically this experience has diminished in depth and quality. A living sensory *connection* to the world of earlier cultures has given way to more distanced *observation and reflection*. What is the reason for this phenomenon?

According to Steiner's investigations, early humanity was more lightly incarnated and possessed a pre-conceptual, dream-like consciousness based on nerve-sense processes that were saturated with more blood and vibrant, life processes. Sense perception was simultaneously a powerful life process and of a nature similar to the creative life processes outside in the environment. Both inner and outer nature constituted a continuum. Sensory impressions flowed directly and relatively unfiltered into human beings who thereby felt a natural, unity and spiritual participation with the universe, albeit dream-like and unconscious. Nature's creative forces were not yet experienced as mental abstractions but revealed themselves on the stage of the human soul as feeling-laden pictures and visions of a host of gods and spiritual beings.

Earlier humanity's vivid *'thinking in pictures'* was supported by bodies that were *'more inwardly alive."* (*Polarities in the Evolution of Mankind*, 1987, p.19). And, although cultures were developing the intellectual part of the soul in Greco-Roman-Medieval times, it was an intellect that was to a great degree still organically enlivened by the life forces of the etheric body and very much tied into the world etheric of 'cosmic intelligence.' People experienced thoughts as being objectively imparted to and through them by the universe and not originating subjectively in the physical brain.

As humanity has evolved, the ancient dream-like, picture consciousness has necessarily given way to a new stage of sensory, mental and intellectual "awakening." Human beings have begun to make a next evolutionary step toward becoming freely thinking, self-reflective individuals. Physiologically, this new "waking up" to the outer sense world occurred because human beings in the mid-fifteenth century started thinking only with their material brains and nervous systems instead of out of an etheric dimension of cognizing. Life processes in the nerve-sense system started to recede. The sense organism became increasingly a devitalizing filter that translates, abstracts, and reduces vivid sense experiences to shadowy images, representations and words.

As thoughts have become filtered and dulled by the physical body, they have turned more and more into *"shadowy images"* and *"spectres of former thinking."*

> *"Since [the Renaissance], . . . people really think with the physical body but . . . this is merely a shadow image of what was once cosmic thinking . . . People today actually have no idea of how much more alive thinking was in former times. In those ancient days, the human being actually felt refreshed while thinking . . . [T]he concept did not exist that thinking could be something tiring."* (*Materialism and the Task of Anthroposophy*, 180-181)

Steiner also speaks of our modern nerve-sense system taking on a mirror-like, virtual quality and only imparting dull reflections. The changed conditions he describes have become even more pronounced at the beginning of the twenty-first century in which the brain and its physical-chemical processes are identified as the 'creators' of our mental life, our psyches, and our egos.

The next step in evolution is now to 're-bloodify,' re-enliven our cognition so that a new level of etheric-based imagination is attained that is not the old dream-like one, but a waking-consciousness imagining. This waking-'dreaming' can be disciplined to objective and scientific, as Goethe has proven, and can help us approaching many of the seemingly intractable problems of our apocalyptic times.

> *"Human beings must become aware that they possess shadow images in their current thinking… [T]his shadow image, i.e. modern thinking, has to be enlivened so that it can turn into Imagination.* (Ibid. p.181)

> *The small child is entirely sense organ.*
> —Rudolf Steiner

Individual Development Recapitulates the Evolution of Consciousness

The historical evolution described above appears to be reflected and recapitulated in human development. Like early humanity, the fresh new body of the very young child, is, according to Steiner, very much one big sense organ saturated with more blood and life processes and entirely open to the in-flow of the world and its formative effects. (Also along these lines, animals similarly have so much vitality in their senses that they are not just connected to their environment, but their behavior is locked into it). The child's innate reflexive response is naturally configured to imitate and be shaped by the actions it so strongly experiences around it. This imitative behavior based in sensory vitality extends markedly up through the first seven to eight years of life and into the beginning of the elementary grades. Swiss Waldorf educator Willi Aeppli notes that *"any good observation shows us the extraordinary freshness and liveliness of the sense perceptions of a seven-year-old. Why? Because so much real life is still at work in the sense processes; they are still mostly life processes."*

Life processes are still in existence (in the imaginative thinking) which can no longer be found behind the purely conceptual thinking of an adult. In the child between 7 and 10 there is still this deep relationship between perceiving and thinking. Only when the thinking becomes abstract, purely intellectual, which means deserted by life, and when the life processes have mostly withdrawn from the sense-organism, do perceiving and thinking separate.

> *Between the ninth and tenth year each child experiences a crisis in development. The cause lies in the fact that, on the one hand, the hitherto imaginative thinking experiences its first intellectual impact, and, on the other hand, one part of the life processes, which has been present up to now, withdraws from the sense organization. The consequence is that the child feels estranged from his environment; he observes it with entirely different eyes and tries to digest his perceptions in a new way, namely, with [a more intellectual] thinking."* (Aeppli, 41-42.)

Aeppli characterizes what Steiner calls *"imaginative thinking"* cited above as *"a soul force to which the teacher can turn in his lessons and which he should foster….[W]e can ask ourselves…whether this 'picture-like' thinking is actually still a 'perceiving' or already a 'thinking'. The answer can only be: It is both simultaneously. On the one hand it is inner 'perception endowed with phantasy',*

but in it already lives the power of young, lively thinking. In imaginative thinking, perception and thinking are one." (Aeppli,41)

Waldorf Education: Re-en-LIFE-ning the Senses in a Digital Age

Steiner predicted that the deadening and blunting of the senses would continue well into the future. He therefore responded to a call for a new kind of education to prepare human beings for this evolutionary trend. He developed Waldorf guiding principles for teachers to help children enhance and expand the rich, life-filled sensory dispositions and capacities with which they are endowed. The long-term aim was is to educate children in such a way that the natural forces of genius in every child are developed and retained into later life as ever renewing sources of adult creativity.

To that end, the Waldorf approach embodies what the poet philosopher Schiller termed "the *aesthetic* education of the human being." The word "aesthetic" interestingly is derived from the Greek *"aesthikos,"* translatable as "of the senses." A truly aesthetic education is one of full development of all sense capacities. To put such a pedagogy into practice, the learning activities and subjects of a curriculum need to be shaped and interwoven into a *whole, interconnected organism* that over time acts on all twelve senses in a lively, balanced way in the child. Every lesson—even in subjects such as science and math—need to be imbued with a *true artistry*. This is achieved by orchestrating and choreographing deep sensory, image-laden experiences, very often involving hands-on and whole-bodies-on movement activities—sensory-motor and performance.

Different subjects emphasize the exercise

of different senses at different times, but in the end all twelve are addressed as integral to a healthy development and an integration of body, soul and spirit. Developmentally, the four lower, internal body-oriented senses (touch, life, movement, balance) are addressed strongly in the lower grades as the foundation for the unfolding of the four higher social, "spirit" senses (of another ego, concept, language, and hearing/listening) with four "soul" senses in the middle. The soul sense of sight is especially exercised through regular practice in the many visual arts and observational exercises in the sciences and other subjects. The sense of warmth (and cold) is developed subtly but pervasively throughout the curriculum through such affective experiences as storytelling, warm and cold colors, a teacher's enthusiasm, specialized heat experiments in physics, warming clay and many other modalities. Exercises to enhance smell and taste are not as frequently done but left to guided life experiences in nature and geography (for example, cooking and eating Mexican food as part of a geography lesson).

Current Neuroscience and the Mission of the Arts

As a Waldorf class teacher, I found that learning is profoundly enhanced by an artistic-experiential way of teaching and learning. Such an approach achieves lasting and integrated capacities of intelligence—intellectual, emotional and volitional (will). Such educating does not aim at training or producing artists, but uses the experiential methodology of the arts to promote capacities that are valuable for all vocations in adulthood. Artistically inspired and permeated "action academics" is not a frill but a time-tested means for young homosapiens

to develop and exercise universal sensory and hands-on motor skills as well as their brains. This was recognized in an issue of *Educational Leadership* magazine (November 1998) devoted to "How the Brain Learns":

"Because our visual, auditory and motor systems are essential to cognition, it's probable that the arts emerged to help develop and maintain them… Evidence from the brain sciences and evolutionary psychology increasingly suggests that the arts [along with such functions as language and math] play an important role in brain development and maintenance—so it's a serious matter for schools to deny children direct curricular access to the arts. The arts are highly integrative involving many elements of human life… [especially] on two key elements: (1) heightened motor skills that we call performance (2) the heightened appreciation of our sensory-motor capabilities that we call aesthetics… Movement is central to life and to the arts." (Robert Sylvester, Art for the Brain's Sake, *Educational Leadership,* 56 (3) November 1998, 31-32)

The current test-oriented mono-focus on reading and math in an increasing number of schools only develops a very limited number of skills, mainly centered in the left-side of the brain. This *one-sided* approach is literally "*narrow*-minded" because it educates only a small fraction and narrow sliver of a child's enormous mind, brain and body potential with a wide spectrum of potential capacities. It neglects the huge resources for learning of the imagery-making and feeling-motivational right side of the brain. We are thereby stunting, prematurely aging and burning out our children and depriving them of their full childhood forces.

Neuroscientist Ian Richardson calls

attention to the deeper cultural roots of this crisis, which have been building over the past centuries.

"Western societies have largely lost the ability to think in images rather than words. … [M]odern neuroscience backs [this up]... .[I]t is the nature of words that they tend to transform experiences into a rather bloodless code that can starve our brains of the rich images that wordless imagining can evoke. [W]ords trigger images as well as other word-thoughts. Yet most of us, most of the time… don't think in images enough… Language is the great achievement of evolution—an essential ingredient in what makes human beings unique on the planet. But there are costs to the way we have grown dependent on the spoken and written word. Imagery consists of the mental sights, sounds, smells, tastes, touch, and other bodily sensations that we can re-create with incredible vividness in that private, infinite universe within our skulls. The human brain is the most complex object in the known universe and it has the most incredible abilities, some which—like imagery—are underused. Imagery is important, but in Western culture, language is king. In school we steadily wrap our children's brains in the 'cool web of language.' It would be terrible if we didn't, but there is a cost to everything. By neglecting imagery we risk the withering of whole set of quite remarkable mental capacities…Children think mostly in images before word-dominated school clouds their mind's eye." (Ian Robertson, Professor of Psychology, Director of the Institute of Neuroscience at Trinity College, Dublin; previously at MRC Cognition and Brain Sciences Unit, Cambridge University, *Opening the Mind's Eye*, 2002, 2-3)

One sees only that which one knows.
—Goethe

Robertson goes on to say what this one-sided intellectual emphasis means for adulthood and how art tries to be a cultural corrective:

"Most of the time we [as adults] see, hear, feel, taste, and smell what our brains expect rather than the sensations themselves. Much modern ART tries to shock or surprise us out of these image-clouding mental habits into seeing more purely with the mind's eye, uncluttered by well worn categories and labels." (Ibid, 4)

"The older we get [it becomes] harder and harder to have an experience that's completely new…When you classify experiences like this, you begin to experience the class and not the event. In other words, your conscious experience becomes once removed from the immediate sensation." (Ibid,12)

"The brain's predilection for prediction and categorization is not confined to the visual sense. It also anticipates what we see, hear, feel, taste, and smell . . . For much of our lives, we taste memories—what we expect—not the raw, fresh complexity of the sensations on our tongues." (Ibid,18)

"But the outside world can hijack our attention…It is…at…rare moments that we are closest to the unfettered, uncategorized seeing that we attribute to young children and to savants." (Ibid, 19)

"Children cry or shout at the 'wide glare' of the looming sky." (Ibid, 20)

In his book, Robertson presents corrective measures for adults aware of the staleness of compulsive mental habits who want to regain a child-like freshness in their sensations and experiences—in addition to being shocked by modern art! *"[You] can train your own mind by practicing imagery"* and thereby connect more directly with the world which includes not just the visual realm but also sounds, smells, tastes, touch, and other bodily sensations. He points out that we also have a mind's ear, a mind's nose and so on. I dare say so much of the brain is devoted to the hand that we also have a mind's hand.

Robertson focuses on the "wordless imagery" but also acknowledges all along that language can be a catalyst for imaging–in poetry and metaphor for example. One can use words artistically so that they "take wing" experientially and "trigger" emotionally moving pictures. And there are many meditational practices for adults to develop and restore inner visualization when the juices of imagination have dried up.

Aesthetic, Moral and Scientific Judgment

Waldorf Education views the elementary school child as especially eager for beauty and an "aesthetic" experience of the world and the adolescent as a seeker for truth. An artistically shaped *action academics* cultivates an general aesthetic judgment rooted in enhanced multisensory awareness, as described previously. Aesthetic judgment becomes the main trunk line from which the two sub-branches of cognitive-scientific judgment and moral judgment organically emerge after age eleven/twelve.

These last two are especially needed by the truth-seeking adolescent to maneuver through the complicated world of "sex, drugs and rock'n'roll." Scientific judgment aims at being as objective and impersonal as possible whereas moral judgment is the opposite. It arises subjectively from within as the voice of personal conscience. Aesthetic judgment can stand in a balanced middle between these two and include both distanced cognitive-objective and subjective qualities. Interestingly, Steiner holds that artistic activity helps transmute eroticism.

Deep artistic experiences intensify a teenager's capacities of observation and thinking in science and learning how to discern truth, goodness, evil and injustice through the humanities. A child educated 'aesthetically' with a well-cultivated repertoire of many senses will develop a greater sense of wonder for and appreciation of the fullness of life. Making beautiful things (lesson books, sculptures, plays, garden beds, gymnastic exercises, etc.) connects and builds "interest," the cognitive/ affective bridge between the child and the world (from the Latin root *"interesse"* = between to be"). An inner voice and conscience will develop as well so that he/she will create and nurture in adulthood rather than destroy.

The "Sense of Beauty" and the Senses of Life and Balance

In the development of aesthetic judgment and appreciation, modeling can play a significant role as educator not only of touch and movement but also of Steiner's two other "body" senses, those of life and balance. These foundational senses connect with other senses (sight, hearing, taste, etc.) to form the complex combination we call our *"sense of beauty."* The sense of balance supports not only our orientation in physical space and its geometrical/mathematical context, but also our aesthetic sense of harmony/disharmony, symmetry/ asymmetry, proportion/ disproportion.

Closely related, the sense of life gives us the ability to feel the quality and integrity of life, the wholeness and wellbeing of ourselves and of things. This sense is rooted in our etheric body as "life body" and master sculptor. Steiner points out that both beauty and sculptural modeling enliven our etheric body and life forces. (Goodness strengthens our astral/emotional body. Truth, the third ideal of Plato, is planted within our physical bodies. Thomas had to use his physical body—his hands—to touch Christ's physical hands to verify the truth of his identity).

The close relationship between living form in sculpture, balance and aesthetics was dramatically demonstrated when Steiner was bringing to life the figures of his thirty-foot elm carving called *"The Representative of Humanity."* A visiting Dutch artist pointed out to him that the whole composition was *"out of balance, Herr Doktor!"* Steiner stepped back, had to agree and added a new compensating sculptural element which he called "World Humor." Might this anecdote also demonstrate that a sense of balance is also related to a sense of humor—and not becoming too serious! (For more details, see Chapter on *Learning from Goetheanum Forms*)

Wellspring of Strength

As stated before, being healthily sense-connected to nature and other human beings can mean that not just knowledge but also the world's abundant energy flows back into us in "feedback loop." Our environment can either wear us out or it can be tapped into for it spiritual nourishment. Steiner made teachers aware of this bountiful resource in a meditation he composed for their profession. This verse helps to renew a person's inner forces and to prepare nightly for teaching the next day (free interlinear translation by A.A.):

Im Schein des Sinneswesens
In the appearances that your senses present to you,

Da lebt des Geistes Wille
There lives spirit will energy

Als Weisheitslicht sich gebend
Offering itself as the light of wisdom.

Und innere Kraft verbergend
And concealing inner force…

The meditation goes on in subsequent lines to indicate how the I-being of the teacher can tap into that hidden force behind the sense world as an ever-renewing wellspring of inspiration, insight and strength. The teacher does so meditatively by bringing warm will energy into thinking and raising thinking into a living etheric-based activity capable of becoming one with the energizing light communicated by our senses. Teachers working in this way find that another capacity comes into play after sleep: *inspiration* for how to meet and teach the children the next day.

Steiner also crafted a second meditation to help teachers develop *intuition* and a heartfelt awareness and relationship to their students. And for collaboration with colleagues and other adults, he gave Waldorf educators an *Imagination* of working together with strength, courage and wisdom.

Fifteen Senses?

There are not just twelve but fifteen senses if one included the three spiritual ways of perceiving just mentioned: the imagination sense, inspiration sense, and intuition sense ! Interestingly, Steiner even characterizes the higher cognitive senses of hearing, word, thought, and ego as "spirit" senses. Intuition has very much to do with sensing the "I" of the other; inspiration, with hearing and word; and imagination with thought.

Imagination Sense

Modeling as image-making is particularly helpful in building *image*-ination. The ego working through the "spirit-permeated hand" (Steiner's term) brings non-physical spirit forms into matter. This activity in the physical develops imagination (small "*i*") in the mind's eye (or mind's ear). This practice on a material "training ground" is a prelude to then lifting the thinking process into a higher plane of cognition. Living images that Steiner calls *Imaginations* are perceived, using the new spiritual sense of Imagination capital "I," Just as the sense of sight needs the organ of the eye, so Imagination has its organ in the non-physical two-petaled chakra organ behind the forehead just above and between the eyes.

In the next chapter, I take up "Enlivening the Imagination," and how to enhance this power in both children and adults. In a later chapter, I go into "What is Imagination?" and its different levels.

Inspiration Sense

Modeling can be thought of as a silent dialogue or musical dancing of our two facing hands with their motions impressing the clay with gestures and the language of form. When not just merely copying, this activity becomes excitingly free, exploratory and full of discovery. With our hands we feel and creatively "dream" new forms. These manual explorers have a life of their own, hit upon unexpected forms for the wakeful eyes to witness and *inspire* us with new ideas.

An inspirational way of modeling is an artistic practice that prepares for inspiration on a higher, spiritual level. The spiritual organ for what Steiner experienced as Inspiration (capital "I") is the 16-petaled chakra situated at the larynx, the organ for sculpting, shaping and vibrating the air into meaningful sound forms. The larynx does eurythmy and speaks/sings forth forms for others to perceive. On a small scale, this is the logos in the human being sounding forth and creating symbolic forms just as the greater Logos speaks forth the alphabet and language of nature and creates the material things of the world. Sound energy forms and shapes, and densifies into matter.

In the Beginning was the Word

Modeling is not just making, but it is also speaking forth forms with the hands. According to Steiner, the etheric body, our inner modeler "speaks" with our hands and limbs and "never with our mouth." (Lecture, Penmaenmawr, August 26, 1923)

Intuition Sense

In our hands we have what Steiner calls "*sleeping will,*" full of unconscious intuitions and intentions waiting to be brought to light and form. Intuition has its organ in the 12 petaled chakra of the heart. Our hands as extensions of our heart/lung rhythmic system are very intuitive in that they penetrate and live into matter and the forms it is going through. This "living into" can be a preparatory activity for a higher spiritual activity, Intuition (capital "I") in which we experience things and beings by being inside of them with our consciousness. This state on a soul level is related to 'empathy,' to being able to "stand in someone else's shoes" and "feel our way" into her situation. Teachers particularly need this perceptive ability to really under-stand and experience what a child is going through: to "be in their shoes."

Spacial Dynamics teacher Jaimen McMillan describes the intuitive faculty beautifully in relation to gymnastics and in a way that can also be related to the hands intuiting through modeling: *"Our own limbs can become organs for intuition through 'first-hand' experiences…It is a gentle reaching out for engagement in a way that allows for something to reveal slowly its secrets as it flows back towards the questioner…"* (Intuition Play and Interplay, *Being Human*, Fall-Winter 2014-15, p. 36.)

Modeling is always an intuitive questioning, a quest: What will be revealed in the clay in my hands this time? Where are these forms coming from?! Where do forms come from in general?!

More on the History of the Senses: Plato, Aristotle and Steiner: Arm Eyes and Eye Hands

When looking at a distant object, Plato experienced that non-physical rays were reaching out from his eyes and grasping at it. Sight perception for him was not a passive receiving but involved actively stretching out to con-*tact* a thing with a sensory and mental energy beam. Our word "perception" is derived from the Latin action verb *"cipere"*

> *The greatest sense in our body is our touch sense. It is probably the chief sense in the processes of sleeping and waking; it gives us our knowledge of depth or thickness and form; we feel, we love and hate, are touchy and are touched, through the touch corpuscles of our skin.*
>
> —Lionel Taylor,

meaning "to take hold of" or "grasp."

In his research, Steiner also experienced the same active will in the sense of sight and described invisible arms of reaching out from our eyes. (*Foundations of Human experience, Lecture* III, 1996, p.66) Conversely, Steiner also characterized our hands as the *"eyes of our rhythmic system."* Our arm-hands, like extending "feelers," extend to touch and grasp a distant object physically, sensorily and mentally.

According to Waldorf educator Magda Lissau, these suprasensory arms extend from the sentient part of our soul. She describes how *"A person's sentient body, the oldest part of the astral body, reaches out into the surroundings and actually touches…the astral counterpart of the objects in the physical world…; astrally our awareness sends out feelers to contact these very objects."* (*The Temperaments and the Arts*, 50-51.)

Overcoming Opto-centrism

Plato's most famous student Aristotle came to question his teacher's emphasis on sight as active and as the most important sense for knowledge. He came to consider the sense of touch as primary in connecting us directly with reality. Richard Kearney summarizes the divergence:

> "In perhaps the first great works of psychology, the 'De Anima,' Aristotle pronounced touch the most universal of the senses. 'Touch is the most intelligent sense… because it is the most sensitive…Touch knows differences…It is the source of our most basic power to discriminate.' Aristotle was challenging the dominant prejudice of his time. The Platonic Doctrine of the Academy held that sight was the highest sense, because it is the most distant and mediated; hence the most theoretical, holding things at bay, mastering meaning from above. Touch by contrast, was deemed the lowest because it was immediate and subject to intrusions and pressures from the material world. Against this, Aristotle made his radical counterclaim that touch did indeed have a medium, namely 'flesh'…[which] was not just a material organ but a complex mediating membrane and accounts for our primary sensings and evaluations.

> "Tactility is not blind immediacy—not merely sensorial but cognitive too…[However] the

Platonists prevailed…Western philosophy sprang from a dualism between the intellectual senses crowned by sight, and the lower 'animal' senses, stigmatized by touch… [This] opto-centrism prevailed for over 200 years, culminating in our contemporary culture of digital stimulation and spectacle. The eye continues to rule in…our 'civilization of the image.' The world is no longer our oyster, but our screen." ("Losing Our Touch", *New York Times*, August 31, 2014)

Steiner also addressed the tension between Platonist and Aristotelian points of view on several occasions including their differences on the senses. In contrast to Kearney, he pointed out that with and after Aristotle the six lower senses (touch, life, movement, balance, smell, and taste) came to be emphasized in Anglo-American and Western culture whereas the higher six (sight, warmth, sound, word, and ego) were characteristic of Eastern culture. Even *"[w]hat is called sight in scientific circles is only a somewhat complicated touching…"* (*Man as a Being of Sense and Perception*, pp. 29-30). The visionary "sight" and *seership* of Plato that beheld visually the archetypal essence of things had given way to a seeing of only surfaces.

En-*Live*-ning *Image*-ination: Mind Sculptures

Nature in her unfathomable designs has mixed us of clay and flame, of brain and mind, that the two things hang indubitably together and determine each other's being, but how or why, no mortal may ever know.

—William James, American psychologist

Modeling as Imagining-in-Motion: Mind Sculpting

The subtitle of this sourcebook is *Expanding Intelligence by Exploring Universal Shapes*. It might just as well have been *"Expanding Imagination."* Because human intelligence functions on the basis of making and *re*-membering images in the miraculous ways cited above, modeling activity proves to be an ideal physical-motor strengthener of mental activity, especially of mental imaging in all of its positive manifestation. The human being, as pointed out before, is at heart an imager, an imaginer and a hands-on image-maker. Modeling as *imagining-in-motion* affirms our humanness.

Steiner recommended that teachers regularly practice this art as way to educate their minds to perceptively behold and live into the stage-by-stage metamorphosis of the developing *child-in-motion*, the *child-in-form-ing*. He showed how modeling activity in particular activates the etheric shaping forces of seeing, sensing and imagining in both teacher and student. He wanted pedagogues to *"imbue themselves with the power of imagination"* as a force in shaping lives. (See Part III: Sources of Imagination.)

Plastic Formations in the Mind

We mold images inside with our minds. We mold images outside with our hands. The hands come into motion and explore and imaginatively think and feel and speak forms. The primal activity of image-modeling externalizes and makes visible in physical matter what the 'I' as mental sculptor does in shaping the "mind sculptures" we variously call mental images, ideas, concepts, thoughts, etc. Hand sculpting works back upon the soul and become mind-sculpting and vice versa. The two reinforce and feed each other in a loop.

Philosopher Immanuel Kant is reputed to have provocatively held that the *"hand is our outer brain."* And as neurologist Frank Wilson asks in his book *The Hand*, *"Who is to say where the brain ends and the hand begins?"* In my communications with him, he made me aware of the management consultancy of John Ward who has business people *"kinesthetically* model" in clay new ideas for their *"company's future"*—new business models!

Modeling and sculpting are *mind molders and mind expanders*. Young and old do well to exercise sculptural faculties regularly for re-creation or for stimulating creativity in a variety of fields and professions.

Modeling Pure Forms is Bodying Forth Shapes Unknown

The small-motor eurythmic activity of hand-modeling is a multisensory experience of *image-making* and *imagination-in-action*. It entails a simultaneous ordering of both material and sense perceptions (touch, movement, sight, life, etc.) and an integration of hands-and-mind. At its basic level, this manner of image-making is significantly influenced by past mental memory images and notions of things we have experienced in the world around us.

At a higher level, imagination takes wing and becomes a creative power to *"body forth shapes unknown."* This *"bodying forth"* is a birthing of new forms. Misnamed, *"abstract,"* or "non-representational" forms are often of this nature, although they may often "remind" us of "something." Such shapes emerge, evolve and bring surprises (inspirations). The activity of shaping new images has the quality of being future-oriented and free of preconceptions—or pre-perceptions!

Clay Images and Mind Sculptures

Having studied the way images are formed in the mind, neuroscientist Ian Richardson came to call them *"mind sculptures."* (Robertson, 1999). Steiner found that in the embryo and early childhood preponderant "sculptural" forces of the etheric body flow down from the large head building out and activating the trunk and limbs. At age 7 a portion of these formative forces are freed into a child's mind to make and retain mental images.

The term *model*-ing connotes making a model, a "likeness," or a *"representation"* of some *thing*, the same words applied in psychology and philosophy to mental images and formations. The word *"image"* is related to the Latin *"imitare."*

The clay-like brain and neural structures in their plastically flexible fluid medium are themselves organic "sculptures." It makes sense that the internal process of mental image-model-making is very closely related to the hand molding of external physical forms. Neuroscientists speak of the brain's plasticity and mind sculptures. Sculptors refer to clay's wonderful plasticity and "clay images." Steiner speaks of spiritual images carrying the archetypes of the human form into a young child's body to form its structure and organs.

Molding Image-Making Minds in Education

In his seminal 1919 course for the first Waldorf teachers, Steiner's advice to them was: *"We must help the children develop* **Vorstellen** *('mental imaging'), feeling and willing,"* substantive: *Vorstellung* (*Foundations of Human Experience,* Lecture II). *Vorstellen* can be translated as both "thinking" and as "imagining."

In the context of the whole lecture, I think, Steiner by using this term instead of *Denken* is here pointing to "imaginative thinking" (although *Vorstellen* can also become quite abstract).

As a result, in Waldorf teaching, live unscripted bringing of imagery through storytelling and related image-making arts becomes a major means to help the children exercise a daily conjuring up of rich mental images. Children are stimulated to make their own "self-created" inner images into concepts that grow with them even into later adult life. Students explore and deeply experience *images* and living concepts with their minds, hands and moving bodies through modeling, painting, drawing, moving and "musicalizing" them.

In Waldorf education there is thus considerable emphasis for both children and teachers alike on developing *image-making and imag*-ination. Such an ability is deemed highly valuable for and supportive of a wide range of life-capacities and skills. These include flexible thinking, grasping whole contexts and keeping track of sequences and interconnections by 'imagining' them. Reading comprehension, for example, is greatly enhanced by this capacity of imagining a chain of events. Above all, mental imaging and imagery is inextricably bound up with our feeling and emotional life and the heart of being human,

Mental Imaging, Memory Imaging, Imagination

Our "mental imaging" capacity produces both memory images and imagination images. But what is the difference and how are they related? There can be considerable confusion of psychological and philosophical terms, attributable to a great extent because the soul, mind and brain are so immensely complicated in their functions and capabilities. Language does not readily fit their almost infinite potential of mental phenomena (See a further in-depth discussion in the chapter in Part III: *Sources of Imagination*.)

In a very enlightening article, Norwegian educator Jorgen Smit points out it is a special challenge to define the process of imagination or imagining because of its very nature:

> "A systematic, scientific description of imagining is already a self-contradiction. It can be compared to a pressed flower or a butterfly on a pin. For imagining is not so systematically conscious. It is not well defined and

ordered. Its core is the overflowing life, the primal forest of surprises, and the wide-eyed wonder over unimaginably great realities, the warm enthusiasm and joy over becoming one with things. When imagination has been productive, we can look back upon it and discover some inherent order. We look back by remembering our observations." ("Remembering and Imagining" Research Bulletin, Autumn/Winter 2015, Vol. XX, No. 2, p. 50)

Smit describes further how imaging and remembering *'supplement each other, much as inhaling and exhaling,"* one an *'organ of the past'* and the other *"of the future."*

> "We always use imagination to help in remembering. Imagination helps both make our memories and recall our memories. Most importantly, imagining helps us fill the holes in our memory, for the memories must be whole if we are to hold onto them well. We color and form all of our memories with the power of our imagination…The power of imagination is like an emerging stream of blood that keeps alive our ability to remember. Without imagination, our memories die. And our imagination would be helpless without the ability to remember…Without our memory's ability to hold continuity, the uncontrolled activities of imagining would be lost in bottomless chaos." (Ibid. p.49)

Smit discovers a *"scale of…forces of remembering and imagining"* mixed in different types of personalities. He shows how teachers can help students *"to enliven imagination so that it grows and develops into exact imagining,"* rather than random fantasizing and dreaming. He recommends that

> "Every school day should have both of these elements: summarizing, clarifying exercises in remembering during which the previous day's products are ordered, digested and

understood; and a new effort, experiencing something new and foreign, always with the power of imagining." (Ibid. p. 50)

The Physiology of Memory, Imagination and Learning

For Steiner, memory and imagination have physiological instruments. Remembering, memory image-making and memorization (*Errinerung*, *Gedächtnis*, *Errinerungsvortellungen*) involve a predominance of "cool-headed" brain-nerve activity whereas in creative-dynamic imagining (*Imagination*, *Phantasie*) there is the involvement of blood-heart activity, feeling and will. According to Steiner, the creative ego is seated and active in the warmth of our "human-creating blood." And it is out of the etheric sculpting life forces in this warm "very special fluid" that the human body is formed. These same body shaping and building forces are lifted by the "I" into our soul and mental life and "build/sculpt" images–*Bilder* in German or"'*mind sculptures*," neuroscientist Ian Richardson's expression.

The Greeks had the perfect image for the relationship of creative imagination and the blood. The intellect and intelligence had their symbol in the horse (e.g. the cleverness of the Trojan horse) but there was one horse that was different. Pegasus is born and springs out of the blood of the Medusa. Creative imagination is intelligence which energetically and actively takes wing with a warm will!

Only looking at her image in his shield, Perseus cut off the head of dread, snake-haired Medusa. Blood poured into the earth and from it sprang Pegasus! Forthwith Athena, Goddess of Wisdom, tamed and presented the white winged horse to the Nine Muses of arts and sciences–the gift of high-flying imagination! (Greek myth)

And in a reverse process full-bodied images can be reduced to the bones of intellect's abstract shorthand of symbols, signs, hieroglyphs and letters.

A healthily functioning human body and mind call for balanced proportions of nerve and bone integrated with blood and muscle. Their integration is mediated by our heart/lung system, our rhythmical "transport" system between head and limbs. Similarly a healthy mind needs a balanced mix and alternation of summoning up past memories and a conjuring up of imaginative creations for new growth. Imagination is our spiritual growing edge.

In modeling, a teacher works artistically between these two poles of memory and imagination to achieve balance over the course of a school year. In modeling, this can translate into an alternation of making 'models' out of memory–for example, rendering a horse or house–or more freely and playfully exploring what evolves with a particular piece of clay. Exercises can also involve a mixed progression of memory and imagination. Playing with pure forms may suddenly remind a student of a horse which then emerges and is articulated as the final product. Even when she has a horse in mind from the start, a child can imaginatively try out different gestures and positions for the horse's body. Preconceived form (memory) can dynamically can evolve and be complemented by imaginative experimentation. In the myth, Perseus uses reflection (in his shield) before imagination springs forth.

Developmental Differences in Imagining

Children in preschool and the early grades tend to be very impressionable and to inwardly experience vivid mental imaging, as is evident in the way they listen "wide-eyed" to folktales, legends and myths. In modeling, they love to imaginatively play with wax or clay to shape human or animal forms, trees, houses and other structures. They become very sculpturally absorbed in mud and sand piles.

Children then typically start to gradually lose the vibrancy of their imaginative capacities as they mature and as left-brained word-based intellect increases and is encouraged. Steiner therefore recommends that teachers maintain an imagination-imbued teaching style, especially at the beginning of adolescence. A healthy imagination becomes vital for a teenager's healthy development of judgment. Wholesome critical thinking and discernment need the flexibility and openness of the imagination which flexibly embraces life's diversity, contrasts, and polarities. Modeling and stone and wood carving in the upper grades continue to be fruitful, additional ways to exercise imagining.

Visual Imagination Blindness

Many children and adults are able to *visually* call up only very dim images in the mind's eye or none at all. Only in dreaming do clear and colorful images appear. But human beings are image-makers and there are other sensory modalities that create images: sound-images in the mind's ear, taste-images in the mind's tongue, smell-images in the mind's nose, and kinesthetic-tacile images in mind's hand.

For the visual mind-image blind, the hands actually compensate and make the visual images appear externally in matter instead of mentally internally.

Modeling as An Enlivener and Balancer for the Imagination of Children of All Ages and Personalities

As educators, we take into account children with a complex variety of maturity, learning styles and mental imaging capacities. This includes visual, auditory, kinesthetic, and tactile learners, as well as other sensory modalities like visual imagination blindness. Steiner also brings attention to memory-oriented and imagination-oriented children, imagination/memory poor children and imagination-abundant-compulsive children (*Foundations of Human Experience*, Lecture XI).

Modeling images in clay is an excellent enlivener and *balancer* for children of all ages and make-ups. This includes the 'imaginative,' as well as 'imagination-and-memory-poor' and Steiner's category of 'imagination-abundant-compulsive' (*Phantasiereich*). His emphasis on a polarity of extremes in children helps us understand the full spectrum of possibilities. Most children are found in the intermediate range in between the two poles he describes.

Imagination/Memory-Poor Children

For imagination/memory poor children, modeling reaches down deeply into the sleeping area of the metabolic growth forces into which *" images disappear easily."* *Steiner* refers to 'imagination-poor' children as being *'more phlegmatic (phlegmatischer) in bringing their images back up'. (Education for Adolescents*, Lecture IV, June 15, 1921, 67). Modeling is therefore very suitable for phlegmatic children, in general, whose temperament and 'watery' consciousness are very strongly seated in their etheric bodies and metabolic systems. Modeling with wet, malleable clay is quintessentially an 'etheric art,' and homeopathically calls on a child's etheric forces and their 'life sense.' Energetic exertion naturally adds 'fire' and warmth to their constitutional 'wateriness."

In working with the wonderful resistance of clay, all students must call up these same metabolic-will forces in their ether-laden blood and let it stream into the moving muscles of their image-shaping hands. In the 'creation space' between their two active hands, they behold and feel memory and imagination images coming to life into concrete, tangible reality. The modeling process strengthens the circulation of metabolic processes 'below' weaving upwards into conscious cognitive formations 'above.' Steiner's ideal method for teachers, in general, is to first help fully educate the action-limb-will of the young child as well as part of the feeling-heart-rhythmical system so that the head-brain-nerve system naturally wakes up and matures "by itself." This method avoids filling the child's head with memorized knowledge and subjecting it to sensory overstimulation (audio, video, etc).

Class teacher and sculptural researcher Hella Loewe describes the working together of metabolic-will with the process of cognitive maturation in a boy in her class. Her approach started with "where was at." For him,

> "all tasks challenging imagination were extremely difficult. There were only three subjects he really enjoyed in the first years of school: the movement game class, painting and modeling with clay. Up into the fourth grade, this boy had the opportunity to regularly engage in modeling with his class once a week in the winter months… In the following years this boy made good progress in his physical body and in soul and spirit (A.A.: His academic achievements are also described); he was able to complete his high school education and graduate after twelve years. In summary we can say this child could not take hold of his cognitive faculties for a long time, a difficulty certainly related to the grave weakness in his metabolic processes." (Loewe, 2006, 93)

As a class teacher, Hella Loewe strongly experienced the therapeutic effect of modeling on this boy's cognitive/emotional development and that of many other children over the years. She challenges educators and therapists to further explore and research its harmonizing, healing value, particularly for metabolic weaknesses:

> "Is it possible that the activity of the inner organs, for example, the intestinal peristaltic, is beneficially stimulated through clay modeling experiences?

> "Is it possible that development and improvement in the metabolic-limb system might be brought about by rhythmically impulse pushing, groping and forming movements of the modelling process?" (Loewe, 2006, 93*)*

From Hella Loewe's descriptions, one can immediately detect how modeling strongly works on the four *'lower metabolic-will senses'* and helps bring about a healthy metamorphosis of the metabolic growth forces involved into the region of the 'four higher cognitive senses.' Modeling, above all, is an activity of the etheric body and its seat in the life sense metamorphoses into the sense of thought. The movement sense transforms into the language sense; the balance/spatial sense, into listening skills; and the touch sense, into a social sense of interaction with other students.

Body-based versatility and dexterity become the foundation for mental capacities and academic work. According to Harvard professor of psychiatry John Ratey,

> "Mounting evidence shows that movement is crucial to every other brain function, including memory, emotion, language and learning…Our 'higher' brain functions have evolved from movement and still depend on it." (*A User's Guide to the Brain,* 2002, 148.)

Or as Steiner similarly expresses it, *"The movements of the fingers are to a great extent the teachers of the elasticity of our thinking."* (*Mystery of the Universe,*121).

Imagination-Abundant Children
Modeling can also be a balancer for highly imaginative children in whose consciousness memory and imagination images tend to surface all too readily. An overabundance of imagining can make such students *more sensitive to and more vulnerable* to strong age-inappropriate imagery and experiences that can become 'stuck' in their minds. I know of one imaginative Waldorf graduate who avoids scary or violent films because images can persist into and disturb a night's sleep.

For the Imagination-overly-rich-child, modeling takes hold of the source of a possible excess of metabolic forces that can shoot into repetitive, unhealthily 'captivating' imaging. Using metabolic-limb activity (the blood in the muscles of arms and hands), it stimulates and expends metabolic blood energy in a *moving* process of physically shaping images. It literally brings images into simultaneous physiological and mental *circulation* so that a child is able to become 'unstuck' and *'can move on.'* Images constantly change from stage to stage. Modeling releases body bound images and energy and encases them as objects in external form to be faced and confronted.

Furthermore, the hands are not just part of what Steiner calls the metabolic-limb system. By virtue of their *rhythmical* shaping movement and their sphere of activity by the chest, they raise the activity up toward the interconnected middle, rhythmical heart/ breathing system, the true human balancer. Steiner remarkably calls the hands the *'eyes of the rhythmical system.*" In modeling, a child's breathing and circulation change and are harmonized—two important functions reaching up into head-brain-nerve system and its imaging function.

(See interesting case examples of different children in my article " Imagination and Memory": in *Helping Children on their Way*: *Educational Support for the Classroom*, Elizabeth Auer, editor, Waldorf Publications, 2017).

Pure Form Modeling in the Waldorf Curriculum: The Stream of the Future

Pure Form, Line and Color as Educators

For decades Waldorf schools have been practicing new experiential methods in educating a practical sense of form, color and beauty in children. Through a new art of dance called eurythmy, for example, students use whole-body movements to sculpt living forms in space in conjunction with poetic speech or music. In formdrawing they practice pure, non-representational forms in the early grades as a preparation for geometric drawing and proofs in the upper grades. In painting, first, second and third graders paint "stories" of pure colors. Primary is the language and dialogue of color —color stories–which may or may not give rise to form as a secondary consideration.

It is interesting to note that Steiner's new approach to the arts in education arose at a time when a new consciousness was also being born in modern art circles. Klee and Kandinsky, for example, were proclaiming in a revolutionary way that pure line and pure color existed as powerful entities in their own right. These elements need not be exclusively considered as secondary tools in representing objects.

Pure Forms out of Self-Activity

Rudolf Steiner wanted sculptural modeling in the elementary school to include the shaping of pure forms. This "pure form modeling" was to be developed as companion

and counterpart to "pure" form drawing. It was to be practiced from the earliest grades on and was especially important before children were too strongly inclined to make naturalistic figures. Steiner specifically recommended that modeling lessons start with basic archetypal geometric forms:

> "Sculptural modeling [*Plastisches*] should begin **before the ninth year, first spheres** [*Kuegeln*], then **other forms** and so on. Also with modeling one should **work entirely out of the forms** [*ganz aus den Formen herausarbeiten*]." (*Discussions with Teachers*, Lecture XV, p. 178. Emphasis in bold added by the author throughout.)

> "**Awaken in the children the feeling for form** [*Formgefühl*] **before the urge to imitate outer objects awakens** . . . Do not let children imitate anything until they have **cultivated within themselves the form through their own activity** [*Selbstätigkeit*] . . . Stick to this principle even when you move on to a more independent treatment of drawing,

painting and modeling [*Bildnerischen*]." (Ibid., *Second Curriculum Lecture*, p. 199)

Steiner recommended an artistic method that entailed free exploration and discovery for the early grades: he wanted students to 'play' with pure forms and only afterwards in a secondary way intellectually conceptualize things which the shapes may call to mind. He himself as a sculptor experienced what he called 'surprises' *(Ueberraschungen)* as he was working on the organic forms of sculpture of the first Goetheanum building, his international conference and performance center. These extraordinary artistic forms, he said, were not ones that were symbolic or allegorical to be intellectualized or interpreted as to what they "mean." Rather they were meant to stand on their own as entities to be experienced on deeper levels.

It is also interesting to note that one of the most formative experiences of Steiner's childhood was the discovery of a geometry book at age nine and the revelation of the spiritual significance of pure geometric forms. He later encountered and promoted projective geometry as a means to expand spiritual imagination. Throughout his varied career, Steiner was deeply involved in research on the mystery of how forms express themselves in matter. One of Steiner's favorite words which he used in a wide range of contexts was *"gestalten,"* to form, to shape.

Applications to Curriculum Studies

Developing an archetypal form sense through modeling has great implications for children's perceptual ability later. For example, in fourth grade animal studies, having practiced pure forms early on, children will have an awakened perception for the formative gestures embodied in the different animals bodies and postures. In modeling, they will thereby not immediately fix on static preconceived stereotypes but will be eager to explore and discover how to capture the otter's slippery sliding or the kitten in its playful pawing. They are able to sense, imagine and model the unique moving contour gestures of the darting, angled eagle body in contrast to the rounded resting cow. Children feel these shapes moving and forming in their creatively flexible hands, hearts and minds. They instinctively want their final piece to project life and animals in movement.

The Streams of the Past and Future

Working first with pure forms before tackling natural figures is not only a good education in dynamic sculptural perception but is also valuable preparation in artistic fundamentals and artistic confidence. Children at times feel intimidated by what a subject is naturalistically supposed "to look like" and even disappointed if their effort falls short of portraying a particular subject. Modeling pure forms is less constraining and allows for variation and experimentation. It has a freeing effect on a child's attitude as he or she discovers forms that are new experiences.

Hella Loewe, class teacher and researcher, associates the exciting process of exploring pure forms with a reaching out to an emerging and unfolding future in contrast to creating out of past knowledge and what is familiar. In her introduction to the pure forms that she modeled with grades one through three, she refers to artistic activities that deeply fire the will out of sense of discovery of something new:

> "I would like to designate the pedagogical stream that activates and strengthens the will forces of children as the 'stream of the

future' in the plastic-sculptural realm. In contrast to this, we can speak of a stream that the children bring with them, the 'stream of the past' that becomes visible in the illustrative drawings and paintings of children and in the little representational figures they model. This stream gradually exhausts itself. It is important that we clearly distinguish the underlying character of the different artistic activities we teach the children." ("Modeling in the Early Grades." *Bund Rundbrief*, Nr. 70, November 2000, translation by A.A.).

In my experience, both streams live strongly in children. On the one hand, youngsters are naturally attracted to drawing or modeling figures which help them represent and process their inner and outer experiences. Children re-member, re-activate, and re-live the forms of the created world which they already have as archetypes within their souls from a past, pre-birth existence and experiences. Modeling helps them to "re-*cognize*" through an artistic medium what they already "know" subconsciously and are waking up to in their encounters with the phenomena of the world.

On the other hand, modeling pure universal forms enables children to experience a complementary "stream of the future" coming towards them with new and as yet unrealized potential. They benefit immensely from "playing" in the universal workshop of pure forms with warm will and enthusiasm. The new organs of a sense and feeling for form gained in this new dimension help them to see more of the rich nuances of reality and bring them into their modeling. In my experience pure form modeling prepares for and continually brings new life to representational modeling by suffusing it with the sense for the dynamic gesture described earlier. Working with the wonderful forms of past creation is complemented and renewed by the warm new energy of reaching out to new forms and future evolution.

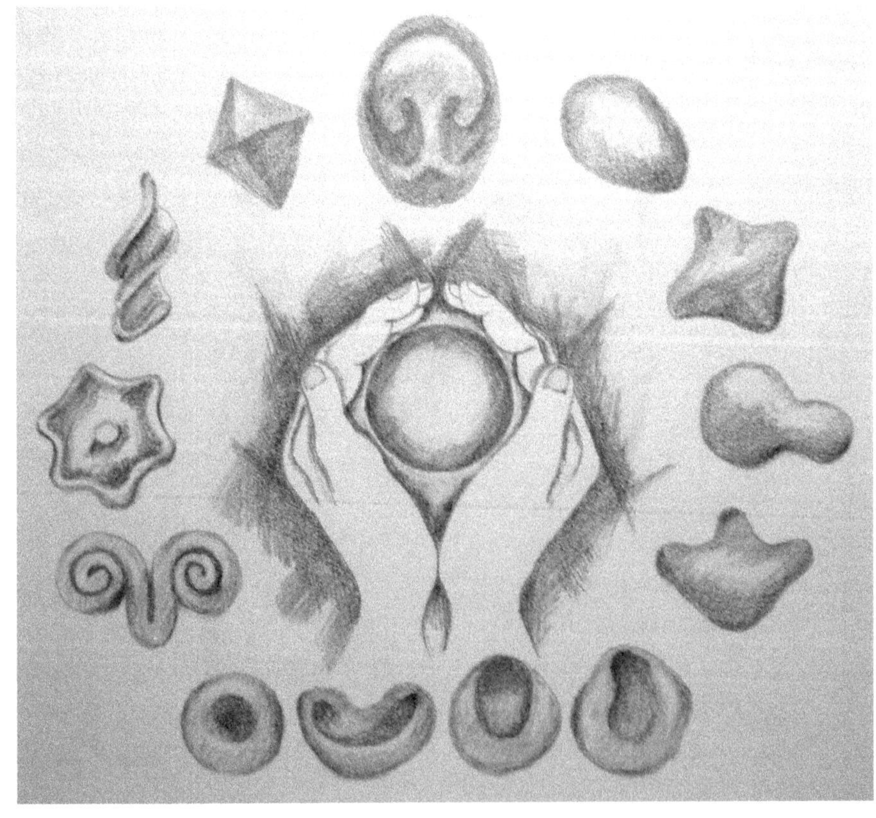

The Wonder of Our Hands

Rudolf Steiner wanted modeling to support Waldorf pedagogy as an *"education of the will."* This meant that to be effective it had to engage a child's motoric effort and primary organs of will, the hands—and not just his/her head and heart. It had to be a real hands-on experiential approach to education that deeply shaped a child's soul right down into its expression in meaningful limb movements and the neural fibers of the brain.

Steiner conceived of Waldorf Education as a pedagogy in which " manual dexterity... stands at the beginning of our teaching." He recommended that in the first lesson of the entire twelve-grade curriculum a first grade class teacher call attention to the fact that each child has two hands, is going to do and make and learn many new things with them (see *Practical Advice to Teachers*, Lecture IV, pp. 59-60). The first assignment for the children was a call to action and an exercise in manual dexterity (*Handgeschicklichkeit*) to shape two pure forms, the straight line and the curve. These are the two fundamental building blocks of all geometry and, according to mathematician and astronomer Johannes Kepler, are what the Creator used to design the entire universe.

Waldorf Education was intended to restore the vital role and intuitive capacities of the human hands. Intellectual subjects were to become an "action academics" and balanced with manual and artistic activities that strengthen the will and the emotional intelligence of children. Working with the hands or "hand-work," as it is called, was also, interestingly, meant to foster a clear and healthy thinking capacity.

Long before the discoveries of brain research at the end of the twentieth century, Steiner at its beginning pointed out the intimate connection between nimble fingers and a nimble mind and thinking. In his words:

> "Someone who knows how to move his fingers properly also has flexible ideas and thoughts and is better able to penetrate the essence of things with his thinking."
> *The Renewal of Education*, Lecture V, p. 67

> "The movements of the fingers are to a great extent the teachers of the elasticity of our thinking."
> *The Mystery of the Universe*, p. 121

Our Limbs and Hands as the Most Human Part of Us

In a revolutionary new way, Rudolf Steiner viewed our limbs and hands and their activity as being instruments of and very close to the creative spirit of the universe. Our hands ray out through the fingertips like stars into the world not only to connect with but also to participate actively in an ongoing creation. They intuitively reach into reality. They have emancipated themselves from the environmental specialization that characterizes animal appendages and are free to create artistically and to make tools.

In a new interpretation of evolution, Steiner held that our uniquely developed limbs, especially our arms and hands as they are connected to the chest and heart region, are the distinguishing physical feature and expression of our humanness rather than our heads. In certain lectures, he joked about the head with its water-filled, mollusk-like shell pompously riding on the body like a lazy king. He recognized the head's indispensable reflective thinking capacities in service to the spirit, but cautioned that we not underestimate the role of our hands in our intelligence and ability to affect the world process. In other words, it behooves us to appreciate how the human organism is a wholeness and perhaps not become "too big-headed."

> *There is indeed no other organ possessed by a living being that can carry out so many movements as does the human hand.*
> —M. Jeannerod, neurophysiologist
>
> *The hand can conform itself to a nearly infinite range of object shapes.*
> —Frank Wilson, neurologist

In a related vein, Frank Wilson, neurologist and author of *The Hand: How Its Use Shapes the Brain, Language and Human Culture* (1998), holds that we would do well to fully acknowledge how the evolution of the hand has contributed to making us into human beings. He brilliantly synthesizes current research in a number of fields including neuroscience and paleontology. Wilson describes how our hands have played a crucial role in the formation of our large brains and the development of speech and culture. Like Steiner, Wilson also cautions against what he calls a cephalocentric," i.e. head-dominated perspective on life that is particularly harmful when applied one-sidedly in education. Young homo sapiens, he advises, have been learning and wiring their neural circuitry for over a hundred thousand years primarily by applying their hands to the world. Today's children, more than ever before, need to recapitulate that evolutionary path. According to him, the only real effective education is hands-on, experiential education.

The Hand as a Sculptural Space-Creating Organ

The human hand, as has been described, is a key to how to go about the modeling process in a natural way. Evolution has embodied an entire universe of form in our flexible hands and their movements. We can discover in their freedom, plasticity of movement and flexible structure how to develop an infinite number of shapes and configurations of space and volume. In a child's hands worlds are born and reborn.

Our miraculous hands create changing forms of sculptural space in, between, and around themselves. They are "space-sensing and space-shaping organs." In their living spaces, substance finds its form because our hands themselves are a manifestation of the creative sculptural life forces active in and around us. We discover a "vocabulary" of archetypal form gestures through their motions and structure-making.

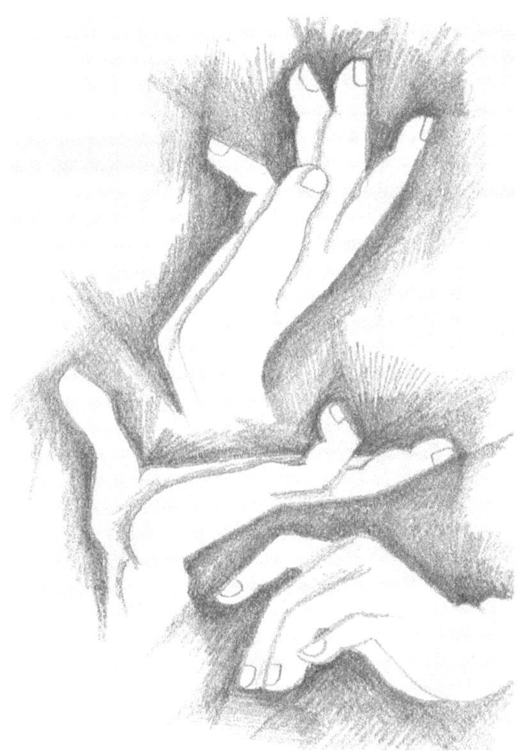

Hands move eurythmically

A Living Heart Space

The hands themselves are living, eurhythmically moving sculptures. The five-fold form of each hand's fingers is reflected in the five-fold pentagon of the palm (see diagram above). Another pentagon is created by the four sections of our bent arms (with hands folded) extending from the chest as the fifth side. We mathematically radiate star-like out into the world with one humerus, two lower arm bones (radius and ulna), three, then four wrist bones and finally five fingers. This raying out in 1-2-3-4-5 is a signature of our interconnectedness with the world. We have the pentagonal form in common with certain nature forms including the living world of many plants. The pentagon was the Pythagorean symbol of health.

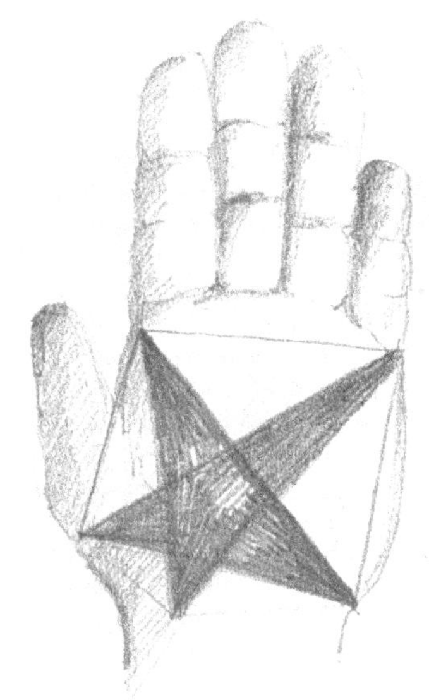

To the Hand
by Rex Raab, architect
*Hand, that comes to grips
with the things of the world,
 and shapes them,
and through your wisdom,
 helps me to grasp existence;
You star come to earth!...
May everything I start,
Carry though, and complete,
 always be helpful,
that I may learn at last
to bless my fellow men
with a healing hand.*

Our cupped or folded hands naturally come together in front of the sternum and heart region to create a "heart form" or spherical bowl-like space of activity of their own. Hands and heart are both organs of feeling and sensitivity, motion and emotion that again connect us with our surroundings. Steiner spoke of the arms and hands as *"the eyes of our rhythmic system."*

143

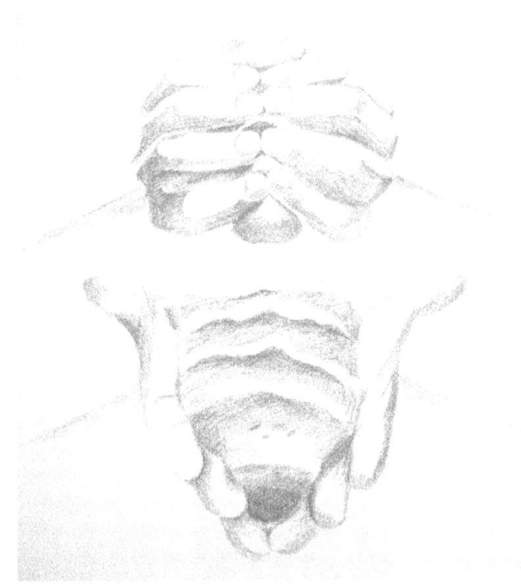

"My Hands are My Heart": Drawing after a photo by Gabriel Orozco exhibited in the Hammer Museum (LA)

All the World and Its Forms in Our Hands: Convex, Concave and Flat/Straight

Like the rest of our body, the hand is not formed out of flat surfaces. Its structure embodies the two elemental and dynamic kinds of curved surfaces—convex and concave. The back of the hand curves out convexly into the world while the other, inner, more sensitive palm and inwardly bending fingers together form a concavity, hollow, a cup, a "cave." Convexity bulges outward, full of life forces as in a bursting bud. Concavity is more receptive, creating an inner world of consciousness and feeling. Our curved palms and the inside tips of our fingers are two of the most sensitive parts of our body. A closed fist emphasizes the convexity of a sphere, but we know that there is a hidden world within. Our fingers curl inward like a water spiral or wave enveloping a warm pocket of air.

In addition to concave and convex, there is another fundamental surface: the flat or straight plane which has a more static, abstract geometric and mineral quality in comparison to the two curves of life forms.

Together these three kinds of surfaces combine to create a multiform world. They generate a myriad of form qualities besides curved and flat such as angular, pointed, sharp, contracted, expanded, balanced, symmetrical, asymmetrical, heavy, light, life-filled, dead, and so on.

Form modeling helps us concretely explore this rich constellation and thereby connects us with the building elements of reality around us.

For more perspectives, see the following chapters in my *Learning about the World through Modeling:* "Hand Movements Sculpt Intelligence," "Thinking through Modeling," and "Rudolf Steiner's Advice on Modeling."

Formed of the Clay of the Earth: Questions about Materials

Invigorating Street Mud

In the quotation cited above, Steiner points out that the main point of pedagogical modeling is for teachers to make a start and have their students activate their hands regularly in creating forms. The forming and form-sensing activity is paramount regardless of what malleable material is used–"even street mud if it is the only thing available it doesn't matter! Elsewhere he called street mud "a very good material" for this important purpose.[2]

Observation of young children playing for lengthy times shaping cool wet mud or sand or cold snow shows us what a primal impulse sculptural activity is for human beings. Our hands want to reshape and transform the earth.

Plentiful earth materials like sand, dirt and clay lend themselves naturally and readily to modeling activity outdoors and indoors. Hella Loewe, a long time Waldorf class teacher found that clay was a wonderfully malleable material and ideal for engaging and invigorating children in the early grades. Her boisterous class developed a passion for their weekly modeling lessons

and was harmonized by them. Following each session, she saw "with pleasure how my children developed healthy, ruddy cheeks; even the delicate, pale ones appeared rosy and stimulated."[3]

Clay for First and Second Grades

Steiner emphasized the artistic value of young children *"handling clay"* and even *"struggling with [such] outer materials."* Their exertion helped them develop will-power and connect actively with the world. In his words:

"Whatever subject is being taught, the child's inherent impulse to play, which is an intrinsic part of its makeup, can be guided into artistic activities. And when children enter the first and second grade, they are perfectly able to make this transition. However clumsy children of six or seven may be when modeling, painting, or finding their way into music and poetry, if teachers know how to permeate their lessons with artistry, even small children as miniature sculptors or painters, can begin to have the experience that human nature does not end at the fingertips, that is at the periphery of the skin, but flows out into the world. The adult being is growing in children whenever they put their being into handling clay, wood, or paints. In these very interactions with materials, children grow, learning to perceive how closely the human being is interwoven with the fabric of the world. These [artistic channels] permit a freedom of inner activity while at the same time forcing the children to struggle with outer materials, as we have to do in adult work." [4]

Waldorf teachers should specially note that Steiner in the quote above is speaking of first and second graders modeling with clay.

Choosing Other Useful Materials

In addition to mud, clay, and wood Steiner also refers to wax and plasticine as suitable modeling materials. (He himself invented his own mixture of plasticine—although not for school purpose—and created numerous architectural models and figures out of it—some quite large.)

Caroline von Heydebrand (1886-1938), one of the twelve founding class teachers in the first Waldorf school in 1919, who practiced modeling and the use of beeswax in her classroom, poignantly described its pedagogical implications:

"Just as the little child digs and plays in his sand pile or in the earth, making little men and animals or baking mud pies, so a little later does the older child occupy his creative imagination with more permanent materials. The nearer he approaches the change of teeth, the more markedly do the formative forces reveal themselves—since their activity in this change of teeth is now, as it were, concluded—in the impulse the child feels to use his creative powers of soul in fashioning forms, in painting and in modeling. And just as the child Jesus [according to legend] was happy when he made his cuckoo-birds out of the moist, clayish earth which he found in the lanes where he played, and with which

he made them look alive as he patted them into shape, so is an other child now satisfied also, if he has a bit of loam or clay which he finds perhaps near at hand. If he can only make something, he will look for his material till he finds it. On the other hand, if his parents can give him beeswax, for example, to model with, then in the very act of kneading this noble material his creative will—working as it does in the circulation of the blood, and warming his hands till they are all aglow— makes itself felt even to the very tips of his fingers. Thus not only is the skillfulness of his hands, increased, but his imaginative capacity is also aroused and nurtured. For we know how similarly the movements and gestures of both hands and feet react when the child is learning to speak: how they help him to learn, to form ideas, and to think… In his play, first of all, is the child's creative activity developed. Later, it shows itself in his happy enjoyment, his eagerness to recreate in his own way the beauty of the world…the road lead[s] from a healthy, wisely-directed play-impulse in childhood to a consciously dutiful activity in mature life." [5]

Similarly, Cecil Harwood (1898-1975), a founding teacher of the first Waldorf school in the English speaking world, characterized the child's early desire to shape objects with the hands as a profoundly organic artistic need:

"[Young children] need all the more to be given artistic food because the desire is still, so to speak, organic. Look at the imagination of children, their make-believe games, their wide-eyed love of stories, their uncontrollable desire to paint and draw, the itching of their fingers to shape and model, even if they have no better material than dirty clay from a back garden, or wax pulled fearfully from the melting wall round the candle flame…Painting, modeling, acting, rhythmical movement, these must become for these young children the very way of knowledge. If you succeed in teaching in this way, you are uniting what is nowadays divided —the forces of the head with the forces of feeling and of movement. You are strengthening the binding point of thought and feeling and will."[6]

Michael Howard, a sculptor who has worked extensively with Waldorf teachers and teacher trainees, encourages them to appreciate the particular capacities that different materials stimulate in children and to avoid prejudging the suitability of materials:

"Teachers who have the children model are to be commended whatever the material they employ. However, since most teachers are not sculptors, they are understandably grateful for any indications that give them direction. In Waldorf schools there is a prevailing view that from pre-school up through grade three children should model with beeswax. Promoting the merits of beeswax typically includes the judgment that clay should not be used with young children because it is harmful to them. The explanation commonly given is that the cold, wet clay robs the children's forces.

"If this is the case, we may well ask if it is harmful for young children to play in puddles, streams, wet sand, mud, snow and the cold water from the sink? Playing with such materials can be messy and thus can cause some inconvenience, but I have never heard anyone say they are harmful. Quite the opposite, it is generally regarded as normal and healthy. If there is any reason for concern it surely is in regard to those children who avoid playing with materials such as sand and snow. One finds the same healthy delight and creative play in a group of children mucking out in a natural clay pit as in a sandbox.

"Such observations alone are reason enough to be wary of the view that clay is inappropriate or harmful in the early years. Those who do not trust their own experience about the healthy nature of clay modeling may look to Rudolf Steiner for the definitive insight. Research by colleagues both in Europe and America has thus far found not one statement from Steiner that hints at harmful effects of clay at any age…

"I raise the issue of clay modeling for two reasons. As a sculpture teacher I feel called to challenge what seems an unfounded dogmatism in my realm of activity. But the use of clay is not the real issue. More significantly, it serves as an example where vigilance is called for. If we recognize a dogmatic mindset creeping into one or two areas of our educational work, however minor in itself, is it not likely that there are others? The issue I raise is the threat posed by a dogmatic mindset per se, where in the name of 'best practice' any principle or method is fixed into the one-right-way. The reason we should be alert to even minor expressions of a dogmatic stance is because as a soul gesture it is the polar opposite of what makes education an art. To judge clay as harmful is to short-circuit a possibly creative pedagogical activity. Instead of judging clay as good or bad, we might ask ourselves: what does each material-beeswax, clay, sand, mud, wood, wool-offer for the development of different capacities? If our inner gesture is experientially open rather than conceptually closed, we open ourselves to appreciate the potential of one material to engage one aspect of human nature while another material may best be used to exercise another capacity."[7]

Clay for Early Childhood Activity

Elizabeth Grunelius, one of the early pioneering kindergarten teachers in the first

Waldorf School in Stuttgart gave enthusiastic endorsement for the use of clay with young children and advice on how to orchestrate modeling with kindergarteners:

"Another general [kindergarten] activity is work with clay . . . First thing in the morning the children help to push their tables together and spread a large oilcloth over them. Then they distribute the boards, one to each place, and bring a good-sized lump of clay for each board. The children can hardly wait to plunge their hands into the plastic material and to start forming it. Sometimes the teacher will set to work too and the children can see how he handles the material. Occasionally the forms of animals, a horse, a cow, a little goat, a duck or even an elephant or a giraffe will emerge, and the children will immediately want to have them and play with them. Of course the children will be free to watch the teacher or follow their own incentives.

"In clay work, as in painting, the results are not made the subject of discussion or comparative analysis; the work is placed on a shelf for the rest of the morning, and after the children have gone home a few pieces of special interest are selected and kept, while the remainder of the clay goes back into the container."[8]

Further Thoughts and Experiences with Clay

For me clay with the right moisture is the quintessential, archetypal earth medium for modeling at all ages, 3 to 103. It gives way to hand pressure with just the right resistance and at the same time holds its form wonderfully. Clay's water permeated texture becomes almost magically flesh-like in feel and look. It is no wonder many ancient cultures associated it with the creation of the human being!

TKhnum the Moulder, the Ram-Headed God shaped human beings and all flesh, modeled the gods and fashioned the world egg on his potter's wheel.

Egyptian mythology

And God formed the human being of the clay of the ground and breathed into his nostrils the breath of life . . .

–Genesis

Remember thou hast made me of clay . . .

–Job

Wise Prometheus modeled human beings out of river clay and in the shape of the gods. He desired fire for his creations.

–Greek Mythology

Clay also lends itself to handling good-sized pieces and "whole-hand modeling." All parts of the "threefold hand" can be fully engaged in the process: concave palm (feeling), fingers (thinking/nerve-sense), and the lower very muscular base before the wrist and muscular thumb (will).

The children in my three class groups in the Waldorf school (1977-1998) loved our weekly clay exercises and special main lesson projects –a whole Adobe village!– and always tackled them with gusto. In past years, I have been invited into the first and second grade to give occasional clay modeling lessons. I experienced that today's children are eager and in need of taking up this therapeutically resistant substance of Mother Earth and imaginatively and passionately transforming it. They found it exciting to be modeling pure geometric forms just as they loved to do two-dimensional ones in their formdrawing lessons. And of course their hands are always "full of" animals, people, and dwellings!

Warming Beeswax

I have also conducted countless exercises and projects in grades 1-5 with colored beeswax to the delight of the children. Beeswax, however, is hard and stiff at first and can offer an unreasonably uncomfortable resistance for young children. There are ways to pre-warm the material so that it would become as malleable as clay. Children can hold it between their warm hands for many minutes while one tells a story or put it down their shirts "into the oven" on their stomachs. Sometimes we put pieces on the window sill in the sun or on the radiator, watching out that it did not become too soft or melt!

In this connection, Hannah Huber, an experienced kindergarten teacher has published a wonderful action research book *Gestalten mit Bienenwachs im Vorschulalter (Modeling with Beeswax in the Preschool Age,* 2001) This manual is sumptuously illustrated with pictures of figures that kindergartners as little builders have constructed out of pieces of soft wax. (It is valuable even for those who do not read German.) In it Frau Huber describes how her children soften beeswax in a warm water bath at hand temperature, and how to put it in the oven at 112° F (50° C) for an hour before use. (I have also heard of a kindergarten teacher who skillfully mixed up batches of warm wax in a pot on the stove and served out soft lumps).

Coloring Beeswax?

Frau Huber also prefers to use beeswax with its natural golden color rather than a colored assortment. She found that "sculptural qualities find their fullest expression in using the one natural color."[9] The emphasis is then primarily on the form experience rather than combining it with a color experience, which is left to painting where form in turn can be secondary or even relatively non-existent.

Sculptor Michael Howard agrees:

"Often the beeswax that is used for modeling is brightly colored. Children and teachers alike may find these colors cheerful and fun, for example, a gnome with a red shirt, blue pants, and a green hat with a yellow feather. What are the pedagogical issues a teacher might consider regarding the color of beeswax? If we want the children to have a color experience, we have them paint. When painting they do not sculpt, they do not give three-dimensional form to the pigment. If we want them to have a form experience, we should help them focus on forming the clay or beeswax. In giving them colored beeswax we are distracting them from a full form experience; we are asking them to paint while they are sculpting. Put another way, using brightly colored beeswax stimulates the sense nerve will. If our pedagogical intent is to develop the feeling-will through sculptural forming, then we would use clay or beeswax that has a simple earth tone."[10]

Fingering Beeswax

I also experienced that beeswax modeling tends to emphasize the nerve-sense pole in the use of the fingertips rather than the palm and muscular base of the hand. With clay one can shape out the whole mass of a piece with the whole hand and then proceed to detailing with fingers and tips as a final stage. Doing a lot of beeswax modeling I find can neglect "whole-hand modeling" and using the fullest potential of our hands' plasticity. Beeswax modeling tends toward what I would call a kind of fine motor, intellectual "picky-ness." Children can become caught up prematurely with fine details to rather than to first artistically capture the primal gesture of a subject. Of course, beeswax is can be very helpful for a child who needs to improve fine motor skills but perhaps that is better achieved in handwork and sewing! (As another perspective, a European Waldorf art teacher with decades of experience visited the United States recently and remarked that he was astounded at how beeswax is so emphasized in American schools and teacher workshops. "We never did it like that!" he exclaimed).

In my opinion, teachers need to continuously evaluate their repertoire of arts and methods for a variety and balance of capacities. Sculptor Michael Howard gives an example of such an ongoing assessment process applied to the two media we have been discussing:

> "We might discover that certain materials are best suited for sense-nerve activity while other materials lend themselves better to feeling-will activity. If we determine that we need to exercise their sense-nerve will, or what is commonly called head/hand coordination, then beeswax is well suited. The inclination to make recognizable objects-bowls, birds, and so forth, but especially, the fine fingertip manner of forming small shapes in wax engage the sense nerve will. If on the other hand we wish the children to exercise their feeling-will, clay is particularly suitable. Clay can naturally be used in larger quantities that invite whole-hand movements. This in turn allows the students to focus more on feeling the quality of the forms rather than on conceptual associations."[11]

Plasticine Magic Mirrors and Spontaneous Hand Dexterity

An interesting medium whose qualities lie between clay and beeswax is plasticine, an earthen material mixed with a non-toxic binder. This material can be costly in comparison to clay and does not lend itself to making large pieces. It can, however, be used over and over.

I found a variety of earth colored brown plasticine that responded more readily to simple hand warmth than beeswax but did not become too soft to retain forms.

My students in the lower grades each flattened two walnut sized lumps of plasticine into two thin, round "magic mirrors" out of which all kinds of forms could emerge. They stored these in a plastic zip bag in their desks. At a moment's notice I could have students bring forth the pieces for quick warming between the palms and for spontaneous modeling and often just short exercises. With a word such as "sphere" or "bird" from me, hands launched into action. After the children held up what they had produced, they reverently curled the form into a rounded lump, smoothed its edges and then flattened it into a magic mirror for future use. Needless to say, my children became very dexterous and flexibly creative over time. Their hands could spontaneously "speak forth" quick forms at a moment's notice!—even as part of the warm-up section of a main lesson.

Daily short hand exercises with plasticine serve nicely as the forerunners to a much more formal weekly modeling lesson with clay which requires more preparation and time.

This chapter appeared as an article "Modeling Clay—for All Ages?" in the *Waldorf Research Bulletin*, Autumn/Winter 2012, vol. XVII, Number 2.

Notes

1 Steiner, R. "Second Curriculum Lecture," *Discussions with Teachers*, Anthroposophic Press, Hudson, NY, 1997, p. 198.

2 Steiner, R. *Kingdom of Childhood*, Lecture 6, Anthroposophic Press, Hudson, NY, 1995, pp. 93-94

[3] Loewe, Hella, "Modeling in the Early Grades," A. Auer, translator, *Bund Rundbrief* Nr.70, November 2000. Frau Loewe's initial articles evolved and expanded wonderfully into a manual *Basic Sculptural Modeling: Developing the Will by Working with Pure Forms in the first Three Grades*, AWSNA Publications, Fair Oaks, CA, 2006.

[4] Steiner, R. "Education and Art," *Waldorf Education and Anthroposophy*, vol. 2, Lecture 3, Anthroposophic Press, Hudson, NY,1996, pp. 58-59.

[5] von Heydebrand, Caroline. *The Child at Play*, Anthroposophic Publishing, London, 1928, card covers, pp. 17-20.

[6] Harwood, C. *The Way of the Child*, Rudolf Steiner Press, London, 1997, p. 32.

[7] Howard, M. *Educating the Will,* AWSNA Publications, Fair Oaks,CA, 2004 pp. 37-39.

[8] Grunelius, E. *Early Childhood Education and the Waldorf School Plan*, Rudolf Steiner College press, Fair Oaks, 1991, pp. 18-19.

[9] Huber, *Gestalten mit Bienewachs im Vorschulalter (Modeling with Beeswax in the Preschool Age)*, Verlag Freies Geistesleben, Stuttgart, 2001, p.9.

[10] Howard, M. *Educating the Will*, p. 40.

[11] Howard, M. *Educating the Will*, p. 39.

Rudolf Steiner's Indications Relating to Pure Form Modeling

Summary of Suggestions for Form Modeling

- Start modeling fundamental forms such as spheres with younger children. Develop other pure forms.

- Model forms for their own sake. Work entirely out of the forms. Discover a similarity to outer natural objects only later on.

- Slip into and become one with the forms. Live with the forms.

- Awaken in children the feeling for form (*Formgefühl*) before the urge to imitate outer objects awakens.

- Allow the children to explore and discover forms on their own and to freely struggle with the material.

- Render and recreate forms freely rather than copy them.

- Use the whole hand in modeling and not just the fingertips. Follow the forms with the hollow of the hand.

- Let modeling strengthen real looking, observing and imagining.

- Educate dexterous hands to promote flexible and penetrating thinking and healthy judgment (discernment).

- Let plant forms and the forming of the human organs and bones be educators of our sense for living, formative forces.

- Let modeling enhance the understanding of organic processes, such as plant growth.

Stockmeyer's Summary

Waldorf curriculum researcher Karl Stockmeyer briefly summarized Steiner's statements on the subject of modeling:

> "Only very few hints and indications exist for modeling. The children should begin modeling in the ninth or tenth years.[*] They should be guided to make plastic forms out of the hollows of their hands and forms for form's sake can be made out of the previous results. A similarity to outer objects should be discovered only when the form is completed. We have been told that a real knowledge of the forms of human organs awakens a desire for modeling in the child, which however, will not result in his copying outer forms." (Stockmeyer, *Rudolf Steiner's Curriculum for Waldorf Schools*,1965, p. 210)

> "Shapes are to be recreated." (Ibid. p.126)

Stockmeyer collected several indications, but he did not cite all. Many others have to be sought out in various and scattered lectures. (See more in "Rudolf Steiner's Advice" in my *Learning about the World through Modeling*).

Readers are encouraged to consult the full texts and lectures and study the quotations in their full context.

---

[*] In the the first quote below, Steiner recommends modeling "before the ninth year."

Start with Modeling Pure Forms for Their Own Sake

Already in the first two week "crash course" in 1919 for the original twelve teachers of the first Waldorf school, Steiner recommended that modeling start with basic archetypal pure forms:

> "Sculptural modeling (*Plastisches*) should begin before the ninth year, first spheres (Kugeln), then other forms and so on. Also with modeling one should work entirely out of the forms. (ganz aus den Formen herausarbeiten)." (Steiner, *Discussions with Teachers*, p. 178)

Steiner deemed the modeling of a sphere to be particularly meaningful for human experience:

> *"To feel . . . a circle in a plane or a sphere in space is **to feel the self, the ego**...When even . . . a fragment of a sphere rouses in him a sense of independence in his own self, then he is learning to **live in forms**."* (Steiner, *Architecture as Synthesis of the Arts*, p. 102)

Pure Forms Before Naturalistic Subjects

Significantly, Steiner wanted this activity of working freely with pure forms and colors to be emphasized in the visual arts before the children matured and had a strong impulse to depict and represent natural forms:

> "Awaken in the children the feeling for form [*Formgefuhl*] before the urge to imitate outer objects awakens. Wait until later before allowing them to apply what they have practiced in drawing forms to imitating actual objects. First have them draw angles so that they understand what an angle is through its shape... do not let children imitate anything until they have cultivated an inner sense for form in its own dynamics which can then later also be imitated. Stick to this principle even when you move on to a more independent treatment of drawing, painting and sculptural forming [*Bildnerischen*]." (Steiner, *Discussions with Teachers*, p. 199)

(English readers note: the word "sculptural forming" is left out of the 1997 translation.

Sensory Openness, Hand and Brain Plasticity

Having a foundation in pure forms enables children to see their expression more readily in the forms of nature later. The early grades are an optimal time of sensory openness before the human organism becomes more fixed, sees what it expects and is in the habit to see. Modeling pure forms keeps the mind open, limber and on the lookout for the new and unexpected. It has been shown in the past decade that the brain has its own incredible sculptural mobility called "plasticity" and this plasticity is closely connected with the hand's plasticity of moving, forming, and inventing. Steiner characterized this relationship decades ago:

> "The movements of the fingers are to a great extent the teachers of the plasticity of our thinking." (Steiner, *Mystery of the Universe*, p. 121)

> " [At the Waldorf school the children's] souls create the most wonderful forms when they have learned to observe certain things in the human being or the animal with a truly artistic feeling for nature . . . The children do not merely 'have an idea' in their heads; they feel the idea, for it flows into heir whole life of feeling. Their being of soul lives in the sense of the idea, which is not merely a concept. The idea is a plastic form. The whole complex of ideas at last becomes a human form and figure and in the last resort all this passes over into the will. The child learns to do what she thinks. [*Das Kind lernt eigentlich alles dasjenige auch machen, was es denken lern*]."(Steiner, *A Modern Art of Education*, p. 198)

Recreating and Growing Together With Forms

Steiner wanted students to become deeply absorbed and immersed in freely rendering and re-creating forms out of a dynamic inner process. Figures were not to be copied and reproduced with pedantic intellectual exactitude:

> "It is totally irrelevant to judge whether something is copied properly and so on. A resemblance to something external should only appear as something secondary. What should live in the human being is the experience of growing together and becoming one with the forms [*innere Verwachsensein mit den Formen selbs*]." (Steiner, *Practical Advice to Teachers*, p. 19)

This principle was specifically demonstrated in Steiner's response to a teacher's question about a modeling assignment in an older grade:

> "You could use a column (pillar) seen from a particular perspective as an example, but you should not make the children slavishly imitate it. You need to get the children to observe, but allow them to change their work." (Steiner, *Faculty Meetings with Rudolf Steiner*, pp. 62-63.)

Whole-Hand Modeling

Steiner wanted children to " follow the forms with the hollow of the hand [*Hohlhand*]" (*Practical Advice to Teachers*, Lecture I). Experiencing forms fully means to take hold of the clay in the full "cups" of the hands and use the whole hand—palms, muscular base, and fingers. Using the finger tips for touching up surfaces is fine, but just using fingers in modeling becomes "picky." Full involvement in form demands full hands as form sensing organs.

Education Toward Freedom: Exploration and Discovery

Waldorf pedagogy seeks, above all, to educate human beings in responsibly directing their own lives. Essential to the development of this self-direction is the creative freedom to discover new ideas and not get stuck in copying fixed forms and intellectual concepts inherited from the past.

> "Modeling affords children and adults a way to develop flexible, imaginative thinking and to freely discover an infinite changing diversity of ideas in concrete form. Concepts are allowed to grow and expand through this medium.
>
> "To lead play gradually over to the creation of artistic forms and then to the practical work…is to act in complete harmony with the demands of man's nature. And it is absorbingly interesting to find that the children's plastic, artistic activity turns quite naturally 'by itself' [*wie von selbst*] to the making of playthings and toys….Our children are allowed the greatest freedom even in their practical work and are allowed to follow their own sense of discovery."
> (Steiner, *A Modern Art of Education*, p. 197)

With the right kind of teacher guidance and inspiration the creation of forms happens substantially through the children's own initiative and " naturally by itself. "

Learning how to learn is a main goal in the Waldorf way of learning and teaching.

Above all, Modeling Activates the Living Forces of the Etheric Body for Lively Learning

Developmentally, while the astral body is being drawn in along the nerves and bearing increasing consciousness, the life energy of the young child is being drawn out more and more outside into making and forming:

> "The etheric body is…a modeler a sculptor…

This modeling force . . . emancipates itself [from forming the physical body] with the change of teeth. It can then work as an activity of soul. That is why the child has the impulse to model or paint forms."
(Steiner, *The Kingdom of Childhood*, p. 92)

Modeling as well as form drawing and eurythmy experiences activate the vibratory resonance of the etheric body during sleep.

"[We] prepare the etheric body of formative forces in [the child's] waking life so that it continues to vibrate, but in its vibrations perfects what has been absorbed during the day. Then the child will awake in an etheric body—and physical body also—inwardly and organically stirred into activity. She will be full of life and vitality."

(Steiner, *A Modern Art of Education,* p. 197)

Modeling Enlivens the Subject Matter of the Curriculum

In my first sourcebook I show how modeling brings the curriculum alive. In the teacher training seminar at Antioch University New England, students model key sculptural motifs of each grade right up through the elementary years. The whole curriculum passes through their hands. I find that modeling helps anchor their understanding.

Interestingly, Steiner indicated that modeling and other arts not only support curriculum themes directly, but also indirectly:

"The teacher should always encourage the young pupils to form shapes of all kinds of any suitable material he can lay his hands on... And if the artistic activities are introduced in the way indicated, other subjects will also come easier. Foreign languages, for example, will be learned with far greater ease."

(Steiner, *Soul Economy and Waldorf Education*, p. 211)

Pure Forms From the Living Language of Plants

Steiner did not think that plants, because of their thinness and fragility, were suitable or practical subjects for modeling or sculpture. He pointed out, however, that all modeling teaches us about plants because of its formative nature.

"Any plastic skill that we develop in the child helps him to understand the formations contained in plants."

(Steiner, *Modern Art of Education*, p. 193)

Paradoxically, Steiner spoke of the leaf as the most perfect sculptural form. In the leaf the life body of the plant expresses its archetypal sculpting gesture: the forming of the surface of a plane. The etheric world in which the archetypal plant lives is two-dimensional and planar.

What Steiner demonstrated was highly suitable sculpturally from the etheric world of plants were metamorphic form motifs. Examples in his first Goetheanum can inspire many modeling lessons. The pillar base motifs express the sculptural forces and gestures of budding, sprouting, leafing but are not depictions of or symbols for buds, sprouts or leaves. Similarly, the architraves are flowing forces of life. (See *Series Five* for examples and the later chapter on *Learning from Goetheanum Forms*).

Human Organs and Bones as Teachers of Form-Making of the Etheric Body

On several occasions Steiner recommended the modeling of bones and organs such as liver, lungs and kidneys. This was not only to learn physiology and anatomy but to experience and engage in the same formative life forces that shape the body itself.

Modeling the kidneys becomes a lesson in symmetry and the lungs a lesson in asymmetry. The femur ball and hip socket are the archetypal embodiment of convex and concave. The muscles undulate in wave forms. The vertebral column is like a rhythmical "running form drawing" but in three dimensions. (See Series Eight for examples.) Because we do not see these organ forms every day, they have to a great degree the atmosphere of coming out of another world. They teach the soul to be *mobile* and open to exploring the not so unfamiliar.

> "At a comparative early age . . . between ten and eleven . . . children learn to know how the bones are formed and built up, how they support each other . . . Then the children model plastic forms . . . Not that the child imitates the forms of the bones, but from the way in which he now models his forms we perceive the outer expression of an inner mobility of soul. Before this he has already got so far as to be able to make little receptacles of various kinds; children discover how to make bowls and things quite by themselves."
>
> (Steiner, *Human Values in Education*, pp. 61-62)

With my groups of students, I made them aware of their skeletons in grade 4 as part of a whole imaginative picture of human form and function. In grade 7 we modeled organs such as kidney, lung, hand and foot and in grade 8 representative bones (femur, etc.) and the ear.

Students are "not to imitate," and copy exactly but to render subjects out of a "mobile" inner sense.

> "[If] you simply let the children work freely it is very interesting to see that you have explained the human being to them, the lung for instance, then out of themselves they begin to model such forms . . . [The] child forms things out of its own human

beingness (*Menschenwesenheit*)."
(Steiner, *The Kingdom of Childhood*, p.93)

Most important of all is to experience artistically one's own "human-forming-forces" [*Menschen-Kraft-bildende*].

Pure Forms Derived from the Language of Architecture and Ornamental Motifs

Studying architecture and ornament can also reveal motifs that express form dynamics rather than "things" and can be developed into modeling exercises. In Series Five of this book there is an exercise of a double spiral derived from and inspired by the Ionic capital of ancient Greek pillar. The pure gestures of different arches in Series Six is another example.

In his book *Living with Forms in Art and Nature,* Michael Martin develops Steiner's insights into the acanthus leaf motif on ancient temple facades and its two aspects of an "earth motif" and a "sun motif." The shape of the earth motif is plant bulb-like and expresses earthly life forces which create convex forms with weighted, rounded bases and gently pointed tops. The sun motif expresses forces streaming from above and creating a corolla-like form, often with palm-like features. These two forms alternate rhythmically on temple facades, pillars, tombs and vases.

Artistic Feeling for Form:
Developmental Suggestions to Encourage Modeling in the Early Grades

By Peter A. Wolf, translated by Arthur Auer

A Lecture Held at the Craft Teachers Conference of German Waldorf Schools in Muelheim/Ruhr on March 28, 1999

Many class teachers find sculptural modeling to be difficult to do regularly or at all with their students. Frequently, responsibility for this activity is given over to specialist art teachers. This can mean that students only begin to model in the ninth grade in high school. Modeling is felt to be messy and dirty and Rudolf Steiner's statements on the pedagogical justification and vital importance of this artistic activity are often overlooked or ignored.

These few short provocative comments at the beginning should already indicate that what we have here is basically a problem of will and courage. And yet we have at our disposal quite a sufficient wealth of warm, enthusiastic insights and basic knowledge to fire up our wills and inspire us to model again with our children.

Curriculum Overviews Can Be Too Abbreviated

The research document *Rudolf Steiner's Curriculum for Waldorf Schools* by Karl Stockmeyer provides a few scanty generalizations as preliminary information to the subject. They appear, however, as rather abstract and are therefore not especially encouraging. In the second half of this book on the curriculum there are a few summary statements on modeling:

- the child should start modeling at the age of 9 or 10

- the child should be taught to feel and follow the sculptural forms with the hollow of his/her hands

- forms should be shaped purely for form's sake (*Formen um der Formen willen*)

- the child should only afterwards discover similarities to outer material objects

- an engagement with the forms of the human organs awakens an urge for sculptural modeling which should not become mere copying.

Such indications call for us to consider and study them in the actual *contexts* in which they appear in the various pedagogical lectures. Only then will they lose their abstractness and reveal—contrary to Stockmeyer's opinion—that there are *many indications*; they have only been "forgotten."

Fundamentals Out of Form-Feeling

In the "Second Lecture on the Curriculum," Rudolf Steiner gave the subject matter for lessons in the grades. Geometric forms are to be developed in grades 1-4 out of form-drawing and the fundamentals of painting introduced; equally important elementary aspects of sculptural activity are also to be practiced. The importance of this subject and its learning goals are made clear:

> "We continue this [fundamental artistic work in grades 1-4] by moving on to three-dimensional, sculptural forms, using plasticine if it is available and whatever else you can get if it isn't—even if it's mud from the street, it doesn't matter. The point is to develop the ability to see forms [*Formanschauen*=Form-Beholding] and to feel forms [*Formempfindung* = Form-Feeling]."

(Rudolf Steiner, *Discussions with Teachers)*

Also, in context with the development of form drawing out of fundamental elements it is stated in the above mentioned lecture:

> ". . . awaken in the children the feeling for form [*Formgefuehl*)] before the urge to imitate outer objects awakens . . .

> "Do not let children imitate anything until they have cultivated an inner sense for form in its own dynamics, which can then later also be imitated. Stick to this principle even when you move on to a more self-reliant treatment of drawing, painting and sculptural exercises [*Bildnerischen* not translated and omitted in the 1997 English translation]." (Ibid.)

In the Third Lecture on the Curriculum there is a brief and unequivocal statement advocating early modeling:

> "Sculptural modeling should begin before the ninth year, first spheres, then other forms and so on. Also with modeling one should work entirely out of the forms]." (Ibid.)

That the modeling Steiner had in mind does not consist of simply making "spheres" will be shown at the end of this lecture.

The idea of penetrating a changing, metamorphosing form with the life of one's feeling rather than a copying of or imitating finished, fixed forms is followed up by Steiner in more detail in Lecture One of the course

Practical Advice to Teachers. Just as with form drawing, the main point of the activity of modeling sculptural forms was to experience and understand a process of transformation by "inwardly growing together with and into the form itself." The similarity of forms with outer objects presents itself only afterwards. The capacity to experience and work with the "inner laws of sculptural formation," as Rudolf Steiner characterized them, cannot be awakened through external imitation. This capacity is optimally developed between ages 7-14. After this time of greatest potential, the ability to acquire this capacity wanes and dies off. When it is not developed at the right time, according to Steiner, "human beings have a difficult time mastering life's struggles."

To help us experience and understand the sculptural process, he provides a methodological insight: just as in drawing the unconscious movements of the hand can be raised into consciousness by following the form with our eye movements, similarly a three-dimensional, sculptural form can be felt by following and touching it all around. In this way, a person can become involved in a process that engages the fullest interest and proceeds from will activity mediated over feeling into the beginnings of conscious awareness. This is an example of an educational method that gradually leads from will activity over to the development of the intellect.

The Theme of Freedom

In the Christmas Course of 1922 we find the following statement:

> "However inconvenient it may be for the teacher, she should always encourage the young pupils to form shapes of all kinds out of any material he can lay hands on. True,

one should avoid letting the children get unduly dirty and messy, for this can be a real nuisance. But what children gain in these creative activities is worth far more than that they should remain clean and tidy. In short, especially during the early years, it is of great value for them to gain experience of the artistic element.

"All that has to come out of the child first has to be brought in a child-like way appropriate to its nature. And if artistic activities are introduced to the child in its first school years [*gerade in der ersten Zeit*] in the way indicated, the learning of other subjects will become easier. Foreign languages, for example, will be learned with far greater ease, if pupils have done artistic work beforehand." (Rudolf Steiner, *Soul Economy and Waldorf Education*, p. 211)

The expression "to come out of " the child has to do with his/her "predispositions" (*Anlagen*): the child is inwardly a "sculptor," that is to say, he/she is forming his/her interior organs with the help of the etheric body that still predominates in the growth process up to ages 9-10; these inwardly sculptural predispositions want "to be drawn out" first through the feeling life which works on the will and then gradually leads to the intellect. From this methodological and developmental basis and point of departure, artistic instruction can be implemented; for this reason the examples of painting and modeling are presented in this lecture (for other insights on the learning of writing and arithmetic, see the lecture of December 31, 1921).

Rudolf Steiner explicitly indicated what he deemed to be the most fundamental guiding thought of the entire art of pedagogy and creates the possibility of the spiritual-soul part of the human being developing out of the physical-bodily part:

"From which educational maxim does such an [pedagogical] attitude spring? It is the outcome of a total dedication towards freedom. It springs from the ideal to place the human being into the world in such a way that he can unfold his individual freedom or, at least, that no physical hindrances should prevent him from doing so."

(Rudolf Steiner, *Soul Economy and Waldorf Education*, p. 203)

The opposite of such an education would be the mere training of ready-made concepts and ideas without any respect for the physical-etheric development of the child.

The Theme of Balancing Out

A further indication for early modeling was given in the Ilkley Course of 1923 (GA *307 A Modern Art of Education,1972*). In Lecture 12, held on August 16, 1923, Steiner attributed a new role to the artistic element, which from the beginning was to be the basis of all teaching: as soon as the principle of cause and effect starts to enter the lessons, such a more intellectual approach needs to be *balanced out* (*auszugleichen*) through the counterweight of an understanding of art. Modeling belongs in this realm:

"Modeling too is cultivated as much as possible, albeit only from the ninth or tenth year and in a primitive way. It has a wonderfully vitalizing effect on the child's physical sight and on the inner quality of soul in his sight, if, at the right age, she begins to model sculptural forms and figures. So many people go through life without even noticing what is most significant in the objects and events of their environment. As a matter of fact, we have to learn how to really see (*Sehenlernen*) so that we stand in the world in the right way." (Rudolf Steiner, *A Modern Art of Education*, p. 192)

In the same lecture Rudolf Steiner said about the practical aim of "learning how to see" [*Sehenlernen*] that sculptural dexterity is also necessary in order to grasp plant formations. The experience of transformations in sculptural activity creates the ability to direct congealed concepts (which can only comprehend mineral and physical reality) into image forms [*bildhafte Formen*].

"By itself…"

In Lecture 13 of the Ilkley Course, Steiner speaks about connections between sculptural modeling and craft lessons; the artistic and practical overlap.

> "To lead play gradually over to the creation of artistic forms and then to the practical work . . . is actually in accord with human nature. . . . And it is very interesting to find that the children's sculptural, artistic activity turns quite naturally by itself to the making of playthings and toys." (Ibid. p.197)

These words "by itself" should not be taken too lightly because they assume that the entire lesson is carried out artistically from the very inception. In the lecture, reference is made to an exhibition of students' work and the theme of "by itself" appears again. Forms are to arise not out of an imitation or copying but out of free creative activity after the children in the lessons on human and animal have "learned to read in the mind of nature."

> "Behind this stands the method of not only occupying the head with knowledge, but also with clothing ideas in images in such a way that they become living ideas and move from feeling into willing. Thus it becomes possible for students to be able also to make what they know. There then arises a special know-how, a special wisdom: a *"Könnendes Wissen"* (capable knowing) and *"wissendes Können"* (knowing capability)."

(*A Modern Art of Education* 1997, GA 307, August 17, 1923)

When one can feel ideas, they are not just dry concepts, but they are living ideas, which grip the entire human being in thinking, feeling, and willing. Rudolf Steiner formulates this paradoxically: "The idea is a sculptural form. The child actually learns to do what she learns to think." That sounds almost like the modern artist Beuys, and who inspired him?

"By itself" does not mean "alone without support," but happens as the result of a developmentally appropriate lesson and of "living ideas" actively alive in the teacher herself. This transfers to the children inspired by the teacher's enthusiasm and capability. A year later in the lecture courses at Torquay, England (*The Kingdom of Childhood*) and Arnheim, Holland (*Human Values in Education*), Rudolf Steiner brought an example of such a living idea. In Lecture 3 of the Arnheim Course, after he has spoken about the introduction of writing, he once again made a plea for early modeling. Besides "painting-drawing" (*malendes Zeichnen*) and "drawing-painting" (*zeichnende Malen*), "we lead the child as much as possible into the artistic element and the modeling of small sculptural works, without wanting anything other than what the child naturally wants to make out of the form from an inner creativity" (*Human Values in Education*, Lecture 3).

Here again the theme of "by itself" is touched upon and Rudolf Steiner gives an example of it for the first study of the human being (in grade four). When students have learned something of the dynamics of human bone structure artistically and not intellectually (following a dry anatomy book) and have modeled bones afterwards, forms even of the simplest things become something else. Such "aliveness" can only come about when a child has a feeling for form; it does not come out of book knowledge in which everything stands next to each other unrelated and without the interconnections being made visible. Rudolf Steiner sets the bar very high for teachers when he assumes that they are entirely at home in the living reality of Goethe's metamorphosis of the bones:

> "At our school, when the children see a vertebra of the spinal column before them, they recognize its similarity to the skull; they get a feeling for what the transformation of bones is. In a lively way they enter directly into human forms and thus feel an urge to express it artistically."

(*Human Values in Education*, Lecture 3)

Imagine! Steiner proposed this for 10-11-year-olds! And again the assumption is that such lofty ideas as Goethe's teachings on metamorphosis are alive in the teacher.

The Etheric Body as Sculptor
Working with the living in order to become alive oneself means none other than to be in the process of understanding the etheric body better and better. In Lecture 4 of the Arnhem Course (July 20, 1924), Rudolf Steiner called it the greatest work of art because its essence makes it both a work of art and an artist at the same time. "*Insofar as we bring the forming forces of art to children and model with them in a free way, we are bringing what is deeply related to the etheric body.*"

Supplementary to this theme, we find in the Torquay Course that the etheric body is a modeler, a sculptor. It transforms the inherited model body of the child into an individualized, personalized one; the plastic, sculptural forces involved in this process become free and active in the soul.

> "This is why the child has an impulse to model forms or to paint them. For the first seven years of life the life body has been carrying out modeling and painting within the physical body. Now that it has nothing further to do regarding the physical body, or at least not as much as before, it wants to carry its activity outside."

(*The Kingdom of Childhood,* Lecture 6)

Again there is the presumption here that the teacher will only be able to provide good guidance to the child when he himself has an artistic picture of the human organism; and mind you! It needs to be a truly artistic one, not anatomical one as demonstrated in the recent exhibitions of dissected human corpses hardened in artificial plastic (*Plastinate*)–the exhibitions in Karlsruhe and Basel called "Body Worlds" (*Koerperwelten*). Rudolf Steiner's recommendations for the training of teachers do not involve the copying of stuffed organs but rather the development of living principles of life. Modeling, according to him, should become a science seminar in which one can grasp the body of formative life forces (see *Human Values in Education*, Lecture 8). He suggests that teachers individually continue to develop further what they do not have time to explore sculpturally in teacher training. In this connection, I recommend the work of Dr. Armin J. Husemann, MD called *The Harmony of the Human Body; Musical Principles in Human Physiology* (Floris Books, 1994). In this book are to be found concrete suggestions for practicing Rudolf Steiner's modeling exercises for the outer human *Gestalt*, for form inversion (*Umstuelpung*=turning inside-out like a glove), and for the etheric body of the lung.

Pathways to Modeling

How can one do justice to Rudolf Steiner's numerous and urgent appeals for early modeling? One can start by allowing important ideas to penetrate one's consciousness such as: the etheric body as sculptor and the sculptural exercises that relate to its activity, Goethe's metamorphosis idea relating to both plants and bones, Rudolf Steiner's idea of the threefoldness of the human organism.

With respect to threefoldness we find stimulating indications for animal studies in the Torquay Course (*The Kingdom of Childhood*, Lecture 3). The human being is in a harmonious form, which brings into balance what lives itself out in the animals as all types of one-sided, specializations of form in a kind of elastic metamorphosis, expanded or contracted, blown up or stunted organ systems and shapes (*Gestalten*)—all wonderful motifs for creative shaping (*Gestalten*) and re-shaping *(Umgestalten)*. Rudolf Steiner describes similar motifs of transformation in the animal world in Lecture 4 of *Human Values in Education*.

A wealth of practical advice is provided in the book of Anke-Usche Clausen and Martin Riedel, *Plastisches Gestalten fuer alle Alterstufen* ["Sculptural Modeling for All Age Levels," Mellinger Verlag, Stuttgart 1969. No English translation is yet available, but the hundreds of illustrations provide many sculptural ideas and make this book universally valuable]. Almost all of Rudolf Steiner's indications for modeling are cited and taken up methodically in this book. One still has to work at developing a fuller picture of the subject for oneself and finding all sorts of interconnections by referring back to Steiner's pedagogical lectures. But the Clausen and Riedel manuals offer a treasure of quotations, suggestions and, above all, superb sketches indicating how to practically engage in the activity of modeling: exercises for experiencing the creative inner space of our hands and the creation of fundamental forms, examples for human and animal shapes and much more! They show how one might creatively and freely work with basic curriculum indications from Steiner such as

> "Sculptural modeling should begin before the ninth year, first spheres then other forms and so on. Also with modeling one should work entirely out of the forms."
> (*Discussions with Teachers,* Lecture 15)

These illustrated handbooks provide inspiration for developing many possible sculptural aspects: round, elongated, light, heavy, symmetrical, asymmetrical, oval, convex, concave, drop forms and countless others that can arise out of the active surfaces of the hands and fingers. Some might find it remarkable that such a "well known book" that has been around for so long is brought up at this time; but new class teachers are entering the work all the time and may come to know how extremely valuable the standard work of Anke-Usche Clausen and Martin Riedel is even if it appears in a perhaps old-fashioned format.

PART III
WONDERING

Imagination bodies forth the shape of things unknown.
—William Shakespeare

The Modeling Process:
Thinking-in-Images

The chapters in this "Part III: Wondering" section are intended to explore further the relationship of the sculptural process to human imagination and the origin of forms.

> *There are people who exclaim, "Oh [in modeling] you need so much imagination!" But the opposite is true; you get ideas in the process of working which you never had before. Powers of imagination are activated and unfold by themselves. The soft, formless clay is a willing helper in your effort.*
>
> —Michael Martin, educator and artist

Urgently Needed: An Additional Capacity of Thinking and Exact Imagination

In addition to healthy intellects, a new, more fluid way of thinking and imagining is what teachers need to understand the unfolding child more deeply. It is also what mankind requires in the present environmental crisis to holistically understand and rescue the living processes of the earth.

Sculptural modeling is a powerful artistic means to change the inner workings of our minds to grasp and experience metamorphosis and change as it happens in human beings and nature. The sculpting hand reaches into and transforms earth material through a rhythmic flow of movement. At the same time it is inviting and teaching the mind to actively "reach into and slip into changing forms" and learn how to "go with a flow." By modeling forms we practice artistically in an earth material nature's processes of transformation. The Australian biologist Nigel Hoffman characterizes this capacity as *"water thinking"* and *"sculptural thinking"* in contrast to our usual intellect which he calls "earth cognition":

"The [sculptural] modeler is . . . the human maker whose activity arises from an imagination of Water. The actualized form of things is grasped through Earth perception [and Earth cognition];however, as the [French philosopher of science] Bachelard shows, through the imagination of Water and the experience of soft substance, what is grasped is the rhythmic arising of form, the activity of formation rather than the formed results of that activity . . .

"These evocations of Water help to awaken the organ of cognition which will here be termed Water thinking or Imagination. Goethe recognized that there is a power of mind which is like the fluid becoming of nature and he called it 'exact sensory imagination' advising: 'If we wish to arrive at some living perception of nature, we ourselves must remain as quick and flexible as nature and follow the example she gives.' Like water, imaginative thought is sufficiently plastic and sensitive to take on the forms of another being. . . . Water thinking 'runs through' the forms of the leaf, the flower, then flows into the forms of the fruit and seed. With our exact imagination we enter into the leaf shapes and move between them, through their sequence of growth . . . In Water thinking, we learn to 'dwell' imaginatively in the form of living beings with a thinking that participates rather than remains as the external observer." (Hoffman, *Goethe's Science of Living Forms*, p. 38)

"Water thinking means that a middle part of the human being has become active in the cognitive process…The conventional scientific view is that feeling impinges on or sullies thinking—and this is certainly true in relation to purely logical and mechanical [Earth] thinking [which apprehends what is dead… in nature]. But …such logical thinking is not adequate to the growth process in organic form. With Water thinking or Imagination we are literally thinking with our feeling—but here we are not speaking of a personal content of feeling or emotion. What is meant is that a certain aspect or capacity of the feeling life is intensified and heightened into an organ of cognition. In relation to water thinking this is the protean power of feeling, its character of continuity and transformation. It is the feeling with which the sculptor forms his works. This is what allows feeling to mold itself to the fluid, metamorphosing form of another being, and it is by virtue of this plasticity that we can speak of Imagination as a 'sculptural thinking.'" (Ibid., pp. 42-43)

Morphological Thinking and Plasticity

Rudolf Steiner, whose research inspired Hoffmann's work, referred to sculptural thinking and imagination as "*morphological thinking*," form-thinking. Steiner's insights were sparked by Goethe's study of the metamorphosis of plant and animal forms. It was Goethe, in fact, who first developed the biological concept and science of what he named "morphology." Steiner characterized morphological thinking as:

"one in which we think in forms [but] not limited in space; [this way of thinking] lives within the medium of time in the same way as our usual [intellectual] thinking lives within the medium of space. [Morphological] thinking does not link up one thought with another; it sets before the soul a kind of thought-organism…[to be considered] as whole . . . Morphological is so inwardly mobile that it calls forth one form out of others, continuously organically membering itself, continuously growing. One adds morphological thinking to one's regular combinatorial thinking; one achieves it by strengthening and intensifying one's thinking. With this [new mode of] thinking, which runs in forms [*Gestalten*], in images [*Bilder*], one attains what . . . I have called imaginative cognition. . . . The forms are as vividly experienced as physical sense perceptions". (*Die Wirklichkeit der hoeheren Welten*, GA 79, pp. 49-50, A.A. translation)

Steiner saw morphology coupled with sculptural modeling as an indispensable means for teachers to learn how to behold and truly grasp child development and the metamorphosis of life forces in the growing human being:

"We understand the etheric life body of formative forces when we enter the sculptural modeling and shaping process (*plastisches Gestalten*), when we know how a curve or an angle grows from inner forces. We cannot understand the etheric life body in terms of ordinary laws, but through the experience of the hand—the spirit-permeated hand." (*The Essentials of Education*, Lecture 3, p. 45)

Such an experience and understanding of life's forming process (*Gestalten*) then informs how a teacher shapes lessons and an environment in which children in turn can shape their whole being naturally and organically. Steiner, one of whose favorite words was *"gestalten,"* likened the young brain to a wonderful piece of clay which the spirit shapes and like a seal, impresses with form. The incredible plasticity of movement of children's hands as spirit instruments plays an essential role in molding this complex neural sculpture

The Gesture: Organically Working From the Whole to the Parts

Sculpting from a whole to the parts is often a way to vividly experience a process that artistically involves a living organic series of changing form. As Michael Howard points out, it ideally entails a feeling-will process that can enliven and bring new warm energy into our whole human state of being including the nerve-sense pole of our thinking.

Howard reveals how such mode of working calls upon a new inner as well as outer mobility, and on new feeling perceptions rooted in the living, forming forces of our etheric body:

> "It is important to understand the deeper reason for working from the whole; otherwise, working from the whole to the part becomes a cliché or formula. We work from the whole in order to create out of gesture. What is the reason for working out of gesture? Although we are making sculptures in a physical material such as clay, when we work out of gesture we are making not merely physical but etheric human or animal forms. We exchange the goal of realism for that of creating form gestures that are heavy or light, contracted or expansive, restful or active. In doing so, we awaken to more subtle feeling

perceptions belonging to the forces of our etheric body and the etheric world. When we work organically, imbuing every part with the overall gesture of the whole, we are engaged in our feeling-will. In feeling-will or head/heart/hand activity, our etheric body mediates between the astral and physical." (Howard, *Educating the Will,* p. 90)

Cleverness is a matter of the astral body, but wisdom is a matter of the etheric body . . . The etheric body works with time . . . the right timing (Kairos). As we have to wait for the right time, so we have to wait for wisdom. We cannot accelerate the acquisition of wisdom. We can however accelerate the gaining of intelligence and cleverness. That works on the astral level.

–Dr. Otto Wolf, MD

Modeling as an Organic Process in Time

Both the astral body and etheric bodies have their own timing: the former is fast; the latter is slow and this has implications for the modeling process. Consequently, as Husemann points out,

> "The more we slow down the movement of our hands and fingers while we are modeling the more we become aware of the life of the etheric body in these movements. Moving at a speed which corresponds approximately to the motion of the chest during relaxed breathing has shown itself to be effective. An equilibrium arises between the sense of touch in our fingertips and the experience of will in the action of the muscles. In this way our feeling can immerse itself in the sculptural activity of the etheric body. Attention to time is an important factor in any investigation of the etheric. Hand movements which are too rapid come too close to the speed of thinking in the

nervous system and lose their vitality. People today, who do not have any experience of modeling, have to make a conscious effort to put themselves in a phlegmatic mood." (Husemann, *The Harmony of the Human Body*, p. 22)

The phlegmatic temperament is rooted in the etheric and the watery element. Chatting is astral and "left- brained." Quiet and simply "speaking with the hands" are most conducive to "right-brained," image-forming modeling.

The Physiology of Sculptural Modeling: Hands, Head–and above all Heart!

The following are some thoughts of Dr. Armin Husemann, translation by A.A.

"When we shape an unformed piece of clay into a sphere, the form arises through movements. These movements originate from our muscles. Our rippling muscles in turn are built up and nourished by the rippling stream of blood. It is interesting that Rudolf Steiner characterized muscles as 'coagulated blood' (*Young Doctors Course*, January 7, 1924); the two are closely related in their composition and red color due to iron content. Blood movement becomes muscle movement. The blood in turn comes from the heart's movement. Following this remarkable process from heart through blood and muscle to sphere-making movements, we realize that we are not just modeling with our hands but also with our heart and the sun forces streaming through it.

"At the same time, our modeling activity catches the attention of our head above with its eyes–also spheres!–looking down on all the marvelous work being done by the energetic hands. If we trace the origins of this parallel physiological process in the head we again realize that the act of looking and seeing also stems from the heart. Streaming blood from the heart forms the six muscles of our eyes and sustains their functions. With the sense of sight we perceive the sphere's color, but to actually see the form we need to add to sight the sense of movement, also called the muscle sense. From a distance the active muscles of our eyes above rapidly move around and survey the contours of the sphere below and add this perception of movement to that of sight. As a result, we perceive the form.

"Thus we sculpturally model with our hands and our on-looking head and above all with our hearts. Heart movement becomes blood movement becomes muscle movement becomes hand movement." (Husemann, "Der plastizierende Mensch: Ein Bild des Lebens," *Menschenwissenschaft durch Kunst*, pp. 175-178, A.A. translation)

Modeling as a Cosmic Life Process: The Whole Earth in Our Hands and the Sun in Our Heart

Husemann sees the surface-making movements of our modeling hands as a microcosmic image of the cosmic influences sculpting from outside the spherical earth as an organism. He describes how in shaping a clay sphere we are artistically emulating with the etheric forces of our hands the shaping of the earth by the planar etheric forces of the sun. The sun is the heart of the cosmic ether filling the planetary system.

"Our hands grasp the unformed clay from outside, pressing it, shifting and turning it about. They do to the clay sphere what the cosmic etheric forces do to the earth from the cosmic periphery. From all sides, from everywhere, the fingers take hold of the evolving sphere." (Ibid. p. 176)

"Just as the peripheral etheric forces of the earth have their center in the sun so do our sculpting limbs-arms-hands have their center in the heart . . . The life center of the forming movements, the heart, [is] a sun within us shining on the earthen sphere. And the clay sphere does warm up gradually." (Ibid. p. 177)

The human being is a transformer of sun energy into creative human energy and consciousness.

The Etheric Body Continues its Work as Sculptor of Our Physical Body in Modeling Through Our Etheric Hands

The human etheric body is the real sculptor of the human form. It builds up and shapes the physical body's foundation during the embryological development and early childhood. This body of formative life forces lives above all in the streaming blood and other fluids and continues to follow the same paths it traveled in producing the human shape initially.

After articulating most of the human form as its sculptural masterpiece by the end of early childhood, the etheric body continues to play a role in its maintenance and healing but these functions do not demand all of the totality of forces the etheric body had at its disposal and used in creating the body in its first phase. Surplus generative forces are left over from that momentous task. They do not go unused, however. At around ages 6-7 this extra formative energy metamorphoses in two main directions:

- into the conceptualizing power to sculpt mental images and thoughts internally as "mind sculptures"–an indication of school readiness–and into creative capacities directed outwards

- to shape and give meaning to the world through art, science and culture–most often via the hands.

The Etherically Permeated Hand

Steiner pointed out that the hands themselves appear to have a special abundance of etheric forces permeating and extending from them.

"The hands are actually wondrously different from all other parts of the body... From the fingers shine forth radiant formations of the etheric body, which glimmer, dim, then sparkle again into space." (*Exkurse in das Gebiet des Markus-Evangeliums*, GA 124, A.A. translation)

The hands are highly intuitive in their activity and are etherically connected with the central human organ of intuition called the twelvefold heart chakra in ancient traditions:

"The etheric organs expressed in the hands and their functions, work far more intuitively, more spiritually, and perform a far higher task than is accomplished by the etheric brain . . . The hands, or the spiritual basis of the hands, are far more interesting and significant organs for gaining knowledge of the world, and are certainly far more skillful organs than the brain . . . The etheric basis of the hands is connected with the activity of the lotus flower [chakra] in the region of the heart . . ." (*Von der Initiation*, GA 138, A.A. translation)

For Steiner, intuition meant entering into and living in another being or phenomenon and experiencing them from inside–becoming one with them without losing one's identity. The hands as intuitive organs are able to enter into and merge with the substance of the world and participate directly in its process of its changing forms.

In modeling, the actual shaping is the result of our etheric body as sculptor flowing though the blood into our hands as instruments to move the material *into* the contours of a form. The etheric body intuitively knows the language of form and the etheric hand expresses that language visibly with the help of the muscular hand.

Modeling as a Warm-Up Activity for a Spirit-Touching of the Etheric

Modeling is very much an art of touching and feeling. For Steiner it is an art that helps us develop the imaginative thinking we need to *touch* and *grasp* the etheric body.

> "We have to take this step, this turning of one's own active thinking into an organ of touch for the soul. The first step [is] to change our thinking so that we feel . . . . The thinking that becomes active is like a snail—able to extend feelers or to draw them in again . . . . Thinking becomes a suprasensory touching and through [it] the etheric or formative forces body can be in the higher sense, both grasped and seen." (*The Evolution of Consciousness,* pp. 13-14)

Modeling, Higher Suprasensory Members and the Ultimate Form Workshop

The etheric body is described above as the sculptor and modeler of our physical bodies and of clay forms. But what actually transpires in the modeling process is far more complicated and involved when considered from a still "higher" suprarsensory perspective than the etheric world. Ultimately, there is a higher agent "directing" sculptural forces, and that is our Spirit-I or Higher Egoself, our I Am. It is the Spirit-I who actually works through the etheric body to do the shaping work. It acts in cooperation with the highest levels of the spiritual world and the creative activity of what Steiner calls the Archetypes (*Urbilder*), the "masterbuilders" of the universe. (See chapters on "Form-Giving Forces" and "Imagining Archetypes.")

Form-Giving Forces

Water as Teacher of Sculptural Thinking

What we perceive around us as "things" in fixed forms are actually all in the process of moving and changing, albeit in many cases very slowly and imperceptibly—some geologically. In the next 10,000 years the wooden table in front of me will have moved on to and into many other things. A comparatively short time ago its substance was in growing trees which then found themselves turning into a table with the help of moving human hands and minds.

Forms appear to be at rest in a particular moment but are really the result of *trans*-formings and trans-*movings*. In any one moment we are seeing things as "frozen movement."

Although many objects and their forms strike us at first as static structures in space, there are others such as living forms and flowing water forms that challenge our minds to loosen up; they teach us how to see that *every*-thing actually has its origin in a moving process-in-time, even granite mountains. In the case of observing a river, we have a wonderful dual experience: we perceive the general meandering form of the river which is experienced as constant, but looking more closely we notice that its currents and interior flowing are changing continuously. The river is both constant and new in every second.

The water researcher Theodor Schwenk in his imagination-expanding book *Sensitive Chaos* helps us immensely in this direction by revealing the true nature of fluid dynamics and its significance for life forms. He quotes the scientist-poet Novalis: *"The resting state originates in movement. There is no doubt that our body is a molded river."* (Aphorism in Schwenk, p. 58) An examination of the flow of cells and fluids in embryogenesis demonstrates this dramatically. Even adult human bodies renew and change their substances—and shape!—about every seven years.

Schwenk calls our attention to different kinds of water waves which become teachers and enhancers of open and flexible observation and thinking. We are familiar with viewing waves moving on water surfaces, but there is a kind of wave phenomenon, that is less noticed. The so-called "stationary" wave remains in one place but is being continuously renewed internally like a living organism:

"It may be observed in every little stream and every river where the water flows over stones or round posts and piers. We have all at one time watched the ceaseless flow of water: the picture is ever the same, and yet all the time new water is passing by. Here it is parted by a boulder and then unites again, swirling from side to side and creating eddies. There it may be seen to jump over a stone and flowing on in waves. But do the waves flow onwards? Closer inspection will show that the same waves always remain behind the same stone and that the water perpetually flows through their constant form." (Schwenk, p. 26)

In beholding such a phenomenon, we let water teach us its special nature. We learn to supplement our fixed-object, intellect-thinking with "water thinking." This kind of cognition is better able to experience the archetypal living organism, the plant, also as a flow being so that we are able to *"think like a plant"* (Holdredge, 2013). The plant becomes a second teacher. As Australian researcher Nigel Hoffman points out, it was Goethe who developed the *"power of mind which is like the fluid becoming of nature"* able to *"flow through"* the forms of the plant— *"an exact sensory imagination."*

Panta rhei – Everything flows.
Everything is changing.
—Heraclitus, 5th century B.C.

The Etheric World

Water thinking helps us to fathom what life is because moving water is the medium through which life forces work and flexibly form living shapes. In various esoteric traditions formative life forces are called "etheric" forces and come together as the "etheric" or "life bodies" of living beings. These forces are held to have their origins beyond the earth in the sun, planets and the rest of the star world. Ancient and medieval peoples experienced that star forces (also called "astral" from the Latin *astra* for stars) molded the structure of the human body while it was planet forces that sculpted the internal organs. Swiss researcher Ernst Marti examined these traditions and in his extensive research developed further Steiner's renewal of the wisdom of the etheric body, its four ethers, and their relationship to the four elements:

"The instinctive view that the shape of man's body is formed by the forces of the zodiacal stars was confirmed by Rudolf Steiner. Aries forms the forehead and head, Gemini the pairs of shoulders and arms, Pisces the feet, just to name a few. The planets form the inner organs—Venus the kidneys, Mercury the lungs, etc. The stars and planets do not fashion all of this directly in the physical (which would bring about substances), but indirectly by means of the etheric body. The stars stimulate the formative force in the etheric which then brings forth the form appearing in the physical…Rudolf Steiner…described the blue firmament as the boundary of world ether. The etheric world reaches up to the firmament, the ocean of the four ethers which carry within themselves the four elements. At the firmament's boundary the stars appear through which the forces of spiritual beings enter the world of appearances. These are astral and spiritual forces. When the astral forces stream in by way of the portals of the stars (or streamed in during creation), they stimulate the [four] ethers and create from them the formative forces. The spiritual forces penetrate more deeply into the elements and create in them the substances. Rudolf Steiner describes the totality of these forces as the Word, the Cosmic Word [Logos], which sounds in and through the stars." (Ernst Marti, *The Four Ethers*, 1984, pp. 7-8).

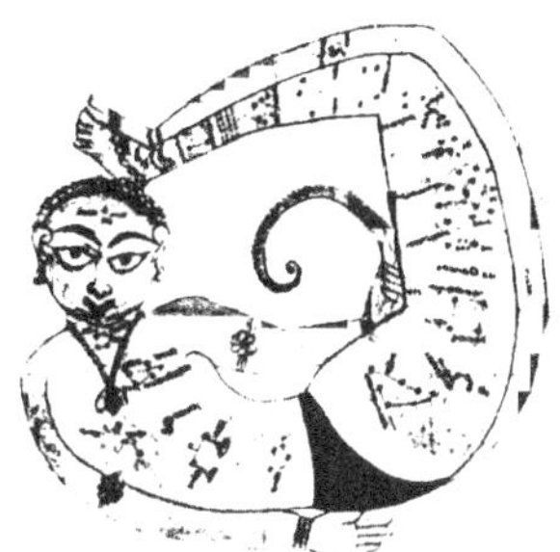

Indian depiction of the cosmic human embryo like form with constellations of the zodiac on the body (from Marti)

According to the perennial wisdom of ancient traditions, the outer structure of the human body is shaped by the star forces. To complete Marti's prior list: the head by Aries Ram star forces; the throat and larynx by Taurus Bull; the symmetry, lungs, shoulders, arms, and hands by Gemini Twins; the rib cage, breasts, and stomach by Cancer Crab; the heart by Leo Lion; the lower metabolic organs, solar plexus, and spleen by Virgo Virgin; the kidneys and loins by Libra Scales; the organs of reproduction by Scorpio; the hips and thighs by Sagittarius Archer; the knees by Capricorn Goat; the calves and ankles by Aquarius Water Bearer; and the feet by Pisces Fish. (See below.)

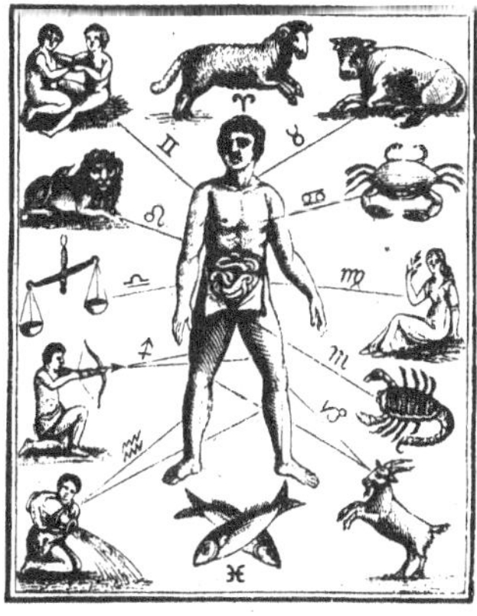

Ancient and medieval correspondences

In addition to the twelve star forces, planet forces form the inner organs within the body structure: Saturn forces form the spleen; Jupiter, the liver; Mars, the gall bladder; Sun, the heart; Mercury, the lungs; Venus, the kidneys; Moon, the reproductive organs. Hence, in total, there are 19 formative forces of what Steiner termed the Cosmic Word or Logos, also traditionally called the Harmony of the Spheres. These sound forth from the stars and planets and shape the human body as microcosm and everything in the universe as macrocosm.

Sound to Formative (Form-Giving) Force to Gestalt (Structured Form)

The star/planet forces are sounding, non-material, wave-like music forces that transform the four ethers into mediating etheric forces. Etheric formative forces then connect and shape substance in differentiated ways. In other esoteric terminology used by Steiner, spirit archetype and astral (star) impulses bear "prototypes" into the world ether and "in-*form*" its four ethers with patterns and plans for structuring the substances of the world. The spiritual (*Geistige*) and astral (*Astralische*) formatively interpenetrate with the etheric which in turn formatively interpenetrates substance. For incarnation into matter, the human being, as directing spirit-I, clothes herself in an astral body made of musical forces which "in*form*" the individual's etheric body of life forces how to take up matter and use it to structure the human physical body.

The following sections are various ways in which the complexity of spiritual, astral and etheric forces can be made visible, experienced and better understood:

- Language, eurythmy, and nature as forces made visible

- The dynamic sculptural reliefs of Michael Howard (Sounding Forms)

- The physics of Chladni acoustical patterns and water sound forms

- Four Ethers: sizing, differentiating, whole-making, aging the plant

- The stars as sculptors in the etheric (Steiner lecture)

- The genetics and dark energy of living forms and of the universe (research of current evolutionary biologist Sean Carroll)

Form-Giving Forces in Language, in Eurythmy as Visible Speech and in Nature

Steiner's research shows that what we perceive as the outer structure of things is formed by the twelve star forces of the Logos. These not only shape out our human body but also magically resonate and condense in us the twelve main cosmic consonants (B, M, D/T, N, R, L, G/K, CH, F, S/Z, H, W). Additionally, seven planet forces form our inner organs and experiences and sound forth as the seven cosmic vowels—Ah, E (pronounced as in day), I (see), O, U (spook), and the double sounds AU (cloud) and long I (eye). According to Marti,

> "Steiner discovered and reported the individual sounds of this [cosmic] Word and uncovered the relationship of the sounds of human speech to the stars. The consonants are related to the forces of the zodiacal stars, B to Virgo, M to Aquarius, etc. The vowels are related to the planets, O to Jupiter, I to Mercury, etc. He did similar research for the world of musical tone." (Ibid., p. 9)

> "All of this can be fully grasped and experienced, and becomes the key to the world of formative forces through eurythmy, the creation of which we owe to Rudolf Steiner. The eurythmic movements are movements of the etheric body made visible by the physical body, which, while performing eurythmy follows the etheric body in every way, as if having slipped into it. Through eurythmy (and in a lesser way through the other arts of word and tone as well) it is possible today to grasp the individual formative forces and find them again in nature." (Ibid., p. 9)

Marti goes on to cite correspondences between forms in nature, eurythmy and the forces of the etheric body:

> "A future science of nature will no longer be possible without this knowledge. All formations of the plant—the leaf formation, calyx, blossom, fruit, etc., and all forms of man and animal—the outer form, the formation of eyes, skin, kidneys, etc. in every detail; the forms of water-wave, surf, drop, etc., become clear and visible as models of action and as forms of the formative forces. In the formation of fruit, of glomeruli, of the eyes, the force of the 'B' sound shows itself, in the formation of a leaf, of a lake, of the breasts, the 'M' sound…" (Ibid. p. 9)

> "Eurythmy is a revelation of the formative forces body. In the movements, gestures, and stances, eurythmy makes visible the entire range (*Umkreis*) of formative forces…

> "How many formative forces are there? There are 12 and 7 (forces of the zodiac and planets) actual formative forces…Substances and formative forces are born of the stars; substances physically, formative forces etherically…

> "Substance itself is a condensation from the region of the stars and can again rise towards them. Then substance becomes process. In Rudolf Steiner's description, metallic gold, as we have it before us, is gold process at rest. The gold process fills the universe all the way to the firmament. But also the liver as physical organ is liver process at rest. The liver process permeates the entire organism

and the universe as well. Thus, each substance has to be recognized as process at rest. In nature, substance and form appear only in combination." (Ibid.,pp. 9-10)

> *What eurythmy and claywork have in common are imaginations.*
> —Dennis Klocek, Esoteric Physiology

Sounding Forms Part One: Michael Howard's Twelve Relief Sculptures Born of Eurythmic Movement

On a path of profound artistic research, sculptor Michael Howard has made visible the formative gestures of the consonants in a dynamic progression of twelve forms in relief called *"Sounding Forms."* He experienced that, just as the moving body of a eurythmist is striving to reveal the workings of the etheric, so *"sculptural form makes the dynamics of the etheric world visible to the senses through embodiment in a material substance."* He calls attention to Rudolf Steiner's statements that *"We find in sculpture the natural laws of our etheric body; we simply transfer this inner order into our works of sculpture…"*(Dec. 29,1914) and *"If one takes the consonants out of the human being, the art of sculpture arises…"* (Dec. 2,1922.) (*Michael Howard,* "Sculptural Form as Visible Speech: The Biography of an Artistic Research Study," *Journal for Anthroposophy,* Michaelmas 2001, Number 73, 24)

The relief forms follow what Steiner gave as an evolutionary sequence of speech sounds. This sequence captures twelve dynamic archetypal, consonant form-making gestures that make up the structure of the human body and the world around us: B, M, D, N, R, L, G, CH, F, S, H, T. Moving through the sequence of forms, one experiences a living organic flow.

Contemplation of each form as an entity with qualities of its own and then relating each to the next one is an enlivening and enriching sculptural revelation. For example, I see the "ball-like" form of the B hanging dynamically in space but with no up or down or apparent direction. The next form M also is suspended in space but now stretches outward toward the world with an undulating gesture in several directions. The third form D reaches "down to earth" and lands on a flat base and feels "grounded"; it also points upward in a two fold angular gesture. Overall it is a vertical form and has entered directional space.

Furthermore, I personally find new associations and applications every time I look at the series which I see daily hanging on my studio wall. The first three archetypal

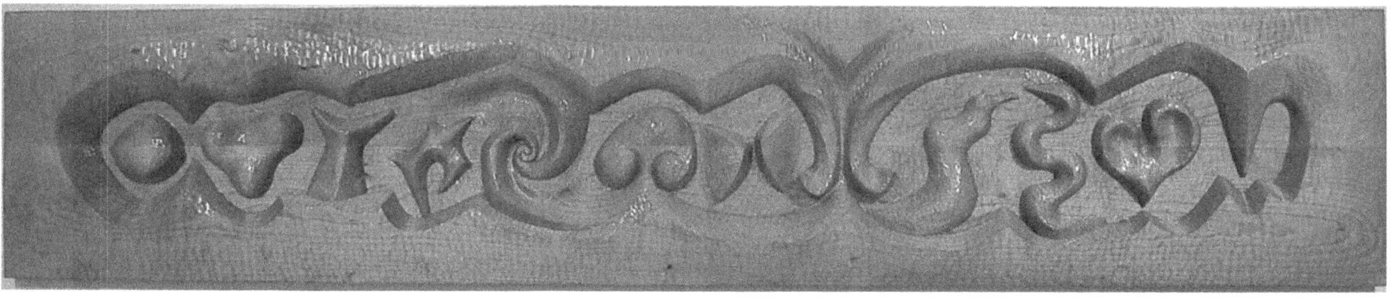

"Sounding Forms"

These forms shown above depict the following left to right:
"B" - Buoyantly Born; "M" -Mediating Medium; "D" – Descending Deed; "N" –Negate Not; "R" – Reverberationg Round; "L"-Life-filled Levity; "G" – Great Gate; "CH" – Human Humor; "F"-Fatefully Free; "S" – Sensitive Sense; "H" – High Hoe; "T" – Taut Trust

form-steps B-M-D resonate with me not only as modeler but also as class teacher. They echo the movements of child development: the round dynamic wholeness of the first grade, the awakening inquisitiveness of second graders, the 'coming down to earth' in third grade. The progression also has the universal gestures of the stages of the embryo: round ovum, differentiating morula, two-lobed neurula in three-dimensional space (See chapter on Embryogenesis.) Michael Howard associates the M-form with conversation. I also experience M's speaking with the world and how it then transforms into the sharper, more awake thinking gesture of the D-form with its upright signature of the 'I'.

Sculptors do not tend to 'intellectualize' about their own works. Steiner himself as sculptor stressed that the metamorphic forms carved in the wood structure of his Goetheanum building were artistic entities in themselves and were not to be intellectually interpreted as symbols for something else. These shapes embody and make visible etheric form-forces and are not symbols of them. (See chapter on "Learning from Goetheanum Forms.") Similarly, eurythmy movements are not to symbolize something else "beyond," but embody movements in the etheric dimension itself.

Sounding Forms Part Two: The Physics of Chladni Figures

In several esoteric traditions, it is through sound that the forms and patterns of the world are created. This perennial wisdom relates to what today's physicists are discovering about the nature of both the large universe as well as its subatomic make up. Both galaxies and sea shells appear to be coagulations of sound waves. (See *Sound Waves May Drive the Cosmic Structure, Science News,* January 1997.)

This wonderful universal phenomenon is demonstrated in a modest but strikingly beautiful way on so-called Chladni plates used in grade six acoustics lessons in Waldorf schools. Salt is sprinkled evenly over a raised metal plate fixed with a center bolt (see below). A young scientist strokes the edge of the plate with the strings of a cello bow causing the plate and salt to vibrate. The salt magically springs into symmetrical, linear geometric patterns.

Stroking different points on the sides of the plate produces different tones and patterns. The higher the pitch, the more intricate the design. Pure tones create the clearest forms; murky wavering tones result in blurry configurations or none at all—chaos!

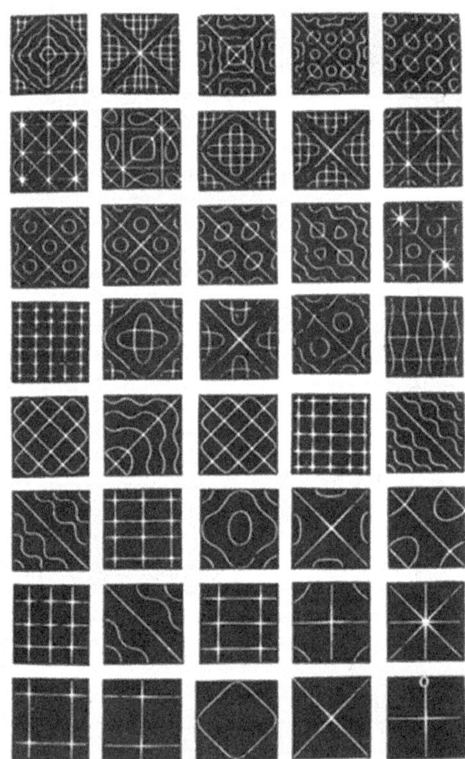

Chladni patterns

The metal plates can be rectilinear, round, oval or other shapes. A piece of paper with a small hole in the middle can be carefully placed on top of the bolted plate and then rubbed all over with a block wax crayon. This "form-rubbing" (technique developed by A.A.) shows the main geometric lines of the pattern.

For students and for adults, the sudden appearance of a form can be an *"awesome!"* or *"wow"* moment. Observers are filled with all kinds of questions. How does that happen?! In spite of what we see, Waldorf science teacher Gerhard Bedding found that "it is hard to describe the fascination of watching the creative moment in the Chladni plate. After the tone dies out, the pattern on the plate remains and can be admired and studied. Yet this is a post mortem—one is looking at a corpse. The living drama unrolls when the sounding tone, as dance master, conducts the dancing particles to their places in splendid choreography."

> "The Chladni plate is a meeting point of two worlds. Material and non-material worlds meet, and it is the not-visible that shapes the visible…The Chladni Plate shows that each tone has its own physiognomy. " (Frits Julius, *Sound Between Matter and Spirit*, pp. 48-49.)

Physiognomy is sculpture—sound is sculpturally modeling faces, formscapes, topologies in matter, but in an unusual, unexpected way.

How does the salt dance over to the geometric lines of a particular figure? The lines are the "nodes," the places where the plate is not vibrating. The grains are bounced off the trembling areas of the rest of the surface into the non-moving linear "grooves," thus marking out a pattern—the post mortem *dead* spots which become a beautiful skeleton! The final figure is the result of the meeting of the polarity of movement and

stillness in which rest wins out because the cello bow no longer causes the plate to vibrate. In fluids and living organisms where the meeting is prolonged or continuous, the polarity creates a rhythmic oscillation and a

> " . . . harmonizing and integration of stillness and movement, of permanence and change as a structured movement and dynamic gestalt." (Alexander Lauterwasser, *Water Sound Images: The Creative Music of the Universe*, p. 32)

The researcher Theodor Schwenk demonstrates this brilliantly in his water research on constant forms through which water is flowing.

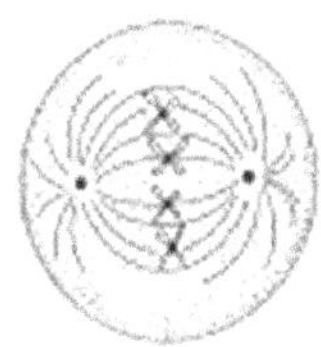

"Chladni form-like" living cell pattern

Interestingly, in the development of the embryo, the patterns initially formed by the pairs of chromosomes remind one of Chladni figures (see drawing above). In cell division, two nodal points (centrioles) appear between which there is agitated activity and the ordering of different symmetrical patterns in a central arena . Furthermore, the appearance of the cartilaginous skeleton and its ossification is like a Chladni form process. Like the lines of the mineral salt on the metal plate, the skeletal structure precipitates and crystallizes magically within a moving liquid matrix of tissue formation. The biologist Hermann Poppelbaum points out that the five- to seven-week-old embryo reminds us of the outer part of the ear. We, as tiny *"ear-like"* form beings, are listening to and resonating with the "silent music" of the cosmos for sculptural "instructions" to shape our bodies.

Historically, it was the physicist and musician Ernst Chladni who conducted the earliest research (1787) on the "sound figures" which came to bear his name. (This was synchronously at the same time that Goethe was experiencing revelations of the archetypal plant formation (1785). In the twentieth century, the British physicist Mary Waller and the Swiss medical doctor Hans Jenny continued to investigate this phenomenon in various media. The Chladni-inspired method is still used today in a more sophisticated way in testing the quality of musical instruments. (See *Scientific American,* Oct. 1981, Vol. 245, No.4, p. 170 "The Acoustics of Violin Plates", by Carleen Maley Hutchins.) The vibrations of the top and back plates are tested to find out how to make superior violins.

Researcher Alexander Lauterwasser ("Purewater!") brings this whole field of sound formation from the medium of earth salt and powder to the more sensitive element of water and its relationship to cosmic music. His beautifully illustrated work *Water Sound Forms: The Creative Music of the Universe* is filled with stunning patterns. Lauterwasser is very much in agreement with musicologist Marius Schneider's tonal vision of the universe:

"The whole world is gradually congealing music, a sum of vibrations, whose frequency increases to the degree that it materializes. IIf all form and shape is coagulated music, aged gestures of liquid sound, is then not the whole world like an echo of these primordial sounds? Would not all shapes and bodies of nature actually be, in the deepest sense, resonance bodies, each one tuned to a special moment of these sounds, a note, an interval, a word, a cadence, a melody?" (Lauterwasser, p. 17)

According to Steiner this is indeed the case:

"Everything going on in nature is permeated by a hidden music, the earthly projection of the "music of the spheres." Every animal incorporates a tone of the music of the spheres. This is also true of the human body." (Rudolf Steiner, *Balance in Teaching*, p.18)

The Plant and Modes of Activity of Four Ethers

Goethe as artist-scientist was able to observe how life forces in general differentiate the plant as a whole. Steiner was able to see how this differentiation was, in fact, due to the usually invisible etheric formative activity of what he called the "four ethers." Swiss researcher Ernst Marti has then taken up Steiner's indications and investigated how these ethers and their different modes of activity work synchronously to form the plant-as-process. Each ether he finds has a different task:

Light ether: enables growth, size and spatiality. It is working in and around the plant and

> "sucks on the earth 'periphera-petally' from all sides toward the sky…visible in the growth of plants which strive away from the earth towards the cosmic sphere…In a dark cellar, light draws the potato sprouts towards the light; it causes the blossoms to turn towards the sun, twisting to follow it." (Marti, 1984, p. 18)

Light ether actively creates space and separates things from each other (envelops and borders).

Tone ether (also called sound, number or chemical ether): creates harmonies, symmetries and polarities.

> "In the forces of growth, [splits] what is uniform and lets it grow apart…into number relationships …[and order]." (Ibid., p. 20)

> "From a trunk, separates out, dividing itself into branches and twigs, into leaves which sometimes differentiate themselves further." (Ibid., p. 19)

> "Steiner also calls tone ether chemical [and number] ether because it is the carrier of chemical activity. The substances relate to each other according to the laws of numbers." (Ibid., p. 21)

Numerical order is immanent in chemistry and music.

> "In Greek, to evenly arrange is *harmonia*, to harmonize. Tone ether, according to its primary nature harmonizes. Harmonizing, building a structure, organizing, presupposes separate entities being brought into a measured relationship. Tone ether does this visibly in the Chladni sound figures or in the positioning of a plant's leaves on its stem." (Ibid., pp. 22-23).

> "The leaf of a plant reveals in a wonderful way the two-dimensional working of water and tone. In its plane-like form it is water; in its symmetry it is tone. In the leaf's veins the sap is flowing; in the separated fields of the net-like structure of the leaf the chemical [tone] processes are taking place." (Ibid., p. 27)

In the formation of things, tone ether is inaudible (Lehrs, 366) to our human ears unless we are a Pythagoras or Goethe who wrote of the *"sun resounding and singing."*

Life Ether: is the principle that makes the plant a unity, a living whole. It heals injury and makes whole again. (Making *whole* and *heal* are etymologically related.) Life ether individualizes and makes an organism an un-dividable *Gestalt*. It has *members* "all-in-one" rather than parts. Each member, for example, each organ, acts according to the intent of the whole which is active in every point and particle. It creates an enclosing skin as expression of an inner nature.

> "Life ether differentiates the whole…creating form from within. It is a plasticizing of form out of itself…All shapes and forms of living beings arise through this plasticizing activity. Life ether creates living bodies; the earth element creates lifeless bodies." (Ibid., pp. 24-25)

Life ether can also be called *Word ether* or *Logos ether*. The Greek word logos means not only "word" but also the whole "essential principle or meaning" of a thing.

Warmth ether: "brings time into existence… That a plant starts to flower at a certain point…is due to warmth ether activity" (Ibid.,31). It makes the etheric body into a "time" body.

Example of a Tree
Size: "The tree's size and spatiality are effect and manifestation of light ether [which creates space]."

Differentiating/ordering: The artistic branching and ordering of the crown reveal the tone ether [which differentiates, harmonizes and creates order].

Wholeness: Life ether is the reason that the myriad leaves, the branches and roots form a whole.

Aging: "The fact that the tree is 70 years old and blossoming at this very moment reveals the creative activity of the warmth ether [which creates time]."(Marti 1984, 33)

The microcosm of the four ethers creating the plant mirrors the four stages of evolution in which there arose time (dimensionless Old Saturn), space (beginning in one-dimensional Old Sun), movement (two-dimensional Old Moon), and finally, solid structured form (Gestalt) in three dimensions (three-dimensional earth).

Examples of Joint Activity:
The ethers work together and produce combined effects:

- Light ether and warmth ether grow the plant to full mature size.

- Light ether and tone ether means the plant does not just grow a simple linear stem, but differentiates into orderly branching and segments.

- Tone ether and warmth ether differentiate and age a whole life in stages of time.

- Warmth ether and tone ether produce chemical processes of ripening of a green cherry into a sweet red one.

- Light and life ether create a growing whole that metamorphoses in changes of form: frog egg to tadpole to adult, baby to child to teenager.

The above are examples of the effects of pairs. However, according to Marti, the four ethers are always working together *"in all possible combinations"* and *"in their fourfold joint activity are the actual life forces."* (Marti, 1984, 38-39)

Higher Formative Forces Make the General Work of the Four Ethers Specific (Species)
The four interworking ethers make up the etheric body of all living beings, but they are not all that is required. According to Marti's interpretation of Steiner, in order for a specific organism to come about, species-formative forces must enter from the cosmos. These superior astral and spiritual formative forces gather up the general life-forming forces of the ethers and guide them to shape a particular species such as a daffodil or rabbit (Marti, 1984, 40). Marti provides other examples:

> "Nature's beings …are formed substance. It is as if the etheric formative force has descended into what can be perceived by the senses and there produces the form. What in its own realm is pure force and movement, here becomes form at rest. The form of a deer, the shell of a snail are formative force come to rest." (Ibid.,p.10)

Steiner referred to the etheric body (*Ätherleib*) also as "formative forces body" (*Bildekräfteleib*). According to Marti, "When one speaks of the etheric body or formative forces body, they are two views of the same thing" (Marti, 1984, 13). It can be pictured as a light-filled body of the streaming formative forces of four activated and interpenetrating ethers!

Warmth Ether as the Chaoticizing Threshold into the Physical
Waldorf teacher and scientist Ernst Lehrs makes us aware that it is the differentiated activity of the four ethers that mediates the coming-into-existence of the archetypal plant and other living organisms. They are the *"agent to which [the] Ur-images and their*

physical reflections owe their existence." (Lehrs, *Man or Matter,* 360). It is the warmth ether, however, that is actually the *Ur*-state and *Ur*-ether of creation. It makes it possible for the other three higher ethers to be active in the material world:

> "Constituting …a border condition between the [worlds of spirit and matter], the warmth ether has, on the one hand, the function of receiving the picture weaving [of arche-typal images] transmitted to it by the higher ethers, and on the other, of bringing physical matter into a state where it becomes recep-tive to the working of the etheric forces. The warmth ether achieves this by freeing matter from being controlled one-sidedly by the center-bound forces of the earth…
>
> "In processes …[such as melting and evapo-ration] we…recognize the physical manifes-tation of a universal function of the warmth-ether…to divest matter of all form and to lead it over from the realm of gravity into that of levity…Its function is to bring about…the chaos…which the earth needs for the ever-to-be-repeated renewal of her life…Chaos is working in the plant, when through the union of the pollen with the seed a state of chaos is produced within the seed, which enables the type to impress anew its form-principle into it." (Lehrs, 361)
>
> "…The archetype [of a plant] imprints its image into the tiny seed…There is in prin-ciple no limitation to the number of such seeds, each of which will bear the complete plant." (Lehrs, 364)

The effects of "chaoticizing warmth ether" can be observed in embryogenesis when a sperm chaoticizes the ovum and when between the fifteenth and twenty-first days there is an exceptionally dramatic "chaotic" remodeling of a planar leaf-like being into a stalk-like being in space. (See chapter on the Archetypal Forms of Embryogenesis). The warmth ether enables:

- the light ether to "grow" and weave the new embryo form into three-dimen-sional space;

- the sound ether to differentiate the top symmetrical branching lobes and other new features;

- the word or life ether to facilitate the "becoming" and solidification of a whole human individual created out of and for the word.

- Warmth ether brings time into existence into which the other ethers can work.

It makes the etheric body into a metamor-phosis-driving time body that causes the embryo to age in visible form stages. Steiner described time as *intensive* movement.

The Four Human Members as Four Princi-ples in the Ethers

- The ego principle expresses itself in the life ether that individualizes i.e. harmo-nizes into an un-divid-able whole, a one-ness with a center.

- The astral principle is a musical-numer-ical one that expresses itself in the tone ether's activity: dividing into ordered multiplicity, symmetry, polarity, contrasts.

- The etheric principle expresses itself in the light ether—the most quintessentially etheric of the ethers—enabling growth and flourishing.

- The physical principle lies in the original warmth energy of creation (Old Saturn) that densified into the mineral body of earth.

Observation Exercise of a Plant-in-Motion: Flourishing and Withering (Life Leaving)

Higher worlds and archetypes are known by contemplating simple things, especially seeds, plants and other living organisms that are microcosms of the greater processes of a living universe. Such exercises expand our range of senses for what is right in front of our noses!

Flourishing: To start to *know* the etheric body, lovingly behold a plant over time. You are seeing the activities of a streaming fourfold etheric body that is made visible because it is/has taken up matter into its "moving-forming": growing in size and space (light ether), branching/leafing (tone ether), metamorphosing always as wholeness (life ether) and aging in time stages (warmth, ripening ether).

Withering: You can also observe an etheric body's effects as it withdraws:

Day 1: Pull up a thriving weed in your garden, place it on a table, and watch what happens, as it goes limp and loses its shape:

- *Orderliness* (tone ether): Its leaves and stem shrivel and curl as overpowering air dries and sucks out its ether-mediating moisture.

- *Fullness* (light ether): No fresh renewing sap presses out leaves and stem (turgor)

- *Wholeness* (life ether)**:** The unified structure collapses into a chaotic heap.

- *Matureness* (warmth ether): The plant prematurely and rapidly *ages* in an un-*time*-ly way. Solid-making earth heaviness forces (gravity) pull down and harden the remaining earth substance.

Day 2: The next day pull a similar weed and place its fresh fullness beside its wilted neighbor.

Day 3: On the third day, pull another and compare all three. The drying-out process results in less and less water to mediate the activity of light ether (photosynthesis),

ordering tone ether, whole-making life ether and warmth ether. This situation results in a precipitous aging! Ethers retreat and the whole falls apart into a shriveled heap.

When you observe a plant, you are looking at an etheric body that is filled in with matter. We first know the etheric body by contemplating its effects.
    –Rudolf Steiner

The Ethers, the Human Organism, Mental and Perceptual Life

All four ethers work in the human etheric body with different emphases on different systems. For example,

> "In the metabolic region, …the warmth ether takes the lead and acts in such a way that the higher kinds of ether are able to work magically into the material processes of the body.

> "On the side of the nerves and senses system, the life ether has the lead, bringing about fixed forms in a salt-like manner." (Lehrs, 386)

Since our thinking is a metamorphosis of etheric forces into soul activity, heavily nerve-based thoughts can rigidify mentally into fixed mental images and skeletally abstract concepts. Or we can bring the metabolic warmth and will into play in thinking as a balance and have more flexible imaginative thoughts that are more suitable for investigating the flowing etheric realm itself.

Ernst Marti, following Steiner's indications, attributes all sense activity and nerve and brain formation to the life ether. When the latter is pulled into gravity, it degenerates into electricity; hence the electrical nature of the nerve-brain-sense system.

Our mental life consists of images resulting from many kinds of sensory impressions

–visual, auditory, tactile, kinesthetic, etc. We experience a thing and have an immediate "co-image" of it. Or time passes and we summon up an older "post-image" (memory image) later from the unconscious. Lehrs coins a third term and concept which he calls a "*pre-image*." Pre-images can be seen by "*the eye-of-the-spirit*" as exercised by Goethe and Steiner who called this scientific mode of perception, Imagination.

Just as there is joint activity between the different ether modes such as light and sound, our modes of sense perception can also share common qualities. Lehrs, for example, cites the

> "overlapping of visual and aural experiences… We…give musical attributes such as 'consonant' and 'dissonant' to colors and to describe tones as 'light' and 'dark'. The reason is that subconsciously we accompany visual experiences with tone-sensations, and vice versa. [Some] people say that they 'see' sounds and 'hear' colors." (Lehrs, 382-3).

Kandinsky and Klee had such extraordinary perceptual gifts (synesthesia) and reflected them in their art.

Harmony of the Spheres: The Stars as Sculptors; from Rudolf Steiner, *Roots of Education,* Lecture 3, pp. 38-41

In this excerpt, Steiner indicates how the etheric body of formative forces is one of levity and lightness and opposite to earth centric-oriented gravity. Its nature in living forms is to be drawn out by peripheral cosmic forces:

> "Observation through the senses and working in the intellect of the brain enable us to observe only the physical body. A very different training is needed to enable a person to perceive, for example, how the etheric body manifests in the human being. This is really necessary, not just for teachers of

every subject, but even more so for doctors. First, we should learn to sculpt and work with clay, as a sculptor works, modeling forms from within outward, creating forms out of their own inner principles, and guided by the unfolding of our own human nature. The form of a muscle or bone can never be comprehended by the methods of contemporary anatomy and physiology. Only a genuine sense of form reveals the true forms of the human body…

> "Now let's look at the physical body; it is heavy with mass and subject to the laws of gravity. The etheric body is not subject to gravity—on the contrary, it is always trying to get away. Its tendency is to disperse and scatter into far cosmic spaces. This is in fact what happens right after death. Our first experience after death is the dispersal of the etheric body. The dead physical body follows the laws of earth when lowered into the grave; or when cremated, it burns according to physical laws just like any other physical body. This is not true of the etheric body, which works away from earth, just as the physical body strives toward earth. The etheric body, however, does not necessarily extend equally in all directions, nor does it strive away from earth in a uniform way. Now we arrive at something that might seem very strange to you; but it can in fact be perceived by the kind of observation I have mentioned. When you look up into the heavens, you see that the stars are clustered into definite groups, and that these groups are all different from one another. Those groups of stars attract the etheric human body, drawing it out into the far spaces. Let's imagine someone here in the center.

> "The different groups of stars are drawing out the etheric body in varying degrees; there is a much stronger attraction from one group of stars than from another, thus the

etheric body is not drawn out equally on all sides but to varying degrees in the different directions of space. Consequently, the etheric body is not spherical, but, through this dispersion of the etheric, certain definite forms may arise in the human being through the cosmic forces that work down from the stars. These forms remain in us as long as we live on Earth and have an etheric body within us. If, for example, we take the upper part of the thigh, we see that both the form of the muscle and the form of the bone are shaped by influences from the stars. We need to discover how these very different forms can arise from different directions of cosmic space. We must try to model these varying forms in clay and we will find that, in one particular form, cosmic forces act to produce length; in another the form is rounded off more quickly. Examples of the latter are the round bones, and of the former, the more tubular bones.

"Like sculptors, therefore, we must develop a feeling for the world—the kind of feeling that, in ancient humankind, was present as a kind of instinctive consciousness. It was clearly expressed in the Eastern cultures of prehistory, thousands of years before our era; but we still find it in Greek culture. Just consider how contemporary, materialistic artists are often baffled by the forms of the Greek sculptors. They are baffled, because they believe the Greeks worked from models, which they examined from all sides. But the Greeks still had a feeling that the human being is born from the cosmos, and that the cosmos itself forms the human being. When the Greeks created their Venus de Milo…, they took what flowed from the cosmos; and although this could reveal itself imperfectly in any earthly work, they tried to express it in the human form they were creating as much as possible. The point is that, if you really

attempt to mold the human form according to nature, you cannot possibly do it by slavishly following a model, which is the contemporary studio method. One must be able to turn to the great cosmic sculptor, who forms the human being from a feeling for space, which a person can also acquire.

"This then is the first thing we must develop. People think they can gauge the human form by drawing a line going through vertically, another through the outstretched arms and another front to back; there you have the three dimensions. But in doing this, they are slaves to the three dimensions of space, and this is pure abstraction. If you draw even a single line through a person in the right way, you can see that it is subject to manifold forces of attraction—this way or that, in every direction of space. This 'space' of geometry, about which Kant produced such unhappy definitions and spun out such abstract theories—this space itself is in fact an organism, producing varied forces in all directions.

"Human beings are likely to develop only the grosser physical senses, and do not inwardly unfold this fine delicate feeling for space experienced in all directions. If we could only allow this feeling for space to take over, the true image of the human being would arise. Out of an active inner feeling, you will see the plastic form of the human being emerge. If we develop a feeling for handling soft clay, we have the proper conditions for understanding the etheric body, just as the activity of human intellect connected with the brain provides the appropriate conditions for understanding the physical body.

"We must first create a new method of acquiring knowledge—a kind of plastic perception together with an inner plastic activity. Without this, knowledge stops short at the physical body, since we can know the etheric body only through images, not through ideas. We can really understand these etheric images only when we are able to reshape them ourselves in some way, in imitation of the cosmic shaping."

Embryology is to me by far the strongest single class of facts in favor of the change of form...

   –Charles Darwin

The evolution of form is the main drama of life's story, both as found in the fossil record and in the diversity of living species. So, let's teach that story. Instead of "change in gene frequencies" let's try "evolution of form is change in development" . . . At the university level, the evolutionary view of life should be as fundamental to a college degree as Psychology 101 or Western Civilization . . . We are stoning our children to utter boredom with little pebbles and missing the big picture.

   –Sean Carroll, evolutionary biologist

The Cosmic Sculpting of the Embryo and Current Genetics (Compare to Steiner Above)

In 2009, the anniversary of Darwin's birth, I attended a special lecture at an international conference of evolutionary biologists at the Museum of Natural History in New York City. The keynote speaker was Sean Carroll, Professor of Genetics at the University of Wisconsin-Madison. The following are excerpts from his *Endless Forms Most Beautiful: The New Science of Evolutionary Developmental Biology and the Making of the Animal Kingdom* (the title of book came from a description of living forms by Charles Darwin).

Sean Carroll describes the cosmic context of what he calls the "sculpting" of living organisms. Nature first geometrizes and marks out the globe of the embryo with maps of patterns (of stripes, spots, etc.)–form drawings!–so that cells "know" where to go and form the contours and organs of the body. Organisms are *"sculpted"* as they grow. According to the current genetic view, the pattern mapping, growth and sculptural shaping of each particular organism are activated and controlled by certain gene *"switches"* and follow the plans of specific gene *"tool kits"* which instruct the making and patterning of body parts. The forces which set these tool kits and switches in motion, however, still remain elusive and invisible. He calls them the unseen *"dark matter and dark energy"* of the genome and likens the problem of their mystery to an analogous one facing astrophysics. We *"see the 'stars' of the genome [and] exactly where genes are encoded in DNA"* but not *"the dark matter in our DNA [which] controls where and when genes are used in development."* (*Endless Forms Most Beautiful*, p.109)

I think Steiner would say that these genetic patterns and activating forces are not just analogous to the nature of the macrocosm but indeed come from the stars! Interestingly, Carroll points out that *"the human [gene] tool kit long predated apes and other primates."* Steiner pointed out that the human archetype (spiritual form kit?!) is the driving force behind and in the emergence and evolution of all living organisms and kingdoms of nature:

"How does the embryo know which part will be head and which will be tail? Or top or bottom? How does it decide where to put eyes, legs?...Marking cells with a harmless dye...to see where [they wind up] ... [reveals that] cells "know' where they are in an embryo and to what tissues or structures they belong. Cells 'learn' their position and identity [as a result of] the collective work of tool kit genes…The key idea is to picture embryos as globes upon which co-ordinates are progressively determined and refined… The geometry of the embryo's coordinate systems, with its parallel and intersecting lines of longitude and latitude, imposes some spatial order on how the program of tool-kit genes unfold. This geometry is also reflected by the physical contours of developing embryos, which are sculpted by periodic grooves, form smooth curves, and have many spherical features. The populations of cells that make up the major subdivisions of embryos, or the positions of developing organs or other specialized structures, are often marked as simple geometrical shapes—bands, stripes, lines, spots, dots, or curves—of tool kit gene expression…These stripes and other shapes are much more than aesthetically pleasing pictures of the tool kit genes in action as embryos develop; they reflect the basic operations through which the complex architecture of animals is progressively built up from simple geometric patterns…" (Carroll, 88-91)

"Once the basic body plan is laid out and the repeating pattern of somites [the embryological building blocks of vertebrate bodies, vertebra, ribs, muscle groups] is far along in its development, positions in the embryo begin to be marked where various organs and appendages will form. Tool kit genes for building three-dimensional structures are activated, and body part construction begins. The four-limbed pattern of vertebrates is ancient and there are many general similarities to limb development among all vertebrates…The limbs begin as tiny buds that grow out of the flank of the embryo at two specific coordinates along the east-west axis…The buds, while initially very small, are three-dimensional and possess three axes along which the top (back) and bottom (palm), front (thumb) and back (pinkie), and proximal (e.g., shoulder) and distal elements (digits) of the limb will form as the bud grows dramatically. Specific tool kit genes organize these axes in the early limb bud… Other tool kit genes turn on in patterns that foreshadow the physical development of the long bones, digits, joints, muscles, and tendons of the mature limb. The development of these elements proceeds in a proximal-to-distal order, with the future position of the upper arm or thigh, forearm or calf, and hand or foot specified in sequence. Bone develops from condensations of cells that first form a cartilage template, which is replaced by bone. The patterning of the limb is visible first as cartilage patterns. But even before these patterns are visible at the cellular level, the expression of the tool kit gene Sox9 prefigures the pattern of condensations. Joints arise in zones between these condensations and even before these spaces are visible at the cellular level, the striped expression of the GDF-5 gene marks the future position of the shoulder, elbow, wrist, and joints between the hand and finger bones in the forelimb and the positions of the knee, ankle, and foot and toe joints in the hind limb. The future position of tendons that attach muscles to bones of the limb is prefigured by expression of scleraxis, another tool kit gene.

"The beauty of the limb is also sculpted by death. The separation of digits in mice, chicks, and humans is due to the death of the tissue between the digits in the developing limb. Within the pad-like hands and feet, these interdigital zones are marked by expression of different tool kit genes that instruct the cells in the zones to undergo programmed cell death. In a cookie-cutter-like fashion, the interdigital tissue is carved away, leaving the digits. Interestingly, in ducks, an additional tool kit member is expressed in the interdigital zones to block the death-promoting signal—and this leaves the interdigital webbing of duck feet. While all limbs are composed of the same structures—bones, tendons, muscle, joints, etc.—these structures differ in size, shape, and number within the limb." (102-103)…

"…The revolution in understanding how animals develop came about… by making the 'simple invisible' visible. The ability to see stripes, spots, bands, lines, and other patterns of tool kit gene expression that precisely prefigured the organization of embryos into segments, organs, and other body parts, provided many 'Eureka!' moments when the role of a gene in a long studied process became exquisitely clear. Stripes that foreshadow segments, patches that revealed powerful zones of organizing activity and other patterns that marked positions of bones, joints, muscles, organs, limbs, etc.—all of these connected invisible genes to the making of visible forms.

"Furthermore, the revealed order of tool kit action in animal development made logical sense. Just as in the construction of a building, where there is an order to the sequence of steps…There is an order to building animals, from the making of the basic body plan to the fine detailing of individual body parts. And, from the logic of this order, we then understand how monstrosities result when the operation of a tool kit gene is damaged by mutation. When a step is omitted, all dependent steps are abnormal….

"…The role of an individual tool kit gene is easy to understand when visualized in action… [and in]…many geometrically simple patterns… But the building of an entire animal is complicated. The complexity arises from the parallel and sequential action of tool kit genes—dozens of genes acting at the same time and place, many more genes acting in different places at the same time, and hundreds of tool kit genes acting in sequence as development progresses. The chain of parallel and successive operations is what builds complexity." (105-106)

"…How do the tool kit genes know where to act and when to shape the development of form? Where are the [operating] instructions for each step [of development and for the tool kit]?…

"There is a handy analogy between the make-up of the universe and the structure of the genome…While much of what can be seen is always becoming better understood—the formation of stars, the structure of galaxies, and the collapse of suns—cosmologists have only recently confronted the prospect that only a small fraction of the matter in the universe is visible (emitting light or radio waves)…The behavior of some visible objects such as galaxies is affected by more abundant, invisible "dark matter' and "dark energy. [estimated at 75 to 90% of the universe invisible!-A.A.]

"The analogy with genetics is that for decades, because of the simplicity of the genetic code, we biologists have been able to see the 'stars' of the genome, to see exactly where genes are encoded in DNA. But we too now appreciate that in most animals' genomes, the genes that we see occupy just a small fraction of DNA. A much larger part of our DNA consists of sequences that are not part of the simple code for any gene and whose function cannot be deciphered simply by reading the sequence. This is the 'dark matter' of the genome. Just as dark matter in the universe governs the behavior of visible bodies, the dark matter in our DNA controls where and when genes are used in development." (109-110)

"…The dark matter in DNA [controls] how tool kit genes are used, it contains the instructions for making and patterning body parts. These instructions are embedded in the dark DNA as genetic switches (my second analogy). You may not have heard about switches before this book. They have not received nearly as much attention, either in the lab or in the press, as they deserve. But this is more a reflection of the challenge biologists have had in finding them and deciphering how they work, not of their importance. Molecular biologists have only relatively recently been able to peer into the dark and reveal the location and properties of switches. The most surprising and crucial feature of genetic switches is their ability to control very fine details of individual tool kit action and anatomy. The anatomy of animal bodies is really encoded and built—piece by piece, stripe by stripe, bone by bone— by constellations of switches distributed all over the genome.

"Switches are key actors in both dramas here—development and evolution. These switches draw the beautiful patterns of gene expression…. It is the switches that encode instructions unique to individual species and that enable different animals to be made using essentially the same tool kit. And switches are hotspots of evolution…. the maker of spots, stripes, bumps, and the like. Part genetic computer, part artist these fantastic devices translate embryo geography into genetic instructions for making three-dimensional form. (111)…

"…The human [gene] tool kit long predated apes and other primates. It is clear that genes were not the drivers of evolution. The genetic tool kit represents possibility— realization of its potential is ecologically driven…" (286)

Dark matter and energy and genetic switching are still the unperceived unknown leading physicists perhaps to consider a non-physical dimension to the universe.

Sources of *Image*-ination

Imagination bodies forth the shape of things unknown.
—Theseus in *A Midsummer's Night Dream*

Understanding the nature of imagination is crucial to understanding the tremendous value of modeling images. Image-making, whether it be in clay or in the mind, is at the heart of our humanity. In psychology for the past four decades there has been a raging "imagery" debate over whether or not the human cognition really functions on the basis of mental images. The counter-argument is that the mind's real "operating system" may be in an abstract code that is the random biological result of evolution and natural selection. Hence this question is vital to our human identity, to the meaning of all the arts and to teachers who use images to generate in-depth learning. Waldorf education was created for the consciousness soul which, according to Steiner, transforms itself (*umwandeln*) into an "Imagination Soul."(GA 145, Lecture 10, March 29, 1913)

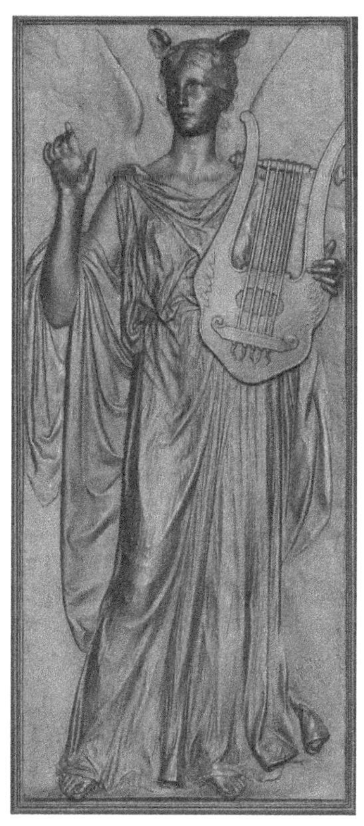

Winged Imagination by sculptor Olin Warner

Not Readily Pinned Down

As Norwegian Waldorf educator Jörgen Smit advises, we had best enter the forest of imagination in a mood of openness and wonder for it is an unusual place full of the unexpected:

> "A systematic, scientific description of imagining is already a self-contradiction. It can be compared to a pressed flower or a butterfly on a pin. For imagining is not so systematically conscious. It is not well defined and ordered. Its core is the overflowing life, the primal forest of surprises, and the wide-eyed wonder over unimaginably great realities, the warm enthusiasm and joy over becoming one with things. When imagination has been productive, we can look back upon it and discover some inherent order. We look back by remembering our observations." ("Remembering and Imagining," *Research Bulletin*, Autumn/Winter 2015, Vol. XX, No. 2, p. 50.)

Given Smit's caution, rather than trying to pin down the wings of imagination, I present here a series of different characterizations of imagination that hopefully will not only shed more light on this mysterious power that rises out of our depths, but also create a rounded mosaic of understanding.

Attempts at Definition

A standard dictionary (Webster) defines imagination as *"The act or power of forming a mental image of something not present to the senses or never before wholly perceived in reality."*

According to this definition, imagination includes the production of memory images derived from the past as well as mental formations of something new ("never before"). But "image" itself is defined as:

- *"A likeness of a thing"*
- *"The reproduction or imitation of the form of a thing"* (the word *"image"* is *"akin to the Latin 'imitare,' to imitate."*)
- *"A representation of something not present"*

These last descriptions of images, as *likenesses, reproductions, imitations,* or *representations* of something, however, seem better suited to the nature of *"memory-images"* which are of a *past* nature and *re*-produced and *re*-presented in the mind. But this description leaves something to be desired when applied to *"imagination-images"* (or *"imaginations"* if you will) which can be entirely *new productions* or at least

very new to a significant degree. Are these also "likenesses" and if so of what? Where do they come from? They appear or are created as a *"never before"* and as if "out of the blue"?

Alan Richardson's Imagination-Images

According to the classic study of psychologist Alan Richardson, the *activity of mental imaging* in general is the *cognitive process* that produces *imagery* as *"concrete representation[s] of sensory, perceptual, affective or other experiential states"* (*Mental Imagery*, 1969, London: Routledge and Kegan, ix). Imagination-images are one of the four main types:

He finds that images fall into four categories:

1. *After-images:* occur immediately after a visual sensory experience and usually fade quickly. For example, a flash of lightning leaves a bright after-image behind as one keeps staring at the night sky as background.

2. *Eidetic images*: are fixed, percept-like, photograph-like images that can last for a long time in the mind. Studies indicate that up to ten percent of children are very impressionable, eidetic imagers, but most often lose this capacity, especially after age 10.

3. *Memory-images*: are the common, everyday images that we *remember* of particular past events. They vary in clarity, and are often hazy, incomplete and unstable.

4. *Imagination-images:* come in a wide-ranging variety including the *"creative imagination imagery"* of artists and scientists, *"meditation imagery,"* the *"dream imagery"* of different sleep states (REM), mental disorder and

drug-induced *"hallucination imagery,"* etc.

A person can have a memory-image of a particular claw hammer, *"but a mental picture of a hammer with a solid gold head and a smooth ivory handle would be an imagination-image because I had never seen such a hammer until a moment ago when I constructed an image of it."* (Ibid.,93-94).

The Multisensory Nature of Imagination and Imagery

In neuroscience today the imagination and image-producing faculty extends to all senses. Many researchers point to the rich multisensory nature of mental images. For example, in a major and comprehensive study, *The Case for Mental Imagery* (2006), top researcher Stephen Kosslyn also describes how mental imagery is not limited to the *"visual modality… and the experience of seeing with the mind's eye,"* but also includes *"auditory imagery… accompanied by the experience of 'hearing with the mind's ear,' tactile images … accompanied by the experience of 'feeling with the mind's skin,' and so on…."* (Kosslyn, 2010, 4). One can imagine sound-images (bell-ringing), taste-images (lemon juice), smell-images (rose scent), touch-haptic-images (sandpaper roughness), pain/quality of life images (nausea) and so forth.

Ernst Lehr's Imagination Compared to Memory

Waldorf teacher and scientist Ernst Lehrs helpfully sheds light on the character of imagination or "fantasy" as he calls it by specifically contrasting it with memory imaging:

> "Both memory and fantasy [German: *Phantasie*, also translatable as imagination] are activities of the soul which lead to the formation of certain mental images, but these images are of opposite nature and have opposite origins. Memory pictures are generally based on past sense-perceptions; they can also be remembered imaginations or dream experiences. Even then, the original impressions, in order to be remembered, must have been fixed in the mind in a way similar to the fixation of outer perceptions. This is always a process engaging the nervous system. We note as a characteristic of memory that it has the task of reflecting past impressions in an unchanged manner and with the details as distinct as possible. Thus it is typical of memory to have a certain static character.

> "Fantasy is of a quite different nature. Here the soul is as much occupied with free production as in memory it is with reproduction. Compared with the static nature of memory, fantasy has a dynamic character. In this respect it shows a striking resemblance to the ever-moving, creatively working blood. In other respects, too, a close relationship can be found between the soul's imaginative actions and events within the body's blood-system. Quite in line with their opposite nature, fantasy and memory are distributed in a characteristic way over the span of life: in early years the soul dwells predominantly in imaginations, and in closing years predominantly in recollections." (Lehrs, *Man or Matter*, 45)

Imagination Rooted in "Mag-ic"?

Waldorf teacher Michael Preston in a *Renewal* essay describes the "The Gift of Imagination" and calls attention to the work of R.K. Elliott, who holds that i**mag**ination is derived from **mag**ical rather than as previously stated **im**itating (Latin: "*im*itare"). The extraordinary power that i**mag**ination-images exert in our minds and over our actions is **mag**ical.

Preston fruitfully approaches the essence of imagination by characterizing what this mental faculty *does*:

- creates what does not and has not existed

- transports us to far-off times and places

- quickens and enlivens our understanding

- synthesizes disconnected experience into a coherent whole

- sees the world from other points of view

- helps us to become empathetic, moral and loving persons

- helps us objectify ourselves and bring about changes in ourselves

- enables us to experience transcendent aspects of reality

And, again, imagination is not just limited to visualizing and picturing.

Philipp Lersch's Imagination in Four Types
In his *Aufbau der Person* (1970), psychologist Philipp Lersch very interestingly differentiates and extends imagination's creative dynamics to include the categories of playing, wishing, planning and creating:

Play imagination: Young children playfully attribute new meanings to objects and experiences in their immediate environment. Play imagination is at the heart of being human and of what the poet-philosopher Schiller called our inherent *Spieltrieb*, play impulse.

Wish imagination: conjures up whole worlds arising out of our desires and dreams in life. Goethe described this beautifully when he wrote: *"Our wishes foretell the capacities within ourselves; they are harbingers of what we shall be able to accomplish. What we can do and want to do is projected in our imagination quite outside ourselves and into the future. We are attracted to what is already ours, in secret. Thus passionate* *anticipation transforms what is already possible into dreamt-for reality."*

Planning imagination: imagines the elements and steps involved in how we go about intentionally doing something .

Creative imagination: the capacity of artists, scientists, doctors, teachers, visionary leaders, etc. (See E.M. Kranich, "Fantasy and Imagination," *Bund Rundbrief,* 7-8.)

All four types are very much related to and can transform into each other : Play imagination arises out of our child-like spirit-ego or higher "spirit self," which is the source of our deepest wishes (*Foundations of Human Experience*, Lecture IV). It is also the self-educating "training ground" for mature creative imagination. Furthermore, the ego can take hold of our wishes and projections of the future and organize them into planning.

> *The human being plays only when she is in the full sense of the word human. And she is fully a human being only when she plays.*
>
> —Friedrich Schiller

> *I can't tell you how the Book of Nature is becoming readable to me. My long practice…suddenly works and my quiet joy is inexpressible… It is a growing awareness of the Form with which again and again nature plays, and in playing, brings forth manifold life.*
>
> —Goethe

Goethe's Imagination in the Service of Science
Goethe, as archetypal artist embodying and exemplifying Schiller's "play impulse" (*Spieltrieb)* trained his creative imagination

to serve science as well as art. By training his imagination to be an objective instrument of knowledge, he came to experience a unity of *"sensory-spiritual"* (*sinnlich-überlsinnlich*) reality in the phenomena of nature and in human creations. Goethe called this power *"exakte sensorische Phantasie,"* *"exact sensory imagination."* This allowed him to "live into" appearances and penetrate to their archetypal essence (*Wesen*).

It was particularly in his botany research that this capacity allowed Goethe to "see" in his mind's eye ("*Geistesauge*") the suprasensory reality of the *Ur-pflanze, the* plant archetype or the form manifesting in and moving through all the plant kingdom—a unity in the multiplicity. Steiner describes how *"Goethe, by means of mobile ideas, wanted to grasp the whole system of plant growth as a unity— so he slipped out of one plant form… into another by metamorphosing the idea itself. This kind of observation with mobile ideas was, in Goethe, doubtless, the initial impulse toward an imaginative way of observing."* (CW 214, 1991, 30)

The unity of the archetypal plant lived so vigorously in his mind that he could even *imagine* plants that did not yet exist but could exist.

Waldorf teacher and scientist Ernst Lehrs translates Goethe's way of knowing into steps we ourselves can follow and practice:

- Use exact senseperception for forming a clear image (*Bild*) of the different single leaf forms as they are arranged upwards on a stem.
- Retain them in the mind using the image-forming power of memory.
- To the memory images first gained by exact sense-perception, apply the second power of image-forming called *Phantasie-imagination* and inwardly *recreate* the transition from one leaf-form into another.

> I had the gift that, when I closed my eyes and with my head lowered thought of a flower in the middle of my organ of sight, it did not linger for a moment in its original form but opened itself out and unfolded new flowers from both colored petals and green leaves, they were not natural flowers but imaginary ones, though as regular as the rosettas of a sculptor. It was impossible to fix the creation that was streaming forth; nevertheless it lasted as long as I wished, did not become exhausted or further intensified… The reason why these appeared so readily could well be that my many years of studying plant metamorphosis, together with my study of painted discs [and after-images] has wholly imbued me with these objects….Here we find afterimage, memory, creative imagination, concept and idea manifesting themselves all at once in the independent vitality of the organ with total freedom and without intentionality or guidance.
>
> —Goethe, Theory of Color
>
> (Quoted in Urieli, *Learning to Experience the Etheric World: Empathy, the After-Image and a New Social Ethic*, London: Temple Lodge, 2000, 87).

Lehrs points out that Goethe was thereby able to unite two polar faculties in a *"new organ of cognition"* for which the latter, as said, coined the term *"exact sensory Phantasie"* (imagination): *"What we are doing is to endow objective memory, which by nature is static, with the dynamic properties of Phantasie, while endowing mobile Phantasie, which by nature is subjective, with the objective character of memory."* (For an excellent guide to Goethe's new "Adventure of Reason," see Chapter V in *Man or Matter*, 1958, 81-112)

> *Every process in nature, rightly observed, wakens in us a new organ of cognition.*
>
> —Goethe

To achieve exact sensory perception, strong afterimages and vivid memory images demanded of Goethe that he practice not only rigorous and *"exacting"* sensory observation (*exakte sensorische*) but also a special kind of discernment which he called *anschauende Urteilskraft"*, the *"power of contemplative/ intuitive judgment"*. This faculty required that he shut out mind-cluttering theoretical abstractions. He meditatively beheld (*anschauen*) a plant many, many times and let its pure being and features resonate in his soul as a vivid afterimage (*Nachbild*). He then patiently and *"actively waited"* for its true character *"to speak"* and *re-create* (*Nachschaffen*) itself *afresh* within his imagination. Since nature herself was imaginatively creative, Goethe asked, *"By contemplation (Anschauen) of an ever-creative nature, may we not make ourselves worthy to be spiritual sharers in her productions?"* (Ibid.,quoted in Lehrs, 84-85). He also called this experience a *"gentle empiricism."*

Goethe's "imagination" of the plant was then not the result of a "flight of fancy," auto-suggestion or hallucination-image, but a mental re-creation rooted and anchored in rigorous and patient scientific observation of material reality. One could also say that the spirit behind nature itself was sharing and "inspiring" archetypal images into his actively receptive consciousness. Our senses and intelligence are themselves gifts of nature to be wisely used.

Although Goethe became most famous for his literary and "poetic imagination" as expressed in his poetry, novels and great dramatic works such as *Faust*, he strongly held that in all forms of true art—literature, drama, painting, sculpture, etc., one could discern objective, universal principles and laws at work just as in science. Reciprocally, serious science needed the sensory and imaginative enhancement that aesthetic perception fostered. (For more on Goethe's imagination see the chapter "Imagining Archetypes.")

> *I must confide to you that I am quite close to the secret of plant creation, and that it is the simplest thing imaginable. The ur-plant will be the strangest creature in the world…With this model and key to it, one will be able to invent plants ad infinitum; they would be consistent; that is to say, though non- existing, they would be capable of existing, being no shades or semblances of the painter or poet, but possessing truth and necessity. The same law will be capable of extension to all living things.*
>
> — Goethe

Coleridge's Threefold Imagination

It was the ideas of Goethe, the German Idealists and Romantics that Samuel Taylor Coleridge brought back across the English Channel from the continent and reforged into his Romantic philosophy of the imagination. As a philosopher-psychologist-poet, he experienced and distinguished three main activities of imagination:

1. *"Aggregating"/recombining already known images from memory*: The basic, *"mechanical,"* and *"passive"* way our intellect *"brings together dissimilar*

images" and a mere *"mode of memory."* Coleridge named this lowest activity *"Fancy,"* which is a highly confusing term today.

2. *Creating images to order sense perceptions:*, Coleridge calls attention to a miraculous power of imagination we take for granted, namely, to *"order"* even the simplest of our sense perceptions into cohesive, meaningful formations in the mind; this normally unconscious activity brings coherence to the myriad impressions which external reality continually makes upon us. Without it, we would experience the world as a chaos of percepts. For example, we see a forest, then "sort out" the individual trees. Coleridge designated this as our *"primary imagination…The living power and prime agent of all our sense perception, and a repetition in the finite mind of the eternal act of creation in the infinite 'I am"* (quoted in Barfield, *What Coleridge Thought*, 74).

3. *Creating images with deeper or higher meanings*: Gareth Knight summarizes Coleridge's next level of imagination which he says *"goes beyond the primary function [#2 above] in that it re-orders and re-arranges the phenomena of sense perception, the images in our minds, into sequences and associations that reveal a deeper level of meaning, and even existence, than the ordinary world. It is the field not only of poetic or artistic creation but also the stuff of myth and legend"* (*The Magical World of the Inklings*, UK: Skylight Press, 1990). The result is a new creative *"modification,"* *"re-creation,"* or *"fusion"* (Coleridge's terms) that is really new and alive. It is more than just a "mechanical" recombining

of ready-made memories; it is brought about more consciously than when the imagination "orders" sense perceptions. Coleridge's confusingly calls this function, *"the secondary imagination."* Such a designation, however, is misleading because, as Barfield points out, both his "primary" and "secondary" describe two equally amazing "forces" of imagination. And Coleridge himself writes that the two kinds are actually *"identical in agency."*

Furthermore, an imagination-with-deeper-meanings applies not only to artists but also to the profound insights of scientists, philosophers, and seers. Goethe as scientist has been cited as a prime example. He, in fact, is someone who combines all three aspects of imagination: carefully intensified "sensory-ordering- imagination" with "deeper-meaning- imagination," e.g. the *"Urpflanze."* Both of these capacities are grounded in a healthy "associative" intellect. As Coleridge points out, "The higher… powers [of imagination] can only act through a corresponding energy of the lower" (Ibid.,quoted in Barfield, 85).

Barfield's Imagination Embracing Polarity

The philosophical stream centering around Coleridge's ideas was very fruitful and flowed across the Atlantic to inspire the Transcendentalism of Emerson, Thoreau, Alcott, Peabody and others. And then it is fascinating how a century later this philosophy of the imagination found a place in the mythopoeic work of the Oxford club of writers called Inklings, It included J.R.R. Tolkien, C.S. Lewis, Charles Williams, Owen Barfield and others.

It was Barfield who strongly represented and promulgated Coleridge's ideas in the group. He was an interesting combination of the clear crystalline intellect of jurist and philosopher and the poetic imagination of a novelist. In one of his brilliant philosophical works, *What Coleridge Thought,* Barfield performs the service of epistemologically articulating and systematizing the dynamic thinking of Coleridge, who used incredibly complex language and was not the most organized writer. He deeply understands Coleridge's ideas because they resonate with his own experiences of imagination.

In addition to thoroughly examining the three major functions of imagination described in the last section, Barfield explores several other key concepts in Coleridge's thinking including the crucial roles of *"polarity"* and *"unity in multiplicity."* He notes that for Coleridge, polarities are intrinsically and organically woven into the fabric of both nature and the human mind. And for him, polarity is not just *"compatible" with imagination,"* but lies at its very heart.

"Polarity is dynamic, not abstract…Where logical opposites are contradictory, polar opposites are generative of each other—and together generative of new product…The apprehension of polarity is itself the basic act of imagination." (*What Coleridge Thought*, Middletown: Wesleyan University Press, 1971, 36)

The dynamic of a polarity-permeated imagination is what creates a living space for new possibilities and the unexpected.

As mentioned, Barfield shows how Coleridge's differentiations into a confusing nomenclature of "primary" and "secondary" imagination are, in fact, better characterized as *"two polar forces"* of the one *"power"* of imagination: " '*As the very powers of growth and production,'*… these [two] forces *"operate, not only unconsciously and half-consciously as life in nature, but also self-consciously as the same life in human nature* (Barfield, 77).

As with Goethe, the power of imagination becomes the bridge that allows the human spirit-individuality as "I am" to participate intimately in a living way in the world process. In Coleridge's words, an act of imagination becomes a *"repetition in the finite mind of the eternal act of creation in the infinite I AM."* (For Goethe, it was a beholding of the eternal act of plant creation and other life forms.)

The human mind is able to achieve a cognitive oneness with the whole. Here Coleridge was influenced by the German Idealist Schelling's idea of *"Ineinsbildung"—"forming-into-one."* Imagination has the power to overcome our separateness from the universe and *"re-unite"* us with the very source of creation.

This subject of unity and oneness is closely related to a second major polarity at the heart of imagination, that of whole and parts:

> "In imagination, [a special quality between the whole and the parts] is [Coleridge's] principle of 'unity in multiplicity." (Barfield, 79).

In an act of deeply meaningful imagination, the wholeness must be living in each part and organically come from 'within' so that there is real unity. Otherwise, the process is just a mechanical adding together from without, of copying and imitating. Barfield cites the examples of Shakespeare's very alive "universal" characters compared to the deadly abstract stereotypes of inferior dramatists. (Barfield, 79)

A.C. Harwood's Imagination of Wholeness

Barfield and C.S. Lewis were dear friends with the great pioneer of Waldorf education in Britain, A.C Harwood. All three (and other Inklings) went on periodic walking tours of the English countryside. Imagination seems to have been nourished by *"perambulation"* (similar to the way the intellect was cultivated by the walking Peripatetics of Aristotle's school).

In a lecture entitled "The Wholeness of Imagination" (reprinted in *Child and Man,* 1959), Waldorf teacher A.C. Harwood describes how awareness of the importance of imagination for humanity wells up in the Romantic movement. This new consciousness is in response to the loss of the instinctive image-forming faculty. Since the Renaissance this loss has separated human beings from nature:

> "Imagination began as a thing, a noun, meaning a concrete pictorial representation;

then at a definite point in history it sloughed off its noun-skin, and appeared all new and glistening as a force, an active principle of the mind, as in essence a verb. This transformation occurred about the year 1800, and was accomplished by the great [Romantic] poets…above all by Coleridge…who gave definition to the new word within a theory of knowing and being…

> "There is deep historical reason why the poets of the time of the Industrial Revolution needed to attach new meaning to the word Imagination…After the sixteenth century… the reasoning mind had separated itself from the instinctive picture-forming faculty, poetry and science had fallen apart…Science …was …divorcing man from nature…" (Harwood, 48)

Harwood became a tireless champion of a holistic education that promoted *"thinking in images"* in new ways and was aimed at healing the ever-widening rift with nature:

> "We become spectators when we think about the world abstractly, we unite ourselves with the world when we think in images…Man instinctively thinks in images because God created the world in images." (Ibid. 49)

For Harwood, Waldorf pedagogy became a vehicle for educating children as enthusiastic "participators" and activists in life as well as good observers. In today's world, human beings need to be equipped with a balance of both capacities. Influenced by Coleridge, Harwood makes a point often overlooked: imagination, in fact, is an all-encompassing faculty that uniquely embraces *both* participatory imagining *and* detached abstraction: Whereas "abstract thought knows only one pole…" and alone can become one-sided, "imagination grasps both poles…and understands life" (Ibid. 51).

This is because *at the heart of imagination*

is polarity and a wisdom that encompasses diverse perspectives. It is able to unite opposites: unity and multiplicity, sameness and difference, the general and concrete, novelty and tradition, the natural and artificial, ideas and images, emotion and order, etc.

An education of the imagination is most effective, according to Harwood, when it takes into account how both poles develop in the student over time: *"[The child] begins by seeing the world in terms of pictures… He does not see the world in the stark matter-of-fact outlines which the modern adult sees…For small children do not have…acute visual perception…They see best what is in movement. The form and gesture of things suggest pictures to them"* (Ibid.,53).

Around age twelve, students start to think more abstractly. For this reason, the Waldorf curriculum has them apply their new powers of intellectual reasoning to sensory experiences in science starting with the physics of light (eye), sound(ear) and heat(touch, warmth). It does so not one-sidedly but "aesthetically," i.e. with enhanced senses so that in a Goethean way the artist and scientist merge.

> "The theories must indeed come. It is a necessary condition of human freedom to detach oneself from the world and consider it abstractly. But this is only one half of the story, and a true education will sow the seeds of imaginative thinking by which ultimately the adult may regain in consciousness that union with the spiritual being of the world from which he fell in childhood. This is also attempted in a [Waldorf] school. The world is interpreted morphologically rather than atomistically. The life-giving principle of polarity is again and again invoked. The exact eye of the scientist is enriched with

the vision of the artist…The creative act of the Imagination…becomes an organ not for the inner life of man alone but for the understanding of the world." (Ibid.,53-54)

By "morphological interpretation" I think Harwood means first seeing unified wholenesses of form before analyzing components. In grade 5 botany student experience the whole plant before considering its specific parts.

Rudolf Steiner's Creative Imagination

As Barfield expresses it, the ideas of German and English Romantics *"come of age"* in Steiner's work. This is particularly true of what Steiner says about the experience of imagination. He characterizes imagination as a basic capacity supporting perception and thinking which can be enhanced through stages along a scale of increasing power to a high level of perceiving how the spirit works in matter.

At the end of *Foundations of Human Experience* (Lecture XIV), Steiner points out that since the second half of the nineteenth century, cultural forces have been working intensely to discredit the value of imagination as an "untruth" in education and other fields. For him, however, the opposite needs to be the case. To serve students effectively, teachers, above all, need to *"keep their imagination alive"* and model it artistically and responsibly in their teaching style and lessons and in their lives. Steiner encapsulates in a verse what he deems to be a "categorical imperative" for teachers:

> *Imbue yourself with the power of imagination* [*Phantasiefähigkeit*].
>
> *Have courage for the truth.*
>
> *Sharpen your feeling for soul-responsibility* [*seelische Verantwortlichkeit*].

In the context of what he had just previously spoken about in the lecture, he means by the second line, I think: "Have courage for the truth" *revealed through imagination*.

It is not so obvious that the last line of the verse is also directly connected to imagination, but again in the context of the foregoing lecture theme, I think, he wants teachers, at least in part to" sharpen your feeling for soul-responsibility" *and meet this responsibility by teaching with imagination.*

Young souls need to be met with imagery to be healthily nourished and to become participants in life. And indeed in the last part of Lecture XIV just before ending with the verse above, Steiner makes the interesting developmental point that it is even more critical to be highly *imaginative with teenagers*. In a later lecture cycle, he points out that *"genuine powers of imagination (Phantasie) find their birth only during puberty, for they can come into their own only after he astral body is born."* (*Soul Economy*, 227). At this critical time of growth, education needs to nurture and exercise them lest they be stifled by a one-sided intellectuality.

Protean Imagination Seated in Healthy Senses and Vitality

Steiner sees imagination as a multi-talented Proteus with several functions. It plays a critical role in the development of healthy discernment and judgment of the world (*Urteilen*) and underlies our primary ability to have sense perceptions:

> "If your imagination is strong enough (and in normal life this occurs only unconsciously), if it is so strong that it permeates your whole being **right into the senses**, then you have the ordinary imaginations (*Imaginationen*) which enable you to mentally imagine (*vorstellen*) external things. Such imaginations, which deliver sense perceptions [*sinnliche Anschauungen*] of things arise out of the activity of imagination [*Phantasie*] and will…" (R. Steiner, *Foundations of Human Experience*, 56, bold by A.A.)

> "When the imaginative sense directs its activity inward, there arises what we normally call an outer sensation of something ('*Empfindung*'), an outer perception ('*Warhnehmung*') The activity of the imaginative sense has to be directed inward to see what is outside us. Everything we sense outside ourselves we can perceive only because what appears in the imaginative sense works in us." (R. Steiner, A Psychology of Body, Soul and Spirit, 39)

It is the imaginative sense that makes percept-images (*Wahrnehmungsbilder*) and "makes sense" out of our perceptions both physical and spiritual.

Steiner attributes image-forming to our breathing (inspiration and expiration):

> "The life of breathing gives image quality (*Bildhaftigkeit*) to the fleeting life of the senses that tends to preserve itself. We are able to have Bild-images of the outside world because the breathing rhythm is in touch with the currents that pass through the nerves. Abstract thoughts (*Gedanken*) are still entirely bound to the nerves, but anything to do with images is connected to the life of breathing. When we breathe, we have creative (*bildend*) life, a life we may call the image-creating life." (*Cosmosophy II*, 87)

It is breathing that makes it possible for etheric body to become active as image sculptor: "The breathing is where our etheric body truly becomes a body of creative powers (*Bildekräfteleib*) that designs images. (*entwirft Bilder*)" (Ibid., 90).

The nerves are there to hold and keep the images, but what they are able to catch hold of and extract is only a shadow of the living reality which comes to lie deeper in our image-forming life forces:

> "[Our everyday] Vorstellung-images contain living spiritual Imagination-images. The Vorstellung-images we have in everyday life are a kind of extract of those Imagination-images. The imagining process (*Imaginieren*) extends back into the bodily, and the pale and gray reflection comes to conscious awareness as our everyday Vorstellung-images . . . The Imagination-images slip down and live in the general vitality, or vital activity, of your organism."
> (R. Steiner, *Cosmosophy II*, 124-25)

Imagination is literally at the core of a healthy vitality! Everyday mental imaging can be intensified into higher capacities of creative and spiritual (capital 'I') Imagination.

> *Vorstellung [in the Foundations of Human Experience] is like the photograph you take of a finished object...; Phantasie is more like the first inspired sketch an artist makes, vital, unformed, evocative, capable of evolution and growth.*
>
> —Michael Wilson, Scientist and Musician

> *In the Study of Man, Steiner draws a sharp distinction between … Vorstellung, an end product, a formed picture stemming from the past…and Phantasie, a new beginning, a germ or seed drawing upon the future, working through sympathy to creation.*
>
> —A.C. Harwood, Educator

Steiner's Polarity of *"Vorstellung"* and *"Bild"*

In Lecture II of the *Foundations of Human Experience* Steiner emphasizes the importance of teaching with *"Bilder"* (pl. of Bild), *that is, with images* that are freshly conjured up out of the *Phantasie*-imagination, warm

will, and vitality of the lively teacher. The *Bild-images* to which Steiner is referring are saturated with life, sensory richness and are full of meaning. They can build on everyday *Vorstellung*-images (representation–images based on memory), but the latter must *be transformed* and *re-en-live-ned* !

Hence the teacher needs to *"live imaginatively into"* the deeper archetypal essence of a lesson's subject matter. Out of the deep well of *Phantasie*-imagination, she brings a topic in such a lively, new way that the subject comes to life with immediacy and real presence. The vitality in the children resonates with the vitality of the teacher. Teachers become transformers and resurrectors of drily conceptual and abstract *Vorstellung*-images back into a more animated *"sensory-soaked"* and vibrant *Bild-image state.* Pedagogical examples from Steiner and Wiechert follow in the next sections.

> *Aliveness in the teacher must pass over into aliveness in the children.*
>
> —R. Steiner, *The Kingdom of Childhood*

Steiner advises teachers to avoid teaching with too many untransformed *Vorstellung*-images because they are faded and often abstract images of experiences in the nervous system. They are rooted in the constricting fixity of past memories both from this life and even from prenatal existence:

> "If you one-sidedly emphasize the life of Vorstellung-images, you actually direct the entire human being back to the prenatal life. You will injure children if you educate them rationally because you utilize their will in something they have already completed . . . You must bring in more Bilder. Why? These Bilder, these Bild-images are living Imagination-images, that go through

the Phantasie-imagination and the forces of sympathy." (R. Steiner, *Foundations of Human Experience*, 61)

Steiner's living *Bild-images* are ones that take root in the life processes of the physical and etheric bodies and are blood-stirring. They are full of nourishing wisdom, are warming, easily breathed in and digested and stimulate further creativity and action. They reach down through the child's soul life into the whole organism and into the toes:

> "We sow Bilder into children, which can become seeds that germinate because they are planted in bodily activity…Your activity with Bilder works upon and resonates through the whole human being…" (Ibid., 62)

Such alive images continue to vibrate in a health-bringing way during sleep when experiences are consolidated, assimilated and creatively reshaped.

When Steiner says that teachers experientially *implant Bild*-images into *"whole human being"* and into *"bodily activity,"* he literally means into all the deeper layers of the human being. Well-orchestrated artistic experiences sink deeply:

> "The 'I' is, first of all, essentially bound to sense perceptions. Sense experience is taken up into the 'I.' A [pale] Vorstellung-image is attached to it and settles into the astral body; it exercises the force that then makes the memory of it possible by settling, as a movement, into the etheric body…In the physical body, at first quite unconsciously, there comes into being from what lives in the memory, a Bild-image. . . We always have in the physical body, where a movement from the etheric body stops, an impregnation a Bild-image; this Bild-image can naturally be reached with imaginative Vorstellen-imaging

One thereby sees how the physical body is a carrier of all these Bild-images." (CW 206, *Menschenwerden, Weltenseele und Weltengeist*, 124-26, translation by A.A.)

Bild-images are *"impregnated"* most deeply of all into the physical body which becomes their *"carrier."*

In lecture nine of the *Foundations of Human Experience*, Steiner describes how profoundly what teachers sow into young souls plays a role in shaping out their whole being right into their physiognomy. *Bild*-images become the concepts (*Begriffe*) that impress themselves deeply into soul and body:

> "All the concepts [i.e. as Bild-images] poured into the child's soul shine back from the face of the mature person… Through the formation of concepts, our teaching leaves its imprint (*Siegeldruck*) on the person, right down into the body." (R. Steiner, *Foundations of Human Experience*, 152)

Teachers come to and are "in-spired" with such *Bild*-images by contemplating and living with humanity's rich treasures of archetypal wisdom and through artistic practice. They are working on both their own and the children's physical and etheric bodies. As Dr. Otto Wolf has pointed out, wisdom lives in and is *"a matter of the etheric body."* Hence this body of living forces is nourished and educated by highly meaningful experiences and images that penetrate deeply.

Too many "pale" and abstract Vorstellung-images give the child a deadening sense of "having been there, done that." They encourage passivity, weariness, and physiological unhealth. In contrast, alive Bild-images stimulate not only new active imagining in the students but also motivate and warm their will into action. Such freshly created images reach into the heart and stir the blood flow in the muscles. Children sit up in their seats with attention and interest. They are primed to enthusiastically transform their inner experience into outer artistic and technical action.

Nevertheless at the end of *Foundations* Lecture II, Steiner qualifies his advocacy for teaching with *Bild*-images. He urges teachers to use *"as many as possible"* (*"möglichst viele"*) and liberally *"mix"* (*"einmischen"*) them into lessons to enliven the experience. Teachers, he points out, have at their disposal *"two systems"*: one based on the use of *Bild–images and* imagination; the other system based on *Vorstellung*-images and memory. The process of *Vorstellen*-imaging belongs to the innate cognitive inheritance of our pre-birth experiences. These are built into us to give us not only our "jump start" in life, but also our freedom and independence as modern human beings. We need both the capacities of imagination (*Phantasie*) and everyday thinking activity (*Vorstellen*) just as we need not only blood and muscle but the support of a nervous and skeletal system as well.

In our one-sidedly intellectualized culture, teachers can help students immensely in this process of developing a balance of capacities. They do so if they can take upon themselves and continue the creative image-making activity (*"Bildtätigkeit"*) of the whole cosmos which is an amazing image-maker! The use of *Bild*-images opens students up to healthily imagining their own potential future and finding their way into *life*.

Steiner's Spiritual Imagination
In his 20s and 30s, Steiner learned from Goethe's practice of *Phantasie,* creative imagination with both aesthetic/poetic and

scientific applications. Through this experience, he activated his own dormant capacities and then extended what Goethe had achieved as a new way of observing and knowing. For example, in his *Philosophy of Freedom* (1894), Steiner developed the socially creative aspect of imagination which he called *moralische Phantasie*, moral imagination as a basis for ethical individualism.

Years later, in 1911, Steiner described how genuine creative *Phantasie*-imagination becomes a bridge between our basic everyday *Vorstellung*-based mode of thinking and that of very advanced spiritual Imagination:

"Goethe, who was well acquainted with the artistic process, so often stressed that Phantasie-imagination is by no means an element that assembles phenomena in an arbitrary manner, but that it is subject to the laws of truth. The laws of truth work entirely out of the world of Phantasie-imagination. Only because they take effect in everyday life do they undergo change and interweave with the everyday content of consciousness, shaping the world of ordinary percepts in a free way. Thus we have in genuine Phantasie-imagination something midway between mere Vorstellen mode of mental imaging and one of Imagination." (R. Steiner, *Pneumatosophy*, 197-98)

Steiner refers to the *"Phantasievorstellungen," the imagination-images* we have everyday in our everyday thinking when we, for example, imagine doing something ahead of time. I have an *imagination-image when I am sitting still and I imagine myself moving*.

Hence the intermediary step of creative *Phantasie*-imagination in the arts, mathematics, and other fields can, if cultivated, *turn* into the transcendent experience of psychical and spiritual dimensions. The

Swiss artist Paul Klee, for example, held that his "abstract" paintings (*Bilder*) made the *"invisible visible."*

The Imaginative Sense

Also in keeping with the idea of a progression of a lower to a higher faculty, Steiner characterizes *Imagination* as a spiritual sense, as our *"imaginative sense"* (*"imaginativer Sinn"*). In a rising hierarchy of senses, it comes just above and after our twelve physically-based senses as our thirteenth sense if your will. Two levels below is our *Vorstellungssinn*, our *"sense of thought or concept."* From the foregoing discussion of "scale," one can assume that it is this *Vorstellung*-sense that can be intensified and developed into the *imaginative sense.*

The imaginative sense, according to Steiner, has its center in the spiritual vortex-like organ of the soul traditionally called the "two-petaled" chakra located between the eyebrows and in the forebrain. He describes the activity of this two-fold organ as two *"capture-arms"* (*Fangarme*) of the astral body reaching either inwardly or outwardly. The imaginative sense becomes active

"in human beings with spiritual sight when it stretches out as two capture-arms [*Fangarme*]. Just at the place where the two-petaled lotus flower develops in human beings with spiritual sight, ordinary people have two such [astral]…arms, directed inward and crossing each other in the area of the forebrain… When the imaginative sense directs its activity inward, there arises what we normally call an outer sensation of something, an outer perception. The activity of the imaginative sense has to be directed inward to see what is outside us. Everything we sense outside ourselves we can perceive only because what appears

in the imaginative sense works in us." (R. Steiner, *A Psychology of Body, Soul and Spirit,* 39)

It is the imaginative sense that mentally and creatively "makes sense" out of our perceptions both physical and spiritual.

In order for the imaginative sense to switch from perceiving everyday to spiritual realities, it must be turned in the opposite direction. This is what Goethe had started doing when he turned his imaginative gaze outward to behold spiritual archetypes working in nature.

> *The inner life of the mental image [Vorstellung]…which allows itself to be guided [symbolically toward higher perception] leads beyond itself as a mere mental image [Vorstellung] and becomes something that, though it is not a judgment [Urteil], makes a meaningful image, pointing beyond the soul. This is what we may call Imagination in the term's true meaning.*
>
> —Rudolf Steiner, *Pneumatosophy*

Through symbolic mental images and/or rhythmic mantric verses, a meditant can turn the ordinarily inward-directed attention and consciousness (astral capture-arms) of the imaginative sense "outwards" i.e. away from the limiting effects of the physical body, brain and nervous system. This is similar to what happens in sleep when one's astral body-ego leave the physical-etheric, but here one remains awake. Meditative exercises are meant to "wake," "move," and "lift" a person toward and into a transcendent etheric state of consciousness. They also generate the right accompanying "feelings" needed to activate the outreaching astral arms so that they become receptive and can "feel" and be "touched" by the spirit:

"Through the [meditative] process, mental imaging ("*Vorstellen*") moves into…the imaginative world…In imagining ("*imaginieren*"), [the soul] feels itself in touch with…an external world of the spirit. When the spirit lives into mental images (*Vorstellungen*) that are really pressing toward Imagination, that spirit is as compelling as the material world is. We find it difficult to imagine ("*vorstellen*") a tree as golden. Mental imaging ("*Vorstellen*") rises to the level of imagination" ("Imagination")… In ordinary life, mental images fill themselves with the content derived from percepts conveyed by our eyes and ears and so on…In imagining (*imaginieren*), we allow the spirit to do the filling of mental images." (Ibid, 195-196)

Although Steiner describes two opposite directions of attention here, I think there must be intermediary states on a scale or spectrum of turning from the "ordinary" to the suprasensory via *Phantasie*-imagination. Just as our life sense (*Lebensinn*) metamorphoses into our thought or concept sense (*Vorstellungsinn*), so the latter must organically metamorphose and turn into our "imaginative sense" on a progression of transformation from one state into the other. Steiner's use of *Vorstellung* as a lower form of imagination in many contexts can be understood as being on the way to toward higher *Imagination*. He even refers to symbolic "*imaginative Vorstellungen*" and "*Phantasie-Vortsellungen*." Furthermore, all three levels of sense—"life sense," "*Vorstellung*-sense," and "imaginative sense" share a common reservoir of spirit in the inner world of the human being.

In 1921, Steiner related how in sense perception we are actually experiencing the spirit and *Imaginationen*-images, albeit unconsciously. What we become aware of is the reflected *Vorstellung*-image:

"People are actually in the world of the spirit when they make sensory perceptions and have Vorstellung-images. Sensory perceptions depend on dead matter, purely physical apparatus, being embedded in the organism, with only the ether body present in them… The content of sensory perception is definitely spiritual by nature. It is merely that when we form the Vorstellung-images we extend the sensory activity to the nerve organization [which is] in a process of dying. Organic activity has to be excluded… Vorstellung-images are spiritual experiences, but in Bild-images. When it comes to Vorstellung-images we are in fact aware that they are abstract by nature and that the images they give are not rich and full (*nicht intensive gesättigte Bilder*). Things turn pale and gray when we move back from sensory perception to the life of Vorstellung-images. That grayness exists only for our conscious life, however, for in reality all Vorstellung-images…contain Imaginationen-images…but they do not come to conscious awareness. The Vorstellung-images we have in everyday life are a kind of extract of those Imaginationen-images…Every time you have a Vorstellung-image you also have an Imaginationen-image , but whilst the Vorstellung remains in the conscious mind, the Imaginationen-image slips down and lives in the vitality, of your organism…It enters into every organ—it lives in the brain, in the heart, in the lungs, in the kidneys, everywhere. It unites with our general vitality." (R. Steiner, *Cosmosophy II*, 124-125)…

"In so far as we live in the element of spirit we know it only as Bild-image. The physical body is however created out of the spirit, and if we develop our faculty of Imagination, we can gain living insight into the imaginative life that lies at the back of it." (Ibid., 126-127)

"Going through the gate of death, human beings begin to experience as their reality the things they only experienced as images before… Everything is always completely the other way around." (Ibid.,132)

As we shall see in the next chapter, the process of turning around our consciousness is very much related to the subject of *Umstülpung*: Turning Inside-out. At its conclusion, the Dutch medical doctor van Emmichoven describes a turning-inside–out process wrought by Steiner's greatest mantric verse, the Foundation Stone Meditation.

> *We must be able to live in suprasensory worlds while simultaneously being able to return at anytime to stand firmly on two feet.*
>
> —Rudolf Steiner, *The Mission of the Spirit*

Recent Research on Imagination

Based on Steiner's indications and his own experiences, researcher Dr. Andreas Heertsch sees in the progression from everyday *Vorstellen-imagining* through intermediary *Phantasie*-imagination to advanced *Imagination* and their interplay, a rising *"scale of knowing."* As a stage or type of knowledge, he finds that imagination indeed *"has its beginning in everyday consciousness"* i.e. in *Vorstellen* or everyday "imagining." ("Ein Tor zum Eigentlichen: Zur Skalierbarkeit von Imagination, Inspiration und Intuition," *Die Drei* November, 2016, 21).

Psychologist and meditation workshop leader Terje Sparby builds on Heertsche's discussion of the gradations of and steps in imagination, and explores what he calls an intermediary realm between the everyday and suprasensory states of consciousness. ("The Realms and Steps of Higher Knowledge," *Die Drei,* 12/2017, 19-28). Sparby finds, for example, that the sculptural recognition of shapes such as the human face, in general, can be designated as a physical-sensory imagination. In working with many groups of people, Sparby found that intermediary perceptions of forms and subtle color experiences can be intensified through meditation and the arts and lead toward and into the suprasensory imaginations (Ibid., 21.

The fact that imagination may be gradually developed along an evolving spectrum is encouraging for those beginning on a basic level. Whether through hand sculptures or meditation-mind-sculptures or a combination of both, the direction toward and into the transcendent can be similar.

In the second phase of his life work, Steiner enlisted the *imaginative* arts in the service of spiritual development. He recommended the activity of modeling images in clay, for example, to develop and perceive the working of the etheric forming forces (**Bild**ekräfte), the ***image***-forming forces in the vitality of the human body.

Umstülpung: Turning Inside-Out

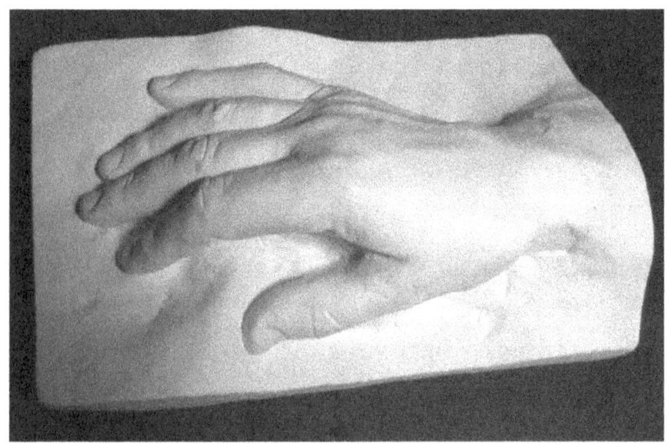

Hand of Goethe at age 72

Gestalten

As mentioned in a previous chapter, one of Rudolf Steiner's favorite words was *"gestalten"*—variously rendered as to *shape, form, mold, sculpt, model,* etc. He himself was an "amateur" sculptor who loved to return to his studio after a long lecture tour to carve wood or model in clay or in a plasticine which he himself invented.

Plastisches gestalten, rendered as *sculptural modeling*, has a double emphasis since *"plastic"* itself is derived from the Greek *"plastikos "* and *"plassein"* meaning *"to mold"* and *"to form."* The quality of being plastic, malleable, and flexible is *"plasticity"* and is used to characterize, for example, brain formation and hand movements. Steiner spoke of a child's brain as being like supple clay waiting for the spirit to sculpturally shape its convolutions and interior configurations.

> *We can see in a child how physical nature is plastically formed by the spirit. What precisely is the brain of a child when it is first born, according to our modern natural science? It is something like the clay which a sculptor takes up when he prepares a model. And now let us look at the brain of a seven-year-old child when we begin his primary education; it has become a wonderful work of art.*
>
> – Rudolf Steiner

Metamorphic-Morphological Thinking

Steiner correlated mental plasticity with brain plasticity. Working out of the soul,

> "thought has a plastic [sculptural] effect. It becomes imprinted on the brain …We recognize …in ordinary memory, the plastic nature of thinking, similar to the formative processes in the physical body . . . The plastic nature of thinking has a 'sculpting' effect in life." (R. Steiner, *Education, Teaching and Practical Life*, 85-86)

The forms we call forth can be relatively *static*, as for example, in fixed memory image formations. We can also imagine *changes-of-form* or *trans-form-ations* of one object in a series of shapes. (*"Umwandlungen"* or *"Umgestaltungen"*). When we do this, we are heading in the direction of an enhanced mental capacity Steiner called *"organic-morphological"* or *"metamorphic"* thinking. Goethe developed this ability to behold changing organisms in his mind's eye (*Geistesauge*), what he himself called "*exakt sensorische Phantasie*," exact sensory imagination.

Unlike our everyday "object thinking" which is primarily space-oriented, morphological thinking lives very strongly in the stream of time. This capacity is able to keep track of a full living process by imagining transitions that do not necessarily manifest spatially-materially. For example, in the spiral of metamorphosing leaf forms up the stem of a plant—it is the same leaf type taking on different shapes in a series of iterations. And this applies to sepals, petals, pistil, etc. The plant is all leaf according to Goethe—there are surprising leaps from one shape to the next. The metamorphic mind is able to imagine the visible as well as the invisible intermediary changes occurring in between, in an etheric dimension and pure state of being. It mentally bridges the apparent physical gaps. As Ernst Lehrs describes,

> "The spiritual principle of the plant [is] engaged in a kind of breathing rhythm [of expansion and contraction], now appearing, now disappearing, now assuming power over matter, now withdrawing from it again."
> (E. Lehrs, *Man or Matter*, 92-93)

Morphological *thinking-in-time* can be a valuable capacity especially when added to object thinking in space, which we need in order to stay grounded. Steiner compares the two different but complementary ways of thinking:

> "In our ordinary thinking everything is arranged spatially…Ordinary thinking is a combining way of thinking, one that collects scattered elements…Morphological thinking, one in which we think in forms… is not limited to space; it lives within the medium of time, in the same way thinking lives within the medium of space. This thinking does not link up one thought with the other; it sets before the soul a kind of thought-organism. When we have a conception, an idea or a thought, we cannot pass over at will to another. Even as in the human organism we cannot pass over at will from the head to any other form, but must first pass over to the neck, then the shoulders, the thorax, etc., even as in an organism everything has a definite structure which must be considered as a whole, so the thinking which I characterized as morphological thinking must be inwardly mobile…. It is inwardly so mobile that it produces one form out of another, by constantly growing and producing an organic structure…

> "Our thinking must become mobile and our thoughts must be inwardly connected with each other. Mere combining thought cannot grasp the life which proceeds from the spirit, this can only be grasped by an inwardly living thinking."
> (R. Steiner, *Die Wirklichkeit höheren Welten*, Lecture 2, 35-36,)

Umstülpung: Super-Morphological Thinking

Goethe reshaped his mind to include the morphological mode of thinking and to see the continuous metamorphosis of the plant archetype, the *Urpflanze*, in his mind's eye. According to Steiner, he was able to intensify this capacity to its highest level and achieve Imagination. (See CW 214, The *Mystery of the Trinity*, p. 49.) Goethe also made great strides in applying the same way of imagining to animal and human formation. This enabled him to discover for the science of anatomy the intermaxillary bone hidden and fused in the human jaw. He further made the observation that "*all skulls have arisen through a transformation of the vertebra.*" (Diary, 1790)

According to Steiner, Goethe was on the right track, but lacked the full experience of bone metamorphosis because it requires the special capacity of Inspiration (ibid, 49) which he calls *"umgestülpten Denken,"* *"umstülped-thinking"* or *"thinking turned-inside-out."* (Goethe also could not go the next step because he did not realize that this inverted relationship involved the rein-carnation of past lower body forces into re-embodied head forces.) This "supermor-phological" (*übermorphologischen*) think-ing capacity enables a person to imagine a subject turned-inside-out.

> **Umstülpung:**
> *(literally "around-turning) is usually trans-lated as "turning-inside out." This process interestingly encompasses the possibilty of two directions: to turn inside-to-out-side ("ausstülpen") or outside-to-inside. ("einstülpen"). I recommend adopting new Englishified terms: an "umstulp" (noun), "to umstulp" (verb); "to instulp"; or "to outstulp." The Latinate terms "inversion," "invert" or "revert" seem too abstract. The root "-vert means "to turn."*

Through *umstülped*-thinking one mentally pictures the transformation of not only ver-tebrae into cranial bones, but also of other bones in the lower body. Steiner compares the process of *Umstülpung* to the turning-in-side-out of a glove:

> "It is not enough to derive the cranial bones through just a morphological examination… one must go further to understand the rela-tionship between the head and the rest of the human organism (we are focusing now on the skeleton for the time being). How, for example, do the arm and leg bone forms relate to those of the head bones? One only understands the metamorphosis of one form

emerging from another when one realizes that it is not just a spatial re-configuration, but something quite other: an *Umstülpung*, an inversion of form involving a turning-in-side-out-and outside-in . . .

"To understand the mutual relationship between a leg bone and a head bone, one needs to compare the outer surface of the head bone with the inner surface of the tubular bone. [For example], the inside of the thigh bone must be turned outwards . . . so that it then corresponds to the outer sur-face of the cranial bone. And vice versa: the outer surface of the thigh bone corresponds to the interior surface of the cranium . . .

"You need to imagine this process like the *Umstülpung* of a glove; the inside is turned out and the elasticity also simultaneously changes . . . The glove is not just turned inside-out (*umgestülpt*), but through new forces of elasticity it takes on a fully different form.

"You see, I bring you quite a complicated indication of this third kind of thinking… which not only lives in changing shapes (*Gestalten*), but a thinking that is able to turn the formation of an inside to the outside and thereby change the form. This only becomes possible when one no longer lives in time, but with this process of *Umstülpung* one's thinking in space and time transitions into a reality beyond space and time . . . This third kind of thinking is quite different than combining thinking and sculptural thinking [and] plunges into spacelessness and time-lessness; the changed form appears with the inside turned outside and the outside turned inside . . . It is quite another quality of thought… "

(Rudolf Steiner, *Die Wirklichkeiten hoeheren Welten*, Lecture 2, 59-60. A.A. translation)

Two years earlier, Steiner had described this important and "very difficult concept" of

Umstülpung to the first Waldorf teachers:

> "If you think of a vertebra pushed and pulled in various ways, you will create the bowl-like form of the skull . . . You can relatively easily picture a skull transformed out of the vertebra of the backbone. . .
>
> "However, it is not so easy to get the shape of the tubular arm or leg bones from the bowl-shaped head…You must use the same procedure you would use when you put on a sock or a glove and first turn it inside-out… If you made a sock elastic so that you could artistically form it with all kinds of bumps and dents and then turned it inside-out…[and the outside toward the inside]. The human limbs are…a skull turned inside-out." (*Foundations of Human Experience*, 162-63)

Dr. Johannes Rohen, an international expert on functional anatomy and famous for his textbooks, has followed up on and investigated Steiner's indications in great detail. He illustrates how the basic archetypal vertebra shape metamorphoses and simplifies up the spine to the pivotal form of the so-called "atlas" and undergoes an Umstülpung into the head bone forms:

> "All vertebrae share a basic structure but differ considerably in their structural details depending on where they are located in the spine…The vertebral processes… become smaller and more delicate at the top of the spine and are reduced to mere stumps in the atlas [the topmost vertebra]…"
> (J. Rohen, *Functional Morphology*, 348)
>
> "If we pursue these metamorphosing forms…into the base of the skull, we discover two closely associated bones (the sphenoid and occipital bones) that together exhibit all the structural elements of a vertebra, but with front and back reversed (*umgestülpt*) … The sphenoid and occipital bones, collectively called the os basilare, are surprisingly similar in structure to the vertebra (such as the lumbar vertebra)…In this [os basilare] bone we can see not only a metamorphosed individual vertebra but also a formation that encompasses the structural elements of all vertebra in idealized form. The os basilare integrates the entire spine into a single ideal structure. This principle of integration is the real mystery of vertebral metamorphosis. At the level of the atlas, a null point is reached. "A complete reversal (*Umstülpung*) of back and front occurs. But the form also enters a new space, where it manifests uninfluenced by the earth's gravitational field. This is the only way to explain the wonderful winged shape of the os basilare, the skull's 'foundation.'" (Ibid., 351-353)

Polarity of Forming Forces

The wing-shaped vertebra is the signature motif that we see ripple up the spine and into the head. The spirit plays metamorphically on winged white calcium keys as on a piano keyboard. In fact, Steiner experienced the skeleton acoustically and "inspirationally" as a musical creation and sequence:

> "Do not merely look at [the skeleton] in its various forms but listen to it; listen to how one bone changes into another—the spinal column with its wonderfully sculpted vertebrae layered one upon another, with the ribs extending from it which bend and curve in front and are so wonderfully articulated together; the way in which the vertebrae are changed into the bones of the skull… [Hear these forms] for this is a wondrous gathering of instruments in a splendid orchestra that resounds in the most wonderful way."
> (R. Steiner, *Mysteriengestaltungen*, Lecture 6, 86-87, A.A. translation)

The spinal forms are Chladni sound figures crystallized in calcium and shaped by the musical forces of the universe.

In considering this metamorphosis from lower to upper body, scientist Andreas Suchantke brings attention to the primary role of polar forces. In the upper body forces tend to sculpt spherical forms and in the lower body different forces shape radial-axial long forms. In between there is a balanced transition of form (*Metamorphosis*, 16-26).

Some of his main points are:

"Goethe recognized, however dimly, that the vertebra could be regarded as the archetypal element of the skeleton, not because all the other bones were materially identical to it and thereby derivable from it (i.e.'homologous'), but because—more clearly than any other part of the skeleton—it unites the two formative polarities that else where appear in a more or less one-sided fashion." (25)

"The spine appears as a bridge uniting two morphogenetic fields [of forces] that display a polar relationship." (23)

"On the level of morphogenetic activities—… let us call them formative forces—two polar fields of force are discernible. The one is responsible for the [inwardly oriented] spherical forms with the protective function. It is most active in the region of the cranium and from there extends its influence into the spine…strongest towards the top…where it appears in dominance in the neural arch [of the vertebra]." (25)

"[The spherical influence] diminishes as the distance from the head increases and is replaced more by the polar counterpart, the tendency responsible for [peripherally oriented] axial forms which are expressed in the increasing dominance of the vertebral body." (25)

"From the middle of the thoracic (chest) upwards, the vertebral body becomes ever smaller and weaker, until, in the uppermost vertebra the atlas, it disappears altogether… At the same time there is a corresponding expansion of the [spherically-oriented] neural arch…At the very top, in the atlas… the neural arch prevails." (22)

"In the other direction the opposite occurs. The vertebral bodies become ever more massive, achieving their largest size in the lumbar region—where they…have an increasing load to bear. The neural arches… become ever smaller." (22)

"This axial tendency…[is also]evident most clearly in the limbs, but also in the ribs, and especially in the columnar form of the spine itself. Diametrically opposed to this is the spherical tendency that has both its center and its culmination in the form of the cranium." (25)

> *Modern education teaches people to know only what is turned-to-the-outside, and they have a concept only for half a human being. They cannot comprehend even the limbs because the limbs have been turned inside-out by the spirit.*
>
> —Rudolf Steiner

The Vertebral Column like a Plant

Interestingly, the metamorphosis of the vertebra forms from lowermost to uppermost spine reminds one of rhythmical changes of leaves up a stem. In particular, the leaves of many plants tend to be rounded and fleshy at the bottom (closest to water and earth) and give way up along the stem to more differentiated and spiky, angular shapes and finally to simplified forms at the top.

Similarly, larger, heavier vertebrae below with more rounded features give way to more pointed and delicate forms in the middle of the spine. Centrum bodies, very dominant below, shrink as they form upwards until the centrum is completely absent in the last vertebra, the atlas. The neural spine and side processes (the wings!) decrease in size, become more delicate, and are reduced to stumps in the atlas which is *"relatively shapeless."* (Rohen, 2007, 348) In this upward progression, the arch and foramen (hole) enlarge at the top.

Goethe considered the leaf the archetypal form of the plant from which all other parts are metamorphosed. The vertebra similarly appears as the protean form mediating between the polarity of rounded head bones above and limb long bones below.

"Goethe recognized, however dimly, that the vertebra could be regarded as the archetypal element of the skeleton… because— more than any other part…— it unites the two formative polarities [of spherical and axial] that appear elsewhere in a more or less one-sided fashion." (Suchantke, 25) The vertebra form also encompasses a fourfoldness: (1-2) the ponderousness and roundedness of the centrum (physical-etheric), (3) the star-like wing-like or star-like side processes (astral), and (4) the formamen (hole) for the upright spinal cord (ego).

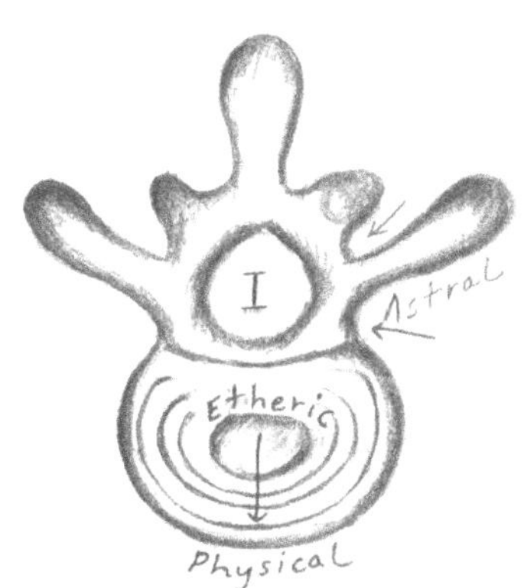

Rounded etheric and wing-like astral forms with I-center

Secrets of the Skeleton

Another fascinating book for lifelong study is L.F.C. Mees' *Secrets of the Skeleton: Form in Metamorphosis*. In it he considers the metamorphoses of lower body bones into head bones and how different bones are variations on certain form-themes. Some of his insights include:

"An archetypal theme—a vertebra with two ribs transforms itself into the girdles [pelvic and shoulder] with limbs and finally into the central part of the skull, the temporal bone with the jaws." (61)

"A remnant of the limb principle, mainly the fingers, can be found in the grooves of the jaws where the teeth are situated." (66)

"The hollows of the hand and foot together… become the hollow of the mouth." (66)

"The milk teeth can be seen as a metamorphosis of the ten fingernails and ten toenails." 66)

"One can imagine a metamorphosis of the muscles of the limbs into the muscles of the face…Our gestures are…up to a point a kind of talking." (69)

"Is it not possible to think of the heart—as organ between arms and legs—continuing to live as a metamorphosis in the tongue between the jaws? Both are composed only of muscles. Both organs never grow tired in our lifetime." (69)

"The convolutions of the intestines… [remind one] of the convolutions of the brain." (69)

"The trunk, rolled up and turned back to front, becomes the head of the next incarnation." (70)

"[After death] the trunk detaches itself from the mortal remains; the head remains behind. Our principal activities on earth are connected with the trunk…This shape is taken back, enlarged, assimilated, played upon… in a world we call heaven…The new head contains…the secrets of the past and shows the heavenly stamp in the magnificent dome of the skull. Creative beings add a new trunk and the development continues." (73)

***Umstülpung* of Other Systems**

In his study *The Harmony of the Human Body*, Dr. Armin Husemann extends the idea of *Umstülpung* from the skeleton to the sensory, nervous, muscle, blood and speech systems:

The Skeleton: The brain resides in an *umstülped* skeleton. The skull is an umstülped vertebra or tubular bone. (See prior section on Umstülpung for examples.) Huseman makes us aware that this allows thoughts to come about inwardly that reflect what the body, especially the very interactive lower torso-limb body, is experiencing outwardly. Outer experience is umstülped into the inner experience of images. "The formation of thoughts… resides in an umstülped space in relation to the rest of the skeleton." (Huseman,1989, 59) Our thinking is an Umstülpung!

The Sensory System:

The Eye: Husemann describes the development of the eye as an example of how a sensory organ arises: "At the point where the lens becomes transparent the whole process has reached the state of *Umstülpung*: what began as a separate movement inwards in the form of an eye vesicle has broken through to the light on the opposite side." (Husemann, 1989, 60)

His illustrations show how life-filled tissue responds to the light forces outside, embraces them, internalizes them and creates the lens organ as crystallized light within.

The Ear: In his 2010 study of human hearing, Husemann also develops Steiner's indications (CW 218, lecture of Dec. 9, 1922) on how the inner ear is a metamorphosed, transformed limb:

"the spiritual forces of the deeds of legs and arms are *umstülped* and reincarnate as the ear bones (ossicles) in the next life. Foot and calf become the hammer, the kneecap becomes the ambos (anvil), and the thigh becomes the stirrup." (Husemann, *der Hörende Mensch*, 37, A.A. translation)

The transformed foot, the hammer, dances on the ground of the drum! Hearing is *umstülped*-will.

The Nervous System: undergoes an *umstülpung* on the way from the spinal column into the brain. The grey matter is "arranged centrally in the spinal cord, coated by the mass of fibers, the 'white matter.'…In the cerebrum the grey matter lies at the periphery as the so-called 'cerebral cortex.' It surrounds the white matter which lies within it…With the transition from the spinal cord to the *umstülped* skeletal space of the skull, the network of nerves also changes its spatial orientation. The right side crosses over to the left and pathways which up to that point run on the left cross over to the right (which is the reason why the right side of the body is connected to the left cerebral hemisphere and vice versa). Pathways which lie at the front move to the back and those at the back to the front. The area where this takes place is called the 'brain stem.'…Essentially it is the cerebrum which is *umstülped* as far as grey and white matter is concerned, forming that part of the brain which, in the way that it overlies the old parts of the brain, has developed most strongly in human beings, in contrast to the animals…It is through the *umstülped* cerebrum—in connection of course with all the other human characteristics of the organism— that we possess alert, self-conscious thinking.

> *Were the eye not of the sun, how could we behold the light?*
>
> *The eye owes its existence to the light. Out of indifferent animal organs the light produces an organ to correspond to itself; and so the eye is formed by the light for the light so that the inner light may meet the outer.*
>
> —Goethe

The Muscular System: is also affected by such *Umstülpung* in the region of the neck. The muscular surfaces at the hyoid bone [just above the larynx] give a clear picture of the high degree of confusion between body and head muscles in this area. (63)

In the *Umstülpung* zone, two currents of forces are coming together in a creative chaos to bring about the switchover.

The Blood system:

"[In embryonic development] the brain begins the infolding process and takes the blood vessels with it …[where they] …produce the cerebro-spinal fluid…which gives buoyancy to the brain…The blood becomes cerebro-spinal fluid. Heaviness becomes lightness." (64)

Speech:

"[In exhaling] almost at the point of excretion [of the poison of carbon dioxide] the muscles of the larynx are able to stem the outflowing air and transform it into sound…Through the 'I', new spiritual life is infused into the dead-end-product of the metabolic process, thus forming language. This [is] an *umstülpung* process of the metabolic products of the physical body into the life of the spirit…Language contains the essence of the activity of the 'I'…that…fills the sound made by the astral body, also produced by animals, with meaning." (67)

Tissue:

"Physical organic tissue is extended by the etheric body, hollowed by the astral body and *umstülped* by the 'I.'"(65)

"The *umstülpung* process takes place in the human being's etheric body through the activity of the 'I' in the star [astral] body." (70)

Simple Inside-Out Modeling Exercises

In lectures, Steiner turned a glove inside-out to demonstrate the basic idea of Umstülpung, although he stressed the process was much more complex. He also described a sculptural exercise which is featured in Husemann's study *The Harmony of the Human Body* (1994):

"Imagine you have an elastic sphere. You make an indentation in the top in such a way that what was pointing up has now been pressed to face downwards so that the sphere turns into a kind of bowl…Imagine further that the sphere is folded in on itself not only until the indentation touches the lower wall at the bottom, but passes beyond it, penetrating it….but as it come out the other side, its substance has changed consistency." (Husemann,1989, 57-58)

Exercise: Torso-Limb Longness *Umstülped* into Skull-like Bowl-ness

The simplest way to experience *Ümstulpung* is to observe the positioning of bone in your own two-part skeleton. Your skull bone is on the outside as an exoskeleton. The bones of your lower body are mostly embedded inside muscle as an endoskeleton, especially in the limbs.

Below is a simple exercise in plasticine to experience a long limb-like form turning inside-out into a thin curved hemispherical form.

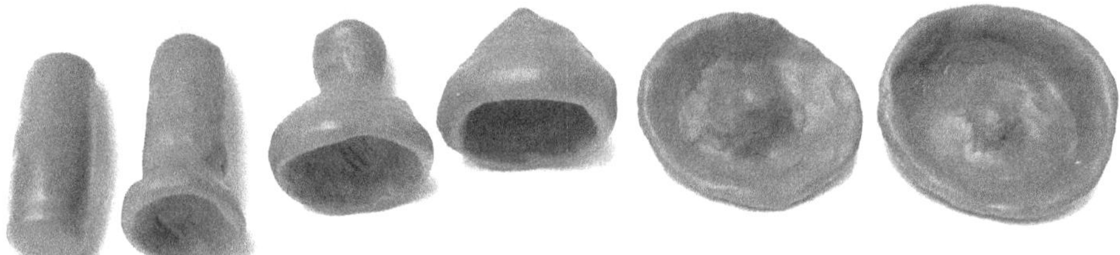

1. Form an approximately 3"h x .75"w cylinder to symbolize the quality of longness of the torso-limbs).

2. Press into the cylinder's base so that it gradually widens into an acorn-cap-like form.

3. Turn the form's edges up so that the outside becomes the inside and it becomes a rounded bowl-like shape.

4. Make a new cylinder and place the bowl-like form on top.

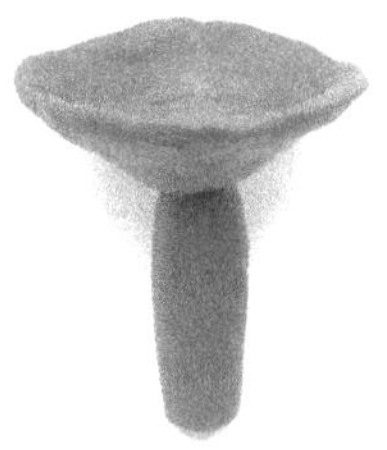

The bowl-like form is analogous to the bottom half of the skull. The second cylinder represents the lengthening nature of a new torso-spine-limbs extending from it. In the embryo the new trunk grows down from the initially predominant head form. Limbs lengthen out from it. This is only a crude procedure like turning the glove inside-out to activate imagining the real process.

Why Umstülpung for Teachers?

Steiner characterized the process of Umstülpung as "very difficult to imagine," in spite of his glove demonstration. Why was it so important for teachers to become familiar with this concept? The reasons are multifaceted and have many implications for Waldorf education and its foundations in anthroposophy:

Re-embodiment: Above all, for Steiner, the idea of Umstülpung is the key to understanding the process of human reincarnation. The forces of our former torso-limbs metamorphose into those building up the head of our next life:

"After we have passed through the period between death and a new birth, our present body, except for the head, will become the head of the next incarnation…The head is always lost. Naturally, we are talking about forces. Of course, the material of the rest of the body is also lost. But this material is not the essential thing…. These forces are transformed into the forces of the head…" (*Das Rätsel des Menschen*, Lecture VI)

The human being brings these metamorphosed forces into life and begins as a head-like embryo (ovum) which extends into a torso and then out into limbs, genetically inherited vehicles for a new biographical agenda of deeds!

Developmental Insights: Steiner wants teachers to be aware that the way lower body forces are *umstülped* and compacted into the next life's head gives useful clues to many of the functional relationships between a child's current head and current lower body. Some of the more prominent connections to be taken into account are:

- The head is inherited from the past, but the new torso and new limbs are there for the future. Steiner advises teachers therefore to educate primarily the future-oriented limbs of the child and part of the chest which lives in the present. The head inherited from the past will wake up organically of its own accord and be re-modeled and rejuvenated—made younger and more child-like to serve the spirit! From feeling-willing to feeling-thinking is the natural developmental path to awakening intelligence rather than stuffing heads with information and making them prematurely "senile." The dried out abstract intellect is old, whereas living thinking and imagination are youthful.

- The forces of our *gesturing* hands, dancing legs and entire metabolic-limb system of a former incarnation are metamorphosed into jaws and teeth which amazingly come to serve our *gesture-filled* speaking in this life. Language development remains connected to movement and is supported by eurythmy, gymnastics, movement and practical activities throughout childhood—and adulthood! The sense of word is a metamorphosis of the sense of movement.

- Past life finger forces form our new teeth which we use for speech formation (dental sounds!). They develop "soul teeth" for taking hold of language in grammar and strengthening the "I." Furthermore , a surplus of tooth forces in turn is freed around age seven and metamorphoses into forces of thinking, memory and learning. In Steiner's startling words, at school age the child begins to *"think with teeth forces"* which are metamorphoses of finger forces! (*A Modern Art of Education*, 80) By exercising their new fingers, children are not only activating their present

brain processes but are also building up forces that will go forward into their head formation, teeth, speech and thinking in a future incarnation

Teaching and learning involve very long term development!

- Our past interior abdominal metabolic forces *umstülp* into the more outward activity of chewing (catabolism) and transforming the foodstuff energy of nature into the light energy of consciousness and thinking. Thinking interestingly involves both a catabolic aspect in its capacity for analysis and an anabolic one for synthesis of concepts into ideas. (*The Renewal of Education*, Lecture 10) The synthesizing process is head-centered while analyzing is in the lower body. (*Curative Course,* 19) A healthy balanced pedagogy requires both building up and taking apart, being allowed to *"chew on things"* and to "digest" and to *"make* what we have learned *our own."* There are many other features of Waldorf education that show how cognitive activity is intimately bound up with motor and organ functions. The whole body is an interrelated instrument of intelligence, memory, imagination, and learning.

- The interior lung forces of our past life (formerly the vehicle of our soul living within the body) *umstülp* into our new nose and nasal passages. The nose is not just an entrance for air but also an olfactory organ related to our capacity for making mental images and moral judgments in our prefrontal cortex. In human evolution *"only a little piece at the bottom of the olfactory nerve has remained. The rest of it has been metamorphosed and is here below the forehead. …With this organ we form our mental* images… We cannot smell like a dog, *but we can make mental images"* (*The Kingdom of Childhood*, 46).

Also, according to Steiner, the large evolutionary decrease in once immense olfactory powers (similar to that of today's animals) has meant their metamorphosis and reallocation into our powers of moral discernment. Soesman develops this indication of smell as the basis for morality and cites the wise saying that lingers in the language about bad situations: "That stinks!" One can think of others: "Something is rotten in the state of…", "I had to hold my nose", "I could smell something was wrong," etc.

Moral Imagination and Pedagogical Morality: Steiner wanted imagination and moral discernment to join together pedagogically into the higher human capacity of *moral imagination* which when applied in the classroom becomes alive, fresh, moral "technique" and practice. At the end of his first course to teachers, he sums up all that he was talking about in the first two-week teacher training course:

"Teaching has a certain inner morality, an inner responsibility. Teachers truly have a categorical imperative:… Keep your imagination alive! If you feel yourself becoming pedantic, then say to yourself: For other people pedantry may be bad, but for me, it is immoral! This must be the teacher's attitude. If it is not the teachers, attitude, then teachers must consider learning how to use their knowledge of teaching for another profession. Of course, in life we cannot accomplish these things and achieve completely the ideal; however, we must at least know the ideal. You will not have the proper enthusiasm for pedagogical, morality if you do not fill yourself with something fundamental—that is, the recognition that the head itself is already a complete human being with stunted limbs and chest. You must know that each limb of a human being is a complete human being, but with the head and chest stunted, and that in the chest the head and limbs maintain balance. If you use this fundamental thought, then you will receive inner strength from it so that you can fill your pedagogical morality with the necessary enthusiasm." (*Foundations of Human Experience*, 211)

Steiner's main mission on earth was to bring a new picture of the developing threefold human being (*anthro*-posophy)that would inspire and incite people to action and transform all the major endeavors of human life—social forms, education, science, medicine, agriculture, the arts, psychology, self-development, etc. Not only was this living ideal picture of the human being to give them enthusiasm but it would become a driving force in their lives and the source of strength and will to carry through with these ventures.

The first twelve teachers, who already had an extensive background in anthroposophy, must have also realized that Steiner was in his first educational course synthesizing his "philosophy of freedom" and his new experience of reincarnation and human metamorphosis (*Umstülpung*) into an education towards freedom and love. The developing human being was a being evolving towards increasing emancipation and perfection through a series of lives.

Cosmos-centered Will-Organs for an Education of the Will: A child's human limbs are the tiny in-radiating tips of great spirit-roots or spirit-radii originating in the spirit-periphery, their actual center. True limbs, which only humans have attained, are the last forms to appear in evolution (from sea onto land) and are a signature manifestation of incarnation of the spirit ego—its radiating and stretching into matter. In our journey from land to sea, we developed *landing gear*! Head forms (cephalopoda) and then trunk forms (vertebrata) came first and are more related to our earlier animal-like form and existence in the seas.

To help teachers imagine this reality of spirit center of the limbs, Steiner recommended that they bend and re-sculpt their minds through exercises in modeling and in synthetic or projective geometry. Through the concepts of a sphere or plane at infinity as center, one can picture how from a cosmic center at infinite periphery the limbs ray in and insert themselves into the torso. Through incoming cosmic power lines, will energy streams into the blood and muscles of the moving child. In lecture 10 of the Foundations course, Steiner geometrically *umstülps*:

- the head with its center in its physical middle

- through the rhythmic system with its midpoint out of the torso and "faraway" in the surroundings

- to the limbs with their center at infinity, raying in and inserting themselves into the torso.

This mobile geometric meditation was presented to help teachers plastically imagine how the tubular will-bones of the lower body turn inside-out into the bowl-shaped skull. The inside-out reversal also helps one understand the same *umstülping* process for the vertebrae into head bones.

Since 1919, observations of embryogenesis have shown how limb bones crystallize from the outside inwards until they insert themselves into the torso (legs last on days 42-44). The fleshy, physical growth expansion of limb buds has the appearance of an outward direction. *But the real telling limb development story lies in the* interior anatomy. The endoskeletal process shows the opposite direction of arm and leg bones forming from the periphery: radiating fingers and toes are the first to "crystallize," then the middle part of the hand and foot; next the lower parts of the arms and legs are followed by the upper, which insert into the shoulder and pelvis only late in the process (approx. 42nd to 44th day). This radiating inwards of the limb bone and muscle formation is precipitated by the I and soul body of the new individuality who needs these organs of will to actualize a new life agenda. Following on head and trunk formation, these new limbs are our "landing gear" for stepping out into life and shaping the world.

The Riddle of Sexuality: Understanding the true nature and origin of the human limbs was also to help teachers fathom the *"riddle of sexuality,"* the female/male polarity (or spectrum?) and embryogenesis as cosmogenesis. (See Chapter on Embryogenesis.)

The male member has the character of an extending, i.e. convex, limb and is in fact referred to in German as a *Glied*, translated as both *limb* or *member*. The same organ in the female has held back so that formative energies can specially develop an inner space, a concavity (womb) in which cosmic will forces ray in to form a new human body. After birth, these forces continue to ray into the mother's limbs and down through milk lines into the breast to produce milk. Milk is veritably "limb-will juice" to naturally help the child's spirit awaken and incarnate further.

Education of the Will: According to Steiner, every human "I" is a gift of the Elohim of Moses's Genesis, also called "Spirits of Form" (*Exusiai*). They are the *Gestalters*, the shapers of the universe. Each ego is an ur-spark of their divine will energy which then metamorphoses into its other expressions as feeling and thinking. "The incarnating spirit ego itself being" entirely of a will nature" (*willensartiger Natur, Cosmosophy* I,

73) directly connects into and thrives in the warm blood and warmth-generating muscles of the active human being. Ultimately, the Waldorf appoach is an education of the will of this "I-Being"or more exactly of her 'feeling will" ("gefühlmässige Wille") because feeling (eg.desire) is a form of will "held back" and will "in becoming" (Foundations, 79).

Waldorf as Education of the Will: Since the primary organs of will are our limbs and heart, Steiner saw that the modern world's over-emphasis on the extreme opposite pole, the reflecting head and brain, overlooked and neglected the *"most spiritual"* and *"most human"* part of us, our hands and feet and arms and legs and our heart with is own special intelligence. Real, deep learning comes from heartfelt doing, interaction with and participation *in* the world. Child development is healthiest when cognition awakens organically as a result of the child's spirit-limb immersion in life experience. Head thinking and judgment follow as a concomitant reflective process.

Children incarnating from the world of spirit as will-beings are primarily "verbs." They know that spirit is action and want to learn with their moving limbs and with the outreaching of "the limb nature" of their very active senses taking hold of nature's objects.

An educational approach therefore needs to start where consciousness is greatest, in the active limbs (ages 1-7), then to add emphasis on the nurture of the emotional life (7-12) and finally to nourish the blossoming imaginative-intellectual head life (12-18). The path of awakening consciousness from hand to heart to head is opposite to the direction of body growth (physical-etheric) which starts in the large head (embryo), proceeds to the torso (breath maturity) and finally to the lanky limbs (sexual/earth maturity).

Contemplative Cosmology

In addition to the projective geometry imagination described above, Steiner also gave an Umstülpung Meditation to teachers facing the riddles of children "in need of special care:"

"Every evening let live in your consciousness: 'In me is God'... (RS draws blue circle with yellow center point)

"In the morning let shine: 'God is in me'... (draws a yellow circle with a blue center point)

"Understand that a circle is a point and point is a circle. You remember the drawing I made for you of the metabolism-and-limbs man and the head man...That was what you have ...in this simple figure for meditation... The I-point of the head becomes in the limb man the circle...

"When the point claims a place for itself in the body, it becomes the spinal cord. There you have the inner dynamic of the morphology of the human being. Taking it as a starting point, you will be able to build up a true anatomy, a true physiology...You will acquire the intuition that can perceive in how so far the upper and lower jaws are limbs...[and] how the teeth and toes are in a polarity to one another. For you only have to look at the attachments of the jawbones...[to]...see the stunted toes...hands and feet." (*Curative Education*, 178-179)

Later in another lecture Steiner re-emphasizes the meditation's importance and relates it to embryonic development and:

"Over and over again let...the circle steal into the point, let the point expand to the circle...

"You will find that something reveals itself to you, namely, how the metabolism-and-limbs organization comes into being out of the head organization." (*Curative Education,* 201)

He also pointed to the esoteric significance of the Cassini curves, particularly the lemniscate or Figure 8 in which outer becomes inner and vice versa:

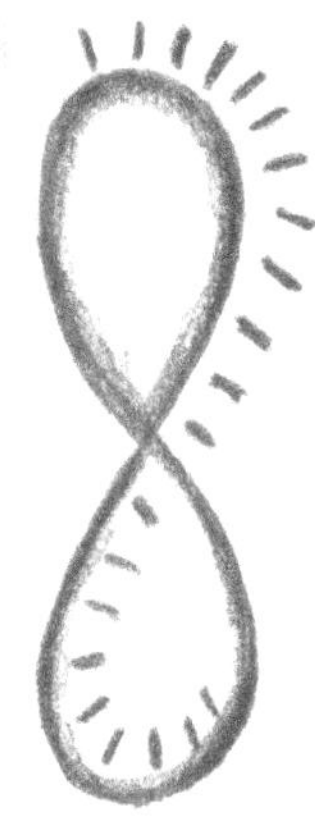

Outside crosses into inside

A prolific poet, Steiner crafted hundreds of verses, mediations and mantra, many of which contain *umstülpungs*:

When seeking your self,
Seek out there in the world;
When seeking the world,
Seek inside your self.

The inner we find in the outer.
The outer we find in the inner.

Steiner's entire *Calendar of the Soul* (52 seasonal verses) is based on the principles of symmetry and umstülpung. Compare the beginnings of these two paired verses:

Verse 1 (Easter)

When out of world-wide expanses
The Sun speaks to the human mind,
And gladness from the depths of soul...

Verse 52

When from the depths of soul
The spirit turns to the life of worlds
And beauty wells from wide expanses...

**More *Umstülpung*:
Anthropogenesis and Cosmogenesis**

Umstülpung pervades all of Steiner's later thinking about the universe. In a lecture on the "The Cosmic Origin of the Human Form," Steiner describes how our existence in the spiritual world is an Umstülpung of our life in the physical:

"The kind of experience we have in the spiritual world is very different from that in the physical, but the two are related. The relationship is such that we are turned completely inside-out (*umgestülpt*). Imagine if we could turn a human being here inside out so that his inside—the heart, for example—becomes the outer surface…If this could be done taking hold of the human being in the inmost heart and turning him inside out like a glove, then he would …enlarge into a universe. If we had the faculty to concentrate in a single point within our heart, and then turn ourselves inside out in the spirit, we could become this world that we otherwise experience between death and a new birth. That is the secret of the inner side of the human being…The heart of the human being is the world turned-outside-in (*umgestülpt*). That is how the physical, earthly world is really connected to the spiritual world. We must get used to this 'turning inside-out or outside in.'" (*The Mystery of the Trinity*, 108)

"When we are in the life between death and a new birth we are in the very same world that is outside here on earth. All that you see…as an external world becomes your inner world…You regard the sun and moon as your organs, as being in you…Outside us is a lung, is a heart…Everything we carry within our skin becomes more and more our outer world, our universe, our cosmos…our view… is exactly opposite…" (Ibid., 94)

"The closer we approach to a new life on earth, the more this universe that is the human being contracts for us. We become increasingly aware of how this majestic universe…is shrinking and contracting, how out of the weaving of planets… [and] the fixed stars of the zodiac…all this shrinks together, it shapes itself to become first a spirit body and then an etheric body. And not until it has grown very, very small is it taken up in the mother's womb and clothed there with matter." (Ibid., 96)

–Thomas Traherne (1637-1674), Metaphysical Poet (He remembered prebirth, birth and his very first months of life.)

"We see, far in the distance like a single point, the human embryo that is to be. We see, like a single entity, what has become of sun and moon drawing near our mother… We know that when our cosmic consciousness has completely vanished, when we go through a darkness (which happens after conception when we become submerged in the embryo) that we will have to turn this inside-out. What is on the inside then comes to the outside. What the sun and moon have been you must turn inside-out and then a tiny opening appears; through this you must go with your I, your ego and this becomes a copy or image of your human body on earth. …You must turn the whole thing around and push what is inside outward and go though a tiny opening.

"In this way we work out the formation of the several parts of the human body. We gather together what we experience as the entire universe and give to every part its destined form. Only then does what has been formed in the spirit get clothed, and permeated by a plastic material—matter. The matter is only taken on; but the forces that form and shape us we ourselves had to develop from the entire universe." (Ibid.,103-104)

"The human being builds his entire body from the constellations of the stars and their movements…The human being is indeed a kind of copy or image of the world of the stars. A large part of the work we do between death and a new birth consists of building our body from the universe. Standing on the earth the human being is indeed a universe, but a shrunken universe… This [human] form is created first in the astral and etheric realms and only shrinks and contracts in order to be clothed in physical matter." (Ibid., 105)

Umstülpung as a Principle of Creation and Consciousness

Hans Bonneval has collected all of Steiner's main references to *Umstülpung* with much valuable commentary. For example, he summarizes the progression of creation as a series of *Umstülpungs*:

"The Creator umstülps himself into the spiritual Creation from which the human being also and above all goes forth. The spiritual, archetypal human being umstülps himself into the fourfold human being in the physical. Man's companion creatures, the animals, plants and minerals also umstülp into the physical…That which in higher spheres was the surroundings of a gigantic cosmic man, the macrocosmos, umstülps into the physical man as microcosm. As such, the human being perceives and thinks about the surrounding world and umstülps it still again into himself as an image (*Abbild*) which ignites feelings and above all actions. With will impulses and deeds the human being out of his inner point-being (*Punkt-Wesen*) acts back upon the world and changes it… The consequences of my deeds, that is, my umstülped life of deeds come to meet me as karma from the new world around me." (*Umstülpung als Schöpfung- und Bewusst-seinsprinzip,* 2005, Verlag Ch.Moellman, 47, A.A. translation)

The idea of the human being as a miniature version of the universe lives in many esoteric traditions and myths such as that of the Norse cosmic giant Ymir and the Hebrew Adam Kadmon.

Bonneval also relates the concept of Umstülpung to modern developments in cosmology which are predicting highly unusual states of the universe. For instance, he cites a 2004 article in the science journal *Bild der Wissenschaft* with the very interesting title "The Umstülped Big Bang" (*Der umgestülpte Urknall)*. In it is described the challenges of imagining an umstülped cosmos:

"[Einstein's] general relativity theory predicts a boundary in which the laws of physics break down and the theory itself loses it validity: space and time shrink to nothing, whereas space curvature, energy, density pressure and temperature grow immeasureably." (Bonneval, 14)

Bonneval connects his research to the efforts of geometricians to create umstülpable forms out of paper, poster board and other materials. One of the most notable is

Paul Schatz's umstülpable "Invertible Cube." For more information, go to: https://www.kuboid.ch/

Umstülping into a True Universal Humanity
Modern humankind has penetrated the structure and workings of physical matter in great depth, but has, in the process, lost a sense of what life is. According to Steiner, a main evolutionary need of our times is to experience and understand the "etheric" and the cosmic formative forces animating all biological processes. Such an achievement will aid us greatly in meeting the apocalyptic social and environmental crises we now face on our tiny planet with 7 billion people. (The population in 1776 was 800 million.)

Steiner created many exercises to help people develop a sense of the nature of the living. Many of these practices use the plant as a "teacher" and the simplest embodiment of life. Themes include metamorphosis, growing and withering, the power of the seed, etc. Perhaps the most profound of these exercises is the Foundation Stone Meditation.

The Dutch medical doctor Zeylmans van Emmichoven describes how its rhythmic verses are intended to help the "I" via the astral body (soul body) to experience the etheric body of life forces. This mantric pathway initially leads inward but then turns one's consciousness "inside-out" into the universe:

> "When, through the exercises, the Ego ["I"] penetrates ever deeper into the hidden parts of the human being, it experiences the etheric body through the astral body. It should be emphasized that the etheric is not experienced inwardly in the same way as the astral body with its different soul-members.

Rudolf Steiner, especially in the last years of his life, often pointed to the law of turning-inside-out (Umstülpung). The forces of the physical body are centripetal, oriented toward the center of the earth. But if the etheric is to be recognized, attention must be directed to the centrifugal forces which work out from out of the cosmos. The astral body, on the other hand, has the tendency to close in on itself, because it provides the human soul with an inward self-contained life. But when the Ego breaks through to the etheric forces, it suddenly experiences a kind of turning-inside-out from the earthly into cosmic existence…" (*The Foundation Stone*, 69-70,)

Emmichoven then describes how this process of Umstülpung gives birth to a new sense of our true humanity and interconnectedness:

> "[Through the Foundation Stone Meditation] the human being is led from his individual Ego to the Ego-power of mankind as a whole as it lives in the cosmos. As a physical human, one can feel separate from one's fellow humans, but not as etheric human. Although the forces of the human being's own etheric body represent a link with the individual Ego, the etheric nevertheless spans and penetrates mankind as a whole. In the etheric, we are already on the way to becoming humanity. When the etheric body is transformed by the Ego into Life-spirit… then a stage has been reached in which the human being is no longer merely an individual but simultaneously bears within him those forces which enable him to unite with mankind as a whole." (Ibid., 70)

The experience of the etheric takes place in a new dimension—in a sun space where

> Day-bright light pours into human souls,
> Light that illumines wise heads,
> Light that warms simple hearts…

The Foundation Stone Verse is made up of seven stanzas and itself undergoes an Umstül-pung in its language from the first six into the seventh and last stanza.

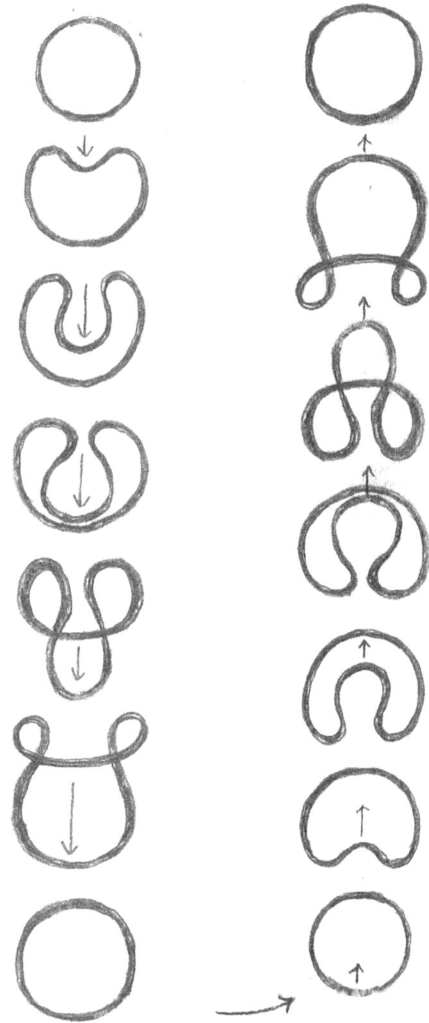

Watch the outside turn inside
And an inside turn outside

Imagining Archetypes

Knowledge is perceiving the eternal in things. –Goethe

Goethe's Child-like Perception of the Archetype

In beholding imaginatively and intuitively (*anschauend*) the archetype of the plant, (*Urpflanze*) as a "sensory-spiritual" phenomenon ("*sinnlich-übersinnlich*"), Goethe was able to lift his consciousness into the purer, embryonic-like, etheric state of the living thinking. (See also "Goethe's Imagination" in the previous chapter *Sources of Imagination*) Fellow poet and philosopher Schiller at first did not recognize the special nature of Goethe's way of knowing when he reacted to the latter's account of the *Urplant*: "*But that's only an idea!*" This pronouncement upset Goethe considerably and he retorted: "*Then I see ideas with my very eyes!*" Schiller had a strong analytical, Kantian mind-set and was too quick to judge the experience as only an abstract concept.

However, having offended Goethe, Schiller, who was hoping to gain the famed older man's respect, realized his mistake afterwards and in a letter apologized for his hasty comment. In it, Schiller described what he had come to realize: that Goethe had an extraordinary living cognition and imagination similar to that of the ancient Greeks; and that he was, in fact, feeling stifled in the harsh, restrained intellectual climate of northern lands. Schiller's intuitive communication touched Goethe deeply. His younger colleague had revealed something of which neither was consciously aware—namely, that Goethe in a past life (according to Steiner), had been a sculptor in Plato's Athens (Steiner, *Karmic Relations* IV, 148). Schiller's letter not only healed the rift, but initiated one of history's great creative friendships and a uniting of two opposite, yet complementary personalities.

Goethe was a patient observer of nature, especially of plants and the workings of light, darkness and color. He first allowed phenomena to make impressions on him and allowed the afterimages of these experiences to sink deeply into his soul. He then *waited* and after a time found that the phenomena and images began to "speak" to him. He learned to hear and to "*read in*" the book of nature, which whispered her "*open secrets*" (*offenbare Geheimnisse*) to him and revealed the essence of her moving forms. Allowing what was observed to inwardly *gestate* as vivid afterimages nurtured what Goethe called his '*exact sensory imagination*' (*exact sensorische Phantasie*"). He was able to inwardly, vividly and objectively recreate, for example, the metamorphosis of the plant from seed to flower in his "mind's eye." (*Geistesauge*).

Goethe's "*Phantasie*" (imagination) should not be confused with self-willed, highly subjective and very personalized imagining. What is generally thought of as *"phantasy"* or *"fantasy,"*(two spellings) can indeed be erratic and contrary to waking consciousness. Goethe's method involved a rigorous scientific self-training in what he termed *"anschauende Urteilskraft,"* rigorous contemplative or intuitive discernment, a *beholding with complete openness.* Such actively receptive mental activity employs what he also called a *"gentle empiricism,"* a gentle will that resists jumping to intellectual conclusions and imposing abstractions on nature. Instead, this capacity leads an *"alliance of the eyes of the spirit with the eyes of the body."* Scientist Ernst Lehrs points out that it is

> "this eye-of-the-spirit [that] becomes capable of perceiving the levity-woven archetypes (ur-images) which underlie all the physical eye discerns in the world of ordinary space… Rudolf Steiner called this mode of perception…Imagination. …Imaginative perception rests on reawakening in the eye (and thus in the total organism behind the eye) certain infant forces which have grown dormant in the course of the growing up of the human being." (Lehrs, 380)

Hence it is the creative forces of childhood that must be revived and renewed. Goethe as artist retained these child forces throughout adulthood. It was their cultivation and retention that allowed him to lift his conscious into the higher etheric realm of a living thinking and imagination and at the same time still have "his feet on the ground" of acute sensory awareness. In this sensory-spiritual state of mind he experienced how *" all formative action in nature is prompted by certain archetypal (ur-) forms or images."* (Lehrs, 360)

> *…Imagination [is] the sense of perceiving the ur-images of the world with an eye-of-the-spirit which has been made strong enough to require no support from the physical eye, the metamorphosis of a faculty possessed by all human beings before birth and still in early childhood… We see that to require this faculty of Imagination means carrying through consistently the training inaugurated by Goethe.*
>
> –Ernst Lehrs

Singing Form-Giving Archetypes

On several occasions, Rudolf Steiner pointed to the Chladni pattern phenomenon (shown in the chapter on Form-Giving Forces) as a way of imagining how sound and tone mediate between spirit and matter in the universe albeit in a more complicated manner. In his research, he experienced that tone is more than just the vibration of matter. While tone uses air and water as a *"body"* and *"support,"* it has a higher, non-material dimension that directly reveals the very inner essence of things: *"All objects have a spiritual tone at the foundation of their being, and in his deepest nature, the human being is such a spiritual tone."* (The Inner Nature of Music, p.5)

He agreed, in part, with Schopenhauer's instinctive sense that through music nature is directly communicating with human beings. In producing tones in music, *"the true artist reproduces the archetypes—not the mental representations (Vorstellungen) that the human being normally has, which are copies…[The musician/composer] puts his ear to the very heart of nature…stands in an intimate relationship to the Thing-in-itself and penetrates to the innermost nature of things."* (Ibid., p. 2-3).

According to Steiner, the musical artist, in fact, is able to be a faithful receiver of archetypal musical compositions directly from the dimension of the spiritual world in which,

"The archetypes …resound…in an ocean of … sounds and tones…chords, harmonies, rhythms, and melodies… the 'music of the spheres'. . ."
(R. Steiner, *Theosophy*, 125-26)

As the highest region of the spiritual world, the Spirit Land is:

"where the archetypes of things arise… This is the laboratory of the cosmos wherein all forms are contained, whence creation has proceeded; it is the home of the Ideas of Plato, the 'Realm of the Mothers' of which Goethe speaks in Faust…"
(R. Steiner, *Esoteric Cosmology*, 65-66)

"Physical things and beings are copies (*Abbilder*) or imitations of their archetypes (*Urbilder*)…In the spiritual world everything is in constant activity, constant motion, constant creation… The archetypes are creative beings (*schaffende Wesenheiten*), the master builders of everything that comes into existence in the physical and soul worlds… Their forms change quickly, and each archetype has the potential to assume countless specific forms. It is as if the specialized forms well up out of them—one form has hardly been created before its archetype is ready to let the next one pour out….Archetypes do not work alone, but stand in closer or more distant relationship to each other. One archetype may need the help of the other to do its creating, and often innumerable archetypes work together so that some particular being can come to life in the soul world or the physical world…" (Ibid.,124-125)

And significantly, the archetypes are not silent in their work. To those who, like Pythagoras, can "hear " the cosmos, they sound and 'sing' as they form and build the world.

In a mind-bending challenge, Steiner calls on us to imagine the world of physical objects from the 'other side' and from the perspective of the spirit land of archetypes that closely interpenetrates the earthly realm. From there, our earthly landscape and its objects appear as negative spaces surrounded by sounding form-forces:

"Imagine a finite space filled with a wide variety of physical bodies, then imagine that the physical bodies are gone and visualize hollow spaces of the same shapes in their places. Imagine that what used to be empty spaces between the bodies is filled with a wide variety of forms that relate to the former bodies in many different ways. This is somewhat similar to how things appear in the lowest region of the world of the archetypes: Things and beings that are embodied in the physical world exist as hollow spaces here, and the mobile activity of the archetypes and the spiritual music goes on in between them. When the time comes for physical embodiment, the hollow spaces are then filled in with matter…"
(R. Steiner, *Theosophy*, 127)

In *An Outline of Esoteric Science*, Steiner gives a concrete example.

"The space occupied by a mass of rock in the physical world appears [in the spiritual world] as a cavity of some sort, but the force that shapes the form of the stone is seen all around the cavity."
(*An Outline of Esoteric Science*, 92)

Again, these forces hovering around physical thing-spaces are experienced as resounding music.

Steiner found that "*The physical world is a kind of condensation that has been crystallized out of the astral soul world*" i.e. out of a sounding star world composed of music. (*The Inner Nature of Music*, 4).

The archetypes themselves exist at an even higher level (Higher Devachan) as zero dimensional " *seed germ points of life*"(*lebendige Keimpunkte*) which creatively project into three lower' worlds. When these intend to manifest in the physical world, they first condense into *"spirit formations"(Gebilde)* that appear in the one dimensional soul-astral world (Lower Devachan) as astral archetypes. These further condense and project into the lower elemental or etheric world (two-dimensional, planar) as etheric archetypes. *"The etheric body is the etheric archetype of the physical body."* (*The Inner Nature of Music and the Experience of Tone*, 6) The etheric *"body of formative forces"* (*Bildekräfteleib*) draws up and sculpturally shapes physical matter into the three-dimensional frameworks of living organisms. In the creation of the human bodies, it is the astral body that carries from the soul world the "astral archetypes" or "prototypes" (*Vorbilder*) into the sculpturing etheric bodies. (*Esoteric Science*, 65) The etheric body uses these 'architectural plans' to shape the physical body. In summary, the astral and etheric bodies are the archetype intermediaries between the highest spirit archetypes and material embodiment.

To illustrate this complex process of densification and interpenetration more concretely, Steiner often uses the analogy of water (spirit) crystallizing into ice (physical things). To really understand material objects, we need the "water thinking" described in the previous chapter. Water thinking enables us to flexibly grasp how solid appearances arise out of always changing "fluid" spirit dynamics.

The water/ice analogy can be expanded and differentiated more to encompass other elements so that imagined in reverse the order would be: ice (physical solid) melts into water (etheric forces) which rarefies into steam/air (soul/astral forces) and finally into fire/warmth energy (spirit forces). In many traditions, fire is experienced as the threshold into spirit. Steiner's Old Saturn was spirit becoming a warmth body. The counterpart in today's physics is that the origin of matter lies in energy, heat, and light– E=MC squared.

While one may be tempted to picture the process too materialistically and as a great linear "chain of becoming" along a descending "path" from the highest to the lowest region, Steiner urges us to transform the 'water to ice" analogy into a non-spatial imagination because

> "The soul and spirit worlds are not 'next' to or 'outside' the physical world, not separated from it in space." (*Theosophy*, 97)

> "The different levels or regions [of the different kinds of archetypes are] interpenetrating rather than layered or piled up on top of one another." (Ibid.,127)

> "During bodily existence we live in all three worlds at once …the sense-perceptible world…the soul world…[and] as thinking human beings we are citizens of the country of spirit beings… Sense-perceptible things are of the same substance (*Stoff*) as the soul and spirit worlds surrounding them but they stand out because of certain characteristics that make them perceptible to our senses… Figuratively they are condensed spirit and soul formations. The spirit world can change into the soul world and the soul world into the sensory world just as water can turn into ice." (Ibid.,147-8)

The archetypal spirit, soul, and etheric worlds are right in front of our noses–and part of our noses!—not in some world beyond.

> *Nature is the incarnation of a thought, and turns to a thought again, as ice becomes water and gas. The world is mind precipitated.*
>
> —Ralph Waldo Emerson

We can begin to experience different ever-present dimensions and layers of reality if we change our consciousness. We can do this by gradually extending and expanding our thinking power as a spiritual activity which is able to perceive and "intuit" the presence of other worlds. We can accomplish this because *"The spiritual world [itself] is woven out of the 'substance' constituting human thought …[which] appears in human beings [as] only a shadowy image or phantom of its real being"* (Ibid.,123). Our normal thinking is the first level of a spiritual activity that can be enhanced step by step to penetrate other realities and beings working around and in us.

"Only because sense-perceptible things are nothing other than condensed spirit beings can we human beings—who can lift our selves up in thought to the level of spirit beings—think about and understand them. Sense perceptible things originate in the spirit world and are simply another manifestation of spirit beings; *when we formulate thoughts about things, we are simply inwardly directed away from their sense-perceptible forms and toward their spiritual archetypes. Understanding an object by thinking about it is a process that can be compared to melting a solid body so that chemists can study it in its fluid form.* The spiritual archetypes of the sense-perceptible world are to be found in the different regions of spirit country. In the [highest] regions, they still exist as living germinal points (*lebendige Keimpunkte*), while in the four lower regions they take shape as spiritual formations (*Gebilde*). When the human spirit tries to come to an understanding of sense-perceptible objects by means of thinking, it perceives shadowy copies or imitations of spiritual formations." (Ibid.,149)

Steiner was not only a "faithful thinker" but also an artist and *"practical* Idealist" who made the activity of the archetypes artistically visible in the first Goetheanum. Its entire architecture and sculptured interior details (columns, architraves, statue, paintings, etc.) were *" frozen music"* from higher archetypal realms, meant to be melted into movement by the musical and sculptural imaginations of viewers. The metamorphic forms of its pillars proceeded musically from one to another and sang the seven tones of the planetary scale and twelve musical keys of the star world. Performances of eurythmy, speech, drama, and concerts brought cosmic life into a sacred earthly space, a resounding sun-space. The building was also called the *House of the Word*, of the resounding, form-giving Logos. (See the last chapter on Learning from Goetheanum Forms.)

Is Steiner's Vision of the Archi-tecture of the Universe Like an Inverted Cosmic Plant?

Steiner held that all around us even the mineral element originates in life processes. As we have seen, his is a living universe which is formed out of archetype beings as "living *seed germ* points" (*lebendige Keimpunkte*). When these *seed* points are moved to materialize, they appear in the soul world to the observer as dynamic lines which are analogous to the linear *stems* of plants.

"[In the soul world] . . . a blossoming flower conjures up a particular line before our souls, while a growing animal or dying tree gives rise to other lines."

(R. Steiner, *Knowledge of Higher Worlds*, 40-41)

The archetypes then manifest further in the etheric plane of the elemental world analogous to expanding *leaves*. Finally, in the last stage, archetypes hover around three-dimensional spaces which fill in with matter and 'build' the world's objects—the final *fruit* of their spiritual activity. From point-like to linear and planar and finally into the three-dimensional is the same path of manifestation followed by plant formation.

> *Do you seek the highest, the greatest?*
> *The plant can be your teacher. Be with will what the plant is will-lessly. That is it!*
> —Friedrich Schiller

Archetypes Expressed as Living Ideas in the Brain Fluid

Researcher E.M. Kranich characterizes how spiritual archetypes (*Urbilder*) work in the human mind as living ideas (*lebendige Ideen*) and congeal into mental image representations (*Vorstellungen*). He identifies the cerebro-spinal fluid as the physiological "medium" for these living ideas which exist between the archetypes in higher realms and their reflections in brain-filtered, representational *Vorstellung*-images. Here are excerpts from Kranich's *Der innere Mensch und sein Leib: Die Spiegelung der lebendigen Ideen und deren Wirkung im Gehirn* ("The Inner Human Being and His Body: The Mirroring of Living Ideas and Their Effects in the Brain," 162-166, A.A. translation)

"Through a connection to a particular percept content, Vorstellungen-image become fixed i.e. congealed into particular forms; in themselves they are flexibly movable and mobile [*beweglich*, in the mind] . . .Rudolf Steiner stressed that *Vorstellen*, the activity of mental imaging, is 'a movement of *Bild*-images.'" (161)

"One must differentiate between a fixed *Vorstellung* (mental representation) and a *Vorstellungsbild*, capable of movement (*beweglich*). When turning to the sense impressions—let us say, of an equal-sided triangle, a water lily or a horse—particular mental images (*Vorstellungen*) are formed (*gebildet*). Then our moving *Bild*-images freeze into one of many possible forms, just as fluid water turns into ice " (162)

"Our fixed *Vorstellungen*-images, which configure themselves in the perception process, originate in the initially moving *Bild*-images in *Vorstellen*, the activity of mental imaging. All *Bild*-images of a triangle, for example, are single form states of a general mobile triangle; similarly, all *Bild*-images of plants are congealed states of a general mobile plant-image (*Pflanzenbild*). The same is true for the *Bild*-images of animals, minerals, etc. A *Bild*-image that can take on different forms is an *Urbild*, an archetypal ur-image or archetype . Goethe described the archetype of the plant world in his *Metamorphosis of the Plant*; he wanted to show how individual plants are special form variations of one archetype, the *Urpflanze*, the Ur-plant (type). He also sought to discover the archetype of the animal world.

"Now these archetypes are actually mobile *Vorstellung*-images (*bewegliche Vorstellungen*). And just as every *Vorstellung*-image (when not a creation of fantasy) points to reality and is a *Bild*-image of it, so do archetypes (*Urbilder*) point to a creative spiritual reality out of which, for example, the laws of the formation of different plant forms issue forth; this spiritual creative principle is active in the plant world. The mobile *Vorstellung*-images in the mind of the human being are reflected image-copies (*Abbilder*) of these creative archetypes." (163)

"How does it happen that the human mind has these image-copies of the living, creative archetypes….and through them attains the perception of objects? The individual must have experienced these archetypes before they became mere *Bild*-images of *Vorstellung*-images (*blosse Bildern der Vorstellungen*) in the brain. . . " (164)

"A living idea (*lebendige Idee*) is like an echo of the creative archetype… Its medium is not the structure of the brain, but rather the moving, flowing cerebral-spinal fluid that permeates and surrounds the brain and the spine (liquor cerebrospinalis)…In this fluid the human ego takes hold of a living idea (*Idee*) and brings it to those areas of the brain…related to the senses. This is possible because this fluid not only surrounds the brain but also flows through fine pores into its outer layers and into the white matter . . ." (164-165)

"How then do these vibrant living ideas then become schematic, unliving *Vorstellungen*-images? When the human being in thinking takes hold of a living idea living unconsciously in the cerebral-spinal fluid, the idea… enters the living substances of the nerve paths of the associative regions of the brain…The living idea seizes the life forces and separates them from the living substances which die …[and] pass over into a condition of hardening and passivity." (165)

It is possible through spiritual exercising to lift one's consciousness away from the ponderous physical brain/nerve structure and think only with the finer, higher etheric forces which interpenetrate the fluid. Such activity does not get caught up in the obscuring process of dying nerve structures and secretions which can only reflect it. One

moves one's mental activity intentionally in a higher, non-physical etheric medium which connects one into the World Ether in which the archetypes express themselves as living ideas. The World Ether is a where all thoughts live and where there is world memory (Akasha is cosmic etheric), a living record of all that has happened in the universe.

Interestingly, although regular reflective thinking is filtered and limited, it does take place in the "lower" etheric medium of the electro-chemical. Electricity, according to Steiner, is a "fallen" state of the etheric; hence, all the research with EEGs. One could therefore say that regular intellectual thinking uses the physical-chemical, "fallen etheric"/electric processes of the nervous system.

> *Education consists in teaching children how to breathe properly.*
>
> —Rudolf Steiner, *Foundations of Human Experience*

Breathing Rhythms and Living Thinking at Home in the Archetype

Steiner repeatedly brought attention to the significant effect the pressure of breathing has on the cerebro-spinal fluid and brain. It is through this interaction that etheric forces meet astral forces to activate and support cognition. In Waldorf education, Steiner therefore stressed how important it was to help children *"to breathe properly."*

Dr. Armin Husemann has further developed Steiner's insights by investigating the physiological process of respiration. According to him, the rhythmical breathing motion presses the "astral-laden air" up against the ventricle wall holding the cerebro-spinal fluid around the brain. The astral forces are then able to penetrate into the watery fluid. Through the medium of air in respiration, the musical, wave-like forces of the astral body (soul) flow and bear consciousness and patterning into the life forces of the nervous system. This brings about a remarkable process whereby the body-building forces of the etheric body in the blood metamorphose into mental-image-building in the brain fluid:

> "The activity of the thinking preparing to manifest itself, is the same as the activity of the etheric body—first forming the physical body in which its thought processes are then reflected. The etheric body which flows in the blood is suddenly deprived, with the transformation of blood into watery [cerebro-spinal] fluid, of the instruments with which it forms the physical body. It loses its hold in the pure, slightly salty fluid: but it is taken hold of by the astral body which agitates the fluid through respiration. The generative activity of the etheric body, liberated from the physical body, becomes conscious in the astral body through respiration. Life forces turn into 'experience.' Every artistic, every thought and experience arises because respiration intercepts in the cerebro-spinal fluid the motions of the etheric body which are set off in the latter through sensory perception or through the development of ideas…

> "…Through this Umstülpung, the etheric body is separated from the physical body in the fluid human being. Instead it unites with the astral body which penetrates the cerebro-spinal fluid through respiration. This reveals qualities of the head…namely the etheric body resonates in harmony with the astral body in the cerebro-spinal fluid. The generative forces are thus enabled to enter the consciousness as living forces…

In the head, the etheric body is forced out of the physical body and is brought in harmony with the respiratory rhythm of the astral body. By this means the activity of the etheric body is brought to consciousness in the head…The type of thinking which is tied to the senses, which understands the laws of mechanics and of physical matter is linked to the inner extension of the senses, the brain. *The living thinking, which is at home in the archetype, and its metamorphosis into different forms is brought to consciousness in the cerebro-spinal fluid. Thus Rudolf Steiner speaks several times specifically about the 'fluidic nature' of the archetype.* It is the awakening of our own embryonic generative forces in consciousness. " (A. Husemann, *The Harmony of the Human Body*, 75-77).

Rather than the mechanical operations of dense brain matter, it is the interpenetrating and surrounding fluid that becomes the vehicle for the vitalization of thinking powers. The etheric forces interpenetrating the cerebro-spinal waters, mediate and connect the activity of intentionally enhanced thinking with the etheric world of living ideas:

> "It is simply a matter of the intensity with which we conduct our thinking as to whether we observe the ideas which serve to put our perceptions into context as living ideas. This become evident in truly active and not machine-like passive thinking. The world of ideas (*Ideenwelt*) from which we take the concept we combine with sensory perception is …the etheric world…Steiner describes the etheric world as flooded with cosmic thoughts." (Ibid., 80)

Our minds tap into a sea of cosmic thoughts that allow us to become aware of the archetypal ideas in nature.

Thinking with the Etheric Body: An Intermediate Level of Higher Cognition

Goethean biologist and researcher Wolfgang Schad also describes "*thinking with the life [etheric] body of the brain*" and relates it to Steiner's '*Ideal cognition or knowledge*' ('*ideelle Erkenntnis*'). This he characterizes as an intermediary level of enhanced consciousness which taps into the world of living ideas (*Ideenwelt*) and becomes aware of the *idea* in reality.

"Steiner characterizes a transitional dimension of consciousness (*Übergangsbereich*), between the sense world and the higher suprasensory worlds [of Imagination, Inspiration and Intuition] which he calls that of 'ideal knowledge' ('*der ideellen Erkenntnis*'). Such knowledge happens without sense perception by focusing its interest and questioning only on the content of concepts and ideas discovered through sense experience...[It] is more concerned with an understanding (*Verstehen*) of the 'how' of things rather than the 'what. It is not yet the body-free understanding of suprasensory research nor is it a processing of impressions with the physical brain; instead it is an understanding that calls upon the force fields pregnant with life in the brain organ (*lebensträchtigen Kraftbereich des Gehirnorgans*). Ideal knowledge thinks with the life body of the brain . . ." (Wolfgang Schad, ed. *Evolution als Verständnisprinzip*, 36-37, A.A. translation)

Schad shows how "*ideal cognition*" characterizes Steiner's early first phase of research which build on Goethe's way of perceiving and thinking combined with his own ideas for a philosophy of knowledge and freedom. Steiner's early works foreshadow and metamorphose into his later development of the advanced stages of consciousness, Imagination, Inspiration, and Intuition. According to Schad,

- *The Theory of Knowledge Implicit in Goethe's World Conception* (1886) is the imaginative stage of ideal cognition.
- In *The Philosophy of Freedom* (1894) *we have* the inspiration stage of ideal cognition.
- *The Riddles of Philosophy* (1900, revised and expanded 1914) is the living example of the intuitive stage of ideal cognition.

At the beginning of the twentieth century these three stages intensify into Steiner's advanced spirit research:

- *Theosophy* (1904) embodies the method of Imagination
- *An Outline of Esoteric Science* (1910) embodies the method of Inspiration
- The "Karma Lectures" (*Karmic Relationships* vols. I-VIII, 1924) embody the method of Intuition.

The Embryo in Fluidic Motion as Teacher of Archetypal-Sculptural Thinking

Our brain floating buoyantly in its cerebrospinal fluid looks very much like an embryo floating in amniotic waters!

There is a remarkable relationship of cognitional conception and mental *re*-presentation and biological conception and *re*-production. Both mental conceptualization and physical conception are amazing "instruments" of the archetypes working musically-sculpturally through a fluid etheric medium.

Contemplating and imagining the embryo-in-motion in a dynamic progression of forms—especially in its first two months educates living, mobile thinking.

The next chapter on the Archetypal Forms of Embryogenesis and the related exercises in Series Ten are intended as aids in fluidly imagining and modeling the most amazing sculptural-musical process in the universe.

> *I have…told you about the ability to bring forms into the etheric body of the head. This makes it possible to see through the time body, the etheric body, all the way back to birth. It also brings the soul to a very special mood with respect to the cosmos. One loses one's own bodily nature…but feels oneself living into the cosmos. Consciousness expands…into the widths of the ether. One can no longer look at a plant without becoming immersed in the growth. One follows it from root to blossom. One lives in its juices, in its blossoms, in its fruits….But it is necessary that we be able to return again and again…We must be able to live in suprasensory worlds while simultaneously being able to return at anytime to stand firmly on two feet.*
>
> —Rudolf Steiner, *The Mission of the Spirit*

> *The living thinking, which is at home in the archetype, and its metamorphosis into different forms is brought to consciousness in the cerebrospinal fluid. Thus Rudolf Steiner speaks several times specifically about the 'fluidic nature' of the archetype. It is the awakening of our own embryonic generative forces in consciousness.*
>
> —Armin Huseman, *The Harmony of the Human Body*

The Archetypal Forms of Embryogenesis

This chapter is meant to supplement Series Ten (see pp. 61-66) with background for adults on the esoteric significance of embryology. It includes resources for further study. While most of these insights are not taught to students, they can stimulate in adults the wonder and enthusiasm that are critical ingredients in inspired teaching rooted in a deeper understanding.

Research on Embryo Form and Gesture

Gaining an ever widening and deepening picture of the developing human being is of tremendous value for teachers and parents and should always be the main informing and the driving force behind all education. In Waldorf schools, this picture expands beyond a physical-psychological framework to take into account a person as a reincarnating soul and spirit.

As an educator, I have found it very thought-provoking and enlightening on many different levels to study Steiner's indications on how the incarnation of an individual's "spirit germ" (*Geistkeim*) and other higher spiritual elements (life body and soul body) are reflected in the changing forms and gestures of embryonic development. In addition, I have studied the works of several researchers who have developed Steiner's insights further.

My initial interest started when I met Dr. Thomas Weihs and then much later read his book *Embryogenesis in Myth and Science* as well as Dr. Karl König's monograph on *Embryology and World Evolution*. Both Weihs and König were doctors and colleagues in the Camphill Community and correlated the microcosmic stages of the developing embryo with Moses's macrocosmic myth pictures of the six days of world creation. König also described a correlation with Steiner's four stages of the earth's evolution (Old Saturn, Sun, Moon, Earth).

> *Embryology will have to become one of the main subjects for the general study of man…In the developing embryo we see cosmic images which cannot be pinned down. These images call for truly imaginative thinking. [This] does not mean to give rein to phantasy, but to look until suddenly one begins to hear, to perceive from the form and the structure, what the gestalt has to say, to sing, to tell.*
>
> –Karl König

My perspectives in this field have also been immensely deepened by meeting the embryologist Jaap van der Wal and the educator and sculptor Christian Breme. In addition, I have found the works of Otto Hartmann, Fritz Wilmar, Wolfgang Schad, and Kaspar Appenzeller to be very informative. (See annotations in the Bibliography).

As a result of my comparative research looking at a the descriptions of a dozen different embryologists, I have been artistically developing and using over several years a series of thirteen modeled figures in adult education workshops to foster an experience of the amazing otherworldly forms of the first eight weeks of the human being. These exercises are shown and described in *Series Ten* in Part I of this sourcebook and are very applicable in the high school. In Waldorf schools, embryology is usually taught in the tenth grade (in North America) or eleventh grade (Europe).

These thirteen separate milestones are meant to artistically stimulate the imagination so that the real flowing sequence of the changing forms of a tiny water being (93% H2O to start)—the embryo in flow motion—can be seamlessly pictured in the mind's eye. They are only a part of the total maternal ecosystem and do not include the equally important surrounding cosmic sheaths (chorion, amnion, allantois, yolk sac) in which the individuality is also working before its activity focuses on sculpting the central physical body. (For modeling exercises including the outer sheaths, see Christian Breme's booklet *Embryology*).

Exercises in Series Ten

(See pp. 61-66 for illustrative photographs)

Sphere
Spiral
Two, Four, Eight-fold Divisions
Morula
Blastula
Nest
Leaf Disk
Neurula: Seedling-like
Serpent-like
Mammal-like
Emerging Human

Summary from Series Ten: An Inspiring Series of Archetypal, Universal Forms

- The first eight weeks or two months of physical human development are called the "embryo" stage followed by the last seven months of the "fetus" stage.

- The mysterious forms of the early embryo and of anthropogenesis are perhaps the most extraordinary series of sculptural transformations that we can encounter. This anthropogenesis reflects a cosmogenesis.

- In the course of this metamorphosis, the human being *recapitulates* the form gestures of mineral, plant and animal so that the familiar, identifiable human form can emerge. The modeled forms help us experience how the invisible spirit is made visible, how the universal becomes individualized.

Forms 1-2: Sphere and Spiral (Week 1)

The sphere is both a whole encompassing universe, the macrocosm, and at the same time the microcosm, the life of an emerging centering self. The spiral is another universal form, one of life (helix), motion and change.

The sphere is also the Beginning, the Oneness which begins to divide and differentiate. What biologists technically call "embryogenesis" is cloaked and hidden in the myth pictures of Moses' *Genesis*:

> In the Beginning, the Elohim created the heaven and the earth. And the earth was without form…The Spirit of the Elohim moved upon the face of the waters…and said, Let there be light…and the Elohim *divided* the light from the darkness.

Forms 3-6: Morula: Geometric Division into 2, 4, 8, 16 (Week 1)

The 16-division at three days is what biologists call the *morula,* Latin for "mulberry" (last form on the far right above). Steiner described how an initial stage of the present universe was a giant sphere composed entirely of warmth which took on a "mulberry" shape by differentiating into warmth globules (round egg forms). These units became the foundations of the future physical bodies of human beings. Steiner esoterically named this "mulberry" stage *Old Saturn*. It may be correlated with Moses's account of the First Day of Creation and the Hebrew day of the week interestingly called *Saturn-day*.

Form 7: Blastula: Sphere Surface of Leaf-like Planes (Week 2)

The flat-celled surface of the little blastula world has separated gelatinous fluid inside itself from fluid outside.

Steiner esoterically designated the second stage of the universe as *Old Sun*, when etheric bodies of life forces are added to the "Old Saturn" physical bodies of warmth. This may be correlated with *Sun*-day and Moses' Second Day of Creation: *Let there be a firmament in the midst of the waters and let the firmament divide the waters from the waters.*

Form 8: Leaf-like Disk (Week 3-beginning and middle)

The blastula nests in the mother's womb wall (nidation) and forms within itself a 2-chambered inner "egg." Between the 2 chambers of yolk sac and liquid-filled amnion, a beautiful little, flat, round almost dimensionless, *leaf-like* being is suddenly born (embryonic germ disk) At first she is just the circular place where yolk sac (earth) and amnion (heaven) touch and meet as a circular etheric surface. Developing out of and em-*bed*-ded in two, then three germ layers, this sleeping princess swells, and

"awakens." This is the physical germ of the future human body into which the spiritual individuality will show dramatic signs of arriving and making its mark in days 15-21.

As if marked and roused by the "Finger of God" (see Michelangelo's God hand extending to Adam), a magical vertical axis line is engraved down the middle of the embryonic disk. The entering human spirit inscribes its name into flesh: "I". This neural groove is the future site of an enclosed neural tube, the precursor of the spine/vertebral column, the central 'I' axis of future consciousness.

All kinds of wondrous sculptural reconfigurations are thereby set in motion. Transverse folding creates inner spaces for the primal beginnings of new organ systems (primordia).

In animals, this stage of transformations is called "gastrulation" with the form gesture of a double-walled cup called a "gastrula" which does not occur in humans. According to embryologist Erich Blechschmidt,

> "The developmental kinetics taking place here lead to a folding process which is not a 'gastrulation' such as occurs in animals as invaginaton of part of the body surface. *There is not gastrulation in man*." (Blechschmidt, 42)

Geometry of the Embryogenesis: Summary

The point-like ovum sphere, chaoticized by the entry of the linear sperm, expands into the blastula form emphasizing a surface of flat planar cells outside. The planar surface forces then turn into (*ümstulpen*) and focus in the interior where the planar germ disk appears as the flat circular intersection of yolk sac (earth) and amnion (heaven). The burgeoning and sculpting vegetative-etheric life forces thrive and are most active on surfaces as well as in liquid which is full of shearing planes (Schwenk). The thin, tiny being of two and then three layers has yet to expand from two- into three-dimensional space. The advent of a third layer (mesoderm) and threefoldness signals that the human 'I' is ready to step out onto the world stage costumed in its etheric and astral raiment.

Form 9: Neurula: Seedling-like (Weeks 3 - 4)
As a result of transverse folding, the relatively flat disk thickens into Neurula, a cylindrical seedling-like figure with two symmetrical seed-leaf-like formations at its top. It transitions from a flat 2-dimensional plane to three-dimensional space with a top/bottom, back/front and right/left bilateral symmetry—a new world of real volume! On the sides of the middle-axis of this thick upright stem, plant-like segments called somites appear (not modeled or shown). Repetitions of segments and the bilaterality of the "seedling" are a signature of the working of the vegetative-etheric principle and presage the forming of repeating vertebrae. The two top bud-like lobes later on metamorphose into a two-lobed brain.

Although the embryo at the end of week three and beginning of week four is still very much plant-like in its outer formative gesture, it is undergoing a radical transformation indicated by its inner process of folding and creating spaces for future organ development. These changes are signs of the entering soul-astral principle which is remodeling the plant house into a house for a "soul." The inner transformations indicate an 'animal-like ensoulment" (*anima* in Latin means "soul") and can be characterized as an 'animalization' (van der Bie).

In addition to the influence of what I would also call a "soulification", one can also observe and "read" in the forms of week 3 the presence of the individuality, the "I", namely in the vertical straightness first of neural groove and then of Neurula and her cylindrical "seedling" body shape. This gesture presages the ego's future taking hold of the body and lifting and stretching it into an upright posture of the embryo at 8 weeks and later the child walking around age 1. The "I" is the center of the soul; they are often coupled together as "soul-ego" or "soul-spirit."

Sculptural Umstülpung
In weeks three and four, the very complicated foldings and new shapes entail some very remarkable cellular rearrangements. For example, cells exchange locations: eye cells turn from facing each other inside the organism to an outside location on the right and left sides in anticipation of looking out into the world!

Christian Breme characterizes this process as a 'grand metamorphosis': "Within a few days [days 14-28] a tremendous process of inversion (Umstülpung) has occurred, in which besides the substances and the plastic forms, the hollow spaces have also been created, as if sucked in. It is as if a glove that had been turned inside-out was turned over again. What was formed peripherally is now the center after the inversion." (Breme, 21)

According to Steiner, these changes indicate that it is the advent of the human individuality and soul moving into the house of the central body that is responsible for the onset of a tumultuous transformation encompassing week three and week four with the formation of a neural groove and then enclosed neural tube. These mark the beginnings of the process of "neurulation" leading eventually to a vertebral column and a nervous system. According to Steiner.

"With the eighteenth to twenty-first day after conception the individuality, the "I", wanting to incarnate clothed in a new ether body and astral body, takes possession of the physical body which up to that point had been built by the mother.

"With the eighteenth to twenty-first day after conception the individuality, the "I", wanting to incarnate clothed in a new ether body and astral body, takes possession of the physical body which up to that point had been built by the mother."

(R. Steiner, *Menschheitsentwickelung und Christus-Erkenntnis*, CW 100, Dornach 2006,108, cited in Maris 2008, translation by A.A.)

"The taking hold, happens approximately from the eighteen, nineteenth, twentieth, twenty-first day on after conception when that which has descended from a higher world starts working with the developing human being (werdender Mensch). [i.e. the Geistkeim, the Spirit Germ]" (Steiner, *Das Prinzip der spirituellen Oekonomie*, CW 109, 201, Dornach, 2000, cited in Maris 2008, translation by A.A.)

Already at conception, a descending spiritual element called the "spirit germ" (*Geistkeim*) unites with the inherited physical germ. This sets the stage in the first 18 days for the personal individuality to begin entering.

The Fourfold Macrocosmic Birthing Chamber

Steiner also interestingly characterizes the four membranes sheaths surrounding the growing embryo as the *first body* of the prenatal human being and correlates them with the four-foldness of higher bodies:

"...the amnion is the physical correlate of the ether body, the allantois is the physical correlate of the astral body, the chorion is the physical correlate if the I-organization of the grown up human being." (R. Steiner, *Physiologische-Therapeutisches auf Grundlage der Geisteswissenschaft*, CW 314, 308, 1989, 308, cited in Maris 2008, translation by A.A.)

The ego first resides peripherally in the warm blood streams of the chorion which later becomes the placenta; the astral body, in the allantois; the etheric body, in the watery amnion; and the physical principle in the yolk sac. Descending out of the cosmic periphery, the four-fold human make-up of physical, vegetative etheric, astral and "I" principles expresses itself first as a *peripheral* macrocosmic formation in the surrounding "walls" of these four membrane sheaths; and then these four principles turn from outside to focus inside (*umstülpen*) into a microcosmic *centric* being suddenly emerging as if out of nowhere in the middle space of this cosmic "birthing chamber."

Biologist Wolfgang Schad points to the chorion-become-placenta as an excellent metaphorical model for the 'jack-of-all-trades' (*Alleskoenner,*) class teacher generalist, surrounding, nourishing and supporting the growing child in the center. (Schad, 2005, 15,)

In other lectures, Steiner points out that the human 'I' really only comes to live in and use the forces of the centric physical body as a mirroring instrument but actually simultaneously retains its true residence in the cosmic periphery. (R. Steiner, *Philosophie und Anthroposophie*, CW 35, *Bologna*, April 8, 1911). This dual manifestation expresses itself remarkably in the progression of forms we see in embryogenesis—chorion/

placenta outside with embryo inside– and makes visible a complex on-going relationship between the lower and higher 'I's of the human being, a citizen of two worlds.

Form 10: Animal-like Gesture: From Straight to Curved (Weeks 4 -7)
In the second half of week four (days 24-28) the plant-like body is overcome by the soul-astral principle and curves into a distinctly animal-like form and the curved form which Poppelbaum even characterizes in one of his charts as an "gastrula form!" This curvature embraces what is now the actual growth and expansion of the organs which were only primordia in week three. The heart is the first to start forming out of the stream of blood. The heart's beginnings signal a turning point in the embryo's dynamics of the embryo which become more of an animal (astral) nature with the forming of an inner world standing over against an outer world (van der Wal, 2005, 148).

The mysterious fish-like gills (not modeled) which appear are not for breathing but, like ripples in the sand on the beach, are echoes of cosmic vibrations imprinted into the neck in which the sounding larynx will be formed and from which the logos will resound. (See Series Thirteen: Chladni forms created by sound and the Chapter on Form-Giving Forces and tone ether). The entire embryo form at this point is "ear-like" (Poppelbaum, 73) and resonantly listening to the "silent music" of the cosmos for sculptural instructions. The curved concave moon crescent with its development of an inner soul world and organ systems recalls again Steiner's Old Moon when sound ether arose and an animal-like human being was endowed with consciousness and a soul body of sentience.

This stage echoes Moses's myth picture of the Fifth Day of Creation of the first wave of animals: *Let the waters bring forth the moving fish of the seas and the birds of the air.*

The soul body…[sings] and [releases] the forms of the human body.
  —Rudolf Steiner, *Human Values in Education*

Form 11: Mammal-like: From Curved to More Angular (Embryo 6 - 7 weeks)
The head raises itself gradually and swells proportionally larger and larger because of the growing brain. Rounding head forces have been dominant throughout the forming process from the spherical ovum through the circular disk and now to an enlarging dome from which the trunk and limbs grow down. One can say in a certain sense that we start as all head and gradually add a lower body.

Arm-buds become visible in the serpent-like Form 10. The head and the back become less curved and more angular in mammal-like Form 11. In Forms 11-12 above, only the gestalt of the head/torso is modeled here to keep the main gesture of central form within the realm of the suggestive and just on the threshold of crossing over into the "human looking." The lengthening limbs *are left to the imagination*. Modeling the fetal form with articulated limbs can be a further exercise in anatomy (months 3-9).

Sixth Day of Creation: Let the earth bring forth the beasts, cattle and creeping things.

Form 12: Emerging Human: Rounding and Straightening (8 Weeks)
Again, straightening, stretching and unfolding and radial limb development are signs and signatures of the ego at work and

anticipates the upright posture of later life and standing on the earth (at age one).

To develop inner organs the form goes from *straightness* (weeks 3-4) through concave *curvature* (Weeks 4-7) and then to *straightness* again (Week 8 on).

Interestingly, the human organism passes through and *recapitulates* an intermediate animal-like form gesture where the curving inward continues the creation and growth of concave soul space and interior organ growth. Concavity is a sign and signature of the soul/astral principle working (animal-like); convexity, of the life etheric body (plant-like) and straightness of the human ego.

Moses's Sixth Day of Creation continues: *"Let us make the human being in our image."* Old Moon has metamorphosed into the Earth, home of the human "I".

End of the Two-Month Embryo Sequence

The fetal stage is reminiscent of what Steiner calls the 'Atlantean' human being (König). The waters of the great flood break and each child is born into the conscious world of air as a little ark!

We can plunge ever deeper into our observation of nature and seek to read the riddle of its forms and processes. We can explore this or that periodic process and discover the rhythmicity of this or that structural motif. What we want to do is…to learn to 'hear' the process that blossoms in flowers, to 'hear' embryology in its manifestations and apprehend the inwardness of the process.

—Hans Jenny, Sound Form Researcher

The Embryo as a Symphony of the Creative Word (Logos): A Musical Flow of Forming with Four Notes PEAI

Steiner describes the human being as a "symphony" of the creative word or logos of the universe. Indeed, the tiny ear-shaped embryo in itself appears to be not only listening to the cosmos but also to be 'singing' along in a musical sequence of shapes. It is transforming itself according to a score we can 'read' with its fugue-like interweaving and interpenetration of motifs or notes sounding through and structuring the various organ forms. These notes appear in many ways to correspond to the four principles of human nature: the physical principle (P), the vegetative-etheric (E), the soul-astral (A) and 'I' (ego).

Researcher Dennis Klocek points to this connection when he comments that:

"The value that Steiner brings to embryology is viewing catabolic as astral principle, anabolic as etheric principle, and "I"-organization as the guiding force between that balances. The catabolic and the anabolic forces are enacted through the interaction of the nerve in the blood, with the organ formation arising in between as a functional image of the interaction. It turns out that embryology is fugue-like; the motif of nerve and blood is carried out in every organ. Every organ is an image of a particular connection between the blood and the nerve." (Klocek, *Esoteric Physiology*, 141)

Or as embryologist Karl König poetically expresses it, we learn *"to look until suddenly one begins to hear, to perceive from the form and the structure [of the embryo], **what the gestalt has to say, to sing, to tell.**"*

The embryo's fugue-like musical score is full of very complicated repeating and interweaving motifs. The following is meant as a possible framework for beginning to discern and appreciate the 'form-principle gestures at various stages. For me, from one perspective of *predominant* form *action*, they appear in the first 8 weeks as a sequence of

A-I, P-E-A-I, A-I, P-E-A-I

interpreted as:

- **A**: In a tight spiraling movement, the shining seed (Greek: *sperma*) *desires and seeks* out the glistening new world of the ovum, a gesture of the soul-astral principle.

- **I**: The maternal ovum, imagined both as a sphere *and* as a tiny center point, is a *centering* space which the child's individuality focuses on and approaches. *"To feel …a circle in space is,"* according to Steiner, *" to feel the self, the I Am, the ego…"*

- **P**: In cleavage into a morula, we perceive the mother's 'physical principle' at work in 'crystallization' of the similar *mater*-ial units.

- **E**: In the flattening cells and curved planar outer sphere of the blastula and in the sudden appearance within it of the flat round germ disk, we encounter the mother's life-etheric principle active and expressing its character in *leaf-like forms and surfaces*.

- **A**: In the *indentation* of the germ disk by a primitive pit and by a neural groove down its middle, soul-astral forces hollow out a characteristic *concave* trail.

- **I**: In the elongation of the round germ disk into a flat 'pear' shape and in the *straight* linear signature of the neural groove marking a vertical, central axis, a veritable letter 'I' signature , we see the activity of the approaching I-principle beginning to take hold and work

simultaneously as the center of the soul-astral.

- **A**: In the transverse folding of the disk into a cylinder with *inner spaces* for future organ development, we observe the workings of the new incarnating soul and its soul-astral-animalizing principle.

- **I**: In stretching, *lengthening, upright* cylinder form, the I-principle also asserts itself.

- **P**: In filling out into the *three dimensions of space* with up-down, right-left, backfront, the embryo takes on physicality and *mass.*

- **E**: In the bilaterality and *rhythmically pattered segmentation* of the cylinder form, the plant-like forces of the vegetative-etheric are still expressing themselves strongly and dominating in spite of the '*anima*-lization' process.

- **A**: In addition to the transverse folding of week 3, the longitudinal bending of the cylinder into the *curving, curling gesture* of weeks 4-7 show the animalizing forces coming to predominate in the outer form.

- **I**: In week 8 the *re-straightening* and '*uprighting*' of the bent form into an emergent human form, the note of "I" sounds again.

Interestingly, the sequence of P-E-A-I appears also to overarch the first 8 weeks or 2 months of embryogenesis as a whole. It is like a four movement sonata: mineral-Physical movement, plant Etheric movement (leaf-seedling), animal Astral movement (curved form) and finally human-I movement (straightening). As in a musical work, themes are repeated. For example, straightening sounds in the second movement (seedling), disappears and then recurs in the fourth movement.

Furthermore, according to Steiner, in the first months of the fetal stage, there is more intense action of the child's etheric body (E); at 7 months, more of the astral body (A); and just before birth, of the ego (I). And, of course, there is the physical birth (P), the etheric birth at age 7 (E), the astral birth at 14 (A) and standing up in the world at 21 (I). The P-E-A-I motif repetitions go on! What first expresses itself as forming in the body development of the embryo and fetus later expresses itself in action and behavior.

Nevertheless, the above framework is only intended as but one way to start appreciating in the broad strokes a complicated and nuanced interplay of factors. While at any one point, a dominant form gesture may stand out for us , the other three are always present, working and interpenetrating, often to be detected as less dominant, secondary "sub-gestures." Some examples include: the bulging roundness of the ovum projects burgeoning life (E) from within; the 'sphericity' of cells also expresses an etheric fullness (E); the curving 'organ-izing neurula (A) comes to have a bulging exterior heart filling with life blood (E). What is more, we must not forget that the centric embryo body is only part of the new organism which includes the choir of the membranes 'singing' all around it. P is sounding in the yolk sac; E, in the waters of amnion; A, in the allantois; and I, in the warmth-permeated, blood-filled chorion.

ATCG

Interestingly, today's genetic language of body construction is 4-fold. Although there is no correspondence to the four principles above, the current physical model (P) of the spiraling helix (A) of life (E) around a central axis (I) is word-logos-like. It employs the fourfold alphabet of ATCG from which 'words' (codons) and 'sentences' (strands) are made. One can imagine this elegant double spiral as a musical-sculptural score transcribed and conducted by a very special musician?! *Might it involve a coda as well as a code?!*

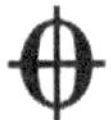

coda symbol in music

The Musical Building of the Human Body

In his *The Harmony of the Human Body: Musical Principles in Human Physiology* Husemann beautifully articulates how the sculptured human form is a *"musikalischer Bau,"* a "musical building." He shows how the body is constructed on the principles of the intervals in the musical scale. Husemann, however, deals mainly with the adult body and only touches on the musical-sculptural formation of the embryo.

This is certainly another area that can be developed in more detail. Looked at musically, we can begin to see how embryogenesis also has its 'intervals:' the ovum is obviously the tonic or prime but is the bilaminar disk its second or the neurula its third? The clear emergence of the human form at the beginning of the fetal stage (at 8 weeks) certainly seems like a fourth with other intervals coming later.

Imagining Musically-Sculpturally

As a practicing artist, Steiner discovered that *"when the sculptural… is taken a step further, it is led over into a kind of musical experience. There is also the opposite step, from the musical element back into the sculptural-pictorial."* (*Art as seen in the Light of Mystery Wisdom,* 1984, Lecture January 2, 1915, 28).

Consideration of embryogenesis teaches us not only to go back and forth in our imagination, but also to imagine (visually and aurally) an organism *"musically-sculpturally"* at the same time. Like the sudden appearance of a Chladni form in salt on a resounding brass plate, the appearance of embryonic forms inspires in us awe and wonder.

EMBRYOGENESIS: Embryo in Flow Motion *by A.A.*

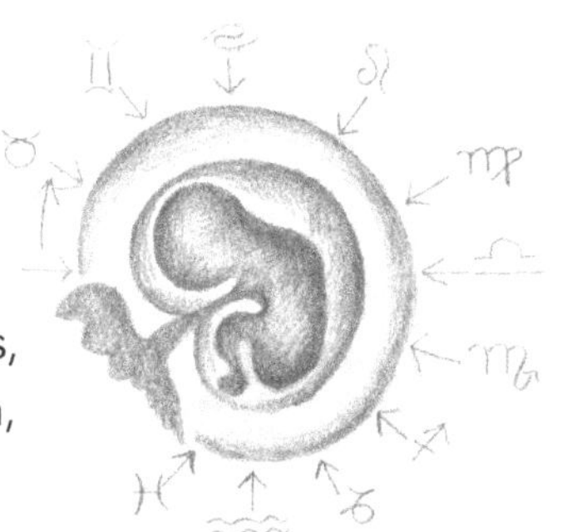

Shining Ovum – Sphere of mostly water
Penetrated by life's spiral
Trembles with the music of creator beings hovering 'round it.
Into chaos, Sphere divides into 2, into 4, into 8, into 16,
A glistening mulberry form, a Morula! – Old Saturn-like.
Morula's multitude of rounded cells flatten into little leaf-like cells,
Float to the surface of a new sphere holding a water world within,
Mulberry Morula becomes Blastula! – Old Sun-like,
A fluid-filled eye ball soaking in the form-giving light of the stars.
Deep within this little water globe,
Land appears dividing waters from waters.
An island disk of diaphanous flatness.
A tiny sleeping Leaf Being is being born in its bed of tissues.
The Finger of the Spirit marks a groove of light down the Leaf's middle.
She stirs, thickens into cylinder-like Seedling, lengthening, straightening.
At her top, two seed-leaves appear.
Seedling curls into a moon-like ear listening to the universe:
How will I rhythmically shape the frame of my body according to the sounding of the stars?
How will I rhythmically shape my organs according to movements of the planets?
How will I make the sun into my heart?
I rhythmically weave my form out of the music of the spheres,
Echoes of Ancient Saturn, Ancient Sun, Ancient Moon resound through me.
I relive urmineral, urplant, uranimal in my body,
Form gestures of serpent, of fish, of mammal ripple through me.
At last, my I AM takes strong hold, straightens me again
and lifts my form into full spirit and Humanness
After nine moons, I feel the waters around me break in a Great Flood.
I flow forth into the world as a little ark
Water Being reborn as an Air Being.
In my first breath, my soul awakens to the call of another New Life,
On Earth.

GESTURES OF THE 4 STAGES OF EMBRYOGENESIS

1. Gesture of Mineral-like Forms (Physical Principle)　　*MINERAL MAN*　　Echoes of Old Saturn-Polaris
Embryo Wk 1: 1st Day of Creation　　　　**(Duplication of same forms)**

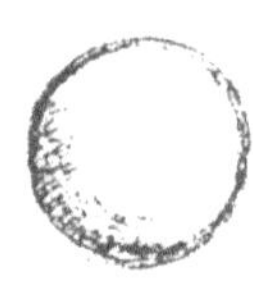 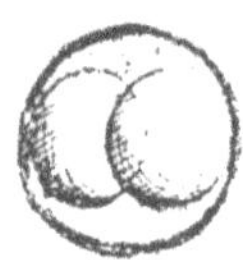 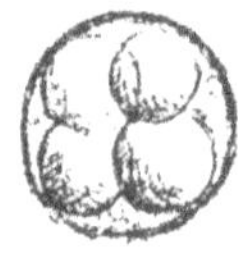 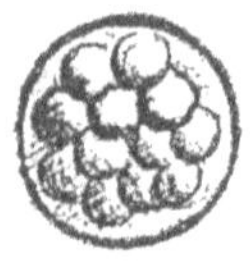 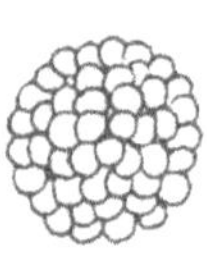

crystalline-mathematical quality

16 Cell 3 days **MORULA=Mulberry**

2. Gesture of **Plant-like Metamorphosis** of **different** Forms (Vegetative-Etheric)　*PLANT MAN* - Old Sun -Hyperborea

Embryo Wk. 2: 2nd Day of Creation　　　　*Embryo Wk. 2 cont.:*　　*3nd Day of Creation*
" parting firmament "　　　　　　　*water mini-universe*　**BLASTULA**　*eye-like + seed-pod like*

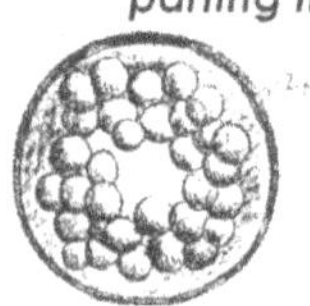 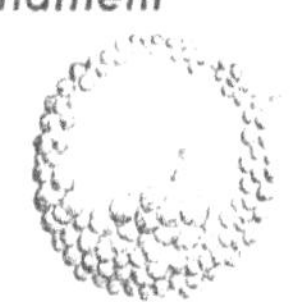　　　　　　　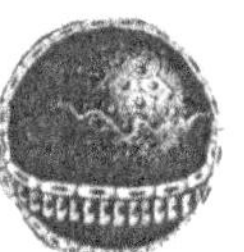

cells flatten to periphery　　　　　　*"land + plants appear"*
bed of germ layers appears as center

Embryo Wk 3 FOLDING into NEURULA: Plant Man in the process of being 'soulified'/'astralized'/'anima-lized':
At its new center: Little Body disc arises from 3 germ layers　　*3rd Day of Creation cont.*

13 days　14　　　15　　*leaf-like forms folding into stem-like cylinder*　　*"Paradise": Urplant*　*Seedling-like*

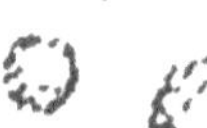 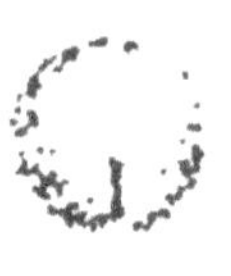 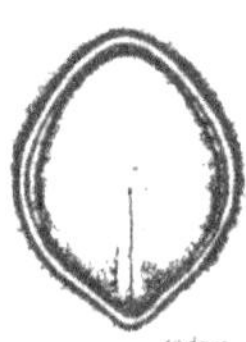 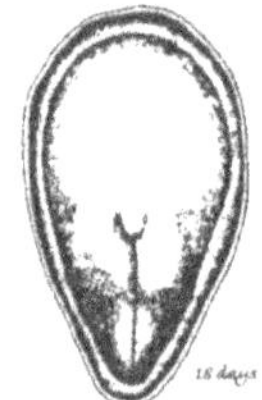 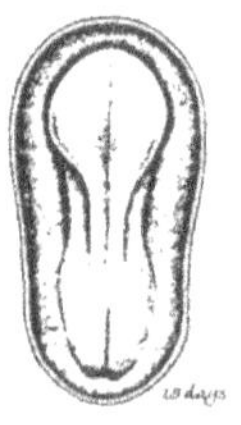 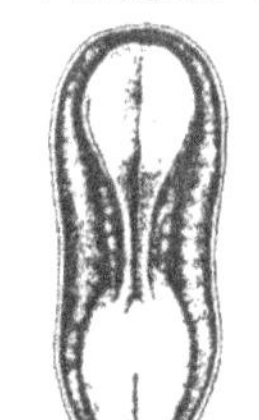 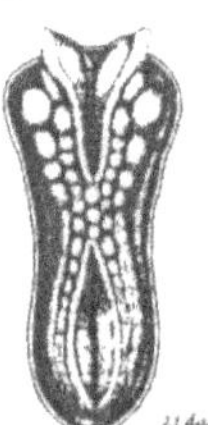 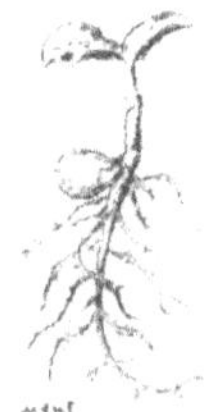

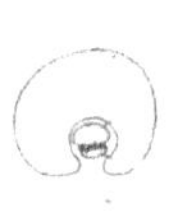 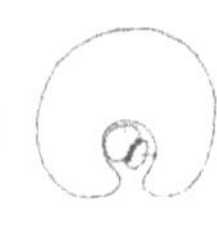 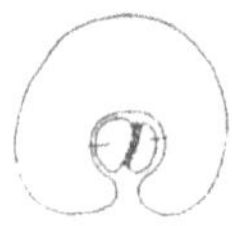 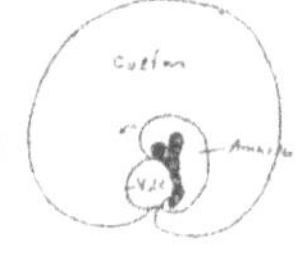

Wk. 3:Little body of leaf-like disc rotates upright in its water world

3.Animal-like form gesture *ANIMAL MAN*　　(Soul-Astral) (inner space/organs)　　**Old Moon -** Lemuria

4th Day of C.　　　　*5th Day of C.*　　　　*6th Day of C.*　　**4. Earth (Ego-Human)-***Atlantis*
*Birth=Breaking of the Waters=***Flood**
Embryo Wks 4-8　(Rohen: Neurulation wk. 4 to birth) **ear-like**　　**Child= An Ark** = water to air bein
From straight to curving form →　　　　　　　　　→ to straightening

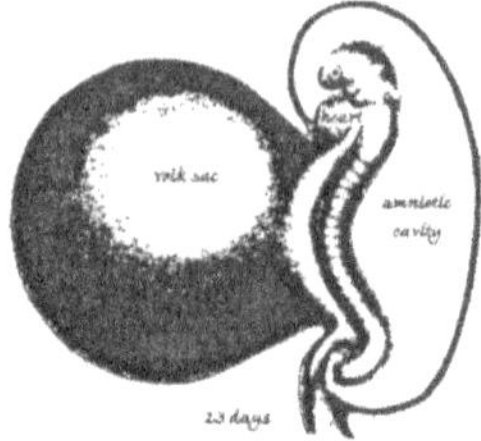 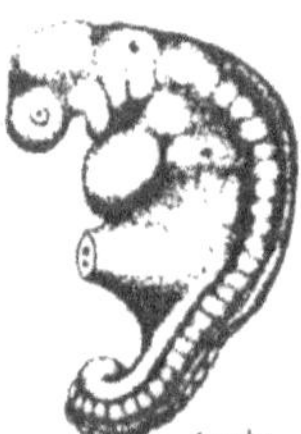 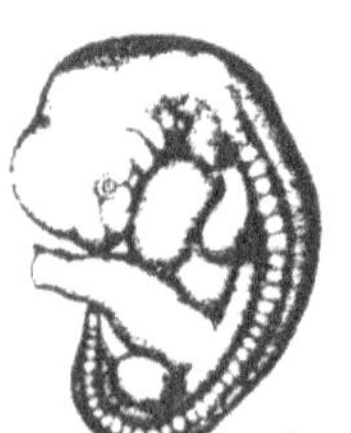 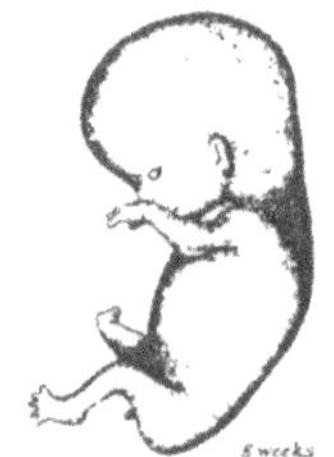

Uranimal:　　　　Serpent -like　Fish-like　　　　　Mammal-like　　**4. HUMAN FORM**
FETUS STAGE (7 mos.)

Drawings after Wilmar, Appenzeller and Rows 3 and 5 by Permission from Wooden Books, 8A Market Place, Glastonbury BA6 8LT, UK.

Learning from Goetheanum Forms

Metamorphic Treasure Trove

The sculptural motifs of Steiner's first Goetheanum building offer an inexhaustible treasure trove of metamorphic forms to study and learn from. Inspired by the living world of formative forces, they were initially modeled in a small format in clay, plasticine or plaster and then carved in different woods. The motifs formed pillars, architraves, and standing sculpture on a large architectural scale.

Artists and teachers have benefited from both rendering and developing further these organic sequences. For example, I found it very enlightening to first draw and then model in clay Steiner's metamorphic series of forms carved around the bases of the columns of the Goetheanum. *See right column.*

These pure forms capture not buds, sprouts, leaves, flowers, fruit, seed and so on, but the *moving force dynamics* of their manifestations and of their metamorphosis from one form to the next. I found that the experience of modeling these universal, archetypal shapes work formatively in and flow into what you then freely develop in your own work in clay or other sculptural media. (See Series Five: Plant-like forms.)

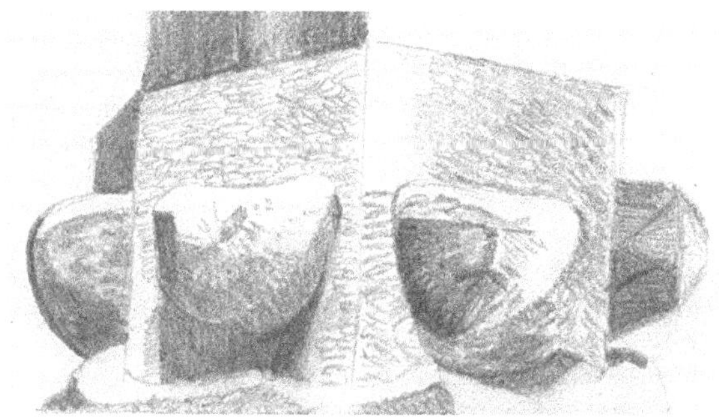

Budding

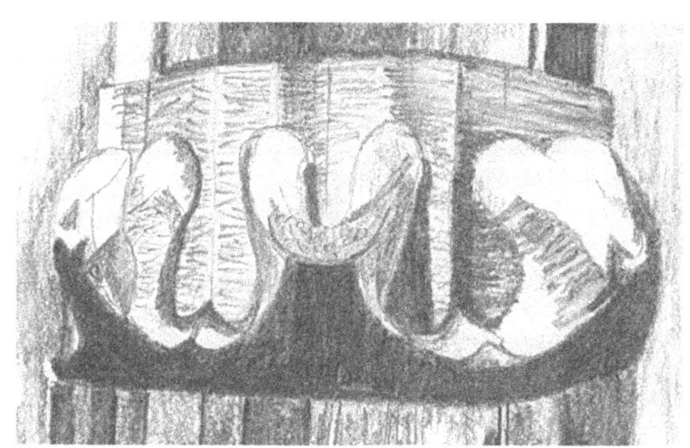

Sprouting

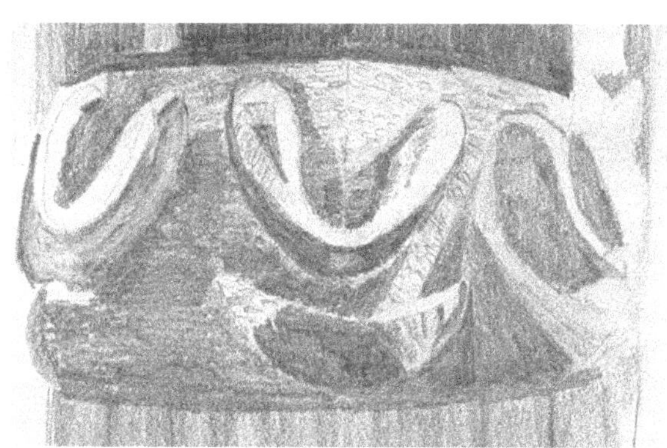

Leafing

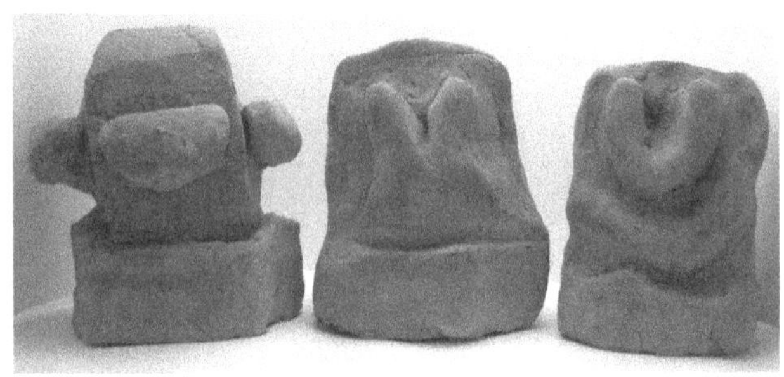

Clay sketches of Steiner's column base models

Below are some examples from my own work done while I was a class teacher. The forms are shown here in wood but they can be rendered in comparable clay formations – always with variation because of the nature of a different material with its own peculiarities.

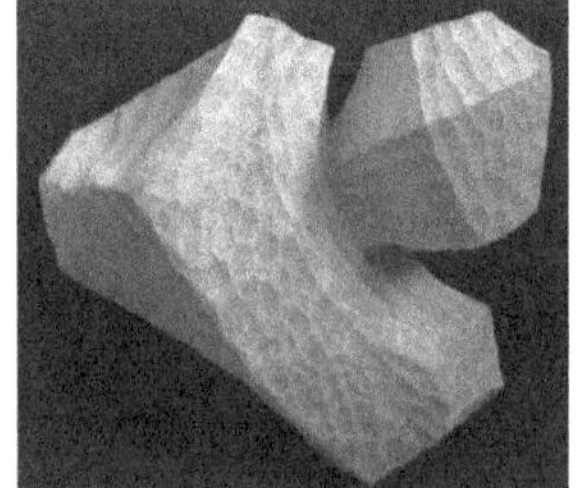

Form gesture of budding

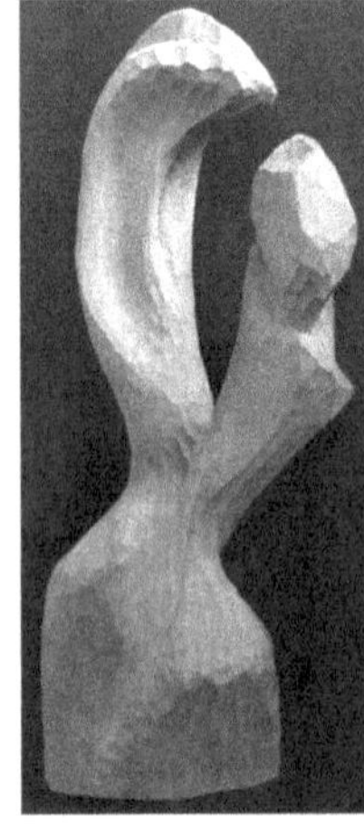

Of leafing and budding

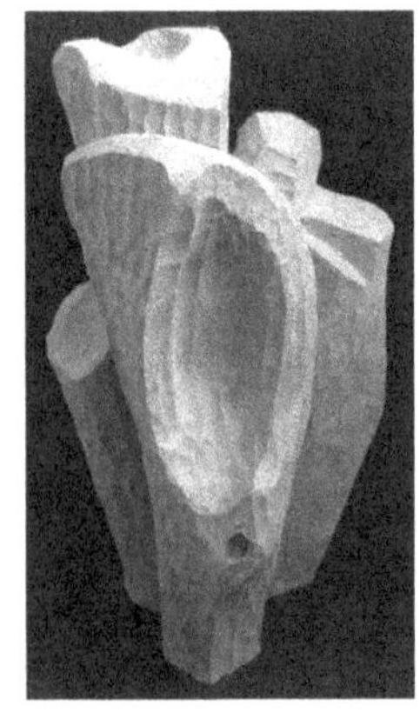

Of withering/falling apart

Form Gestures of Twelve Hands

Steiner's large, central sculpture for the Goetheanum above was called *"The Representative of Humanity."* It dramatically depicts the tension of the creative forces needed in the process of becoming, being and staying truly human. (For further details about its esoteric meaning and background, see Judith von Halle and John Wilkes' *The Representative of Humanity: Between Lucifer and Ahriman*).

Sculpturally, this massive thirty-foot sculpture made of tons of laminated elm is filled with the energy of living form-creating forces. Its language speaks a rich vocabulary of universal polarities and qualities of form: convex-concave, flat, straight, angular expansive-contractive, and light-heavy. The work's upper part is characterized by an exaggerated convexity; its lower part by an exaggerated concavity. In between is the large central figure the "Representative of Humanity" actively harmonizing and balancing extreme tendencies and transforming them into what is truly human.

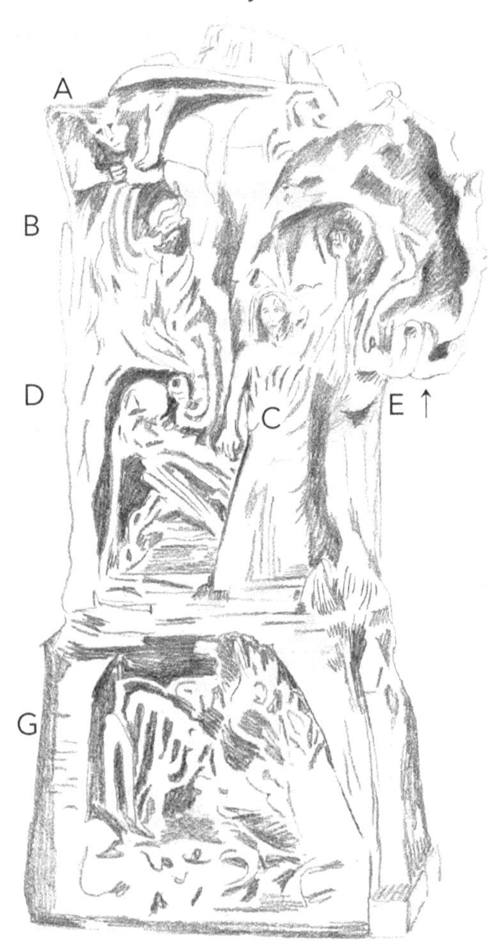

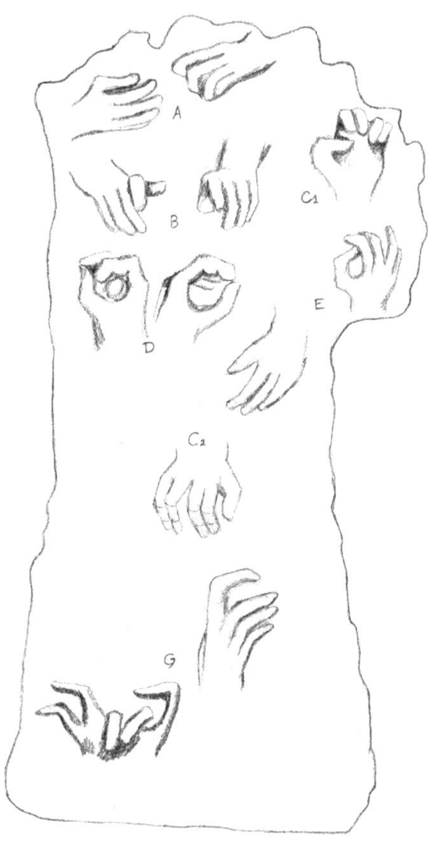

Pairs of hands from the top:
A. Elemental cliff being (also called World Humor)
B. Rising Lucifer
C1. Left hand of the Representative of Humanity
D. Upper Ahriman
E. Falling Lucifer
C2. Right hand of the Representative of Humanity
G. Lower Ahriman

After very busy lecturing schedules, Steiner loved to be in his studio and sculpt and experience the forms emerging out of the wood. He had a special way of carving and produced *"double-curved" surfaces* that radiated the appearance of life. These surfaces organically integrated convexity and concavity in a living, dynamic interplay.

In Steiner's work of complex forms, six figures are depicted, each with a pair of hands in various gestures. Above is a map of the twelve hands and approximately what section of the sculpture they are in. Not all are immediately visible in photographs or even when one visits the work.

The hands mirror in miniature the major themes and dynamic form language of the sculpture as a whole. For example, the convex back of the right hand of the central figure faces frontwards and is directed downwards in a counter balancing way toward the shriveled, angular, sclerotized features of the lower figure and its surroundings. My experience is that this right hand of the central figure creates within itself a spherical sun-space of healing life forces.

In contrast, the left hand is raised high with its cupped concave inside facing outwards. It is directed at a chaotic turbulence of rounded, curving forms billowing above it. Its gesture is one of helping the falling figure and the forces above it to find the healing center and not to drift off into oblivion.

Both hands and arms stretch from above to below in a powerful diagonal that passes through the heart of the central figure. Undulating etheric curves of life are carved in relief over his rhythmic center of heart and lungs.

Artists and teachers associated with Waldorf schools have been studying and learning from "The Representative of Humanity" for decades. I encourage you to contemplate its many meanings and form language from photos or, better still, if you get the chance, see it first-hand in Switzerland. Some visitors sit before it and get to know its forms actively through drawing. I have studied aspects of the work by bringing a small piece of plasticine and capturing forms in this medium. The hands have a way of really "grasping" forms so that the eyes themselves see more actively. The forms then really sink in mentally, emotionally and actively.

Here are a few more observations and thoughts about the hands and figures to consider and study with the help of the map of their positions and illustrations on the previous pages:

- #1: Rising Lucifer's right hand is drawn from a plaster cast made by sculptor John Wilkes to make the shape and gesture of its underside more accessible. The three smaller fingers are curved inwards and downwards in wave forms. The pointer finger is straightening and pointing with the thumb in parallel. See #6 for a side view.

- #2 and #3: These are the pair of hands of the middle figure "The Representative of Humanity," whom Steiner also referred to as " Christus " or "Christos, " the Greek term for the "Anointed One" (Hebrew: "Meshiach").

- # 4: Lower Ahriman's right hand at the very base of the sculpture is the most bizarre and dramatic. It projects extreme angularity, boniness and sclerosis as well as excruciating arthritic pain and the throes of death. It is reminiscent of and as powerful as Grünewald's depiction of crucified hands in the Isenheim Altar painting.

- #5: Upper Ahriman's right hand here has his other characteristic gesture: contracted, cramped, upturned concave, hollowing, emptiness.

- #6 and #7: Rising Lucifer's hands from the side. How are they different in gesture from #8?

- #8: "The Representative of Humanity"

On a final note, the strange winged head with arms at the very top left of the sculpture was added as an "afterthought." A Dutch artist Mieta Waller viewed the work in progress and bluntly expressed her sense that it was tipping too much to the right and appeared

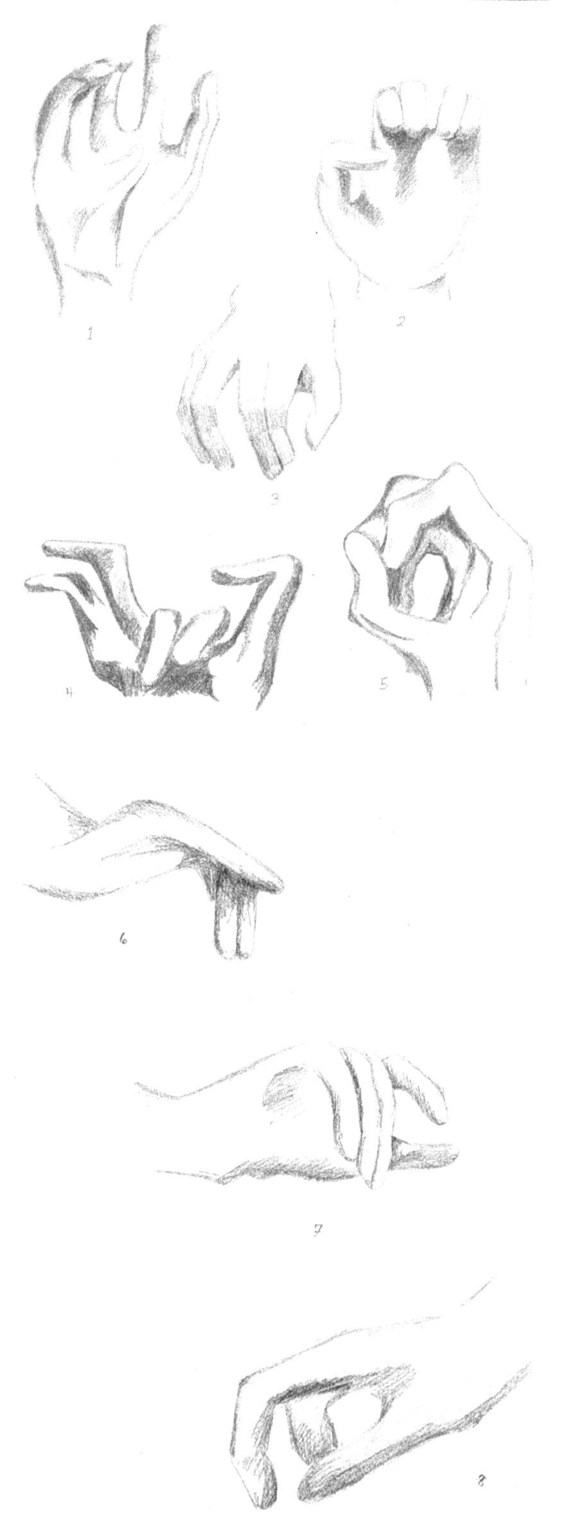

to be ready to fall over. Steiner then realized that it was indeed out of balance sculpturally and added another figure on the opposite side to compensate. He referred to this elemental being as a " cliff being"

(*Felsenwesen*) and also as "World Humor." In his open artistic process, the universe – and a frank Dutch lady – had revealed to the great initiate quite a humorous surprise! And Steiner loved surprises.

The artistic process is one of revelation and exploration.

Adult Exercise

Study and characterize the shapes, gestures and positioning of the hands of "The Representative of Humanity" in comparison to the other hands including the strange "cliff being" and its head with its wing-arms-hands at the very top left of the sculpture. (See Series Seven and Twelve for the related exercise below which can also be enjoyed by adults.)

(See Hand Appreciation Exercises in Series Twelve)

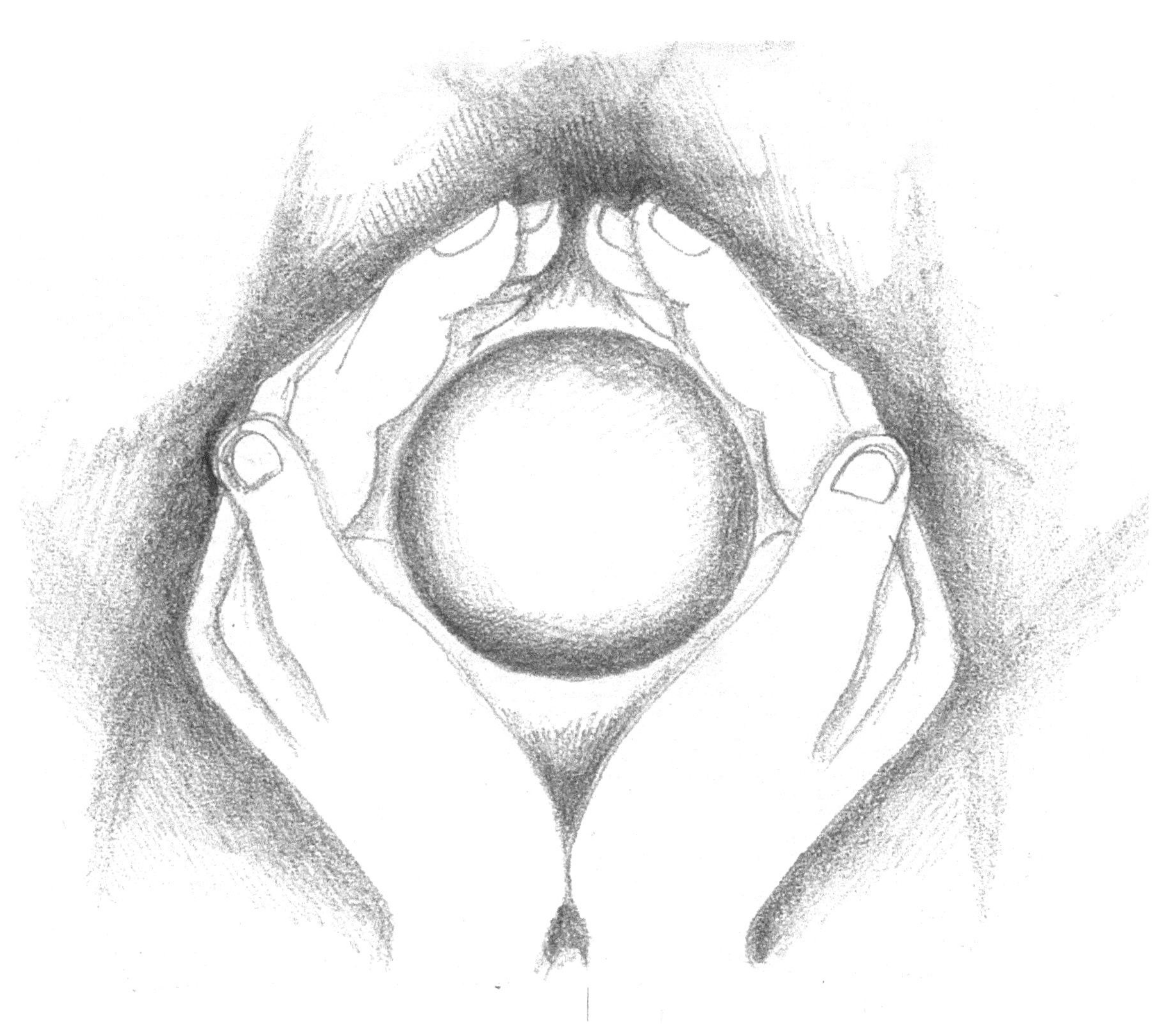

Part IV
Supplementary

The Spirit-Permeated Hand
A Lecture Opening the 2004 Antioch Waldorf Summer Session
By Arthur Auer

HANDS, Heart and Head

We are of the universe!
Stars ray into hands
To transform the earth.
Feet listen to earth and stars
And draw us to our destiny.
Hearts know the way.
Heads mirror the light of stars.
Of the universe are we!

In human development the child first grasps objects, then grasps words, then grasps thoughts. Hand grasping is the neurological catalyst for speech and mental grasping. We have the idea of grasping hidden in our Latin-based word *concept* from the Latin *concipere* meaning *"to grasp together."* And of course there is the interesting relationship of dominant handedness on one side of our body to the formation of a speech center on the other side.

Hands Build the Brain

Neuroscience has been recently discovering more and more about how the functions of the hand affect a very large part of our brain and how hand activity builds our intelligence and even brain mass and structure. In 1998 some remarkable research came together under the title of *The Hand: How its Use Shapes the Brain, Language and Human Culture*. Its author Frank Wilson, a California neurologist, says that between 100-200 thousand years ago the hand reached its present anatomic configuration and attained a new capability with *enormous implications*: The ring and little fingers were able to cross over to touch the opposing thumb resulting in an oblique squeeze grip. (Try it yourself.) This meant that the hand could conform itself to a nearly infinite range of object shapes and control them precisely, delicately or powerfully. Small objects could be taken apart and put back together again or made into new things.

At the same time Wilson points out during this evolution toward a new hand design, grip and dexterity, the brain concurrently tripled in size, resulting in a new species called homo sapiens. The new modern hand discovered how to take hold of the world in new ways. And in response the brain plastically sculpted new structures for control, for cognitive and imaginative life and for speech. The infinite plasticity of our hand movements worked together with the neuroplasticity of the brain to sculpturally model new neural formations and expand brain capacity. It is interesting to note the eighteenth century philosopher Kant characterized our *"hand as our outer brain."*

Implications for Education

The implications of this new view of joint

hand-brain development are enormous for education. According to Wilson, young homo sapiens have been learning and building their brains for over a hundred thousand years by processing the world through their hands in conjunction with the direct, unmediated use of their senses. Children therefore need to educationally recapitulate this evolutionary path in order to build their brains. And any culture that neglects this plan of nature does so at the peril of civilization and health.

Wilson warns against what he calls a "cephalocentric," i.e. head-dominated perspective on life that diminishes the vital role of the hands and relegates them to a menial status. The intellectual snobbery of the head is particularly harmful when it one-sidedly dominates education. For Wilson, real, life-changing education is experiential, hands-on education. (And Wilson by the way, knows of Waldorf education and refers to it when lecturing. He and I have corresponded by e-mail and he ordered copies of my modeling book. He even referred me to a friend of his who uses clay modeling to help business executives brainstorm corporate ideas or better said—*hand-storm* them!)

Manual Intelligence

What Frank Wilson has been proclaiming at the end of the twentieth century, Rudolf Steiner was putting into practice at its beginning. Steiner conceived of Waldorf Education as an education of the will that recognizes the true and remarkable capacities of the human hand. In his words," manual dexterity...stands at the beginning of our teaching." Working with the hands was to be at the heart of the Waldorf method not only to bring about good motor skills, but also by means of the arts, to charge learning with tremendous sensory and emotional engagement and to foster healthy thinking.

Decades before the so-called Decade of the Brain in the 1990s, Steiner was pointing out the intimate connection between nimble fingers and a nimble mind. "Someone," he said, "who knows how to move his fingers properly, also has flexible ideas and thoughts and is better able to penetrate the essence of things with his thinking."

> The movements of the fingers are to a great extent the teachers of the elasticity of our thinking.

Steiner in fact characterized our hands as being a "very fine thought organs". We can think with our hands and paradoxically from a certain point of view according to him… "the hands—taken from the perspective of their life forces—are much more significant and adept organs of knowledge [than] the human brain…With our fingers…we can think much more brightly than with the nerves of the head…. [And] when we do not merely grasp with our hand but think with it …we follow our destiny."

Hand Awareness

In the first lesson of the entire Waldorf Curriculum journey, Steiner asked first grade teachers to call attention to the children's hands and how the children are going to start learning by *doing* something with their hands.

> *Children, you have come to school to learn something...You have two hands. These are for working, you can do all kinds of things with them... Now I am going to do this. And now you can take your two hands and you do it too.*

Two hands and doing were to be the starting point for an action education of the spirit. And for Steiner, spirit is active and stands in contrast to a merely reflective education of what the British call 'mind.' For Steiner, mind is essentially passive and not really creative. Moreover, he recommended that the children not just know that they have two hands but that they gain an awareness of the wonder of their hands as primary instruments of the creative human spirit.

It is not a coincidence that the start of each day in Waldorf schools begins with a warm handshake, a most important act of the so-called Waldorf method. There are all kinds of ways teachers can promote hand awareness and I have begun assembling a beginning list for hand awareness in various subjects in grades 1- 8. (See list at the end of this book)

Most Human Part
In fact, the aspect of hand awareness is also a key to the anthroposophical, the "humanosophical" basis of Waldorf education because it is our hands in a sense and not our heads that are the most human part of us and closest to the spirit from a certain evolutionary point of view. In earth evolution, it is our unique human limbs which have come last along with our spiritual human ego. It is with our limbs that we are able to directly penetrate and transform the earth. The head, in contrast, is like Plato's cave in which we sit back in imprisoned isolation and view only shadows of reality projected into it. On occasions Steiner humorously put the head in its place by characterizing its water-filled, oyster–like shell as our oldest and most animal-like part. He also joked about the head as a lazy king pompously riding about on a hardworking body or once even referred to the head as a kind of parasite.

Like Frank Wilson, Steiner cautioned society against one-sidedly glorifying the head and its clever intellect. In his view, the role of our hands in developing overall intelligence should not be underestimated, especially when it comes to understanding living organisms, whole systems, flow processes, and especially human development. That is why Steiner recommended sculptural modeling as one of the essential activities in ongoing teacher development. In his words,

> We cannot understand the body of formative life forces in terms of ordinary laws, but through the experience of the hand–*the spirit-permeated hand*. Modeling should take a foremost place in the curriculum of …[teacher] training…, for it provides the means whereby the teacher may learn to understand the body of formative life forces. The following may be taken as a fundamental principle: a teacher who has never studied modeling really understands nothing about the development of the child.

On this basis, modeling needs to be part of a teacher's career-long continuing education and practiced together in faculty meetings in order for teachers to tune up and remodel their organs of cognition for grasping the etheric.

Threefold Hand Form
So what is this spirit-permeated hand as Steiner calls it? How does the spirit use the hand to bring about this potential of an almost infinite number of creative movements and forms? Frank Wilson ended up calling his ten-year research study and book a

meditation on the human hand and if indeed we contemplate and study the hand's remarkable activity, we begin to discover all kinds of ways in which the human spirit makes use of it. In the time remaining, I would like to share a few further thoughts on the subject of the spirit-permeated hand.

First of all, it is of the great significance that the spirit in evolution has freed our hands up from having to adapt too strongly to the demanding rough earth. Our human hands do not have to harden and specialize, for instance, in knuckle walking as do those of our primate kin. To achieve their unique capacity to serve the spirit, our hands and limbs interestingly hold back from becoming too specialized as happens with animal appendages. Our hands are what noted biologists like Stephen Gould and others call paedomorphic which means they are arrested in their development. They remain plastically young, embryonic, soft, pliable and free so that they can create this infinite variety of forms. According to the noted neurophysiologist Jeannerod, "There is indeed no other organ possessed by a living being that can carry out so many movements as does the human hand." (*Encyclopedia of Psychology*, "Psycho-motorics," 1994)

Our hands have been lifted up from the earth into our chest sphere and have become "chestified," "rhythmified," "speechified" extensions of our middle system. (In fact, Steiner even characterized our hands as "the eyes of our rhythmic system.") Our two cupped hands naturally position themselves in front of our heart region to create a warm heart form or spherical sun-space. Both hands and heart are related to each other as organs of feeling and sensing, of motion and e-motion that connect us with our surroundings.

We can find the threefoldness of the whole human being in miniature in the form and functions of the hand. We have a thinking part in the head-like finger tips half covered by little hard skull-caps and packed with nerves. As the blind know, the fingers have eyes that can see in the dark. In the curved hollow of our hand we have a sensitive, intimate inner feeling space, which children know is very tickly. And then in the bottom third of our hand willing comes to its fullest expression where it is more muscular and tougher, with a thick heel and muscular ball of the powerful thumb. And this unique opposing thumb of the human hand one could say is a stodgier, thicker type finger, and gets pulled into the sphere of the will and is the most 'willified' finger, stubborn and oppositional. It is characteristically our most human finger. Its development has been closely correlated by biologists with the development of our uprightness, bipedality and to our becoming human in evolution. It is the last of the fingers to develop in the embryo and has the flattest and least claw-like finger nail. But talking about the thumb is a very complex side track. So at this point I will just leave you with Sir Isaac Newton's curious conviction about the thumb that "In absence of any other proof, the thumb alone would convince me of God's existence."

Just looking in general at our fingers, hand and arm we see a marvel of mathematical musical sculpture of *one* bone, *two* bones, then three followed by four wrist bones and finally five fingers. 1-2-3-4-5, a simple but elegant radiation pattern out into the universe; and our five fingers ray out from a five sided pentagonal palm. Another pentagon is created by the four sections of our bent arms with our chest as one side. Biologists tell us the number five has been in the evolutionary plan of pentadactyly for millions of years. Five, we know mathematically, is the number generating the golden ratio in our hand and body geometry, is related to our five milk teeth in each mouth quadrant, and to our 1+4 architecture: 1 thumb plus 4 fingers and the star form of 1 head plus 4 limbs radiating out from the trunk.

Womb of Worlds

Now there are many fascinating aspects about our hands and limbs that could be mentioned, but one of the best ways I have found to experience the meaning of our cosmic form is to simply act it out with young children. When first graders stretch out in a five pointed star of two arms, two legs and a head, they know how to become stars; they have an instinctive sense of how our shape is a living parable of our heavenly origins.

Through Spacial Dynamics, projective geometry and anthroposophy, we learn how our true spirit's being and home center is actually way out there expanded at infinity in another dimension beyond space and time. From there our spirit streams to earth and only a tiniest fraction of our mighty being and who we really are materializes into what we see as our physical bodies. In embryonic development the last delicate tips of our mighty being to sprout from our trunk are our hands and then feet. Interestingly Rudolf Steiner characterizes even our fully developed hands as being really only Keime, as germinal seeds. What might he mean by this? We thought we had highly perfected hands

that can do all kinds of amazing things. If we consider the spiritual significance of seeds in nature, we can see them in a sense as the spirit's open gateway through which living formations enter from another dimension. Seeds are forms which allow for something to come through and to unfold.

To experience the deep significance of this phenomenon in nature, Steiner often pointed to the fruitfulness of contemplating simple seeds. The simplest and humblest seed can reveal the highest. Seeds are portals to the world of creation and to what are called the archetypes. In our phenomenal world, everything is fashioned according to non-physical patterns or archetypes in another dimension, a dimension some modern quantum physicists like David Bohm are calling another implicate universe, an invisible one woven into ours. In spiritual terminology, these creative patterns or archetypes of everything originate in the highest part of the spirit world and live in a state Steiner characterizes in his book *Theosophy* as *Keimpunkte*, germinal seed points. And remarkably this happens to be the same way he describes our hands. In other words, our embryonic, seed-like, bud-like hands are created in the Image of the Highest. Their earthly form reflects the divine the state of being of the very same creative archetypes they serve. Our seed-like hands thereby are able to put us in direct touch with the seed potency of the spirit. We have the spirit world literally at our finger tips. When we move our hands in purposeful actions, we are "swimming and splashing in the spirit." Our hands are the threshold where spirit form mysteriously integrates itself with matter and actively transforms it. I have always found it fascinating how a nondescript lump of clay moving playfully between my hands can come to take on so many forms. And personally I find that many of the forms that take shape in my hands I never imagined beforehand. Where do they come from?

In fact, using the hands activates the warm stream of imagination in us and allows unexpected possibilities to well up. This activity connects us with something new and oriented to the future streaming toward us. Our active hands bring the energy of will into our imagining and visualizing and teach our seeing to become active looking that reaches out into and grasps the world. Our hands making music bring will into our hearing and teach our ears to actively listen to the world. Hands-on activity supports visual learning, auditory learning and legitimizes the deep experiences of the kinesthetic learner in the repertoire of learning modes. There are many different ways and images to describe how the will of the spirit ego uses our hands to energize our human faculties and actualize itself. We can experience the space in and around our hands—our hand space —as a living, flowing womb space in which spirit forms are born into matter mediated by the moving element of life in physical reality. Or expressed in modern, more mechanistic terms, through our moving antenna-like fingers and satellite dish-like palms we capture incoming star patterns from the spirit world and participate in an ongoing creation. Our hands bring spirit movement into matter, freeze it and fix it there for a time.

Whatever images we use to describe this remarkable spiritual activity, it is in the essential nature of our spirit-permeated hands to want to continuously make the invisible spirit world visible. And that has always been the main mission of what culture has called Art.

Hand, Heart, Head

And so we come back to where we started: Art as education, education as an art: *Children you have two hands and are going to do and work and learn with them:* Waldorf education as an education of the will and manual intelligence, an action education, a spirit education, an education that enables us to do what we need to do. The word art, or in German *Kunst,* actually means "to be able." Waldorf education is an *I am able education*, an enabler, an enabling education as Waldorf graduates have described it. Through the magic of the artistic way of working, Waldorf education thereby also becomes an *I am human education*, a humanizer, a human-making education which connects us with our true humanity and true human center out beyond our finger tips and into the world. Steiner very simply and beautifully describes this connection in terms of everyday school activities, when he says

> Even [first and second graders] as miniature sculptors or painters…, [whenever they put their being into handling clay (Ton),[or] wood, or paints] can begin to have the experience that human nature does not end at the fingertips,…., but flows out into the world…. In these very interactions with materials, children grow, learning to perceive how closely the human being is interwoven with the fabric of the universe.

Rudolf Steiner is said to have reflected before his death on the first pioneering years of Waldorf education and expressed the wish to turn it around 180 degrees into the artistic. People often wonder and discuss what he meant. For me a simple step in that direction is to start saying and thinking *HANDS, heart and head*. Why does the head always have to get first billing on our bumper stickers? Let us have affirmative action for the hands in our consciousness.

A practical step in lesson planning is to evaluate each subject with this question in mind: In what ways does this particular subject, for which I am now preparing, lend itself to a more fully experiential, hands-on, approach; an approach that will charge the learning process with deep feeling, directly engage as many senses as possible and fire the will? Going in this direction, of course, most often proves to be messier, more involved and more" inconvenient" than a simple "academic pencil and paper approach" but ultimately we know it fosters real life changing capacities and builds intelligence. For me this approach entails finding ways for students to exercise what can be called the feeling-will so that they can become so physically and emotionally involved in what they are doing that they lose track of time. And watch out! You as teachers might also lose track of time!

Another valuable question to ask *regularly* as part of your review is : What has each child made today? Mental images? Conversation? Words on paper? A drawing or painting? Hand-braided knots translated afterwards into geometric formdrawing? Vigorous body movements in a skit or dance or game ? A playful sword fighting or wrestling practice in drama? Modeling a huge castle with magnificent towers and parapets? Making the classroom clean and tidy with our hands? What have the children made and really done today? And when were there moments in which they were warmly absorbed with their feeling will?

Sculptural modeling, of course, is one of those more "will-full" and messier options… but today's children in my experience are longing for teachers who get out the good mother earth clay on a regular basis and let hands speak and think and hand-storm the forms of the universe. Children especially love large group projects. You can check out my book on modeling for some concrete ideas.

In the end, however, the crucial catalyst for me is hand awareness. We all know that we have two hands but are we really aware of the spirit potential of what lies miraculously right in front of us every day–these two selfless helpers of the spirit? Frank Wilson admits that even he, as a neurological hand specialist, had not been really aware of his own hands for most of his career until it hit him one day. He woke up to his hands and plunged into discovering how to do new things with them including teaching himself piano at a mature age. Our hands are what the artist/scientist Goethe called an open secret, a secret right under our noses. And so in the coming three Antioch weeks, as you model clay, or sculpt airspace with your hands in eurythmy, or use your hands in many different ways, you might well pay more attention to what these two old friends are really doing right in front of you. And I hope that some of these thoughts today have served in some way to re-introduce these two precious companions to you. Thank you very much for your attention.

Imprinting spirit on the physical

"We work and create in the physical world as *spiritual* beings. What we imprint on physical forms, materials and forces, our spirits think out (*ersinnen*) and form out (*ausbilden*). Our task as messengers of the spiritual world is to incorporate the spirit into the material world. (Rudolf Steiner, *Theosophy*)

As much modeling as possible

"Sculptural modeling should be practiced [with students] as much as possible." (Rudolf Steiner, A *Modern Art of Education*)

Immersion into nature's forces

"[In sculpture] what you depict you create not through mere imitation of a model, but by immersing yourself into the forces out of which nature herself has formed and created…" (Rudolf Steiner, *Der Dornacher Bau)*

God sculpturally forms nature

"'God geometrizes' – this expression is attributed to Plato; creative Nature 'imaginates' (*imaginiert*), she thinks in images' – this saying is one of Steiner's…In the final analysis, there is no difference since the geometrizing God of Plato sculpturally models (*plastiziert*) Nature just as a geometrician forms his ideal constructions: through His creative *Phantasie,* His power of imagination (*Imaginationskraft*). Whether we observe the shape of a plant or human being, we are always looking at a revelation of 'imaginating' (*imaginierend*) Nature." (Lorenzo Ravagli)

Surprising ideas and imagination activated

"There are people who exclaim, 'Oh [in modeling] you need so much imagination!' But the opposite is true; you get ideas in the process of working which you never had before. Powers of imagination are activated and unfold by themselves. The soft formless clay is a willing helper in your effort. (Michael Martin, Waldorf educator and artist)

Child both shaped and shaper

"Nature works as artist in shaping a child; the child herself in turn becomes a shaper of things. When the child does not have the opportunity to actively form things around her, her life forces and creative joy are lamed leading to a sluggish digestion and listlessness. If the natural energy for activity cannot express itself in a healthy manner, it bottles up in the body and becomes the cause of nervous restlessness." (Caroline Heydebrand, Founding Waldorf Teacher)

Enlivening of fundamental senses

"In a beautiful way sculptural modeling enlivens all four of the child's lower senses… The sense of sight is strongly de-emphasized. It is wonderful at times even to model blindfolded. The sense of touch becomes more active as the hand continuously feels the surfaces and bumps. With our mobile hands, the sense of movement perceives all these surfaces, contours and angles. The sense of balance is active in weighing and aiming for an artistic unity and balance, even when a piece does not involve symmetry. All sculptural modeling is a living organic process of creating…The sense of life is intensively involved in sculptural activity." (Willi Aeppli, Swiss educator)

Forming=Living !
"To create forms means: to live!" (Matisse)

Metamorphosis=Key
A shape is a mobile, changing (*werdendes*), and passing (*vergehendes*) phenomenon. The knowledge of shapes is one of transformation (*Verwandlung*). Metamorphosis is the key to all the kingdoms of nature." (Goethe)

Water-like thinking grasps the arising of forms
"The [sculptural] modeler is…the human maker whose activity arises from an imagination of water… Through the imagination of water and the experience of soft substance, what is grasped is the rhythmic arising of form, the activity of formation rather than the formed results of that activity… Like water, imaginative thought is sufficiently plastic and sensitive to take on the forms of another being…Water thinking 'runs through' the forms of the leaf, the flower, then flows into the forms of the fruit and seed. With our exact imagination we enter into the leaf shapes and move between them, through their sequence of growth… In Water thinking, we learn to "dwell" imaginatively in the form of living beings with a thinking that participates rather than remains as the external observer."
(Nigel Hoffman, biologist)

Protean power of sculptural thinking
"…A certain aspect or capacity of the feeling life is intensified and heightened into an organ of cognition. In relation to water thinking this is the protean power of feeling, its character of continuity and transformation. It is the feeling with which the sculptor forms his works. This is what allows feeling to mold itself to the fluid, metamorphosing form of another being, and it is by virtue of this plasticity that we can speak of Imagination as a 'sculptural thinking.' " (Nigel Hoffman*)*

Releasing gesture
"The sculptor shapes forms which the eye sees but weakly… It is a direct transfer of the sense of touch into the sense of sight that the sculptor serves. The sculptor attempts to release into gesture the static (*ruhige*) form which is otherwise solely an object of the one-sided perspective of the eye. (Rudolf Steiner, *Kunst und Kunsterkenntnis*)

Plasticizing
"Modeling as a creative activity should have another more appropriate name 'plasticizing.' The term means: 'the capacity for changing form' – an ability one does not acquire by 'copying models' i.e. modeling." (Anke Clausen and Martin Riedel, Waldorf educators and artists)

Hollows and bumps
"Sculpture is the knowledge of hollows and bumps." (Rodin)

Life creates out of convexity, roundness
"What are the formative forces? Those forces that create out of roundness stand closest to our experience; these are the etheric forces, which we know as growth forces in the plant. They unite everywhere with the element of that which is watery and streaming, flowing

continually, shaping rhythmically. Things that resist these forces in running water [such as river stones] are transformed into round, convex forms… The archetypal manifestation of the spherical tendency when it comes to rest is the raindrop. (Michael Martin)

Drying air hollows inner concave forms
"The drying air consumes all growth. The air is creative in the hollowing out of substance, opening forms to space, and creating inner spaces. Through this kind of formative force there arises the [concave, cup-like] blossom of plants. This force shapes a multitude of different hollow, concave forms." (Michael Martin)

Sphere as archetypal
 "The Creator made the world in the form of a sphere, round…the most perfect…of all figures. This he finished off, making the surface smooth . . . (Plato, *Timaeus*)

 "The sight of a sphere gives us inner peace… It rests in itself; and it needs only the smallest surface to stand on . . . "(Michael Martin)

Modeling grasps the life forces
"We understand the etheric life body of formative forces when we enter the sculptural modeling and shaping process (*plastisches Gestalten*), when we know how a curve or an angle grows from inner forces. We cannot understand the etheric life body in terms of ordinary laws, but through the experience of the hand–the spirit-permeated hand." (Rudolf Steiner)

Into the fingertips
"What use is nature shining before your eyes, What use are all those art works around you, If creative power does not lovingly fill your soul

And flow into your finger tips to shape new works of beauty." (Goethe)

The human body is a molded river
"Many of the movements and forms we… [see] in water reappear as body and movement in the lower water animals…jellyfish… sea-stars, sea urchins, snails and many shells. 'The resting state originates in movement.' (Novalis, *Aphorism*) There is no doubt that our body is a molded river." (Theodor Schwenk, water researcher, author of *Sensitive Chaos*)

Sculptural thinking needed to create a better world
"We need sculpture and sculptural thinking. I would like to see it applied to biomechanics, to government and social structures and so on. I do not mean in the sense of dictating how the structures should be but rather to utilize an analysis of form and connect this with ideals and even moral imperatives. I can imagine the work of artists becoming more an integral part of the form of social-political institutions, pedagogical practice, agriculture, forestry, ecology in general, nutrition, human relations, justice and the resolution of conflicts. I actually believe that sculpture more than any other artistic or cultural activity is an instrument to create a better world." (Tony Cragg, contemporary British sculptor)

Modern art jolts us out of mental habits
"We only 'see' a fraction of what is before our eyes. Most of the time we see, hear, feel, taste, and smell what our brains *expect* rather than the sensations themselves. Much modern art tries to shock or surprise us out of these image-clouding mental habits into *seeing* more purely with the mind's eye, uncluttered by well-worn categories and labels. When we cultivate imagery and

visualization in the mind's eye, we use parts of our brain that are not triggered by verbal thoughts." (Ian Robertson, Professor of Psychology, Director of the Institute of Neuroscience at Trinity College, Dublin)

HENRY MOORE

Mystery behind familiar objects

"As a sculptor, I am trying to expand people's vision, to see the outer dimensions, the mystery behind familiar objects. When I create a sculpture, I try to do it from inside outwards, to imbue life."

"Sculpture should always at first sight have some obscurities, and further meanings. People should want to go on looking and thinking…"

Discovering the whole time

"Being a sculptor means…you must be discovering the whole time. A sculptor wants to know what a thing is like from on top and from beneath—a bird's eye view and a worm's view. It's infinite. "

Obsessed

"I am a sculptor because I am obsessed with the shapes of things."

A variety of shapes

"There is in nature a limitless variety of shapes and rhythms…from which the sculptor can enlarge his form-knowledge experience…"

Form from nature for its own sake

"In my collection of found objects in my studio—stones, pebbles, bones, pieces of wood—for me they are all interesting shapes though some may find them exaggerated or distorted…You don't want a perfect ball or perfect square because there is no surprise… What I have tried to do is to evaluate and appreciate form for its own sake…The older you are, the more observant you are of… nature and forms; and the more easily can you invent. But it has to come from somewhere in the beginning, from reality, nature. Space, distance, landscape, plants, pebbles, rocks, bones, all excite me and give me ideas. "

What the artist makes of his observations

"Nature produces the most amazing varieties of shapes, patterns, and rhythms… Observation enlarges the sculptor's vision. But merely to copy nature is no better than copying anything else. It is what the artist makes of his observations by giving expression to his personal vision and from his study of the laws of balance, rhythm, construction, growth, the attraction and repulsion of gravity – it is how he applies this to all of his work that is important…I am trying to add to people's understanding of life and nature, to help them to open their eyes and to be sensitive. Nature is inexhaustible."

Form blindness

"There are many more 'form-blind' people than there are color blind…The sensitive observer of sculptures must learn to experience form purely as form and not as a description or memory of some particular thing. He must, for example, perceive an egg as a basic, pure form fully independent of its significance . . . as something from which a chick hatches."

Penetration into reality and life

"[A sculptural] work…may be a penetration into reality . . . The provision of pleasant shapes and colors in a pleasing combination [is] not a decoration to life, but an expression of the significance of life, a stimulation to greater effort in living."

"Abstract" closer to reality

"[People] think that abstraction means getting away from reality and it means precisely the opposite —that you are getting closer to it, away from a visual interpretation but nearer to an emotional understanding. When I say that I am being abstract, I mean that I am trying to consider but not simply copy nature, and that I am taking account of the material I am using and the idea that I wish to release from the material."

Life force from within

"[In] the best Greek sculpture [the artists] knew what was beneath the surface, so they were able to release the life force which gave an added strength and vitality to their work. "

"I would like to think my sculpture has…a force,…a strength,…a life,…a vitality from inside it, so that you have a sense that the form is pressing from inside trying to burst… trying to make itself come to a shape from inside itself…"

MORE QUOTES BY OTHERS:

Sculptural modeling's sun-life center in the heart

"Just as the peripheral life forces of the earth have their center in the sun so do our sculpting limbs-arms-hands have their center in the heart…The life center of the forming movements, the heart, [is] a sun within us shining on the earthen sphere. And the clay sphere does warm up gradually." (Armin Husemann)

"Our hands grasp the unformed clay from outside, pressing it, shifting and turning it about. They do to the clay sphere what the cosmic etheric forces do to the earth from the cosmic periphery. From all sides, from everywhere, the fingers take hold of the evolving sphere…" (Armin Husemann)

Become quick and flexible as nature

"When we study forms, especially organic ones, nowhere do we find permanence, nowhere rest or completion. Everything is in ceaseless flow. For in nature no sooner has something formed than it is immediately transformed "If we wish to arrive at some living perception of nature, we ourselves must remain as quick and flexible as nature and follow the example she gives…" (Goethe)

Breathing soul hollows, wears out

"The sphere is the fundamental form into which the soul works, hollowing it out. The soul presses into and consumes the round form. The cause of this lies in the capacity of the soul to carry waking consciousness in the human being. Consciousness destroys the life forces of the etheric. The result is tiredness. If our day consciousness went on and on [uninterrupted by sleep], our physical health would degenerate." (Michael Martin)

Reading soul's hollow forms

"Round, convex forms are relatively easy to 'read' in Nature…It is more difficult to discern the [soul astral] forces shaping hollow, concave forms because they work from the periphery and produce a whole range of very different forms such as the star-like flower blossom cup (calyx), the dried out cones of conifers…; In animals and in humans they conceal themselves in the concave, pocket forms of organs. Still more challenging…is the human form as expression of the spirit I…We find the 'I' revealed not in any one form but in a harmony of forms…" (Michael Martin)

Hands naturally form spherical

"Indeed, on our entire body we do not find

one single straight surface…Our hands are not formed out of flat surfaces. If we want to choose and work on a form that corresponds to the quality of our human form, it must be round. When we behold the inside surfaces of our hands…[we see] that together they form a round bowl and lend themselves most naturally to forming a sphere out of clay! (Michael Martin)

Spheres float in the universe
"But how should we put…a [sphere] form down? It has no base, no up, no right or left? Its sole relationship to space is 'inner' and 'outer.' Are spheres somewhat strangers on the earth in contrast to other objects that have a clear up and down? We come to the conclusion: a sphere has to float in space and continually move and circle around to be true to the nature of its form. That is what the planets and their moons do along their paths in the universe." (Michael Martin)

"The sight of a sphere gives us inner peace… It rests in itself; and it needs only the smallest surface to stand on…" (Michael Martin)

Thinking = spiritual grasping and touching of objects
"By practicing [certain modeling] exercises…a person develops the eye of the spirit and the ear of the spirit. One can then see how thinking, which is primarily an activity of the etheric body, is really a 'spiritual grasping' or 'spiritual touching of the objects around us." (Steiner, *Roots of Education*, Lecture II)

Laboratory of all forms and masterbuilders
"[The Spirit Land] is where the archetypes of things arise…This is the laboratory of the Cosmos wherein all forms are contained, whence creation has proceeded; it is the home of the Ideas of Plato, the 'Realm of

the Mothers' of which Goethe speaks in Faust (Rudolf Steiner, *Esoteric Cosmology,* Lect.12)

"Physical things and beings are copies or imitations of their Archetypes…In the spiritual world everything is in constant activity, constant motion, constant creation… The archetypes are creative beings (*schaffende Wesenheiten*), the master builders of everything that comes into existence in the physical and soul worlds…Their forms change quickly, and each archetype has the potential to assume countless specific forms. It is as if the specialized forms well up out of them – one form has hardly been created before its archetype is ready to let the next one pour out….Archetypes do not work alone, but stand in closer or more distant relationship to each other. One archetype may need the help of the other to do its creating, and often innumerable archetypes work together so that some particular being can come to life in the soul world or the physical world…" (Rudolf Steiner, *Theosophy*)

Rodin on Sculptural Surfaces
"… [Rodin] kept coming back to beauty which is everywhere for him who rightly understands and wants it, to things, to the life of these things… He detaches [the shape] from them, makes it, after he has learned from them, into an independent thing, that is, into sculpture, into a plastic work of art. For this reason, a piece of arm and leg and body is for him a whole, an entity, because he no longer thinks of arm, leg, body…The following was extraordinarily illuminating in this respect. …[His little daughter] brought the shell of a small snail she had found in the gravel…He took it in his hand, smiled, admired it, examined it and said suddenly: 'It is a question for me, that is, for the

sculptor par excellence, of seeing or studying
not the colors or the contours but that which
constitutes the plastic surfaces. The character
of these, whether they are rough or smooth,
shiny or dull (not in color but in character!).
This little snail recalls the greatest works of
Greek art: it has the same simplicity, the same
smoothness, the same inner radiance, the
same cheerful and festive sort of surface . . . "
(from Rodin's personal secretary Rilke's Letter
to his Sister Clara, 9.5.1902)

Quotations and Excerpts
Relating to the Significance of Hand Activity

See additional quotes in Learning about the World through Modeling.

The brain as an extension of the hand into our soul

"The hand has been called an extension of the brain, an outer brain and a mirror of the soul. Much of our personality and identity is contained in gestures and movements of the hands. The hand reflects our mind, expressing our innermost thoughts and wishes. With our hands we communicate with people. The hands plead, bless and love; they express hope, despair, disgust and hatred. They welcome, caress and punish…Our sense of touch lets us discover the true character of what the eye sees – *seeing is believing, but touching is understanding*. The hand 'sees' in the dark and the sense of touch can even substitute for the loss of other senses…Representation of the hand takes up a large area of the brain, and this area expands as sensory inflow and hand activity increase – yes, the hand shapes the brain. Perhaps we can even regard the brain as an extension of the hand into our soul." (Goran Lundborg, *The Hand and Brain*, London: Springer, 2014, vii)

The hand teaches the head

"Steiner's initial work-oriented pedagogical principle that the hand teaches the head is profoundly confirmed and very actual today." (Hans Hunzel, Waldorf educator)

Hands' infinite movements

"There is indeed no other organ possessed by a living being that can carry out so many movements as does the human hand." (M. Jeannerod, neurophysiologist, *Encyclopedia of Psychology,* "Psychomotorics)

Lesson content lives itself out in hands and forms

"Because of the artistic handling of the lessons, the children have been inwardly gripped by what they are doing. It enters their will, not only their thoughts and heads. And we can, therefore, see, as they concentrate on their work, that this continues to live in their hands. The forms change according to the content in our lessons. It lives itself out in forms. We can see in the form the children produce what they experienced in the previous main lesson, because their lesson ought to enter and grasp the whole of the human being." (Rudolf Steiner, *Spiritual Ground of Education*, Lecture VIII)

"…[The human being] thinks with her entire body." (Steiner, *Curriculum Lecture* in *Discussions with Teachers*)

Spirit-permeated hand grasps life

"We understand the etheric body of formative life forces when we enter the shaping process, when we know how a curve or an angle grows from inner forces. We cannot understand the etheric life body in terms of ordinary laws, but through the experience of the hand—the spirit-permeated hand. Thus there should be no teacher training without activities in the areas of modeling or sculpture, an activity which arises from the inner human being." (Steiner, *The Essentials of Education*, Lecture III)

Hand reaches into and splashes about spirit

"In purposeful activity we do not just splash about in the spirit; rather, because we act purposefully, we slowly draw the spirit in. When we reach out our hand to purposeful work, we connect ourselves with the spirit." (Steiner, *Foundations of Human Experience*, Lecture XIII)

Hand as our most spiritual part

"If you look at the palms of your hands and the soles of your feet, you will see that a kind of pressure continuously exists that is the same as the pressure from inside upon your forehead, only in the opposite direction. If you hold the palm of your hand up to the world, or place the sole of your foot upon the ground, the same thing streams in through your palm or your sole as streams from inside against your forehead…You can see that the spirit-soul is a stream that flows through the human being…The human limbs extending out beyond the torso are really the most spiritual part of the human being because in the limbs the process of creating matter occurs the least. The metabolic processes the abdomen and chest send into the limbs are all that make our limbs material. Our limbs are spiritual to a very high degree, and as they move, they consume our body. (Steiner, *Foundations of Human Experience,* Lecture XIII)

Fingers think in forms

"One's head suddenly becomes empty. Thoughts leave you and something begins to stir in other parts of your being. Namely, one's arms and fingers begin to become tools of thoughts, but the thoughts now live in forms. And one has become a modeler, sculptor." (Steiner, *The Mission of the Arts*)

"Our etheric hands are real spirit organs in the elemental world or etheric body. A much more intuitive, spiritual activity is carried out through these etheric organs which lie at the basis of the hands. These etheric organs lead over into the world of spirit. One could paradoxically say: The human brain is the most unsuitable organ of perception for the world; the hands – taken etherically– are much more significant and adept organs of knowledge. (Steiner, *On the History of the Esoteric School*)

Hands radiate life

The hands are actually wondrously different from all other parts of the body…From the fingers shine forth radiant formations of the etheric body, which glimmer, dim, then sparkle again into space. The fingers of a joyful person radiate differently from a sad one… The back of the hand shines differently from the inner surface of the hand…indeed the hand with its etheric and astral parts is a wondrous formation. (Steiner, *Exkurse in das Gebiet des Markusevangeliums*)

Hands understand the unity of things

"The density of nerve endings in our fingertips is enormous. Their discrimination is almost as good as that of our eyes. If we do not use our fingers, if in childhood we become 'finger-blind,' this rich network of nerves is impoverished, which represents a huge loss to the brain and thwarts the individual's all-around development… If we neglect to develop and train our children's fingers and the creative formbuilding capacity of their hand muscles, then we neglect to develop their understanding of the unity of things; we thwart their aesthetic and creative powers." (Matti Bergstrom, Swedish neurophysiologist)

Hands sculpt the soul

"Every action of the hand and the eye sculpts the soul. Piaget called the process accommodation, the development of new cognitive structures." (Arthur Zajonc, professor of physics)

Hands teach our thinking to have plasticity

"The movements of the fingers are to a great extent the teachers of the elasticity of our thinking." (*Mystery of the Universe*, Lecture IX).

Hand as mirror of the brain

"The hand is a mirror of the brain; therefore there can be no such combination as dexterous hands and clumsy brains." (John Napier, MD, hand specialist and professor of anthropology, University of Chicago)

Hands contribute to healthy discernment

"The faculty of judgment is indeed essentially enhanced by the activity of the hands."(Steiner, *Education for Adolescence*, Lecture 2)

Hands as thought organs

"The hands are thought organs (*Gedankenorgane*) just as the etheric part of the head is…[In the hands] it is a matter of something very fine, subtle: a very weak, scarcely glimmering thinking developed by the human being and coming to expression in artistic activity…The hands are a thought organ for destiny…In the hands, which develop an unconscious thinking, destiny is

being thought." (Steiner, *Erdensterben und Weltenleben*)

Thinking with our hands

"We know nothing of our destiny because we always think only with that most superficial of organs, the brain. The moment we begin to think with our fingers – and just with our fingers and toes we can think much more brightly than with the nerves of the head –…our thoughts are the thoughts of our destiny. When we do not merely grasp with our hand but think with it …we follow our destiny…when we allow [another person's] hands to make an impression on us, so that we interpret these hands and think that in every movement of the fingers, there lie wonderful revelations of the human being's inner nature. Yet that is only the smallest part of what moves when [he]walks, or takes hold of something with his hand, or just moves his fingers. For it is the human being's whole moral nature which moves; his destiny moves with him; everything that he is as a spiritual being…After the human being has passed through the gate of death, .. spiritual beings, together with[him] develop out of the form he had in his previous earthly life what will be his form in his next life…This spirit form will finally connect with the [new] embryo in physical life. But in the spiritual world feet and legs [of the previous life]are transformed into jawbones, while arms and hands are transformed into cheekbones . . . this metamorphosis is . . .most wonderful." (Steiner, *Man as Symphony of the Creative Word*, Lecture 12)

Hands as organs of intuition

"The etheric organs expressed in the hands and their functions, work far more intuitively, more spiritually, and perform a far higher task than is accomplished by the etheric brain …The hands, or the spiritual basis of the hands, are far more interesting and significant organs for gaining knowledge of the world, and are certainly far more skillful organs than the brain…. The etheric basis of the hands is connected with the activity of the lotus flower (chakra) in the region of the heart… " (Steiner, *Initiation, Eternity and the Passing Moment*, Lecture II)

Hands as etheric eyes and etheric speakers

"Our arms [with hands are] more or less the outer representatives for etheric eyes." (Steiner, *Cosmosophy* II)

"The etheric body does not speak with the mouth, but with the limbs [i.e. hands, arms, legs]." (Steiner, *Eurythmie als sichtbarer Gesang*)

Young humans build brain by using hands

"In the formative years of each human being, the hands need to recapitulate and play their crucial evolutionary role designing and building significant elements of our neural circuitry and capacities." (Frank Wilson, Neurologist, Medical Director of the Ostwald Health Program University of California, author of *The Hand*)

20 million years for the hand to evolve

"The human hand has been on the evolutionary production line for at least 20 million years." (John Napier, MD., Hand Specialist)

Hands as antennae

"The hand is the symbol of our being human. The fingers…grope…towards new realms [of the]…unknown, the uncertain…[as]a symbol of a longing and a penetration into the mysteries of the world of spirit. Sometimes the hands and above all the fingers on them appear like antennae…" (Ursula Mangoldt, author of *Schicksal in der Hand*)

Hands ray out

"In contrast to the closedness of the head, the hands unfold and ray out…directed to the world and in the final analysis to the entire universe." (Stefan Leber, *Kommentar zu Allgemeine Menschenkunde* III.)

Hands seeing, acting, encountering in past, future and present

"In groping/touching there is a kind of seeing…In the actions (*Handlungen*), which the hands carry out, lie the element of the future. In so far as we can speak of a 'seeing' with the hands, they belong to the head. In action they belong to the world of the feet [which lead us on our path of destiny into the future]. In an encounter they belong to the social life . . . [The hands] represent the whole human being in past (thinking), future (willing) and present (feeling) through observation, action, and encounter. (L.F.C. Mees, MD, author of *Secrets of the Skeleton*.)

Thumb opposition and precision grip as hallmarks of human kind

"Perhaps the most important movement of the human hand is opposition…One cannot emphasize enough the importance of finger-thumb opposition for human emergence… It promoted the adoption of upright posture and bi-pedal walking, tool-using and tool-making that, in turn, led to enlargement of the brain through a positive feedback mechanism. (John Napier, MD, hand specialist)

"Precision and power grips in their fullest expression are hallmarks of human kind." (Napier)

"[The] shorter thumb [of the anthropoid apes] makes the precision grip impossible. [They]cannot bring the inner sides of the upper phalanges of their thumbs and fingers together. Anthropoid apes generally use a type of pseudo-precision grip, holding the object between the thumb and the side of the index finger in the grip people use to hold playing cards. Only the very ends of these fingers meet, which does not allow for a secure and precise grip." (Jan Verhulst, biologist)

Thumb proves God's existence

"In absence of any other proof, the thumb alone would convince me of God's existence." (Sir Isaac Newton)

The human hand "specializes in nonspecialization"

"It displays an exceptional degree of primitiveness – an astonishing conclusion if we consider that it is capable of specialized movements and exceptional sensitivity, precision, subtlety and expressiveness." (John Napier, MD)

The intelligence of the hands

from E.M. Kranich, "Die Intelligenz der Haende," in *Erziehungskunst*, May 2002, Number 5, 515-21, translation by A.A.)

"What differentiates the human hand from similar appendages in the animal kingdom is above all the **position of the thumb** in relation to the other fingers and its incomparable mobility. The human being can cause the thumb and fingers to interact with each other in all sorts of ways to grip large and small objects…When one holds an object in the hand…the thumb and the fingers oppose each other with a pressure; this will activity in the thumb and that in the fingers mutually act on one another. Through this interaction, **the human being experiences himself** when he grips an object. He takes the object up into his experience of self; he connects himself as I-Being with the objects and tools he works with. **The hand is a member of the**

human ego-organization, which comes to expression most comprehensively in the vertical posture of the human being. The **free mobility of the human arms and hands is intimately related to this upright position**; it is unthinkable without this.

"There is not only an **intelligence** of the head, but also one **of the hands and fingers**. This 'physical-kinesthetic intelligence' is one of the several important intelligences identified by Howard Gardner…When a child learns [a skill, for example such as knitting] in handwork lessons, very specific processes occur between the brain and the hands…:the child forms a mental picture of the movement in certain regions of the front of the brain in the so-called premotor and supplementary motor cortex. Research has shown that picturing such an activity causes blood to surge into this area…These brain areas responsible for especially differentiated movements are strikingly large and include the hand and finger areas. When a child decides to use her hands, her mental picture of the activity penetrates from the supplementary motor region over the hand and finger areas of the precentral brain convolution through a nerve (Tractus corticospinalis) into the corresponding section of the spine and from there through further nerve pathways into the muscles of the hands and fingers. Here the child's will to move the hands and fingers ignites …

"Simultaneously, these movements exert an influence on the brain…From the senses of touch and movement, impulses travel back along certain nerve pathways to the brain and into the convolution just behind the central groove gyrus postcentralis)… Research of the past decades has discovered how extremely dynamic the influence of hand and fingers is on the brain …A review of these findings leads to the conclusion that the brain areas involving the hands and fingers of children are enlarged as a result of crocheting, knitting and other fine motor hand skills…and that the intelligence of hand and finger exerts an influence on and enrichment of the brain and the thinking process.

"The intelligence of the hands and fingers works into the brain by expanding the area of the postcentral field which] is connected to further regions of the brain – especially to certain regions of the parietal lobe, the temporal lobe, and also the frontal cortex. These are the physical networks for quite differentiated mental picturing and thinking processes. The frontal cortex amongst other things is the organ for the comprehension of complex mental connections. One can conclude that *the* intelligence of the hands works over the motor cortex (gyrus postcentralis) into these regions of the brain and influences how one forms mental pictures and thoughts.

"What does this mean in concrete terms?:… [when a child knits, for example,] there arises a lawful web of interconnections as she directs the movements of her hands and fingers: one element – the next stitch –'inwardly' connects to the previous one because the new stitch is pulled through the old one. The intelligence involved in knitting lives in extremely dexterous fine motor movements . . . and exerts an influence on the thinking process . . . "

Seed-like hands created in the image of the archetypes

"We have fingers and toes because we do not allow our limbs to over develop (*auswachsen*) . . . If they did, they would not just be covered with fingernails but completely stiffened. By **holding our limbs back**, we thereby are able to develop our will in them… The will pole of the human being is an organic formation that has not come to an end…[and remains **germinal**], **an embryo capable of further development**…We have at the ends of our limbs what are like germinal seeds (*Keime*)." (Steiner, *Cosmosophy* II)

"…[In the Spirit land] the archetypes lie ready… like **germinal seed points** of life, waiting to assume the various forms of thought beings. When these seed points are projected to the lower regions, they immediately well up and manifest in the most varied forms (*Gestalten*). The ideas through which the human spirit appears creatively in the physical world are pale reflections or shadows of these **'seed thought beings'** of the higher spiritual world …We must imagine these 'seed thought beings' as composite in nature." (Steiner, *Theosophy*, 130)

LIST OF EXERCISES

THE PROTEUS EXERCISE

SERIES ONE
1. Sphere
2. Ovoid
3. Bumpy
4. Little Hollow
5. Hand Hollow
6. Twins
7. Stretcher
8. Long Stretcher
9. Little Curl
10. Spiral Curl
11. Pointer
12. Curved Pointer
13. Magic Mirror
14. Roll Up and Oval Mirror
15. Center and Edge
16. Raying from Center
17. Widening and Pointing
18. Flat and Curved
19. Curled Up Beside Each Other
20. One Two Three
21. Crescent
22. Wavy and Zigzag
23. Sand Table
24. Sphere on Two Disks
25. Magic Rescuing Ring
26. Straight and Curved

SERIES TWO
1. Flat Bottom Bump
2. Twosome
3. Lopsided Twosome
4. Very Long Spiral Pointer
5. Double Pointer
6. Deep Hollow
7. Double Hollow
8. Double Curve
9. Deep Double Curve
10. Two Meets Three
11. Brother and Sister
12. Triangular Hollow
13. Hollow Cone
14. Crouching Form
15. Widening and Narrowing
16. Two Harmony Friends

17. a + b Three Friends
18. Mirror Forms
19. Pinching a Pentagon
20. Rising Spiral
21. Twin Hollows
22. Two Sides Separated
23. Ring Around a Ring

SERIES THREE
1. Widening and Narrowing
2. Threesome with Big Middle
3. Heart Shape
4. Equal-sided Triangle
5. Magic Square
6. Twist Sideways
7. Hollow Sphere
8. Spiraling Up
9. Narrow Spiral
10. Twister
11. Deepening Hollows
12. Hidden Space
13. Cube
14. Three Four Five Stretchers
15. Lifting and Sinking
16. Disks
17. Hiding in a Hollow
18. Long Hollow with Round
19. Nestling
20. Huddling in Friendship
21. Three Big Protect Little
22. Secret Huddle
23. Two Hug
24. Spiraling Up a Cone
25. Four Crevices – Four Triangles

SERIES FOUR
1. Double Twist
2. Weaving Figure-eight
3. Meandering
4. Hollowed Sphere to Ring
5. Hollow Front and Back
6. Sphere to Cube
7. Full to Flat
8. Fractioned
9. Roll Over
10. Sharp Curving
11. Soft Curving

12. Entrance Between Two Hollows
13. Full of Life and Drying Out
14. Big Protect a Little
15. Lying, Crouching, Standing
16. Vertical and Horizontal
17. Stretching Out
18. Turning
19. Alert
20. Darting
21. Gobbling
22. Sleeping and Waking

SERIES FIVE
1. Folding Ovals
2. Curves and Points
3. Curling Edge
4. Pod-like Seed-like
5. Bud-like Spiraling
6. Branching
7. Opening
8. Four Curved Edges
9. Hollow Cone and Enclosing Cross
10. Three Hold One
11. Three Round on Three Flat
12. Three and Fourfold Hollows
13. Contracting Expanding
14. Spiraling Up
15. Mistletoe-like
16. Coming Together Falling Apart
17. Hive-like
18. Curved Side by Side
19. Ionic Spirals
20. Disk in Crescent
21. Labyrinth
22. Pyramidal Form
23. Mistletoe-like

SERIES SIX
1. Tetrahedron Compared
2. Tetrahedron Moves
3. Arches
4. Entries
5. Spanning
6. Weaving Three
7. Raised Concavity
8. Rounded Bottom Rises to Top
9. Rounded Pointed Straightness
10. Hexagon
11. Parallel Shifting
12. Shell-like
13. Concave Spiral

14. Convex Spiral
15. Upright Convex to Through-Holes
16. River Bed-like
17. Building a Landscape
18. Space Between
19. Hollows Wrapping
20. Wrap Around
21. Front and Back

THE SOCIAL PROTEUS EXERCISE

SERIES SEVEN
1. Budding Opening
2. Inner Space
3. Bulging Flattening Hollowing
4. Straight to Curved
5. Rising Hollows
6. Bottom, Middle, Top-Heavy
7. Rounded and Angular Landscape
8. Lung-like
9. Saddle Forms
10. Convex Concave Mirroring
11. Figure-eight Twist
12. Weaving S-Form
13. Flaming Up and Water Worn
14. Raised Inner Space
15. Flight
16. Octahedron
17. Hull

SERIES EIGHT
1. Uprights
2. Pushing Forward
3. Welcoming Embracing Forms
4. Three Piggybacking Forms
5. Rising Piggyback
6. Two-Lobe Concavity
7. Sphere into Concavity
8. Twirling
9. Mirror Blades
10. Hearing's Dancing Limb
11. Hearing Sharp Sound
12. Torso-Like Forms
13. Smile and Frown
14. Holder Design
15. Vase Design
16. Car Design
17. Eights within Eight
18. Hip-like Twisting
19. Giving and Receiving
20. Three Impressings
21. Convex Falling into Concave

SERIES NINE: PLATONIC SOLIDS
1. Tetrahedron
2. Octahedron
3. Cube
4. Icosahedron
5. Dodecahedron

SERIES TEN: EMBRYOGENESIS
1. Sphere
2. Spiral
3. Two-, Four-, Eight-Divisions
4. Morula
5. Blastula
6. Nesting
7. Leaf-like Disk
8. Neurula: Seedling-like
9. Serpent-like
10. Mammal-like
11. Emerging Human

SERIES ELEVEN: NATURE FORMS
Inspired by the form language of the examples of nature forms in this Series – or better still, ones from your own knowledge and experience – create new forms in clay.

SERIES TWELVE: MODERN SCULPTURE
Inspired by the form language of the examples of modern sculptures, create new forms in clay.

SERIES THIRTEEN: POETRY
Inspired by a sculptural form of your choice, express poetically in words what you experience. This exercise is to be done with both pure forms and with representational sculpture.

Auer, Arthur. *Learning about the World Through Modeling: Sculptural Ideas for School and Home*. Fair Oaks, CA: AWSNA, 2001.
Sourcebook of exercises depicting Waldorf curriculum subjects grades 1-8.

Books On Sculptural Modeling

Auer, Arthur. *Sculptural Modeling: Its Value and Uses in the Classroom*, (1998).
Master's Project manuscript available from the Rudolf Steiner Lending Library of the Anthroposophical Society in America.

Auer, Elizabeth. *Creative Pathways*. Chatham, NY: Waldorf Publications, 2009.

Auer, Elizabeth ed, *Helping Children on their Way*: *Educational Support for the Classroom*, Chatham, NY: Waldorf Publications, 2017.

Auer, Elizabeth. *Learning to See the World through Drawing*. Chatham, NY: Waldorf Publications, 2015.

Bonneval, Hans. *Umstülpung als Schöpfungs- und Bewusstseinsprinzip*. Borchen, DE: Verlag Moellman, 2005.
A fascinating compendium of Steiner's indications on one of his central mind-bending concepts "Turning Inside Out Inversion" that is least understood and discussed! It is the basis of his whole Soul Calendar.

Breme, Christian. *Wieder Erde in die Hand nehmen. Eine Antwort auf die Virtualisierung der Welt*. (Take Earth into Your Hands Again: A Response to the Virtualization of the World) Stuttgart, Germany: Erziehungskunst: July/August 2003.
Breme is a genius at creating modeling projects for elementary and high school students, including forms of human embryological development.

Clausen, Anke-Usche, and Riedel, Martin. *Plastisches Gestalten* (Sculptural Modeling). Stuttgart, Germany: Mellinger Verlag, 1985.
Profusely illustrated. You do not need to know German to "read" its image ideas.

Elsner, Peter. *Metamorphosis in Nature and Art: The Dynamics of Form in Plants, Animals and Human Beings*. UK: Hawthorn Press, 2013.

Fant, Ake, with Klingborg and Wilkes. *Rudolf Steiner's Sculpture*. London: Rudolf Steiner Press, 1975.

Goodwin, Getraud. *Metamorphosis: Journeys through Transformation*. UK: Temple Lodge Press, 2016.
A sumptuous feast of sculptural sequences including her work and that of many others.

Golombek, Evelyne. *Plastisch-Therapeutisches Gestalten*. Stuttgart, Germany:Verlag Freies Geistesleben & Urachhaus, 2000.
Therapeutic exercises.

Hoffmann, Nigel. *Goethe's Science of Living Form: The Artistic Stages*. NY: Adonis Press, 2006.
A profound study of the dynamics of living forms.

Howard, Michael. *Art as Spiritual Activity: Rudolf Steiner's Contribution to the Visual Arts.* Hudson, NY: Anthroposophic Press, 1998
Includes his brilliant Introduction to the significance and "qualities of form."

Howard, Michael. *Educating the Will.* Fair Oaks, CA: AWSNA Publications, 2004.
Insights into the feeling-will and exercises for form modeling with sand and seeds

Howard, Michael. "Sculptural Form as Visible Speech," Anthroposophical Newsletter.
Brilliant account of the development of the twelve archetypal consonants in relief.

Huber, Hanne. *Gestalten mit Bienenwachs im Vorschulalter* (Modeling with Beeswax in Early Childhood). Stuttgart: Verlag Freies Geistesleben, 2001.
Profusely illustrated. You do not need to know German to "read" its image ideas.

Husemann, Armin. *The Harmony of the Human Body: Musical Principles in Human Physiology*. Edinburgh: Floris Books, 1989.
Describes form modeling exercises given by Steiner for understanding human morphology.

Husemann, Armin. *Menschenwissenschaft durch Kunst: Die plastisch-musikalisch-sprachliche Menschenkunde.* Stuttgart: Freies Geistesleben, 2007.

James, Philip, editor. *Henry Moore on Sculpture.* New York: Da Capo Press, 1992.

Kemper, Carl. *Der Bau: Studien zur Architektur und Plastik des ersten Goetheanum (The Goetheanum: its Architecture and Sculpture)* Stuttgart, Germany: Freies Geistesleben, 1974.

Krösche, *Die Doppelte Kruemmung als das einfachste Urphaenomen des Lebens (The Double Convex-Concave Curves as the Simplest Urphenomenon of Life).* Private printing, 2002.
    Profusely illustrated. You do not need to know German to "read" its image ideas.

Lissau, Magda. *The Temperaments and the Arts*, Waldorf Publications, 2003.

Loewe, Hella. *Basic Sculptural Modeling: Developing the Will by Working with Pure Forms in the First Three Grades.* Fair Oaks, CA: AWSNA Publications, 2006.
    A brilliant, pioneering handbook!

Martin, Michael. *Mit Formen Leben in Kunst und Natur* (Living with Forms in Art and Nature). Stuttgart: Freies Geistesleben, 2000.

Mees- Christeller, Eva. *The Practice of Artistic Therapy.* Spring Valley: Mercury Press, 1985.

Mitchell, David, and Livingston, Patricia. *Will-Developed Intelligence.* Fair Oaks, CA: AWSNA Publications, 1999.

Read, Herbert, *The Art of Sculpture.* New York: Bollinger Foundation, 1961.
    A superb history.

Stockmeyer, Karl. *Rudolf Steiner's Curriculum for Waldorf Schools.* Forest Row, England: Steiner Schools Fellowship, 1965.

Rudolf Steiner on Sculpture (*Gestalten*), Image (*Bild*), and other topics

Leber, Stefan. *Kommentar ueber Rudolf Steiners Vortraegen ueber Allegemeine Mesncenunde.* Vol.1-3, Stuttgart: Freies Geistesleben, 2002.

Source of Steiner excerpts, from many sources not yet available in English

Steiner, Rudolf, *Architecture as Synthesis of the Arts,* London: Rudolf Steiner Press, 1999.

_________. *Cosmosophy I and II*, New York: Anthroposophic, 1985.

_________. *Curative Education,* London: Rudolf Steiner Press, 1972.

_________. *Das Plastische Werk*. Basel: Rudolf Steiner Verlag, 2011.

_________. *Der Dornacher Bau* (The Dornach Building). Stuttgart: Freies Geistesleben, 1966.

_________. *Die Wirklichkeit der hochcrcn Welten* (CW 79), Lecture 2: Paths to Knowledge of Higher Worlds, Christiania, Nov. 26, 1921, London: Anthroposophical Publishing Company, 1947.

_________. *Discussions with Teachers*. (including Three Lectures on the Curriculum) New York: Anthroposophic Press, 1997 (Reprint).

_________. *Education for Adolescents*, Hudson, New York: Anthroposophic Press, 1996,

_________. *Education, Teaching and Practical Life*. CW 297a, NY: Waldorf Publicatons, 2007,

_________. *Esoteric Cosmology*. Great Barrington, MA: Steinerbooks, *2008*.

_________. *The Evolution of Consciousness*, UK: Rudolf Steiner Press, 1991

_________. *Faculty Meetings with Rudolf Steiner*. Hudson, NY: Anthroposophic Press, 1998.

_________. *Foundations of Human Experience*. Hudson, NY: Anthroposophic Press, 1996..

_________. *Human Values in Education*. Great Barrington: Anthroposophic Press, 2007.

_________. *The Inner Nature of Music,* Hudson, NY: Anthroposophic Press, 1983.

_________. *Karmic Relationships* Vol. IV. London: Rudolf Steiner Press, 1997.

_________. *The Kingdom of Childhood*. Hudson, NY: Anthroposophic Press, 1995.

________. How to *Know Higher Worlds*, Hudson,NY: Anthroposophic Press, 2002.

________. *Materialism and the Task of Anthroposophy*, Hudson, NY: Anthroposophic Press, 1987.

________. *The Mission of the Spirit*, CW 214, Oxford 8/22/22, Hudson,NY: Anthroposophic Press, 1991.

________. *A Modern Art of Education.* London, Rudolf Steiner Press, 1972.

________. *The Mystery of the Trinity.* Hudson,NY: Anthroposophic Press, 1991.

________. *Mystery of the Universe.* London, Rudolf Steiner Press, 2001.

________. *An Outline of Esoteric Science.* Hudson, NY, Anthroposophic Press, 1997.

________. *Polarities in the Evolution of Mankind*, London: Rudolf Steiner Press, 1987.

________. *A Psychology of Body, Soul and Spirit.* Hudson,NY: Anthroposophic Press, 1999.

________. *Practical Advice to Teachers.* Hudson, NY: Anthroposophic Press, 2000.

________. *Soul Economy and Waldorf Education.* New York: Anthroposophic Press, 1986.

________. A *Theory of Knowledge Implicit in Goethe's World Conception*, Hudson,New York: Anthroposophic Press, 1968.

________. *Theosophy.* Hudson, New York: Anthroposophic Press, 1994.

________. *Waldorf Education and Anthroposophy*, Vol.II. Hudson,NY: Anthroposophic Press, 1996 (Reprint).

________. *Ways to a New Style of Architecture*, Lecture 3, London: Rudolf Steiner Press, 1999.

________. *Welche Bedeutung hat die okkulte Entwicklung des menschen für seine Hüllen und sein Selbst?* GA 145, 1986.

On the Hand

Haebler, Martha." The Perfection of the Human Hand Lies in its Imperfection," in, *Waldorf Schools, Vol. I*, Ruth Pusch, ed. Spring Valley, NY: Mercury Press, 1993.

Lundborg, Goran. *The Hand and the Brain: From Lucy's Thumb to the Thought-Controlled Robotic Arm,* Springer, 2014.

Mackaye Ege, Arvia. "The Human Hand: its Activities and Role in Education," in *Education as an Art* (Journal of AWSNA), no date or volume. Available from the Rudolf Steiner Lending Library of the Anthroposophical Society in America.

Wilson, Frank R. *The Hand: How It Shapes the Brain, Language and Culture.* New York: Pantheon Books, 1998
A profound book which every teacher and parent should study.

Wilson, Frank R. "The Real Meaning of Hands-On Education." *Waldorf Education Research Bulletin*, January 2000, V (1), 2-14.

On the Etheric, Flowforms, Chladni figures, Metamorphosis, Archetypes, etc.:

Holdredge, Craig. *Thinking like a Plant: A Living Science for Life.* Great Barrington, MA: Lindisfarne, 2013.

Julius, Frits. *Sound between Matter and Spirit.* Spring Valley: Mercury Press, 2005.

Marti, Ernst. *The Four Ethers.* Illinois: Schaumburg, 1984.

Klocek, Dennis, *Esoteric Physiology*, Great Barrington, MA: Lindisfarne, 2016.

Lauterwasser, Alexander. *Water Sound Images: The Creative Music of the Universe.* NH: Macromedia, 2006

Lehrs, Ernst. *Man or Matter.* London: Faber, 1958.

Marti, Ernst. *The Etheric.* UK: Temple Lodge, 2017

________. *The Four Ethers. Illinois:* Schaumburg Publications, *1984*

Schad, Wolfgang, editor. *Evolution als Verständnisprinzip,* Stuttgart: Freies Geistesleben, 2009, 36-37

Schwenk, Theodor. Sensitive Chaos: The Creation of Flow Forms in Water and Air. Forest Row, UK: Rudolf Steiner Press, 2001.

Suchantke, Andreas. *Metamorphosis: Evolution in Action*. NY: Adonis Press, 2009.

Van Emmichoven, Zeylmans, *The Foundation Stone*, Temple Lodge Press, UK 2002.
Poetic rhythms leading into the etheric

Von Mackensen, Manfred, et al. *Uprightness, Weight and Balance : Human Biology in Grade Eight*. Fair Oaks, CA: AWSNA Publications, 2004.
Illustrated insights into bone forms.

Wilkes, *Flowforms: The Rhythmic Power of Water*. Edinburgh: Floris Books, 2003.
Water rhythmically flows through beautiful flow sculptures designed by Wilkes

On the Twelve Senses

Aeppli, Willi. *The Care and Development of the Senses*, Sussex: Steiner Schools Fellowship.1955

Kearny, Robert. "Losing Our Touch, " *New York Times*, August 31, 2014.

Steiner, Rudolf. *Anthroposophy: A Fragment*, Hudson, NY: Anthroposophic Press,1996.

Steiner, *Man as a Being of Sense and Perception*, Vancouver, Steiner Book Centre,1981.

König, Karl. *A Living Physiology*. Botton,UK: Camphill Books, 2006.

Sylvester, Robert, "Art for the Brain's Sake," *Educational Leadership,* 56 (3) November 1998.

On Mental Images/Imagination

Halfen, Roland and Neider, Andreas. *Imagination*. Stuttgart: Freies Geistesleben, 2002.

Heertsche, Andreas *Ein Tor zum Eigentlichen: Zur Skalierbarkeit von Imagination, Inspiration und Intuition*, Die Drei 11/2016, 21.

Kosslyn, Stephen, et al. *The Case for Mental Imagery,* New York: Oxford University Press, 2006.

Kranich, E.M. *Der innere Mensch und sein Leib*, Stuttgart: Freies Geistesleben, 2003

Lacey, Simon and Lawson, Rebecca. *Multisensory Imagery*. New York: Springer, 2013.

Richardson, Alan. *Mental Imagery*. London: Routledge and Kegan, 1969.

Robertson, Ian. *Mind Sculpture*. NY: Bantam, 1999.

Robertson, Ian. *Opening the Mind's Eye*. New York: St. Martin's Press, 2002.

Sacks, Oliver. *The Mind's Eye*. Toronto: Knopf, 2010.

Smit, Jorgen. "Remembering and Imagining." *Research Bulletin*, Autumn/Winter 2015, Vol. XX, Nr. 2, p.50.

Sommer, Robert. *The Mind's Eye*. New York: Dell Publishing, 1978.

Sparby, Terje The Realms and Steps of Higher Knowledge, Die Drei, 12/2017, 19-28.

Urieli, *Learning to Experience the Etheric World: Empathy, the After-Image and a New Social Ethic*. London, Temple Lodge, 2000.

Rudolf Steiner on Embryogenesis

Steiner, Rudolf. *Menscheitsentwickelung und Christus-Erkenntnis* (GA 100). Dornach, 2006,

________. *Das Prinzip der spirituellen Ökonomie* (CW 109). Dornach, 2000.
The "I" takes hold of the embryo body during days 18-21.

________. *Physiologische-Therapeutisches auf Grundlage der Geisteswissenschaft* (CW 314), 1989.
Fourfold human being in fourfold membrane sheath around central embryo body.

Others on Embryogenesis

Blechschmid, Erich. *The Ontogenetic Basis of Human Anatomy: A Biodynamic Approach to Development from Conception to Birth*. Berkeley: North Atlantic Books, 2004.

Carroll, Sean. *Endless Forms Most Beautiful: The New Science of Evolutionary Developmental Biology and the Making of the Animal Kingdom*. New York: Norton, 2005.
Current genetics of embryo morphology.

Anthroposophically-oriented Embryology Researchers

Appenzeller, Kaspar. *Die Genesis im Lichte der menschlichen Embryonalentwicklung*. Basel: Zbinden Verlag, 1989.
Moses' Book of Genesis in the light of human embryo development.

Breme, Christian. *Embryology Experienced through Modeling in Clay: A Path of Exercises in 5 Stages Practice in Five Steps*. Basel, Switzerland, AAP-Verlag Publishers, 2008. infoaap-verlag.net (Distributed by Rudolf Steiner College Bookstore),
Breme has created large plaster forms to study as part of "Relationship Education" (*Beziehungskunde*), known as Sex Education in the U.S. This is truly an inspiring and transformative approach for teenagers and adults.

Hartmann, Otto. *Dynamische Morphologie. Embryonalentwicklung und Konstitutionslehre als Grundlagen praktischer Medizin*, Frankfurt, Klostermann Verlag, 1942.
"Dynamic Morphology. Embryo Development and Physical Body Constitution as the Basis of Medical Practice": A pioneering anthroposophical study of the mineral, plant, and animal gestures of the human embryo.

Maris, Bartholomeus. "Befructung, Empfängnis und Inkarnation: Embryonalentwicklung zwishen Vererbung und Individualsierung" (Fertiliziation, Conception and Incarnation: Embryonic Development between Heredity and Incarnation). *Die Drei* 8-9, 2008.

König, Karl. *"Embryology and World Evolution."* In the British Homeopathic Journal, reprint from vol. LVII (1968) and LVIII (1969). London: Headley Ltd.
Dr. König correlates Steiner's evolution of Saturn, Sun, Moon, Earth and Moses' Genesis with the stages of embryology.

Poppelbaum, Herman. *Man and Animal*. London: Anthroposophical Publishing, 1960.

Rohen, Johannes W. *Functional Morphology*. Hillsdale, NY: Adonis Press, 2007.
See pages 37-63 for "Human Embryological Development: Steps in Taking Hold of Space."

Schad, Wolfgang. *Die Vorgeburtlichkeit des Menschen*. Stuttgart, 1982.

Schad, Wolfgang. *Die verlorene Haelfte des Menschen* (The lost half of the human being) 2005.
A developmental history of the placenta: Its cultural history and role in development: an excellent metaphorical model for the class teachers surrounding, nourishing and supporting the child in the center.

Van der Bie, Gus. *Embryology: Early Development from a phenomenological point of view*. Driebergen: Louis Bolk Institute, 2001.
A compact and concise booklet outlining the gestures of the stages.

Van der Wal, Jaap. "Dynamic Morphology and Embryology" in Van der Bie, Gus. *Foundations of Anthroposophical Medicine*. Edinburgh: Floris Books, 2003.

Van der Wal, Jaap. See Embryo in Motion at www. embryo.nl
Various workshop and seminar publications and DVDs available.

Wachsmuth, Guenther. *Reincarnation as a Phenomenon of Metamorphosis*. Dornach, 1937.

Weihs, Thomas. *Embryogenesis in Myth and Science*. Edinburgh: Floris Books, 1986.
An amazing correlation of the stages with the Seven Days of Creation as remarkably and graphically illustrated in a medieval miniature painting.

Wilmar, Frits. *Vorgeburtliche Menschwerdung: Eine Betrachtung ueber die menschliche fruehembryonale Entwicklung* (Pre-Birth Becoming Human: Observations of Human Early embryo Development). Stuttgart: Mellinger Verlag, 1979.
In the spirit of researcher Frits Wilmar's quote below, I have tried to live into the varied and sometimes contradictory perspectives of twelve anthroposphical researchers of embryology and come up with an artistic sculptural sequence, hopefully with understandable instructions and commentary:
"If one compares the descriptions of my book with the publications of other researchers, one may find contradictions.…A subject however can be presented from very different points of view. These varied perspectives complement each other— especially when it comes to the coming-into- being of human being (Menschwerdung) before birth. " (Wilmar, 131)

Acknowledgements

The author is deeply grateful to Elizabeth Auer for her artistic inspiration, beautiful illustrations, encouragement, and devoted attention to the manuscript.

A special thanks to Michael Howard and Peter Wolf for their chapters and to Patrice Maynard, Douglas Gerwin, Michael Holdrege, Hugh Renwick, and Carol Renwick for their suggestions in the development of the text.

The author is indebted to many artists whose work and ideas have influenced the development of exercises and ideas in this sourcebook. They include: Rudolf Steiner, Hella Loewe, Christian Breme, Michael Martin, John Wilkes, Michael Howard, Peter Wolf, Anke-Usche Clausen, Martin Riedel, Marie Kroesche, Evelyne Golombek, Peter Elsner, Henry Moore, Barbara Hepworth and Jean Arp.